# Managing Diversity, Innovation, and Infrastructure in Digital Business

Nilanjan Ray
*Adamas University, India*

A volume in the Advances in
Human Resources Management
and Organizational Development
(AHRMOD) Book Series

Published in the United States of America by
    IGI Global
    Business Science Reference (an imprint of IGI Global)
    701 E. Chocolate Avenue
    Hershey PA, USA 17033
    Tel: 717-533-8845
    Fax:  717-533-8661
    E-mail: cust@igi-global.com
    Web site: http://www.igi-global.com

Library of Congress Cataloging-in-Publication Data

Names: Ray, Nilanjan, 1984- editor.
Title: Managing diversity, innovation, and infrastructure in digital business
    / Nilanjan Ray, editor.
Description: Hershey, PA : Business Science Reference, [2019]
Identifiers: LCCN 2017061444| ISBN 9781522559931 (hardcover) | ISBN
    9781522559948 (ebook)
Subjects: LCSH: Information technology--Economic aspects. | Information
    technology--Social aspects.
Classification: LCC HC79.I55 .M359 2019 | DDC 658--dc23 LC record available at https://lccn.
loc.gov/2017061444


This book is published in the IGI Global book series Advances in Human Resources Management and Organizational Development (AHRMOD) (ISSN: 2327-3372; eISSN: 2327-3380)


British Cataloguing in Publication Data
A Cataloguing in Publication record for this book is available from the British Library.

All work contributed to this book is new, previously-unpublished material.
The views expressed in this book are those of the authors, but not necessarily of the publisher.

For electronic access to this publication, please contact: eresources@igi-global.com.

# Advances in Human Resources Management and Organizational Development (AHRMOD) Book Series

ISSN:2327-3372
EISSN:2327-3380

Editor-in-Chief: Patricia Ordóñez de Pablos, Universidad de Oviedo, Spain

## MISSION

A solid foundation is essential to the development and success of any organization and can be accomplished through the effective and careful management of an organization's human capital. Research in human resources management and organizational development is necessary in providing business leaders with the tools and methodologies which will assist in the development and maintenance of their organizational structure.

The **Advances in Human Resources Management and Organizational Development (AHRMOD) Book Series** aims to publish the latest research on all aspects of human resources as well as the latest methodologies, tools, and theories regarding organizational development and sustainability. The **AHRMOD Book Series** intends to provide business professionals, managers, researchers, and students with the necessary resources to effectively develop and implement organizational strategies.

## COVERAGE

- Performance Improvement
- Disputes Resolution
- Employee Benefits
- Strategic HRM
- Change Management
- E-Human Resources Management
- Organizational Behavior
- Skills Management
- Employee Communications
- Upward Feedback

IGI Global is currently accepting manuscripts for publication within this series. To submit a proposal for a volume in this series, please contact our Acquisition Editors at Acquisitions@igi-global.com or visit: http://www.igi-global.com/publish/.

# Titles in this Series

*For a list of additional titles in this series, please visit:*
*https://www.igi-global.com/book-series/advances-human-resources-management-organizational/73670*

*For an entire list of titles in this series, please visit:*
*https://www.igi-global.com/book-series/advances-human-resources-management-organizational/73670*

701 East Chocolate Avenue, Hershey, PA 17033, USA
Tel: 717-533-8845 x100 • Fax: 717-533-8661
E-Mail: cust@igi-global.com • www.igi-global.com

# Editorial Advisory Board

# Table of Contents

# Detailed Table of Contents

## Chapter 1
*Nermeen Atef Ahmed Hegazy, Cairo University, Egypt*

Social media has changed not only people's lives but also business's life. The internet has transformed the way companies do their business. Most companies create an entire business function commonly referred to e-business, which is the use of internet and information technology in a company's operations. Social media is not only a communication tool for entertainment. It is also an important part of marketing strategies in firm's business life. Therefore, firms can use social media as a strategic marketing tool to help firms gain a competitive advantage, so social media and social media marketing are gaining importance all over the world, especially from marketers and researchers in order to understand how social media works and to understand its techniques.

## Chapter 2
*Ivana S. Domazet, Institute of Economic Sciences, Serbia*
*Sladjana Neogradi, Addiko Bank, Serbia*

The aim of this chapter is to investigate the impact of the implementation of digital sales channels on improving the bank's business performance (i.e., improving the market position of the bank). The authors look at different types of sales channels and their contribution to increasing the number of clients in the bank, and in particular, they focus on the advantages of the Viber Platform in reaching more clients. A survey on digitalization of the banking sector was conducted, that is, on the integration of digital communications and sales channels, that bringins with it new elements and possibilities for expanding the portfolio of bank services, and thus new opportunities for increasing profits. Based on the results of the survey, it was concluded that banks use digital communications to improve and make more effective and efficient communication with clients, while trying to bring them closer to the offer. With this approach, banks will achieve greater satisfaction and consequently a greater loyalty of their clients.

**Chapter 3**

    *Anshu Rani, REVA University, India*
    *H. N. Shivaprasad, DVHIMSR, India*

In the digital age, consumers have changed their roles from passive receivers of marketing messages to active information suppliers about products through various digital media. The communication between consumers which occurs online is termed electronic word of mouth (eWOM) communication. Electronic word of mouth communication is an integral part of e-commerce. With the exponential growth of internet users and their adoption of eWOM for product information, it has become important to study the factors responsible for the effectiveness of eWOM. This chapter investigates the traditional WOM and eWOM literature to explore its status. A summary of eWOM communication has been presented to summarize prior studies of eWOM which is aligned with basic communication processes. The research papers (literature) have been segregated into eight categories: WOM, eWOM, eWOM impact, source credibility, message characteristics, receiver characteristics, eWOM platform, and response after eWOM adoption. Finally, several strategies are discussed for theoretical and empirical exploration.

**Chapter 4**

    *Esra Güven, Celal Bayar University, Turkey*
    *Volkan Yakin, Abant Izzet Baysal University, Turkey*

Consumer-to-consumer communications in online environments are of a vital importance to the consumer decision-making process. This process consists of five phases, each affected by eWOM communications deeply from the stimulation to the post-purchase behavior. Among all other factors having an impact on this process, the impact of eWOM has a distinguished role. As the technology grows and the consumers use internet and the reviews via internet, they become more and more attached to these reviews to make a purchase decision. In this chapter, the authors make a comprehensive explanation about the consumer decision-making process and explain the relationship of the decision-making phases with eWOM communications.

*Soraya Sedkaoui, Djilali Bounaama University, Algeria & Montpellier
University, France & SRY Consulting, France*

This chapter examines and identifies the factors that influence the implementation of predictive marketing in Algeria enterprises. A structured questionnaire was used to collect data from 30 respondents comprised of CEOs of selected enterprises. Some analytical methods were applied to analyze the data and evaluate the point of view of the enterprises with regard to the adoption and implementation of predictive marketing techniques. The major findings of the study indicated that the adoption of predictive marketing requires the relevant tools and software to extract knowledge "data mining." In addition, the existence of start-up (for analytics) and the level of development of e-commerce and digital marketing in Algeria will undoubtedly encourage the use of these techniques. This chapter also provides some suggestions for further research.

*Michael Sony, Namibia University of Science and Technology, Namibia*

Green marketing meets the present needs of the consumer and business, while also preserving or enhancing the ability of the future generations to meet their needs. The chapter deals with customers' willingness to pay for green marketing initiatives. The chapter explores the managerial perspective using a qualitative inquiry using interpretative phenomenology approach. The customers are willing to pay for green initiatives provided 1) the green initiative does not cost a lot of inconvenience, 2) hotel has a good image, 3) customer profile environmental consciousness moderated the relationship between the customer profile and willingness to pay. Recommendations on how to implement the green strategy in hotels are discussed. The direction of future research sections important research areas in green marketing for an academic contribution.

*José Duarte Santos, Polytechnic of Porto, Portugal*
*Fernando Luís Almeida, University of Porto, Portugal*

Social networks, originally built as channels for personal interaction, are being used in the commercial market as a support for product sales. The use of applications integrated in social networks appears as an opportunity to explore by companies.

Facestore emerged in 2013 as the first e-commerce solution integrated in social networks, allowing the creation of online stores within Facebook, without the customer having to leave the social network interface. Operations like looking into the catalog, choosing the product, and paying the transaction is carried out without the customer need to open a new website. The use of Facestore offers direct and indirect benefits on the different areas of an organization. At the direct level, there are changes in processes in terms of customer service and marketing and sales. However, its use also potentiates indirect benefits in other organizational areas, such as operations, finance, administration and information technologies support, human resources, and research and development.

This chapter investigates the role of digital tools in the value co-creation process of creative contests. Based on a multidisciplinary literature and a discourse analysis of existing creative and innovation contests, the authors identify four categories of tools that affect the value co-creation process: proactive and reactive, trial-and-error, and social learning tools. A synthesizing framework presents how the integration of these tools is beneficial to the exchange of resources between the different stakeholders of creative crowdsourcing. The authors further identify practical tools (i.e., instructive and promoting, creativity supporting, collaborative, and evaluating tools), which intervene in the three phases of crowdsourcing activities (i.e., before, during, and after).

The impact of identity on brand loyalty has taken precedence as an area of focus in recent marketing research. This has taken place in an era defined by technological revolution, which has created market disruptions, and there are implications for customer-brand relationships. Nonetheless, existing research has failed to acknowledge the impact of socio-psychological attributes and functional utility maximization. Knowledge that illuminates how firms can reposition themselves to sustain brand loyalty when disruptions occur in today's complex and globalized business environment is also required. This study will present an empirical investigation into the phenomenon of brand switching behavior among consumers in a specific competitive market, the smartphone industry. It explores how resistance could be built from an identity theory perspective, as emphasis has historically been placed on the functional utility of products at the expense of social meanings. This study provides consideration for market disruptions in the smartphone industry and confirms that the literature does not capture other non-utilitarian factors such as socio-psychological benefits, hence there are underlying factors that motivate consumers to continue buying brands they buy.

# Preface

The Internet represents a tremendous opportunity. For customers, it gives a much wider choice of products, services and prices from different suppliers and the means to select and purchase items more readily. For organisations marketing these products and services it gives the opportunity to expand into new markets, offer new services and compete on a more equal footing with larger businesses. For those working within these organisations it gives the opportunity to develop new skills and to use the Internet to improve the competitiveness of the company. This proposed volume will present a variety of practical application tools, skills, practices, models, approaches, and strategies that are proving themselves in practice, demonstrating effectiveness with managing diversity and innovation. This volume will also present a several visionary proposals for transforming societies, citizens, and professions so all concerned are better prepared to embrace diversity and do their part in creating valuable and necessary innovation that positively impacts the global community. The overall objectives and mission of this proposed volume are to share a different pattern of research work that will provide a platform for new avenues in overall digital infrastructure, digital modern business infrastructure, business automation, and financial aspects of modern businesses. Industry executives, marketing managers, and consumers have expressed concerns about the ability of today's students to create value within our increasingly global, diverse, and sophisticated marketplace. Industry executives, marketing managers, and consumers have articulated concerns about the ability of today's students to create value within our increasingly global, diverse, and complicated marketplace. Targeted in its scope and broad in its sources, the book will become a key reference for digital marketing/business educators looking for quality text about how to promote brilliance among students in the 21st Century.

This volume has focused to present a variety of practical applications, tools, skills, practices, models, approaches, and strategies that are proving themselves in practice demonstrating effectiveness with managing diversity and innovation.

Chapter 1 focused on Social Media become very important for marketing decision-making process; it seems to have "taken over the world". So this is the reason behind why social media attracting this much more attention. When we are talking about social media, we are talking about one of priority strategic tools, so we should know how to make this strategic tool more useful for firms because it would be very beneficial for firm's competitive growth. Social Media term covers the usage of online tools and web sites that allow users to interact between each others in order to share information, opinions and interests.

Chapter 2 discussed on the financial services market has undergone significant changes in recent years. Information technology, including models of modern information architecture, databases and data warehouses, data protection, data management, computer communication, modern statistical software and other IT tools, contributed to an enormous increase in the speed of data processing, the introduction of ATMs, the functioning and processing of various types of credit and payment cards and a like. This technology advancement enabled financial organizations to offer a wide range of quality products and services to the market. In addition, due to the exponential growth of digital communication channels, and in particular social networks, the role of digital marketing takes on an increasingly important item in determining the overall marketing budgets.

Chapter 3 discussed on the rapid growth of digital technology is changing the way businesses worked so far. The field of marketing is exploring new profitable models of business in computer mediated environment. The Internet based marketing models are highly customized, relevant and powerful where consumer create, exchange & choose the information they want (Fernando & Whitelock, 2007). The internet and digital technology have changed the balance of power between buyers and sellers in favour of buyers (Kucuka & Krishnamurthy, 2007). One of the most important capabilities of the Internet, in comparison with previous mass communication technologies, is its bi-directionality (Dellarocas, 2003). It has been observed that the early development of Web is controlled and static. Earlier business institutions on web used to control the content on internet but due to popularity of Social media, blogs, bulletin boards, chat rooms, review sites, e-tailersites, and virtual discussion rooms, the information given by markets have lost this effect (Goldsmith, 2006).

Chapter 4 focused on consumers today need to make numerous decisions and therefore deal with information loads increasing day by day. To be able to cope with this mental load, they develop some short cuts or certain habits. The introduction of online and internet platforms into our lives is causing the markets having been controlled by the marketers for long years to pass on consumer hands. The consumers being able to reach all the information through online environments have started to dominate in the markets, and this has caused the marketers to go through their strategies they have used persistently. Especially the social media platforms by means of web 2.0 following web 1.0 can be said to have a great impact on this shift. Consumer generated online environments, one of the biggest advantage of emerging social media platforms, not only provide the consumers with reaching the information in a rapid and efficient way but also offer a flexibility in time and evaluation opportunities.

Chapter 5 discussed the internet and the web has attracted considerable attention and research from both academics and practitioners. Numerous studies anticipated a "marketing revolution" (Hoffman & Novak, 1997; Keeny & Marshall, 2000) as businesses changed their modes of operation and customers adapted to novel and different ways of purchasing goods and services. With the advent of digital technology and smart devices, a large amount of digital data is being generated every day. Individuals are putting more and more publicly available data on the web. Thus, not only the quantity of digitally stored data is much larger, but the type of data is also tremendously diversified, due to various new technologies (Sedkaoui & Monino, 2016).

Chapter 6 focused on business activities are a part of the social fabric of society. Therefore, the survival and development of business activity are depended on the environment in which it operates. The business environment includes the ecological environment. Thus, it is our duty to protect the ecological environment so that economic activities are carried on without harming the environment. Economic well-being is not the only reason for preserving the environment, but it can also impact the existence of mankind. Thus, protecting the ecology is the societal obligations of both the individual and business. Marketing discipline being an important cog in business activities plays an important role in linking ecology with economic activities.

Chapter 7 focuses on a specific form of social commerce: the virtual stores of Facebook. This social network, with more than 2 trillion active users in September 2017, was the first social network to incorporate the concept of store social commerce (Statista, 2017b). As a first step, we analyze the evolution and different perspectives of social commerce as, for example, communities, social selling, social cashback, presence of virtual stores on social networks, and also how to incorporate in the company's strategy. We intend also to look for the main motivations that may be at the origin of the decision by companies in joining the social commerce. Then, we make a short presentation of the Facebook's role in marketing and we examine the contribution that f-commerce can provide to improve sales and customer relationships, especially in terms of customer retention strategies, the creation of value and the construction of brand loyalty.

In Chapter 8, crowdsourcing is a problem-solving model that takes advantage of the Internet (Brabham, 2013). Jeff Howe, who first coined the concept in 2006, describes it as the act of taking a job, traditionally performed by a designated agent (usually an employee), and outsourcing it to an undefined, generally large group of people in the form of an open call (Howe, 2006). Crowdsourcing is typically characterized by a proactive crowd, an outsourced task and an empowering online environment (Djelassi and Decoopman, 2013). Among the most popular and most promising types of crowdsourcing is creative crowdsourcing, often organized in the form of creative contests (e.g., idea or design competitions) (Terwiesch and Xu, 2008). Contests are used for both, problem-solving and decision-making tasks, in a variety of industries. They help reducing market failure rates of new products and services, accelerating the innovation process, reducing traditional outsourcing costs, and strengthening the relationship between brands and customers (Brabham, 2013, Hanine and Steils, 2018). Even though the principle of outsourcing a task to a group of people is not fundamentally new, the digital environment lifts the usage and usefulness of crowdsourcing to a whole new level.

In Chapter 9, the impact of identity on brand loyalty has taken precedence as an area of focus in recent marketing research. This has taken place in an era defined by technological revolution, which has created market disruptions and there are implications for customer–brand relationships. Nonetheless, existing research has failed to acknowledge the impact of socio-psychological attributes and functional utility maximisation. Knowledge that illuminates how firms can reposition themselves to sustain brand loyalty when disruptions occur in today's complex and globalised business environment is also required. This study will present an empirical investigation into the phenomenon of brand switching behaviour among consumers in a specific competitive market, the Smartphone industry. It explores how resistance could be built from an identity theory perspective, as emphasis has historically been placed on the functional utility of products at the expense of social meanings. This study provides consideration for market disruptions in the Smartphone industry and confirms that the literature does not capture other non-utilitarian factors such as socio-psychological benefits, hence there are underlying factors that motivate consumers to continue buying brands they buy.

Last but not the least, this volume is focused to present a variety of practical application tools, skills, practices, models, approaches, and strategies that are proving themselves in practice—demonstrating effectiveness while managing diversity and innovation. The overall objective and mission of this volume is to share a different pattern of research work that will provide a platform for new avenues in overall infrastructure, socioeconomic conditions, and modern tourism business infrastructure.

## REFERENCES

Brabham, D. (2013). *Crowdsourcing*. Cambridge, MA: MIT Press.

Christopher, M. (1998). *Logistics and Supply Chain Management: Strategies for Reducing Cost and Improving Service* (2nd ed.). Harlow, UK: Prentice Hall.

Christopher, M. G. (1998). *Logistics and Supply Chain Management; strategies for reducing costs and improving services*. London: Pitman Publishing.

Dellarocas. (2003). The Digitization of Word of Mouth: Promise and Challenges of Online Feedback Mechanisms. *Management Science, 49*, 1407–1424.

Djelassi, S., & Decoopman, I. (2013). 'Customers' Participation in Product Development through Crowdsourcing: Issues and Implications. *Industrial Marketing Management, 42*(5), 683–692. doi:10.1016/j.indmarman.2013.05.006

Fernando, F., & Whitelock, J. (2007). International advertising strategy: The standardisation question in manager studies. *International Marketing Review, 24*(5), 591–605. doi:10.1108/02651330710828004

Hanine, S., & Steils, N. (2018). *Crowdsourcing: A Double-Edged Sword Outsourcing Strategy*. Academic Press. . doi:10.5772/intechopen.74531

Hoffman, D. L., & Novak, T. P. (1997). A New Marketing Paradigm for Electronic Commerce. *The Information Society, 13*(1), 43–54. doi:10.1080/019722497129278

Howe, J. (2006, June 6). *A Definition*. Retrieved from http://crowdsourcing.typepad.com/cs/2006/06/crowdsourcing_a.html

Keeny, D., & Marshall, J. F. (2000, November). Contextual Marketing: The Real Business on the Internet. *Harvard Business Review*, 119–125. PMID:11184966

Kucuka, S. U., & Krishnamurthy, S. (2007). An analysis of consumer power on the Internet. *Technovation, 27*(1-2), 47–56. doi:10.1016/j.technovation.2006.05.002

Monino, J., Sedkaoui, S., & Monino, J. (2016). *Big Data, Open Data and Data Development*. London: ISTE. doi:10.1002/9781119285199

Terwiesch, C., & Xu, Y. (2008). Innovation Contests, Open Innovation, and Multiagent Problem Solving. *Management Science, 54*(9), 1529–1543. doi:10.1287/mnsc.1080.0884

# Acknowledgment

First and foremost, I would like to thank my parents Sri Nirmalendu Ray and Smt. Rina Ray for their unending inspiration and standing beside me throughout my career and for writing this book.I would like to thank to my wife Trina Ray for providing me moral support and inspiration as well as the necessary time and resource toward the applications and maintaining databases. I would like to especially thank to my Doctoral Supervisor and my teacher Dr. Dillip Kumar Das, Asst. Professor and Head of the Department, Department of Tourism, The University of Burdwan India to guide me and develop the applications for this project and for giving me the freedom to manage my projects and provide the necessary time and resource toward the applications and databases.

I acknowledge my indebtedness to all the members of editorial advisory board and technical reviewers of this volume. I am also grateful to all the authors whose valued contributions have enriched the volume. I wish to thank the officials at IGI Global Publications for their invaluable efforts, great support and valuable advice for this project towards successful publication of this book.

*Nilanjan Ray*
*Adamas University, India*

# Chapter 1
# Firm's Competitive Growth in the Social Media Age

**Nermeen Atef Ahmed Hegazy**
*Cairo University, Egypt*

## ABSTRACT

*Social media has changed not only people's lives but also business's life. The internet has transformed the way companies do their business. Most companies create an entire business function commonly referred to e-business, which is the use of internet and information technology in a company's operations. Social media is not only a communication tool for entertainment. It is also an important part of marketing strategies in firm's business life. Therefore, firms can use social media as a strategic marketing tool to help firms gain a competitive advantage, so social media and social media marketing are gaining importance all over the world, especially from marketers and researchers in order to understand how social media works and to understand its techniques.*

## INTRODUCTION

In recent years, Social Media become very important for marketing decision-making process; it seems to have "taken over the world". So this is the reason behind why social media attracting this much more attention. When we are talking about social media, we are talking about one of priority strategic tools, so we should know how to make this strategic tool more useful for firms because it would be very beneficial for firm's competitive growth. Social Media term covers the usage of online tools and web sites that allow users to interact between each other's in order to share information, opinions and interests. According to "The State of Small Business Report, 2010"

DOI: 10.4018/978-1-5225-5993-1.ch001

sponsored by Network Solutions, LLC and the University of Maryland's Robert H. Smith School of Business, the study results show that almost 1 out of 5 small business owners actively uses social media as part of his or her marketing strategy (University of Maryland, n.d.). The study also shows that 75% of small businesses have a company page on a social networking site.

## BACKGROUND

We have witnesses a rapid and accelerated growth in social media in the last few years. Social media and social media marketing are gaining importance and popularity all over the world especially from marketers and researchers in order to understand how social media works and also understand its techniques, which is increasingly common and fast growing. According to "The State of Small Business Report, 2010", the study show that different industries are adopting social media marketing at different rates (University of Maryland, n.d.). There are many firms depending on social media marketing and direct mail such as Firms in the education, health, and social services sector. Many organizations, including small, medium-sized, and large organizations used social media now in regular operations. So in order to the rapid changes which happening in the social media and technology, Firms should know how to adapt to these changes in order to have and maintain a competitive advantage.

## LITERATURE REVIEW

### Differences Between Social Media and Social Networks

There are several differences between social media and social networks (Hartshorn, 2010, Cited in Edosomwan et al., 2011); the differences include semantics, features, functions and the way to use these websites. We can summarize the differences between them as shown in Table 1.

### A History of Social Media

When we are talking about social media as we know today, we should know its origin and how does it appear, in order of that we can illustrate the history of social Media as shown in Table 2.

## *Table 1. Differences between social media and social networks*

|  | **Social Media** | **Social Networks** |
|---|---|---|
| Definition: | A media which is primarily used to transmit or share information with a broad audience. | An act of engagement as people with common interests associates together and builds relationships through community. |
| Communication style: | It is simply a system, a communication channel. | It is a two-way communication, where conversations are at the core. |
| The return on investment (ROI): | Difficult to be determined precisely. | ROI is a bit obvious. |

(Data Source: Edosomwan et al., 2011)

## *Table 2. The history of social media*

| **Stage** | **Year** | **Description** |
|---|---|---|
| 1. The Birth of Social Media "The Early Years" | 1997 | The first recognizable social network site launched in 1997 was SixDegrees.com which allowed users to create profiles, and list their friends; It help people connect and send messages to others. |
|  | From 1997 to 2001 | A number of community tools began supporting various combinations of profiles and publicly articulated Friends. Such as: AsianAvenue, BlackPlanet, Ryze, and MiGente which allowed users to create personal, professional profiles. |
|  | 2002 | Launched a Friendster as a social complement to Ryze. It was designed to compete with Match.com, a profitable online dating site. |
| 2. The First Social Media Surge "SNSs Hit the Mainstream" | 2003 | Many new SNSs were launched; some are professional sites such as: LinkedIn, Visible Path, and Xing which focus on business people. The social media and user-generated content phenomena grew; websites focused on media sharing began implementing SNS features and becoming SNSs themselves, such as: Flickr (photo sharing), Last.FM (music listening habits), and YouTube (video sharing). |
| 3. Facebook and Twitter | 2005 | Facebook began in early 2004 as a Harvard-only SNS for students. While in September 2005, Facebook expanded to include everyone. |
|  | 2006 | Twitter a service that had the unique distinction of allowing users to send "tweets" of 140 characters or less. |
| 4. The Rest of the Pack | Around 2010 | There were dozens of other websites providing social media services of some kind such as: Tumblr, Foursquare, Pinterest, Instagram, Google Buzz, Loopt, Blippy, WordPress and Groupon. |
| 5. Social Media | Today | Social media today consists of thousands of social media platforms, all serving the same – but slightly different purpose. Of course, some social media platforms are more popular than others, |

(Data Source: Boyd & Ellison, 2008; History Cooperative, n.d.)

## MAIN FOCUS OF THE CHAPTER

This chapter focuses on firm's growth in social media age; as one of the most important industries in the world, and how to make social media more beneficial for firms. Beside the important role of social media in promote businesses, increase firm's sales, and making money. Social media are gaining popularity and now are used in regular operations of many organizations, including small, medium-sized, and large organizations. In order to the rapid changes which happening in the social media and technology, Firms should know how to adapt to these changes in order to have and maintain a competitive advantage. So the overall objective of this chapter is to have an overview about social media as a competitive advantage for firms, highlighting this issues and challenges being faced in this chapter as follows.

According to Harvard Business Review Report (2010): "The exponential growth of social media, from blogs, Facebook and Twitter to LinkedIn and YouTube, offers organizations the chance to join a conversation with millions of customers around the globe every day."

## What Does Social Media Marketing (SMM) Mean?

- **Social Media Meaning:** Social media is a unique phenomenon because it's transform the communication and interaction of individuals and also companies throughout the world (Edosomwan et al., 2011).
- **Social Media Marketing Meaning:** SMM means techniques that aim to promote products or spread brand awareness through social networks and its applications, it can also defined as a form of internet marketing that implements various social media networks in order to achieve marketing communication and branding goals (techopedia.com).

After knowing what does Social Media and SMM mean; we also should know what does Social Networking Services (SNS) mean? A SNS is defined as a Web-based software application that helps users connect and socialize with friends, family members, business partners, or other individuals (Gnyawali et al., 2010).

## Social Media Platforms

There are many platforms for social media people use such as:

- **Facebook:** A social networking website launched in February 2004. Users of Facebook can create a personal profile; add other users as friends, and exchange messages, including automatic notifications, photos and comments when they update their profile.

- **Twitter:** A social networking website allows users to publish short messages known as "Tweets" that are visible to other users. Twitter was founded in 2006.
- **YouTube:** The world's most popular online video community, where millions of people can discover, watch and share originally-created videos.
- **LinkedIn:** A social networking site designed specifically for the business community. So LinkedIn goal is to allow registered members to establish and document networks of people they know and trust professionally.
- **Pinterest:** A social media website that allows users to organize, share images and videos from around the Web.
- **Instagram:** An online photo sharing service. It allows users to apply different types of photo filters to their pictures with a single click.
- **Google+:** An interest-based social network that is owned and operated by Google Inc.
- **MySpace:** A social networking website that allows its users to create blogs, upload videos and photos, and design profiles to showcase their interests and talents in their webpage's to interact with other users. It became the most popular social networking website in the United States in 2006.
- **Flickr:** A website that allows users to share photographs and videos.
- **Wikipedia:** Wikipedia is a free, open content online encyclopedia created through the collaborative effort of a community of users. The site's name comes from wiki, a server program that enables anyone to edit Website content through their Web browser.
- And many others

As we illustrated above that there are many platforms for social media, so when any firm want to choose the best social network which it suitable for her it should take into her consideration some things:

- Time
- Resources
- Potential customers

## Social Media Characteristics

After clarifying what social media (SM) and social media marketing (SMM) means, we should know the characteristics of social media as follows (Bradley, 2013):

- **Participation:** Social media allows users to collaborate with each others, and participate in social media. There is a lack of clarity between media and audience.
- **Collective:** Social media helps participants to collect and distribute information, for example people collect videos to share or distribute them on YouTube.
- **Transparency:** Social media provides transparency in the way that participants made their participation. They can see, critique, validate, and rate each other's contributions on social media.
- **Independence:** Every participant has the opportunity to be independent in his/her contribution from any other participant; participants also can collaborate with each other's no matter where they are or whoever they are.
- **Persistence:** The fruits of participant contributions are captured in a persistent state for others to view, share and augment; it differentiates social media from synchronous conversational interactions where much of the information exchanged is either lost or captured.
- **Emergence:** There is no possibility to predict, model, design and control all human collaborative interactions and optimize them as a fixed business process.

## Business Development Via Social Media

When we are going to talk about social media marketing, we should never forget that social media marketing has a lot of benefits. We can mention some of these benefits as:

- Free and easy marketing
- Help in brand building
- Relationship building with customers
- Wide audience reception
- Offer a special way for firms to position themselves

While talking about social media marketing benefits, there are also many challenges facing social media marketing such as follows:

- Managing social media marketing take time
- Social media marketing results are hard to track
- If you don't have a smart strategy, you will be in trouble

So in this part we want to answer an important question which is: *Does Social Media Marketing work for business?*

To answer this important question you should know about Social Media Marketing *Benefit*s. According to Stelzner (2015) marketers found that there are really many benefits from social media marketing. 90% of marketers found that social media Increased Exposure, and 70% found that social media activities Increased Traffic to their websites. Also 69% of marketers found that social media Building a Loyal Fan Base and 68% of them see that social media provided Market Place Insights that they didn't previously have. Beside all the benefits mentioned earlier there are also more benefits as: improved sales, gain partnerships, reduced marketing expenses.

## Finding Business Purpose in "Social Media"

Social media can use as a marketing strategy to reduce the marketing cost in firms. There are three ways to use social media to get the results you want for your business as:

1.  **Sell Products or Services:** The instant nature of social media is ideal for sales, so this is the reason why social media became important marketing channel.
2.  **Become a Leading Industry Resource:** Content marketing professionals recognize social media channels as conduits and use them to pass information to fans, followers and customers.
3.  **Provide Quality Customer Service:** All companies want to give their customers the best experience possible, and right now that means providing customer service on social media.

Business capabilities are influenced by using Web 2.0 tools, and basically affect business performance in firms, these factors can be represented in (Andriole, 2010).

## How to Develop a Successful Social Media MKT Strategy

Social media marketing is like other form of marketing, it requires strategy, planning, resources, measuring etc. But in social media marketing Planning, business objectives and strategy are the most important keys. So to develop a successful social media marketing strategy there are several keys including:

1.  **Business Goals Development:** The first task of the firm will be to define the business goals it want to serve with social media marketing, Such as: Improving customer loyalty, brand awareness and reputation, increasing sales, promote businesses, and getting new prospects.

2. **Objectives Definition:** Firms should make objectives "SMART", which means to make them Specific, Measurable, Achievable, Realistic and Timed. In order to achieve these objectives firms should know; what does it expect from a Social Network Strategy? What is the result that firm wants to achieve by using social technologies?

3. **Deliberate Process of Execution (Messages Formulation and Platforms Identification):** Firms should determine results wanted from messages and communication to? Does it have to build its own Social Networking system or use an available platform (e.g. Facebook, etc.).

4. **Metrics Selection:** "You cannot manage what you do not measure." Internet-based platforms provide plenty of information and metrics allowing firm to obtain immediate feedback and to make adjustments early. So defining the right key performance indicators and choosing the proper tools to measure are very important.

5. **Manage Processes, Plan, Resources, and Budgets:** Social Network Strategy has an effect on firm's governance structure and business plan, it affecting human and financial resources allocation in the organization. These changes can be very useful to the firm, because these changes can help firm to be more innovative, open and interactive.

6. **Analysis and Measure Results:** Analytics are a pivotal element to help in achieving social media goals. In the Internet age, strategy review and adjustment is an essential issue to stay up to date and adjust strategic actions.

## Employees and Social Media Use

Employees are very important assets in any firms because of the important role of manager and employee which affects the firm's survival and its success.

Employees' social media use in the Social Media age is very important and essential for any firm. The reason behind that could be that employees play an important role in the social media area; they also know their company's business so they can represent their brands as "brand ambassadors". Employees can positively influence target customers, building strong and valuable relationships with target audiences. In order to what mentioned, we can conclude that Employees' social media use can benefit firms in many ways.

On the other hand there are three main problems that make social media difficult for organizations (Smith et al., 2010):

- Using social media requires control from firms, while the use of social media cannot be fully regulated or controlled.

- Social media is everywhere; therefore social media risks can have wide-reaching effects on the reputation of a firm, because things said on social media may last forever and everyone can reach it.
- Social media is highly emotional and functional.

In order to the previously mentioned problems these risks can cause reputational damage, destroy careers, and lead to productivity losses.

Hence, every firm should have social media team to provide their employees and executives with guidance and support, to be responsible for establish guidelines and policies, and to provide best practice examples and training for employees (Dreher, 2014).

## Firm's Competitive Growth

Competitive advantage can be defined as an organizational capability to perform in one or many ways that competitors find difficult to reproduce now and, in the future, (Kotler, 2000). So, firms must compete to keep or gain market share in addition to attract people or customers in order to search for the growth opportunities.

When we are talking about competitive advantage, we should mention that there are many factors influencing it as:

- Human skills
- Technological skills
- Factors related to firm as:
  - Firm size
  - Firm capacity
- Competitive industry
- Social media utilization

Therefore, most companies are searching for the best practices and metrics in order to understand where to target their social media activities and build their own competitive advantage by creating their own strategies.

The successful use of information technology (IT) can give the firm a competitive advantage to be able to compete with competitors. So communication technology system (ICTS) can be a significant source of competitive advantage to firms.

According to "*Harvard Business Review Report*" (2010) there are many benefits of use social media are:

- Increased awareness of your firm, products, and services among target customers.

- Increased traffic to website.
- The ability to know what is being said about your firm.
- Better understanding of customer perceptions of your brand.
- Improved insights about your target market.

So Firms can collaborate with social media agents in order to help firm to create and strengthen its competitive advantages, especially for micro, small, and medium enterprises (Al-Mommani et al., 2015). Marketing in micro, small, and medium firms differs from marketing in larger firms (Carson et al, 1995), because marketing in micro, small, and medium firms is considered to be easier and more efficient. So by using internet network and social media these firms can reduce cost, enter new markets, and build strong relationships with customers.

The organizational knowledge can also be a base of the competitive advantage in the field of strategic management.

## Social Media Marketing After Economic Recession

The global recession raises challenging questions for the vitality of the business climate and how it influences marketing budgets and aims (Kirtiş & Karahan, 2011). Global financial crisis has appeared in the last quarter of 2008 with the collapse of various large United States financial firms and spread promptly leading to a global economic turmoil (Ellaboudy, 2010).

When firms face an economic crisis, they try to decrease costs by reducing marketing budgets, this is because firms are also affected through different ways by economic crises. Some firms may need to close down and many others may reduce their production capacity. In order to that, marketing decision makers should increase their online budgets; however lower the budget for the traditional marketing tools. For this reason, firms try to find out how to use social media to develop their CRM (Customer Relationship Management) as well as ongoing relationships and creating loyalty (www.ameinfo.com). Social media is very important for both small and large businesses when using the internet to get success. The crisis can also be an opportunity to develop new policies, vision and strategies. It might be the time to firms to shift from traditional media to social media; this is because Firms are looking for more innovative, new and cost reduction ways to market their products or services.

## Digitization and Globalization Age

Nowadays firms have been affected by the digitization and globalization, Social Media affect the interaction way and communication between firms and customers.

So firms have to develop successful strategies and looked for new tactics for this global challenge. Knowledge has become an increasingly essential factor of growth and competitiveness for firms, its market value has increased. New technologies, Globalization, and the Internet affect firms in an enormous way. The growth of social media gives firms the chance to join conversations with millions of customers around the world every day.

According to "*2015 State of Small Business Report*" about marketing tools using by companies, they found that Social Media take the lead of marketing tools used by companies by (61%), which shows the importance of social media in marketing (Wasp Barcode Technologies, 2015). There are also many other important *marketing tools used by companies* mentioned in the report such as (ranked according to the percentage of use each of them by companies): E-mail marketing (46%), Print advertisements (37%), Press releases (36%), Direct mail (32), Trade shows (30%), Search engine optimization (30%), TV and/or radio (20%), Blogging (19%), other (18%), Online Ads (12%), Product or customers' videos (12%), Outsourced public relations firm (9%), Telemarketing services (5%).

Also Harvard Business Review Analytic Services survey (2010) said that nearly two-thirds of the 2,100 companies participated in survey are either currently using social media channels or have social media plans in the works.

In order to the previous reports and surveys; online competitive intelligence service (Compete.com) found that the top three social networks are: *Facebook, Twitter, and LinkedIn.*

## SOLUTIONS AND RECOMMENDATIONS

Social Media can add value to the firm's competitive growth, if proper marketing plan and strategy can be built and implemented, so firms should give social media marketing more attention. Furthermore social media has a significant impact on firm's business promotion, increasing firm's sales, reaching customers, and gain better market position. So by using internet network and social media firms can reduce cost, enter new markets, and build strong relationships with customers. The organizational knowledge can also be a base of the competitive advantage in the field of strategic management.

## FUTURE RESEARCH DIRECTIONS

The author indicates some directions for future research. This study is highlighting the firm's competitive growth in the social media age. Future research may work on examining the growth of the social media industry impact on firms depending on global environment changes. Furthermore focus on the impact of social media on firms can be an important ingredient of economic development.

## CONCLUSION

Social Media Marketing has been found to be an effective marketing strategy for all types of firms in just about every industry - in both Business-to-Consumer and Business-to-Business environments. Social media also offers huge opportunities for firms to increase their marketing share; it is also destined to play an even greater role in the coming years. Finally, we can say that social media has become a popular marketing tool using by companies.

This chapter has shown the importance of social media, there is no doubt that social media marketing has a significant impact on firm's growth. It opened new domains and new opportunities for these firms to attract new customers and promoting to their products and services. So we advise firm's managers and marketers to give both social media and social media marketing more attention because of their tremendous importance.

## REFERENCES

Al-Mommani, K., Al-Afifi, A., & Mahfuz, M. A. (2015). The Impact of Social Networks on Maximizing the Competitive Value of Micro, Small, and Medium Enterprises. *International Journal of Management Science and Business Administration*, *3*(1), 64–70. doi:10.18775/ijmsba.1849-5664-5419.2014.13.1005

Andriole, J. S. (2010). Business impact of Web 2.0 Technologies. *Communications of the ACM*, *53*(12), 67–79. doi:10.1145/1859204.1859225

Barkan, T. (2008). *How to develop a successful "Social Network Strategy"*. Retrieved from: http://www.globalstrat.org/

Boyd, D., & Ellison, N. (2008). Social Network Sites: Definition, History, and Scholarship. *Journal of Computer-Mediated Communication*, *13*(1), 210–230. doi:10.1111/j.1083-6101.2007.00393.x

Bradley, A. J. (2013). *A New Definition of Social Media*, Social Media: *Cultivate Collaboration and Innovation*. Retrieved from: http://blogs.gartner.com/anthony_bradley/2010/01/07/a-

Buchnowska, D. (2013). Social Business: A Conceptual Framework. *Informatyka Ekonomiczna Business Inforatics, 4*(30).

Bulankulama, S.W., Ali, K., & Herath, H.M. (2014). Utilization of social media in an organization and competitive advantages: Development of a conceptual framework. *International Journal of Economics, Commerce and Management, 3*(2).

Carson, D., Cromie, S., McGowan, P., & Hill, J. (1995). *Marketing and Entrepreneurship in SMEs: An Innovative Approach.* Harlow: Prentice-Hall.

Dreher, S. (2014). Social media and the world of work. *Corporate Communications, 19*(4), 344–356. doi:10.1108/CCIJ-10-2013-0087

Edosomwan, S., Prakasan, S. K., Kouame, D., Watson, J., & Seymour, T. (2011). The History of Social Media and its Impact on Business. *The Journal of Applied Management and Entrepreneurship, 16*(3).

Ellaboudy, S. (2010). The global financial crisis: Economic impact on gcc countries and policy implications. *International Research Journal of Finance and Economics, 41*, 180–193.

Gnyawali, D. R., Fan, W., & Penner, J. (2010). Competitive Actions and Dynamics in the Digital Age: An Empirical Investigation of Social Networking Firms. *Information Systems Research, 21*(3), 594–613. doi:10.1287/isre.1100.0294

Golden, M. (2011). *Social Media Strategies for Professionals and their Firms.* John Wiley & Sons Inc.

Harvard Business Review Analytic Services. (2010). *The New Conversation: Taking Social Media from Talk to Action.* Harvard Business School Publishing.

History Cooperative. (n.d.). Retrieved from: http://Historycooperative.org

Howley, E. (2010). *Harness the power of social media: An Alternative Guide for Design & Construction Firms.* Zweigwhite.

Kirtiş, A. K., & Karahan, F. (2011). To Be or Not to Be in Social Media Arena as the Most Cost-Efficient Marketing Strategy after the Global Recession. *Procedia: Social and Behavioral Sciences, 24*, 260–268. doi:10.1016/j.sbspro.2011.09.083

Kotler, P. (2000). *Marketing Management Analysis, Planning, and Control* (5th ed.). Prentice-Hall.

Merrill, T., Latham, K., Santalesa, R., & Navetta, D. (2011). *The Business Benefits May Be Enormous, But Can the Risks -- Reputational, Legal, Operational -- Be Mitigated?* ACE Limited.

Ngai, E., Moon, K., Lam, S., Chin, E., & Tao, S. (2015). Social media models, technologies, and applications. *Industrial Management & Data Systems*, *115*(5), 769–802. doi:10.1108/IMDS-03-2015-0075

Smith, N., Wollan, R., & Zhou, C. (2010). *Social Media Management Handbook: Everything You Need to Know to Get Social Media Working in Your Business*. Hoboken, NJ: John Wiley & Sons Inc.

Stelzner, M. (2015). *Social Media Marketing Industry report: How Marketers are Using Social Media to grow their Businesses*. Social Media Examiner.

Stokes, R. (2014). eMarketing: The essential guide to marketing in a digital world (5th ed.). Quirk eMarketing (Pty) Ltd.

Wasp Barcode Technologies. (2015). *State of Small Business Report*. Author.

## ADDITIONAL READING

Aimiuwu, E. E. (2012). Building a Competitive Edge through Social Media, *Proceedings of the Conference on Information Systems Applied Research*. New Orleans Louisiana, USA.

Arend, R. J. (2003). Revisiting the logical and research considerations of competitive advantage. *Strategic Management Journal*, *24*(3), 279–284. doi:10.1002mj.285

Argote, L., & Ingram, P. (2000). Knowledge Transfer: A Basis for Competitive Advantage in Firms. *Organizational Behavior and Human Decision Processes*, *82*(1), 150–169. doi:10.1006/obhd.2000.2893

Arora, P., & Predmore, C. E. (2014). *Social Media as a Strategic Tool: Going Beyond the Obvious, Social Media in Strategic Management, Advanced Series in Management* (pp. 115–127). Emerald Group Publishing Limited.

Baird, C. H., & Parasnis, G. (2011). From social media to Social CRM: Reinventing the customer relationship. *Strategy and Leadership*, *39*(6), 27–34. doi:10.1108/10878571111176600

Barney, J. (1991). Firm Resources and Sustained Competitive Advantage. *Journal of Management*, *17*(1), 99–120. doi:10.1177/014920639101700108

Bharadwaj, S. A. (2000). A resource-based perspective on information technology capability and firm performance: An empirical investigation. *Management Information Systems Quarterly*, *24*(1), 169–196. doi:10.2307/3250983

Brito, M. (2012). *Smart Business, Social Business: A Playbook for Social Media in Your Organization*. Indianapolis, IN: Pearson Education.

Bughin, J. (2009). How firms are benefiting from Web 2.0. *The McKinsey Quarterly*.

Bulankulama, S., Khatibi, A., & Shokri, T. (2014). The Effect of Utilization of social media for competitive Advantage in Sri Lankan Hotel industry, *International Journal for Innovation Education and Research*.

Caldeira, M. M., & Ward, J. M. (2003). Using resource-based theory to interpret the successful adoption and use of information systems and technology in manufacturing small and medium-sized enterprises. *European Journal of Information Systems*, *12*(2), 127–141. doi:10.1057/palgrave.ejis.3000454

Chaffey, D., & Bosomworth, D. (2012). *Creating a social media marketing plan*, Need to know guide. Smart Insights (Marketing Intelligence) Limited.

Eastman, J. K., & Iyer, R. (2006). The impact of cognitive age on Internet use of the elderly. *International Journal of Consumer Studies*, *29*(2), 125–136. doi:10.1111/j.1470-6431.2004.00424.x

Eren, E., & Vardarlier, P. (2013). Social Media's Role in Developing an Employees Sense of Belonging in the Work Place as an HRM Strategy, 9th International Strategic Management Conference. *Procedia: Social and Behavioral Sciences*, *99*, 852–860. doi:10.1016/j.sbspro.2013.10.557

Evans, D. (2008). *Social media marketing: An hour a day*. Indiana: Wiley Publishing Inc.

Flynn, N. (2012). *The Social Media Handbook: Policies and Best Practices to Effectively Manage Your Organization's Social Media Presence, Posts and Potential Risks. San Francisco, CA.: Pfeiffer, Friedrichsen, M., & Mühl-Benninghaus, W. (2013). Handbook of social media management: Value chain and business models in changing media markets*. Berlin, Heidelberg: Springer-Verlag.

Garrigos, F., Alcamí, R., & Ribera, T. (2012). Social networks and Web 3.0: Their impact on the management and marketing of organizations. *Management Decision*, *50*(10), 1880–1890. doi:10.1108/00251741211279657

Hitt, M. A., & Hoskisson, R. E. (2013). *Strategic Management Cases: Competitiveness and Globalization. South Western*. USA: Cengage Learning.

HUBSPOT. (2015). Social Media Benchmarks Report.

Ismail, A. I., Rose, R. C., Abdullah, H., & Uli, J. (2010). The Relationship between Organisational Competitive Advantage and Performance Moderated By the Age and Size of Firms. *Asian Academy of Management Journal, 15*(2), 157–173.

Jagongo, A., & Kinyua, C. (2013). The Social Media and Entrepreneurship Growth (A New Business Communication Paradigm among SMEs in Nairobi). *International Journal of Humanities and Social Science, 10*(3).

Jantsch, J. (n.d.). Let's Talk Social Media for Small Business. *Version Two.*

Kaplan, A., & Haenlein, M. (2010). Users of the World, Unite! The Challenges and Opportunities of Social Media. *Business Horizons, 53*(1), 59–68. doi:10.1016/j.bushor.2009.09.003

Kietzmann, J. H., Hermkens, K., McCarthy, I. P., & Silvestre, B. S. (2011). Social media? Get serious! Understanding the functional building blocks of social media. *Business Horizons, 54*(3), 241–251. doi:10.1016/j.bushor.2011.01.005

Kimani, E. (2015). Role of Social Media Marketing On Organisational Performance in Kenya, *IOSR Journal of Business and Management (IOSR-JBM)*, 17(1), P. 101- 105.

Linke, A., & Zerfass, A. (2012). Future trends in social media use for strategic organization communication: Results of a Delphi study. *Public Communication Review, 2*(2). doi:10.5130/pcr.v2i2.2736

Liu, C. H., & Liu, H. S. (2009). Increasing competitiveness of a firm and supply chain with Web 2.0 initiatives. *International Journal of Electronics Business Management, 7*(4), 248–255.

Lorenzo-Romero, C., Constantinides, E., & Alarcón-del-Amo, M. (2014). *Social Media as Marketing Strategy: An Explorative Study on Adoption and Use by Retailers, Social Media in Strategic Management, Advanced Series in Management* (pp. 197–215). Emerald Group Publishing Limited.

Manpower Inc. (2010). Employer Perspectives on Social Networking: Global Key Findings. *Survey (London, England).*

Merchant, N. (2012). *11 rules for creating value in the social Era.* Cambridge, MA: Harvard Business Review Press.

Miller, R., & Lammas, N. (2010). Social media and its implications for viral marketing. *Asia Pacific Public Relations Journal, 11*(1), 1–9.

Newman, J. (2013). *Social Media for Internet Marketers: How to Take Advantage of Facebook, Twitter and Google.* USA: Papaplus.

Nguyen, T. U. H. (2009). Information technology adoption in SMEs: An integrated framework. *International Journal of Entrepreneurial Behaviour & Research, 15*(2), 162–186. doi:10.1108/13552550910944566

Oh, J. (2015). *Social Media as Firm's Network and Its Influence on the Corporate Performance*, The International World Wide Web Conference Committee (IW3C2). Florence, Italy. 10.1145/2740908.2741754

Öztamur, D., & Karakadılar, I. (2014). Exploring the role of social media for SMEs: As a new marketing strategy tool for the firm performance perspective, 10th International Strategic Management Conference. *Procedia: Social and Behavioral Sciences, 150*, 511–520. doi:10.1016/j.sbspro.2014.09.067

Pentina, I., Koh, A. C., & Le, T. T. (2012). Adoption of social networks marketing by SMEs: Exploring the role of social influences and experience in technology acceptance. *International Journal of Internet Marketing and Advertising, 7*(1), 65–82. doi:10.1504/IJIMA.2012.044959

Peteraf, M. A. (1993). The cornerstones of competitive advantage: A resource-based view. *Strategic Management Journal, 14*(3), 179–191. doi:10.1002mj.4250140303

Piskorski, M. (2014). *A Social Strategy: How we profit from social media*. Princeton University Press. doi:10.1515/9781400850020

Polat, V., & Akgün, A. (2015). A Conceptual Framework for Marketing Strategies in Web 3.0 Age: Adaptive Marketing Capabilities. *Journal of Business Studies Quarterly, 7*(1).

Porter, M. E. (1985). *Competitive Advantage: Creating and Sustaining Superior Performance*. New York: The Free Press.

Premkumar, G. (2003). A meta-analysis of research on information technology implementation in small business. *Journal of Organizational Computing and Electronic Commerce, 13*(2), 91–121. doi:10.1207/S15327744JOCE1302_2

Qualman, E. (2011). *Socialnomics: How Social Media Transforms the Way We Live and Do Business*. Hoboken, NJ: John Wiley & Sons, Inc.

Rodriguez, M., Peterson, R., & Krishnan, V. (2012). Social Media's Influence on Business-to-Business Sales Performance. *Journal of Personal Selling & Sales Management, 32*(3), 365–378. doi:10.2753/PSS0885-3134320306

Schultz, R.J., Schwepker, C.H., & Good, D.J. (2012). An exploratory study of social media in business-to-business selling: salesperson characteristics, activities and performance, *Marketing Management Journal*, 22(2).

Smith, W. R., & Vardiabasis, D. (2010). Using social media as a competitive advantage the case of small businesses. *Problems and Perspectives in Management*, 8(4).

Srivastava, M., Franklin, A., & Martinette, L. (2013). Building a Sustainable Competitive Advantage. *Journal of Technology Management & Innovation*, 8(2), 7–8. doi:10.4067/S0718-27242013000200004

Swift, T., & Zadek, S. (2002). *Corporate Responsibility and the Competitive Advantage of Nations*. The Copenhagen Centre & AccountAbility.

Teo, T. H. S., & Piang, Y. (2004). A model for web adoption. *Information & Management*, 41(4), 457–468. doi:10.1016/S0378-7206(03)00084-3

Thomas, L. M. (2010). *Sending marketing messages within social networking* (pp. 3–4). Journal Of Internet Law.

University of Maryland. (n.d.). The state of small business report, 2010. Network Solutions, LLC. University of Maryland Robert H. *Smith School of Business*.

Van Zyl, A. (2009). The impact of social networking 2.0 on organizations. *The Electronic Library*, 27(6), 906–918. doi:10.1108/02640470911004020

Vorhies, D. W., & Morgan, N. A. (2005).. . *Benchmarking Marketing Capabilities for Sustainable Competitive Advantage*, 69(1), 80–94.

Vrontis, D., & Thrassou, A. (2013). *Innovative Business Practices: Prevailing a Turbulent Era*. UK: Cambridge Scholars Publishing.

Weerawardena, J. (2003). The Role of Marketing Capability in Innovation-Based Competitive Strategy. *Journal of Strategic Marketing*, 11(1), 15–35. doi:10.1080/0965254032000096766

Weinberg, T. (2009). *The new community rules: Marketing on the social web*. Sebastopol, CA: O'Reilly Media, Inc.

Wirtz, B. W., Schilke, O., & Ullrich, S. (2010). Strategic development of business models: Implications of the Web 2.0 for creating value on the internet. *Long Range Planning*, 43(2), 272–290. doi:10.1016/j.lrp.2010.01.005

## KEY TERMS AND DEFINITIONS

**Competitive Advantage:** An organizational capability to perform in one or many ways that competitors find difficult to reproduce now and in the future.

**Facebook:** A social networking website launched in February 2004. Users of Facebook can create a personal profile, add other users as friends, and exchange messages, including automatic notifications, photos, and comments when they update their profile.

**Social Media:** Refers to the wide range of internet-based and mobile service that allow users to participate in online exchanges, contribute user-created content, or join online communities.

**Social Media Marketing (SMM):** Means techniques that aim to promote products or spread brand awareness through social networks and its applications; it can also defined as a form of internet marketing that implements various social media networks in order to achieve marketing communication and branding goals.

**Social Networking Services (SNS):** A web-based software application that helps users connect and socialize with friends, family members, business partners, or other individuals.

**Social Networking Sites:** Facilitate individuals build social relationships and interests among friends and acquaintances (e.g., Facebook, LinkedIn, Google Plus+).

**Tweet:** A short, 140-character message delivered on the micro-blogging platform Twitter by those who have set up a free account on the site.

**Twitter:** The most famous micro-blogging site on the internet, where people can tweet about the things that interest them, as well as retweet—or tweet again—the tweets of others. Twitter was founded in 2006.

**Web 2.0:** A second generation in the development of the world wide web; imagined as a combination of concepts, trends, and technologies that focus on user collaboration, sharing of user-generated content, and social networking. It is including blogs, wikis, video sharing services, and social media websites such as Facebook, Twitter, LinkedIn, MySpace, and Google+. The term Web 2.0 was introduced by the O'Reilly Media Web 2.0 conference in 2004.

**YouTube:** The world's most popular online video community, where millions of people can discover, watch, and share originally created videos. YouTube was founded in 2005.

# Chapter 2
# Digital Marketing and Service Industry:
## Digital Marketing in the Banking Industry

**Ivana S. Domazet**
*Institute of Economic Sciences, Serbia*

**Sladjana Neogradi**
*Addiko Bank, Serbia*

## ABSTRACT

*The aim of this chapter is to investigate the impact of the implementation of digital sales channels on improving the bank's business performance (i.e., improving the market position of the bank). The authors look at different types of sales channels and their contribution to increasing the number of clients in the bank, and in particular, they focus on the advantages of the Viber Platform in reaching more clients. A survey on digitalization of the banking sector was conducted, that is, on the integration of digital communications and sales channels, that bringins with it new elements and possibilities for expanding the portfolio of bank services, and thus new opportunities for increasing profits. Based on the results of the survey, it was concluded that banks use digital communications to improve and make more effective and efficient communication with clients, while trying to bring them closer to the offer. With this approach, banks will achieve greater satisfaction and consequently a greater loyalty of their clients.*

DOI: 10.4018/978-1-5225-5993-1.ch002

# INTRODUCTION

The financial services market has undergone significant changes in recent years. Information technology, including models of modern information architecture, databases and data warehouses, data protection, data management, computer communication, modern statistical software and other IT tools, contributed to an enormous increase in the speed of data processing, the introduction of ATMs, the functioning and processing of various types of credit and payment cards and a like. This technology advancement enabled financial organizations to offer a wide range of quality products and services to the market. In addition, due to the exponential growth of digital communication channels, and in particular social networks, the role of digital marketing takes on an increasingly important item in determining the overall marketing budgets.

In order to be competitive, the financial organization must focus on fostering customer loyalty, integrating various communication channels, lowering operating costs and good risk management. Financial organizations (banks, insurance companies, leasing companies, investment and pension funds, etc.) strongly influence the flows of activities in the real economy. Such impact has been particularly noticeable in the last five years in Serbia, but also in the whole world. High degree of competitiveness of the financial services market is, among other things, conditioned by the fact that "production" and the provision of some financial services also involve certain non-financial organizations. Direct and "lateral" competition compel financial organizations to compete for the marketplace by developing innovative activities and offering a richer and more quality product and service range in comparison to the competition. Therefore, the primary activity of financial organizations must be the research of needs, preferences, habits, wishes and demands of present and potential clients and ways of their profitable satisfaction.

In order to identify, anticipate and profitably satisfy the requirements of its clients, and accordingly ensure continuous growth and development, it is necessary that the entire financial organization and the activity of all its employees (especially those who are in constant contact with clients), rely on the modern settings of financial services marketing (with special emphasis on digital marketing).

Some of the postulates of financial organizations' modern marketing are:

- Assets of the organization / company are worth little without its clients;
- The task of managing the marketing of a financial organization is not only to attract new ones but also to retain existing clients;
- New customers can only be acquired by delivering superior value / offer;
- Only satisfied customers can be loyal to the given organization;

- The role of marketing is to create a superior offer and to achieve customer satisfaction, but also to anticipate the future needs of its clients.

All marketing activities use the Internet (web and email) as a channel of communication. The Internet has many advantages comparing to other media and provides much greater opportunities for banks, not just as a channel of communication, but also as a distribution channel. In addition to text and graphics, the Internet also transfers audio and video content to clients. Banks frequently communicate with their clients via e-mails. They are working on an analysis of the target group of clients after which they send out e-mails that need to be concise and clear. After sending the message, they evaluate the results achieved and apply the experience in order to redefine marketing communications. Mobile marketing is increasingly present in the offer of banking services. It includes mobile banking, which is often provided as a part of the clients' current account package. In addition, mobile marketing allows banks to reach customers through a mobile device with some type of marketing message.

Banks devote great attention to credibility in the creation of their web sites, which also represents one of the digital channels for the provision (and sales) of banking services. The website has to be designed in sucha a manner that the information that is necessary for the clients is easily accessible through it. Some banks place the web-chat option on their web site, where clients communicate online with a robot that, through a set of certain Q&A scenarios, directs them to the realization of sales of banking products/services. Websites are constantly upgraded and updated with current marketing campaigns and special offers.

Banks use social media and social networks to realize sales plans, as they strive for greater market share. Social networks represent a type of communication similar to a personal contact that represents the most powerful way of market representation. Customers opt for the products and services that a bank has in its offer based on the recommendations of their friends through Facebook or Twitter or based on personal recommendations.

After receiving the recommendation, clients visit the bank's branches, where they get direct impressions through contact with the employees and verify the truthfulness of the propaganda messages of the financial institution. Their relationship in communication with potential clients is often decisive in gaining loyalty and increasing the portfolio. Sales channels, as a way of providing services to clients, must be adapted to the characteristics of the services themselves.

Special emphasis will be given to the proposed model for the integration of communication and sales channels, which will enable the increase of sales volume and, at the same time, satisfy the needs of customers. Banking institutions analyze the benefits of products for proactive communication with their clients and create the methodologhy and directives for the sales staff to use in sales talks. Cross-selling guidelines should enable the customer-facing employees to recognize the sales potential at the moment when the client performs the transaction. Sales arguments are the basis for a proactive approach to the client. The purpose of the sales arguments is to enable employees in the bank to assure the client of the advantages that he could gain from a particular bank offer/product. For personal sales, sales tools are used to enable the retailer to support communication with the client, to keep the client's attention and to provide advice.

Digital distribution channels in banks reduce operating costs and, for this reason, banks are increasingly applying (CRM) campaigns in order to meet diversified customer needs and achieve better business results. CRM is an important segment of strategic planning and is viewed in the context of marketing and promotional mix. Its goal is to increase the profitability of the company and meet the needs of its customers. The CRM concept ensures a more efficient segmentation of target groups, analytical forecasting of market trends, analysis of the profitability of individual customers, improvement of service quality, ability to sell, shorter sales cycle, intense development of competitive advantage and the reputation of the company as a strong business partner.

## BACKGROUND RESEARCH AND LITERATURE REVIEW

Financial services were the subject of interest and research by many authors, including: Ennew and Waite, 2007; Cheverton, et. al. 2008; Ehrlich and Fanelli 2004; Kangis 2000; Lovelock and Wirtz 2004; Klasens 2007; Mittal 2002; Gronroos 1998; Grove, Carlson and Dorsch 2002; Mortimer 2002; Ljubojević 1998, Veljković 2009; Kancir 2006 etc.. It is generally accepted that the basic dimensions of service quality are: (in) tangibility, reliability, accountability, security and empathy (Marinković, Stanković, 2012, p. 258-259).

Ljubojević (1998) deals with the analysis of financial organizations and the definition of their goals, such as increasing market share, expanding existing markets, developing new banking services in the existing and new markets, increasing profitability, etc. Gronroos (1998) considers that the management of basic marketing mix instruments, towards the application of marketing in the field of services, need certain adjustments in relation to the classic 4P concept, which is often applied in the production sector and physically tangible products. The nature of the service and the high level of interactivity of the servicing process has influenced the extension of the traditional concept of marketing mix by adding elements / instuments that relate directly to *people*. This particularly applies to employees in the first line of communication with clients and the way they communicate; the *physical* environment in which they operate, and the *processes* applied by financial organizations during the provision of services.

Authors Tellis, Chandy and Thaivanich (2000) developed and demonstrated a model that measures the effects of economic propaganda through television. The proposed model provides a comprehensive method to evaluate the effect of TV advertising on consumers by simultaneously separating the effects of the ad itself from that of the time, placement (channel), creative cues, repetition, age of the ad, and age of the market. Based on the analysis conducted, conclusions were drawn about the type of ads that immediately receive a direct response, but their effects disappeared for a short time. Depending on the advertisement model, its repetition at the daily level and the TV station (channel) which broadcast it, varies its profitability.

Bhat, Bevans and Sengupta (2002) presented methods that offer the ability to measure the effects of online (Internet) advertising. They consider that the choice of methods depends on the objectives of the research, the budget and the technique at the disposal of the company and the time during which the research should be carried out. They emphasize that for the measurement of advertising one should take into account the following: the popularity of the website to attract and retain consumer attention, highlighting the benefits for users who visit the site and the efficiency of targeting users. For each of these goals, the authors list specific methods, and some of them are page views, page popularity, number of page visitors, number of advertisement views, duration of page review during first visit, the number of page returns, the time that passes until the user returns to the page again, profiling of visitors. Authors emphasize that there is no best way of measuring online advertising, but that the measurement should be based on the research in respect to achieving set goals and on combining multiple research methods.

Jevremović, Štavljanin, Kostić-Stanković (2016) analyzed the impact of interactive characteristics of web sites as the company's main communication tool on the Internet. Namely, each interactive feature of the website affects the user in a different way and in a different degree. Depending on the goals that the company wants to achieve through the website, it should use a different mix of interactive features. This result of the authors' research suggests that companies can create interactive websites in order to raise awareness about a particular brand of the company. With interactive websites, great potentials for increasing brand awareness have more and more popular video games, provided that the characteristics of the promoted brand are compatible and can fit into the context of the video game, because then the indirect effects of advertising within video games can be expected (Štavljanin, Kostić-Stanković & Cvijović, 2016).

Authors Ehrlich and Fanelli (2004) explore the competition in financial institutions, and the process of decisioning whether to position the offer directly with a competitor, or to focus on the free market. After selecting the target market, a financial organization develops an appropriate marketing strategy for each selected segment that, depending on the characteristics of the target market segment, represents a combination of different marketing mix elements

Wyman (2010) claims there are three key levers that can boost the potential of multi-channel distribution and provide an appropriate integrated and efficient distribution model, while simultaneously maximizing economic profit. Those are: 1) optimizing the potentials of each distribution channel individually, while overcoming obstacles and detecting hidden values; 2) increasing the integration of those channels that customers prefer with the goal of fully accepting this channel and 3) aligning the organization and processes with the goal of further development of multi-channel distribution. The process and the way in which it performs services is very important in gaining a general image about the financial organization and its professionalism. A financial organization that provides quick, accurate and efficient services, has a precisely determined sequence of activities in the services provisioning proces, and that is ready to listen to the client at any moment, will create a very favorable impression and create a path for further successful cooperation (Domazet, Zubović & Jeločnik, 2010)

From passive information consumers, created by professional editors, users of banking services have become active creators and users of word-of-mouth information. They consume information from online communities, user reviews, blogs and, of course, critically compare them with the official information of financial institutions present in the form of promotional videos, e-mails, official webcasts, brochures, etc. (Sakal, Pantelić & Matković, 2011).

Salai and Grubor (2011) put their accent on economic propaganda, which represents a form of inelastic communication about the company and its products. It is transmitted through the media in order to inform their clients. It also represents education on the product in order to create positive predispositions and thereby encourage purchasing. Authors (Dibb, Simkin & Pride, 2011) emphasize that thanks to economic propaganda, consumers compare messages from various competitors because they hear promotional messages repeatedly. In addition, these authors point out that economic propaganda affects the increase in product value and that this positively influences consumer awareness of the particular product. Tavan (2011) states that 60% of retail banks in the world do not use much of the social media to deepen relations with their clients, while recent research (Deloitte, 2013), however, reports that 90% of the world's largest banks are present on Facebook, and 88% on Twitter. The study included five social networks, most commonly used by analyzed banks: Facebook, Twitter, YouTube, Instagram and Linkedin. As seen from the table, have 23 banks Facebook, 12 banks are present on Twitter, 22 have opened the YouTube channel, 12 banks have the Instagram profile, while 24 banks have the Linkedin account (out of which 9 have no registered activity). The analysis shows that the surveyed banks have the liveliest social activities on Facebook and Youtube, with the noteworthy fact that banks dominantly use YouTube channel for uploading video material used in television propaganda activities

Meyer (2011) states that banks should particularly use the potential of Internet banking. Forecasts say that by 2020, 60% of Europeans will use Internet banking. Authors (Kohali & Sheleg, 2011) analyze the first virtual office on Facebook, opened in New Zealand in 2010, which offers banking consultancy services to its clients, but without the possibility of realizing transactions. Regardless of the fact that this channel is still limited, this represents the first phase to exploit the huge potential of social networks.

Tinnila (2012) and McKinsey (2012) dealt with the analysis of trends that affect changes in banking distribution channels. To investigate the impact of economic propaganda on brand choice, the Relevance-Accessibility Model (RAM model) can be used (Baker, Lutz, 2000). By applying this model, the authors made changes in the observation pariod, so instead of the moment of broadcasting the promotional message, the moment of brand choice was taken into consideration. In this sense, they differ *advertising message involvement* (AMI) – namely the motivational construct that influences the motivation of consumers to process the information at the moment of exposure to a promotional message; and *brand response involvement* (BRI) – namely the motivational construct that influences the motivation of consumers to process the information at the moment of brand choice. There are opinions (Alhaji and Rosmaini, 2012) that the application of new technology affects the greatest potential and the development of retail banking. Regardless of all the benefits offered by the new technology, it can be a limitation or even a threat, if the system itself is not sufficiently protected.

The results of empirical research (Domazet, 2012) show that financial organizations in Serbia use all forms of promotion and market communication in their marketing campaigns. The proportion is as follows: 57% of financial organizations use advertising, 6% use sales promotion, 10% use public relations, 5% use personal sales, 7% use direct marketing, 11% use sponsorship, and 4% use other forms (fairs, cinemas, theaters, sports organizations and donations).

Certain authors (Slavić & Sakal, 2012; Sakal, Slavić, & Szretykó, 2013) call young potential users Net-generation because they use Web 2.0 and represent exceptional potential in the field of marketing of the entire financial sector. There are also opinions (Bradić-Martinović, 2013) who believe that the implementation of technology in the banking industry should be focused on the automation of processes and their monitoring. Due to business applications, information in the bank is processed through devices such as ATMs, POS terminals at points of sale, as well as through applications such as electronic and mobile banking

Accenture (2013) estimates that, if they do not innovate their current business model, universal banks in the North American market will lose 35% of its share by 2020 from financial institutions that use Internet and mobile technology. O'Connor, (2014), thinks that a major contribution to the development of payment applications can be assigned to the boost in IT sector that has enabled the creation of databases and their continuous monitoring. At the same time, it was possible for banks to consider risk exposure and its measurement using modern statistical and mathematical models. This gave banks the ability to manage their portfolio.

Digital distribution channels in banks reduce operational costs and increases the productivity of bank employees due to automated processes and migration of transactional activities towards digitalization (Olenrewaju et al, 2014). Sandader (2014) points out that the countries of North America, Europe and Australia have the most developed mobile banking, and the US *JPMorgan Chase Bank* stands out as the market leader among them. This bank has developed the most advanced mobile banking applications used on smartphones while relying on resources such as the web site and two-way short message services. Samar Rahi and Mazuri Abd Ghani (2016), Internet Banking, Customer Perceived Value and Loyalty: The Role of Switching Costs, University of Sultan Zainal Abdin, Malaysi, *Journal Account Mark 2016, 5:4*. Study findings evoked from structured questionnaires indicate that while struggling for customer loyalty, the banks will focus on internet banking services and customers percieved value. Besides, switching costs moderate the relationship between internet banking, customer perceived value, and customer loyalty. Internet banking is the key service for customer loyalty. Moreover, if the managers want their clients to be loyal to the bank, they shpuld focus on the customer perceived value.

# MAIN FOCUS OF THE CHAPTER

## Digital Marketing and Banking Industry

Digital distribution channels in banks reduce operating costs and therefore banks are increasingly applying (CRM) campaigns in order to meet diversified customer needs and achieve better business results. CRM is an important segment of strategic planning and is observed in the context of marketing and promotional mix. Its goal is to increase the profitability of the company while meeting the needs of its clients. The CRM concept ensures a more efficient segmentation of target groups, analytical forecasting of market trends, analysis of the profitability of individual customers, improvement of service quality, ability to sell, shorter sales cycle, intense development of competitive advantage and the company reputation as a strong business partner

In modern banking, digital channels are being increasingly used as the primary communication channel, with the aim to establish better relationships with clients. The use of digital channels is to provide clients with an adequate service at any time and any place. Digital communication channels enable banks a proactive and personalized approach in servicing the financial needs of their clients. The use of social networks, web chat and Viber is a new form of communication with clients. Via the live web-chat (that sometimes includes video chat for better connection), banks directly communicate with their clients, offer online banking services or assist their clients to locate the nearest branch or ATM.

Viber is popular, widespread, free and very attractive. It offers voice and video messages sharing between Viber contacts, and Viber stickers for new way of communication. Viber does not require user account, allows users of their services to send messages of all types and make phone calls to other Viber users free. Viber is synchronized with the contacts directory, so users do not need to add contacts separately. In addition to text messaging, users can share stickers, images, audio and video media. Viber users often use stickers while communicating. This is one of the directions for digital channels development and brand strengthening. The goal of using Viber Stickers in banking is to increase brand awareness, rather then sales, and to encourage users engage with the brand. Viber stickers can also be used in Public Chat, which is a free and attractive tool through which brands develop a loyal and dedicated community. Through Viber Stickers, the bank follows modern trends in communication with younger generations, while at the same time helps in developing good savings habits from an early age. Digital banking on the Viber Platform represents a guideline for financial organizations on how to improve their digital business.

Service users, especially the new generation, will accept the benefits of digital communication tools if they can use them. The first bank in the Serbian market, which bases its digital communication on the use of Viber Platform, is Addiko Bank. Large number of users of the Viber application enables personalized communication by organizing prize games and other forms of rewarding customer loyalty, based primarily on digital tools and measurable indicators of the cost-effectiveness of a promotional campaign. On the other hand, two-way communication allows clients to express their creativity, but also to present the desired way of meeting their financial needs in a digital environment in a timely manner.

Digital communication channels enable banks a proactive and personalized approach in servicing the financial needs of teir clients. The use of social networks, web chat and Viber is a new form of communication with clients. Viber is popular, widespread, free, very attractive application that offers sending of voice and video messages.

The development of digital communication points to the importance of implementing new, modern approaches and the necessity of change in the current business practices, in order to maximize the benefits for the business system with minimal investment. Digital media is available without limitations – we can access them at any time, whenever it suits us, in order to find the information, we need or to communicate. Different channels of communication (mobile phones, the Internet, etc.) are at the same time channels for the distribution of banking products, but on the other hand, precisely because of such development, client expect improvement of the quality of service and more efficient operation. This fact is at the same time a great opportunity, but also a great danger in the sale of banking products and services.

Those banks that move more towards digitalization and transform their physical distribution network, can achieve a significant increase in their efficiency ratio. On the other hand, those banks that do not do that, can become an obstacle to developing new banking models globally and lose their clients. It is obvious that the development of alternative channels for the distribution of banking products and services is of great importance for the survival of banks, and greater attention will be given to the Internet and mobile banking as the bearers of innovations in the banking industry.

Mobile phones have largely entered the everyday use of the modern man. According to a survey conducted in 2014, 87% of US adults have a mobile phone, and 78% of the total number of handsets are considered as "smart phones". Mobile phones and the massive use of smartphones are changing the way consumers pay for products and services. This is supported by the fact that, according to the survey, in 2013, 22% of mobile phone users made payments via their handsets, with the share of smartphone users in this number of 28%. In addition, one of the benefits of "smart phones" is that they provide an opportunity for the user to compare prices in order to find the product at the best price, as well as the ability to find detailed information about a product through product bar codes (Board of Governors of Federal Reserve System, 2015, p. 1-2). Electronic and mobile banking provides 24/7 access to the bank – regardless of working hours, lower costs – because fewer clients go to the bank counter, time saving and online connection that can be established anywhere.

In order to redirect and redesign business practices, the banking sector uses technological innovations that allow access to less available and more demanding prospects. In order to gain new and retain existing clients, financial institutions use social media that represent online resources and platforms that people use to share experiences and perspectives. The basic feature of social networks is the possibility of far greater interaction and individualization than with other direct communication channels. Today, companies can place individualized content through social networks. In addition, companies can interact and dialogue with far broader populations than in the past (Kotler, 2006). Banks that recognize the importance of participation in social networks have already based their marketing strategy on this form of distribution of their products and services. Financial institutions consider that if they have their account on social networks, they emphasize their brand, put accent on direct communication and improvement of customer relationship, and reduce the costs brought by conventional forms of promotion.

Social networks are often referred to as Linkedin, Twitter, Google, Facebook, etc. Linkedin is the largest professional social network. Business people exchange different content on it. The significance of LinkedIn is in staff recruitment. Users want to be noticed on that network and actively comment on other blogs and profiles. The opportunity offered on LinkedIn is paid ads and the company's presentation through their profiles. According to the results of the Performics survey on a sample of 2,997 social network users, 60 percent of respondents said their LinkedIn account was more important than any other social network account (Crowe, 2011). In March 2012 LinkedIn reached 100 million users. Although the development of this professional network is only in the beginning in Serbia, professionals in the USA find LinkedIn ast the most important Network by far.

Search engine optimization (SEO) is defined as a series of actions that are run on web sites, all in order to gain a better positioning of the page on Google. The first step is to choose the key word that attracts visitors to the site. In order to optimize the website, financial organizations check how often a keyword related to a product or service is searched by search engines Banks regularly optimize the site because there is a danger that the site loses its relevance. Website optimization is a very slow process, so it needs to be done carefully and patiently.

Facebook is one of the leading social networks today. It is used to share TV commercials, company blogs, and social actions. Many businesses adapt to modern trends and take advantage of social networks to offer their commercial services to as many potential users as possible. When this social network is used for business purposes, one of the main advantages is continuous two-way communication with fans. Companies use Facebook to improve brand reputation and brand recognition. It is also used as a successful marketing channel for publishing content in the form of new and interesting actions, for following the brand, getting feedback from customers and a like. Reading news in the form of a status or publication reveals various information that remains somewhere in the subconscious.

Twitter is a free social networking and micro-blogging tool that allows its users to read others' and send their own micro-textual entries, so-called tweets. Communication and information provided through Facebook pages are mainly information regarding services provided by banks, or activities that they organize and support, so it can really be useful to be a fan of your bank on Facebook. Twitter is often described as 'Internet SMS' because the site provides users with the opportunity to send and receive new entries using various tools, so it is often not necessary to use the original site itself. This flexibility has enabled the site to gain more popularity than it would have been if users were forced to visit the original site in order to use this service. Banks use Twitter to share information with those who are interested in their products and services quickly and easily, bringing together existing and potential customers. In this way, they try to animate clients and encourage them to come to the branch office or to open an account through online application.

YouTube is the most popular Internet service for exchanging video contents, where users can upload, review and evaluate video clips. In order to upload the content, it is necessary to register, while this is not required for reviewing. The members of this site can create personal profiles and upload favorit video recordings through them. YouTube's functiuonality allows users to easily copy and upload content to blogs, Twitter or Facebook profiles. There are thousands of short videos on this service, which people have recorded with their cameras, phones, and webcams. In addition, many inserts from films, TV shows and various other video materials have been stored. A company or individual can take advantage of this service by promoting shows and movies, music and advertising spots. Every day, over 2 billion videos are viewed on YouTube, and 35 hours of content is uploaded every minute.

In addition to social networks, which have dramatically changed communication and sales channels in recent years, CRM (Customer Relationship Marketing) is one of the most important factors in improving communications, enabling banks to acquire potential customers and ensure their loyalty over a longer period, thus enhancing their market share. By combining traditional distribution channels, using CRM, opening accounts via mobile phones and paying via Viber, a high degree of digitization of communications has been achieved, which leads to an increase in profits of financial institutions. By improving various types of communication with clients, banks tend to draw their offer closer to them and establish quality and long-term relationships. Numerous factors influence the decision of the client when choosing a bank. These are, above all, the price and quality of service, speed and simplicity, as well as the kindness of the staff. The quality of service is conditioned by the expertise and interest of the financial organization to assist its clients. Therefore, personal sales, as a form of communication in a financial organization, has a special significance. Through contact with employees, clients get direct impressions based on which they verify the truthfulness of the economic messages of the financial organization. Their relationship with potential clients is often decisive in gaining loyalty.

Empirical research conducted for the needs of this paper refers to the collected data by interviewing more than 100 clients of one bank in Serbia, with the questionnaire model using one question in the field of electronic communications. The question was: "What type of information about the banks' services do you use to meet your needs?"

*Table 1. Information about the services of the bank*

| Information About the Services of the Bank | % |
|---|---|
| By going to Branch of the bank | 12 |
| Advertising on TV | 30 |
| Internet and web site | 23 |
| Recommendation to friends | 14 |
| CRM | 5 |
| ATM | 4 |
| Leaflets | 12 |

Source: Author's survey conducted on a sample of 100 clients of Addiko bank a.d. Belgrade, Serbia

Based on the conducted research, a combination of communication channels, which will be used in the promotion of banks' products and services, can be determined. In order to achieve the planned effects of promotion through the implementation of various marketing mix instruments in the financial services industry (and especially in the banking sector), it is necessary to know the basic characteristics and possibilities of individual media. It is very important to evaluate the performance of the media, their number and availability, quality, content, accessibillity, range, costs and their impact on sales, product image and, most important - their impact on brand awareness

Domazet, Đokić and Milovanov (2017) indicate that the economic propaganda media influence brand awareness to a considerable extent, since the average assessments of the respondents in respect to the influence of the media on their brand awareness are high. Their research shows that the respondents ranked five media by the influence and the average rating of the impact of all media (television, billboards, radio, newspapers and the Internet) is above grade 3, except radio rated with an average score of 2.91, which is the smallest average grade, but closer to grade 3 than 2. Detailed results of the survay reveal that television is the medium that has the greatest influence on the brand awareness of the respondents, followed by the Internet, billboards, newspapers and radio. These results point to the conclusion that television is one of the most powerful media and its impact on consumers is high, especially in the female segment, as the results showed that women gave a greater appreciation of the impact of television on their product awareness than men.

Same authors (Domazet, Djokić & Milovanov, 2017) point out that the Internet is the second medium by the strength of its influence on the respondents' brand awareness. The Internet as a modern medium of economic propaganda highlights its interactivity and targeted consumer orientation. When it comes to gender, the results showd that there is a statistically significant difference between men and women, where men are giving higher average assessment on the impact of this medium on their product awareness than women. Comparing the influence of television and the Internet on the brand awareness of men and women, one can conclude that television would be a better medium for promoting cosmetics, healthy food or footwear and clothing, while the Internet would be a better medium for promoting computers, cars, mobile phones or the like. What is still striking in the results related to the impact of the Internet on the respondents' brand awareness is the statistically significant correlation that exists with regard to age of respondents. The results show that, the younger the respondents are the higher ratings they have given to the influence of the internet on their brand awareness, and vice versa. Based on that result, it can be concluded that an Internet media would be appropriate for the promotion of products or services or events intended for younger people such as places to go out, trendy products, and the like.

Outdoor advertising media used as auxiliary media for the transmission of short and concise messages are billboards. The results of the survey show that they are third in terms of brand awareness and there is no statistically significant difference when it comes to their impact on the brand awareness in respect to gender, education and income. However, there is a statistically significant correlation between the years of the respondents and the impact of billboards on their brand awareness. Younger respondents give higher ratings to this medium and vice versa, suggesting that this medium could be used for products intended for the younger population, as is the case with the Internet.

Traditional media that is most used to provide factual information are newspapers, and the results of the survey show the existence of the largest number of statistically significant correlations among respondents precisely when it comes to newspapers. Namely, older respondents, better educated and respondents with higher incomes, gave the highest ratings to the impact of the newspaper on their brand awareness, regardless of whether they are men or women. These results point to the conclusion that the newspapers would be a good medium for products for which additional information is important to consumers

Radio hoilds the last place as the media with the least influence on the brand awareness. The only statistically significant correlation in the case of radio is among the respondents in respect to theirage, as elderly respondents gave higher grades to the influence of radio on their brand awareness compared to younger respondents.

In generall, women are more susceptible to television, and men to the influence of the Internet. Older consumers are more susceptible to the influence of radio and newspapers, and the younger to the influence of billboards and the Internet. Consumers who are more educated and have a higher monthly income are more susceptible to the influence of newspapers.

## RECOMMENDATIONS AND FUTURE RESEARCH DIRECTIONS

Banks need to focus their business on constant innovations and following global trends when communication and sales channels are in question. That is the only way to get new clients, and innovation in the digital marketing sphere will help in retaining them. Changes in the way of doing business are conditioned by the digitization, which became a part of the integrated marketing communications of modern business systems.

The survey was aimed at determining the representation of the use of various digital communication tools used by banks, where social media and mobile services are in focus. Based on the results of the research it is concluded that the quality of digital communications contributes to more efficient and more economical marketing in financial institutions. The more the digital technologies are used, the greater are the opportunities for the process of managing the service distribution channels. The research also proves that the impact of the implementation and integration of digital communications and sales channels influences the improvement of the bank's business performance, that is, on improving the bank's market position

Based on a sample of 100 clients, the results are analyzed and concrete conclusions are made. Data-related constraints stem from the missing or incorrect responses of the respondents to the survey questions, but the sample size and the assumed randomness of error in responses significantly compensate for the adverse consequences of this type of constraint on the assessment. This empirical research needs to be expanded through future research that will encompass the standpoints of managers of the same bank on the influence of digital communications and their impact on changing the performance of the bank.

## CONCLUSION

The concept of personal sales in branch offices represents the traditional distribution channel, and a personal interaction between a bank and a client. It is also considered safer to use comparing to other channels. However, this channel of sales also represents the cost of buying or renting business premises as well as engaging more employees. Departing to bank and waiting in line at the counter represents a significant waste of time for the client. In this paper, we pointed out that many studies show that the use of alternative channels of selling financial services is the future of banking operations. This is supported by the fact that the application of new technologies in financial institutions, as well as the use of smartphones, especially when speaking about younger clients, reduces costs for the bank. M-banking, E-banking and application of Viber, which are at the initial stage of implementation with banks in

Serbia, make business operations with the bank easier and faster. This represents the future of banking business

For more complex banking transactions, traditional channels of sales such as personal contact will remain irreplaceable, although the application of video chat, co-browsing and desktop sharing, together with PCI compliant tools are bringing the change. Many of the studies and surveys we have mentioned in our work have proven that clients who frequently use Mobile or Interent banking services often establish personal contact with the bank. Customers expect banks to continue to work on improving and modernisation of traditional distribution channels. Banks are working on educating employees, applying simple and straitforward banking. The results of the research indicate that it is necessary to invest in the education and training of employees in the field of digital communications and internet marketing. In addition, banks must follow social media trends and engage in activities on social networks. It is necessary that digital communications is integrated into the marketing activities system, in order to achieve the competitive advantage and market success of financial institutions.

## ACKNOWLEDGMENT

This chapter is written as a part of research projects numbers III47009 (European integrations and social and economic changes in Serbian economy on the way to the EU) and OI179015 (Challenges and prospects of structural changes in Serbia: Strategic directions for economic development and harmonization with EU requirements), financed by the Ministry of Education, Science and Technological Development of the Republic of Serbia.

## REFERENCES

Accenture. (2013). *Banking 2020: As the storm abates, North American banks Must Chart a New Course to Capture Emerging Oportunities*. Author.

Barlow, A. K. J., Siddiqui, N. Q., & Mannion, M. (2004). Development in information and communication tehnologies for retail marketing channels. *International Journal of Retail & Distribution Management*, *32*(3), 157–163. doi:10.1108/09590550410524948

Bergeron, B. (2002). *Essentials of CRM: A guide to Customer Relationship management (Essential series)*. Wiley.

Crowe, M. (2011). New social media study: nearly 60 percent say LinkedIn is most important social network account. *Perfomics*. Retrieved from: https://www.performics.com/new-social-media-study-nearly-60-percent-say-linkedin-is-most-important-social-network-account

Domazet, I. (2007). *Unapređenje konkurentnosti preduzeća primenom CRM strategijskog koncepta*. Ekonomski fakultet Beograd i Naučno društvo ekonomista Beograd.

Domazet, I., Zubović, J., & Jeločnik, M. (2010). Development of long-term relationship with clients in financial sector companies as a source of competitive advantage. Bulletin, 62(2), 1-11.

Domazet, I. (2011). Improving the quality of human resources by implementation of internal marketing, u monografiji. In *The Role of Markets and Human Capital in the Unstable Environmenture*. Karta Graphic Publishing House.

Domazet, I. (2012). *Marketing komunikacije finansijskih organizacija*. Institut ekonomskih nauka.

Domazet, I. (2012). Marketing komunikacije finansijskih organizacija. Institut ekonomskih nauka.

Domazet, I. (2015). Nacionalni brend Srbije kao faktor unapređenja konkurentnosti zemlje. *Strukturne promene u Srbiji: dosadašnji rezultati i perspektive*, 482-496.

Domazet, I. (2016). Improving Competitiveness through National Branding. In Development, Competitiveness and Inequality in EU and Western Balkans. Sofia University.

Domazet, I., Đokić, I., & Milovanov, O. (2017). The Influence of advertising media on brand awareness. Časopis Management, 22(23).

Domazet, I., Hanić, H., & Simeunović, I. (2012). Marketing communication efficiency and effectiveness of the media for various target group. *International Scientific Conference-Management 2012, Fakultet za industrijski menadžment*, 791-796.

Domazet, I., & Simović, V. (2014). *Mogućnosti i pretpostavke za razvoj IKT industrije u Srbiji, u Drašković B. Ur. Zbornik radova "Deindustrijalizacija u Srbiji: mogućnost revitalizacije industrijskog sektora"*. Institut ekonomskih nauka.

Domazet, I., Stošić, I., & Hanić, A. (2016). New technologies aimed at improving the competitiveness of companies in the services sector. In *Europe and Asia: Economic Integration Prospects* (pp. 363–377). Nice, France: CEMAFI.

Domazet, I., & Zubović, J. (2011). Database marketing based business development: the case of Serbian financial sector. In Contemporary issues in the integration processes of Western Balkan countries in the European Union. International Center for Promotion of Enterprises Ljubljana, Slovenia.

Domazet, I., Zubović, J., & Simeunović, I. (2012). Analiza procesa i faza razvoja efikasnih marketing komunikacija. *Ekonomika, 3*, 21-31.

Ehrlich, E., & Fanelli, D. (2004). *The Financial Services Marketing.* Princeton, NJ: Bloomberg Press.

Ennew, C., & Waite, N. (2007). *Financial services marketing.* Oxford, UK: Butterworth-Heinemann, Elsevier.

Eriksson, K., & Mattsson, J. (1996). Organising for Market Segmentation in Banking: the Impact from Production Technology and Coherent Bank Norms. *The Service Industry Journal.* Retrieved from www.fsa. gov.uk/pubs/conhsumer-research/crpr47.pdf

Ewing, M.T. (2009). Integrated Marketing Communications Measurement and Evaluation. *Journal of Marketing Communications, 15*(2-3), 103-117.

Gronroos, C. (1998). Marketing services: The case of a missing product. *Journal of Business and Industrial Marketing, 13*(4/5), 322–338. doi:10.1108/08858629810226645

Grove, S., Carlson, L., & Dorsch, M. J. (2002). Addresing Services' intangibility through integrated marketing communication. *Journal of Services Marketing, 16*(5). doi:10.1108/08876040210436876

Hanić, H., & Domazet, I. (2011). Managing Customer Relationship within Financial Organizations. Polish Journal of Management Studies, 4, 151-166.

Hanić, H., & Domazet, I. (2012). Strengthening Economic SubjectsInternal Capacities: Marketing Management and CRM. *Managing Structural Changes: Trends and Requirements*, 44-60.

Hill, P. (1997). On Goods and Services. *Review of Income and Wealth, 23*(4), 13.

Jevremovic, M., Stavljanin, V., & Kostic-Stankovic, M. (2016). Istraživanje aktuelne i percepirane interaktivnosti veb sajta. *Info M, 15*(57), 42–47.

Kancir, R. (2006). Marketing usluga, 2. izdanje Beogradska poslovna škola.

Kangis, P.Y. (2000). Service Quality and customer retentionin financial services. *Journal of Financial Services Marketing, 4*(4).

Kuenn, B. (2014). *10 Top Content Promotion Tools and Services*. Retrieved December 11, 2014 from http://www.verticalmeasures.com/content-marketing-2/10-topcontent-promotion-tools-and-services/

Levison, J. C., & Rubin, C. (1996). *Guerrilla Marketing Online Weapons*. Hoghtom Mifflin Company.

Ljubojević, Č. (1998). *Menadžment i marketing usluga*. Beograd: Želnid.

Lovelock, Ch., & Wirtz, J. (2004). *Services Marketing* (5th ed.). Pearson Education International.

Marinković, S., & Stanković, L. (2011). Institucionalna osnova zaštite korisnika finansijskih usluga u Srbiji. Marketing, 4(42), 257-266.

Milosavljević, M., & Mišković, V. (2011). *Elektronska trgovina*. Beograd: Univerzitet Singidunum.

Mirković, A. (2009). Društvene mreže – društveni fenomen. *Profit, 16-17*, 12–13.

Mittal, B. (2002). Services Communications: from mindless tangibilization to meaningful messages. *Journal of Services Marketing, 16*(5), 424 – 431.

Morgan, R. M., & Hunt, S. D. (1994). The Commitment-Trust Theory of Relationship Marketing. *Journal of Marketing*, *58*(3), 20–38. doi:10.2307/1252308

Mortimer, K. (2002). Integrated advertising theories with conceptual models of services advertising. *Journal of Services Marketing*, *16*(5), 21. doi:10.1108/08876040210436920

Olanrewaju, T., Smaje, K., & Willmott, P. (2014). *The several traits of effective digital enterprises*. McKinsey Insights.

Pelsmacker, P. (2010). *Marketing Communications: A European Perspective* (4th ed.). Pearson Education.

Radice, R. (2014). *How to Use Visual Content to Improve Social Media Results*. Retrieved November 20, 2014 from http://maximizesocialbusiness.com/usevisual-content-improve-social-media-results-16250/

Stavljanin, V., Kostic-Stankovic, M., & Cvijovic, J. (2016). Effects of indirect advertising in video games: Adverisers' and Players' perspective. *Symposium proceedings from XV International symposium Reshaping the Future Through Sustainable Business Development and Entrepreneurship*, 889-892.

## ADDITIONAL READING

Brousseau, E., & Penard, T. (2016). The economics of digital business models: A framework for analyzing the economics of platforms. *Review of Network Economics*, *6*(2), 81–110.

Carayannis, E. G., & Grigoroudis, E. (2012). Linking innovation, productivity and competitiveness: Implications for policy and practice. *The Journal of Technology Transfer*, *39*(2), 199–218. doi:10.100710961-012-9295-2

Carayannis, E. G., Grigoroudis, E., Sindakis, S., & Walter, C. (2014). Business Model Innovation as antecedent of sustainable enterprise excellence and resilience. *Journal of the Knowledge Economy*, *5*(3), 440–463. doi:10.100713132-014-0206-7

Clark, P. (2016). How the Digital Economy is Reinventing the Business World. Retrieved March 17th 2017, from http://www.digitalistmag.com/digital-economy/2016/04/25/how-digital-economy-reinventing-business-world-04167100

Espinel, V. A. (2016). The digital economy: what is it and how will it transform our lives? Retrieved March 17th 2017, from https://www.weforum.org/agenda/2016/11/the-digital-economy-what-is-it-and-how-will-it-transform-our-lives/

Gonzalez-Pernia, J. L., Peña-Legazkue, I., & Vendrell-Herrero, F. (2012). Innovation, entrepreneurial activity and competitiveness at a sub-national level. *Small Business Economics*, *39*(3), 561–574. doi:10.100711187-011-9330-y

Kehal, H. S., & Singh, V. P. (2004). *Digital economy: impacts, influences and challenges*. Hershey: Idea Group Publishing.

Proskuryakova, L., Meissner, D., & Rudnik, P. (2015). The use of technology platforms as a policy tool to address research challenges and technology transfer. *The Journal of Technology Transfer*. Retrieved March 18th 2017 from http://link.springer.com/article/10.1007/s10961-014-9373-8#/page-1

Vidas-Bubanja, M., & Bubanja, I. (2015). ICT as prerequisite for economic growth and competitiveness – case study print media industry. *Journal of Engineering Management and Competitiveness*, *5*(1), 21–28. doi:10.5937/jemc1501021V

## KEY TERMS AND DEFINITIONS

**Banking:** Business operations in the field of banking services (loans, savings, etc.).

**CRM:** Customer relationship management.

**Digital Communication:** Communication through digital media (social networks, the internet, etc.).

**Financial Services:** Specific services related to banking, insurance, and various types of financial operations.

**Internet Marketing:** Marketing activities carried out on the internet.

**Personal Sales:** A sales channel that uses direct approach when selling a particular product to the client.

**Social Media:** Internet media that are organized as user groups with similar interests.

**Social Networks:** Networks on the Internet that have developed due to the similarity in the needs of certain segments of users.

# Chapter 3
# Electronic Word of Mouth (eWOM) Strategies to Manage Innovation and Digital Business Model

**Anshu Rani**
*REVA University, India*

**H. N. Shivaprasad**
*DVHIMSR, India*

## ABSTRACT

*In the digital age, consumers have changed their roles from passive receivers of marketing messages to active information suppliers about products through various digital media. The communication between consumers which occurs online is termed electronic word of mouth (eWOM) communication. Electronic word of mouth communication is an integral part of e-commerce. With the exponential growth of internet users and their adoption of eWOM for product information, it has become important to study the factors responsible for the effectiveness of eWOM. This chapter investigates the traditional WOM and eWOM literature to explore its status. A summary of eWOM communication has been presented to summarize prior studies of eWOM which is aligned with basic communication processes. The research papers (literature) have been segregated into eight categories: WOM, eWOM, eWOM impact, source credibility, message characteristics, receiver characteristics, eWOM platform, and response after eWOM adoption. Finally, several strategies are discussed for theoretical and empirical exploration.*

DOI: 10.4018/978-1-5225-5993-1.ch003

# INTRODUCTION

The rapid growth of digital technology is changing the way businesses worked so far. The field of marketing is exploring new profitable models of business in computer mediated environment. The Internet based marketing models are highly customized, relevant and powerful where consumer create, exchange & choose the information they want (Fernando & Whitelock, 2007). The internet and digital technology have changed the balance of power between buyers and sellers in favour of buyers (Kucuka & Krishnamurthy, 2007). One of the most important capabilities of the Internet, in comparison with previous mass communication technologies, is its bi-directionality (Dellarocas, 2003). It has been observed that the early development of Web is controlled and static. Earlier business institutions on web used to control the content on internet but due to popularity of social media, blogs, bulletin boards, chat rooms, review sites, e-tailersites, and virtual discussion rooms, the information given by markets have lost this effect (Goldsmith, 2006). Consumers produce their own content and control the effective communication on Internet by sharing their ideas, preferences, opinions, experiences and knowledge on relevant consumption matters across globe. One the one side, availability of multi-channel enhances the opportunities for firms to grow multi-dimensionally and on other side, it increases the competition. Consumers often have ample choices to decide from and this forces them to look after information for reducing perceived risk of purchase . Scholars have commonly come to the conclusion that personal advice, recommendation and suggestions from friends, family and fellow consumers know as "word of mouth communication" have high impact on consumer behaviour (e.g. Engel, Blackwell, & Kegerreis 1969; Katz & Lazarsfeld 1955).

The rapid growth of Internet has gradually replaced interpersonal oral communication between consumers about products, by electronic word of mouth communication (eWOM) in the form of online product reviews & ratings in online websites, communities and social media (Chevalier & D., 2006). As consumption increasingly taking place in social domain, individuals either actively or passively engage in eWOM communication (Hennig-Thurau, 2004). For example, eWOM in form of online reviews provides relevant insights about products to make comparison, fulfil shortage of desired information and enable them to exchange ideas and questions in minimum time and efforts. According to Neilson (2015), 92% of consumer around the world say they trust recommendations from other consumer above all forms of advertising. Thus, eWOM is one of the determining forces in influencing attitude towards product, stimulate purchase intention and finally encourage purchase of product (Cheung & Thadani, 2012).

Besides, The World Economic Forum (2014), estimates that there is a growth of 1.2% in per capita GDP with every addition of 10% rise at internet penetration in emerging economics (Shenglin, 2017). Therefore, the impact of eWOM remains significantly wide for emerging economies with growing internet penetration. Even in the theory of the 'Long Tail Business Model" coined by Chris Anderson, (2004), the researcher supports that the electronic word of mouth in the form of online reviews are a significant attribute to shift demand from niche to hit. The eWOM feedback systems allows consumer to exchange their evaluation and experiences on Internet and amplify digital process (Duan & Whinston, 2008). eWOM has greater influence on consumer behaviour which makes eWOM important for marketers, consumers and business organization to provide attention in understanding the complete communication.

The offline as well as online purchase decisions are based on eWOM message as consumers tend to rely on the opinions of other consumer when making decisions (Dellarocas, 2003). The research field has given attention to eWOM since last two decades (Breazeale, 2009), and there is a need for comprehensive look at existing body of Literature. Though the published studies on eWOM are considerable in volume, little effort has been made to integrate this fragmented area of study. This chapter aims to understand the creation motives for WOM and factors responsible for effectiveness of eWOM. For this, the communication process framework has been used to analyse, classify and summarize the prior studies on eWOM to provide a conceptual model. To make a constructive contribution, several research papers have been segregated in seven categories, which are: WOM, eWOM, eWOM impact, source credibility, message characteristics, receiver characteristics, eWOM platform and response after eWOM adoption. The research methodology used is explanatory research to connect ideas available in literature as on date.

The other objective is to also include the best practices in managing the eWOM system and how the businesses can take the necessary advantage by including eWOM strategies integrated with business model. The case research methodology has been used to connect the real life context with available evident.

## BACKGROUND OF ELECTRONIC WORD OF MOUTH

Word of mouth (WOM) is considered to be most influential source of information for purchase of product since time immemorial. WOM is unbiased and therefore highly effective in shaping consumer attitudes, behavioural intentions and purchase (Wu & Wang, 2011). eWOM is defined as web-based interpersonal communication between virtual persons to deliver the information about product & organization without commercial purpose (Litvin, 2008, Cheng & Zhou, 2010). Breazeale (2009) has analyzed several research works to understand the nature of eWOM. Based upon the content analysis, the researchers have identified several elements that characterize this online phenomenon. eWOM is information sharing between consumers about product experiences where opinion leaders play chief role in content sharing. The communication is network-based, via internet and directed to multiple people. eWOM can spread without time and location constraint. Most of eWOM come from anonymous sources and therefore their credibility can be debatable, still, eWOM has seen to be increasingly affecting consumer decisions.

## Motivation and Consequences of eWOM

This part of literature looks into the aspect of what motivates customer to talk about product. There can be different motivations for different people to engage in eWOM communication. More interestingly, researchers have found that motivation to provide eWOM can also lead to positive or negative eWOM valance. The motivation to give eWOM is also strongly correlated with frequency to visit online platform ((Hennig-Thurau, 2004)).The primary motive of giving WOM and eWOM are product satisfaction, commitment, loyalty, trust, involvement and incentives (Neumann, 2015). On other hand, literature focuses on outcome of eWOM communication. The positive outcome of eWOM persuasiveness is change in consumer attitude, purchase intention and further, sales of brand and product. The negative consequences of WOM have been discussed in existing literature as high expectation and product judgement . Given the complexity of research, the emphasis has been to create the model which provides the comprehensive details of eWOM communication.

## Difference Between Word of Mouth and Electronic Word of Mouth

eWOM is also defined as 'any positive or negative statement made by potential, actual, or former customers about a product or company, which is made available to a multitude of people and institutions via the Internet (Hennig-Thurau, 2004). There are certain fundamental difference between traditional WOM and eWOM. Traditionally, oral, face to face communication used to happen between consumers, whereas, today most of the eWOM communication over Internet is written (Hoffmann & Novak, 1996). This allows resupinate access eWOM communication easily since it remains available for them for longer period of time to read. The reach of such communication is also very high. For example, a consumer from Country X wants to buy a product through online channel in Country Y. In this case, multiple online reviews through various platforms written from different geographical location can influence the consumer decision. The other point of difference lies in type of relationship sender and receivers have. Table 1 represents the differences between WOM and eWOM.

*Table 1. Difference between traditional WOM and eWOM*

| Particular | Traditional WOM | eWOM |
|---|---|---|
| Medium | Talk, Personal meeting, Telephone | Social networking sites, Review websites, Discussion forum, blog, e-tailer etc. |
| Form of communication | Oral | Written |
| Relationship | Real social ties | Mostly Virtual ties |
| Type of Interaction | Face to face | Virtual |
| Ease of Transmission | Difficult | Easy |
| Communication format | Linear | Non-Linear |
| Synchronicity | Synchronous | Synchronous or Asynchronous |

Traditional WOM often occurs where there exist strong personal ties between sender and receiver but eWOM mostly occurs among virtual environment where there is high possibility that the sender and receiver do not know each other personally. The common factor here could be experiential similarity which makes a relationship among any anonymous sender and receiver. It is a common feature of Internet that we can share any content with ease and this also applies to eWOM. eWOM is easy to transmit and very viral in nature as one can effortlessly share through social networking sites and other channels (Huang, 2011). Traditional WOM communication is linear in nature and far more synchronized. On other hand, eWOM needs low synchronicity and exhibit non-linear communication format. Lower Synchronicity even means that there is less need for spatial proximity in case of eWOM (Schütze, 2014).

All of these competencies of eWOM make it more accessible for consumer, marketers and business firms. One side where it provide the opportunity to get real time feedback, conduct market research and know the actual & potential customer's mind, on the other side, it also throws up the challenge of managing eWOM content skilfully. Negative eWOM messages about a product and brand can affect the marketing efforts of business firms and can hinder the growth and profitability (Zhang, Behzad, & Cihan, 2017).

Digital Technologies make it fast and easy for consumer to share information about any brand or product encounter (Morrison, Cheong, & and McMillan, 2013). Due to the crucial fact that Internet communities are growing in today's digital scenario and eWOM has become powerful marketing element, and it has become imperative to know the factors influencing effectiveness of eWOM (McCabe& Curran, 2013; Godes, 2015).

## FACTOR INFLUENCING EFFECTIVENESS OF eWOM

Electronic word of mouth is a popular means of providing, acquiring information and opinion about product and services (Litvin et. al, 2008). A comprehensive theoretical framework to explain the factors influencing the effectiveness of eWOM adoption and purchase intention needs to be discussed elaborately. These are the factors which help laying the foundation for understanding of eWOM communication in present scenario. Studying these factors would help marketers to use the framework to analysis the power of eWOM communication for the product & brand. Just like conventional communication process, eWOM communication is also having a source that codes the message and sends it through a medium to receiver. The case of TripAdvisor represent that how credibility issues can be major factor in eWOM effectiveness and later the discussion about factors has been presented.

## Credibility Allegation on TripAdvisor: A Lesson to Learn

TripAdvisor is largest travel website which offers its visitors advices to plan and book for trips they look for. The main offers of TripAdvisor include, but not limited to, wide variety of travel choices and booking tools by comparing links to find good hotel deals. TripAdvisor creates the brand as largest travel community by allowing 350 million unique monthly visitor reviews and opinion sharing about hotels, restaurants and destinations. TripAdvisor operates and continues growing in multiple countries since its inception in 2000. As reported on website of Radio-Television Slovenia, in 2011-12 the company was under examination against the complaint about fake online reviews by Advertising Standards Authority (ASA). After this grumbles from British hoteliers, TripAdvisor withdrew its slogan of 'reviews you can trust'. As per allegation, the online reviews about hotels, restaurants and destinations were not organically generated by actual customer but were misguidedly generated by fake reviewer. Besides, the case of fictional restaurants and guesthouses with high ratings were also found. It was surprizing that the high graded restaurants and guesthouses which were supposed to be classified as best do not even exist in reality. This raises a question on the credibility of such virtual community and online reviews.

One of the major hotel group representatives has agreed that they generated a lot of positive online review for their hotels by themselves and negative reviews about their competitors on website. This is an ethical violence of rule in virtual business guidelines. For all such wrongs and suspicious reviewers and reviews, TripAdviser was highly criticized. They have also been penalized for publishing misleading information (Fill & Krizaj, 2016).

1.  **Factors Related to Source of eWOM:** The author of eWOM message is regarded as source for eWOM communication. The credibility of author regulates the perception about perceived usefulness of eWOM communication in whole. Source credibility is cues that recipient will perceive a message to be trustworthy, erudite and reliable(Nahed Al-Haidari, 2014). The factors affecting credibility of source, represented in eWOM literature are: Source Knowledge, tie strength, source type & source homophily. This factors are discussed in detail as follow:

    a.  **Source Trustability:** Source trustability represents the level of trust which receivers identify for an eWOM message from source. (Saremi, 2014). The trust depends upon cues of source identity disclosed with eWOM message. Use of 'Real name' in place of nick name along with a display of real profile picture gives more cues of trust. Additional information of source like geographic location, profession and gender helps in identifying the trust element between source and receiver of eWOM communication (Menkveld, 2013).

    b.  **Source Knowledge:** The ability of author of eWOM message to demonstrate the prior knowledge or past experience plays significant role in influencing source credibility while adoption of eWOM message (Cheung, Luo, Sia, & Chen, 2009; Senecal et. al, 2004). The effects of eWOM are stronger when source of message have high expertise. Typically usages of product related technical jargons, giving examples and regularity in content creation are symbols to determine the expertise of author.

    c.  **Source Tie Strength:** Tie strength had been one of most powerful element in WOM (Katz, 1956). Tie strength is defined as the level of intensity of social relationship between source and receiver (Cheung & Thadani, 2012). While comparing tie strength offline and online, it has been found that electronic proximity is created by 'experiential similarity' more than 'structural similarity' (Yan Jin, 2002). The strong social tie between eWOM author and receiver positively influences the effectiveness of eWOM by increasing its credibility (Neumann, 2015).

    d.  **Source Homophily:** Homophily is demonstrated as significant variable in effectiveness of word of mouth process. (Brown & Reingen, 1987; Bruyn & Lilien, 2004; Dellande, Gilly & Graham, 2004; Hawlins, 2008; Steffers, 2009). Homophily has been linked to source persuasion in WOM and eWOM literature as effective elements in relationship formation and persuasion. Studies suggest that people prefer those who are similar to them which increase their interpersonal attractiveness and persuasion abilities (McLaughlin, 2012). Source homophily can be defined as the degree to which individuals are similar in age, gender, education and social status (Chaung & Thadani, 2012). The expressions of similar attitude lead to perceived similarity and trust (Meijinders et al, 2009). Source homophily affects receiver's likeability, persuasion and credibility of eWOM.

2. **Factor Related to eWOM Message:** The eWOM communication is traditionally different from WOM communication as the messages are written, beyond geographical boundaries, viral and timeless. Various studies have examined the message characteristics and message text analysis to understand its impact on eWOM adoption (Yayli & Bayram, 2012). The eWOM message characteristics which influence its effectiveness are: valence, volume, presence, consistency, emotion & ratings. The dimension of credibility in eWOM message depends on valence, volume, consistency, emotions, quality and rating (Saremi, 2014). The assessment of eWOM message elements, presentation and argument supports the credibility and encourage the eWOM adoption (Menkveld, 2013)

*Figure 1. A Framework of factor influencing effectiveness of eWOM*

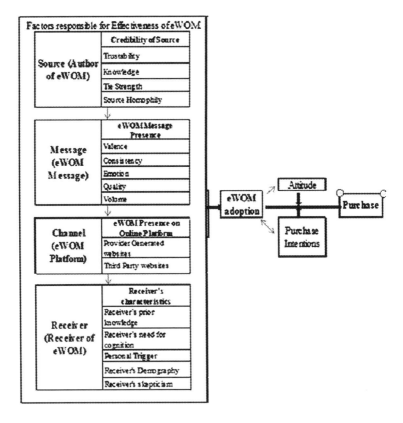

a.  **Message Valence:** The eWOM message valence plays a key role in determining the effect of eWOM in general (Dellarocas & Narayan, 2006; Dematos & Vargas, 2008; Lee, 2008; Park & Lee, 2009). The valence of aneWOM recommendation shows whether message is positive or negative. There is mixed evidence that negative eWOM message influence consumer behavior more than positively framed eWOM. However, there is a likelihood of perceived bias, in case if, a message content is one-sided. Basically, One-sided eWOM presents either the message contain positive or negative information, whereas, two-sided message includes both positive and negative information in the same message. Two-sided eWOM message enhances the completeness of information thus is adopted often for purchase decision (Cheung & Thadani, 2012).

   i.  **Positive Message:** A eWOM message is said to be positive if it contains favorable information about product and brand. In most of the cases, these eWOM are effective.

   ii.  **Negative Message:** Negative information about brand and product is common. Despite the controversy in eWOM research, negatively framed eWOM is more influential than positively framed eWOM (Park & Lee, 2009). Also, negative eWOM is more emotional, novel, valuable and attention drawing than positive eWOM (Klein & Ahluwalia, 2005).

## Amazon.com: Valence, Volume and Consistency in eWOM

Amazon is one of the leading online retailing companies around the world. Amazon has designed its retail website to be consumer-friendly by providing wide range of product in low price to meet consumer requirement. Amazon web services offers technology infrastructure which host product from variety of sellers and bring convenience to both customer and seller in one virtual store. Research shows that Amazon is one of leading website where consumers come to get product information prior to their purchase.

Research has exposed that presence of online review for a product or seller establishes social presence. More the volume of eWOM, more is the acceptability of seller and product is. Amazon offers facility for customer or reviewer to provide open-ended comments and numerical star rating which affect perceived helpfulness. It has been found that moderate reviews are considered as more helpful than extreme positive or extreme negative at Amazon.com. When consumer writes a review in more words and details about product, it enhances the effect of eWOM message. Consumers often find depth of information about product or seller more useful at Amazon. The consistency in eWOM message increases the credibility of product review and influence purchase decisions. Amazon.com can use the eWOM reviews as competitive advantage to formulate more strategies regarding standardization of comment (Mudamb & Schuff, 2010).

    b.   **Message Volume and Consistency:** The available literature indicates that the volume of eWOM is significantly associated with product sales (Cheung & Thadani, 2012). Duan et al, 2000 argues that online eWOM conveys the existence and popularity of product and therefore creates awareness. So, eWOM volume exhibits positive relation with purchase intention and purchase (Duan & Whinston, 2008). Also, related to volume is consistency of eWOM. Information gathering can be done from various online channels and compared by receiver. The consistency of eWOM messages enhances the credibility of eWOM (Yayli & Bayram, 2012).

    c.   **Message Emotion:** Emotion in eWOM message is expressed as extent or type of emotional expressions used (Saremi, 2014). Consumer often get more affected by more emotional expression whether positive or negative (Yin, Bond, & Zhang, 2014). In the eWOM literature, emotional expression in message is said to be influencing the effectiveness of eWOM communication.

    d.   **Message Quality:** The eWOM message quality is determined by argument strength of message (Sia, Tan and Wei, 1999). This holds good for computer-mediated communication as well (Cheung, Luo, Sia & Chen, 2007). Message quality determines the convincing strength of information (Charo & Pershant Sharma, 2015). The quality of eWOM message is related with credibility assessments by the reader, and therefore it influences the effectiveness of eWOM (Menkveld, 2013).

3.   **Factor Related to Medium of eWOM:** There is a need for a channel or a medium for a communication process to take place. Although there are numerous platforms which offer eWOM, they can be broadly classified into two categories- Provider-generated and Third-party generated (Saremi, 2014). Scholars have discussed different platform of eWOM represented in Table 2.

All of these platforms contain eWOM message which are given by other consumers and so perceived to be truthful. However, the eWOM on shopping sites are ready available under every product create a fundamental influence on consumer behavior.

4.   **Factor Related to Receiver of eWOM:** The receiver is the individual consumer who responds to eWOM communication. The effectiveness of eWOM information received varies from individual to individual based on the way they perceive a received message. There are certain receiver's characteristics

*Table 2. eWOM Platforms*

| Platforms | Examples |
| --- | --- |
| Social Networking sites | Twitter.com, Facebook.com |
| Online brand/shopping sites | Amazon.com, Snapdeal.com |
| Online consumer review sites | Epinions.com |
| Online Discussion forums | UKbusinessforums.co.uk |
| Blogs | Blogger.com |

(Cheung & Thadani, 2012)

which influences the eWOM communication (Cheung & Thadani, 2012). The receiver's characteristics which can determine the effectiveness of eWOM communication are consumer's prior knowledge, consumer's need for cognition, consumer skepticism, personal trigger and demographical characteristics.

a.  **Receiver's Prior Knowledge:** Receiver's prior knowledge is receiver's pertinent experience about product which affects the effectiveness of eWOM communication (Cheung &Thadani, 2012; Martin & Lueg, 2013). When consumer is having shortage of information they seek useful information about brand or product through eWOM. The consumers with limited product knowledge evaluate the brand less favorably and so they take help of eWOM for decision making. Also, evaluations are more positive about product when eWOM fits along with prior knowledge of receiver (Hong & Sternthal, 2010). Low prior knowledge of receivers about product allows them to form new attitude with a cognition of empowerment (Cheung & Thadani, 2012).

b.  **Receiver's Need for Cognition:** Individual may differ in the way they process information in general. Need for cognition is receiver's innate desire to think about and process information which they receive. The 'need of cognition' is already a well-researched topic in psychology literature (Cacioppo, 1996). Research findings show that consumer's level of need for cognition determines their motivation to evaluate eWOM (Srivastava & Sharma, 2012; Saremi, 2014). Therefore, receiver having low need of cognition is more likely to accept information of eWOM without evaluating it in much depth.

c.  **Personal Trigger to Receiver:** Consumer's prefer the information that is of their specific purpose. If the information doesn't meet the purpose they generally go through it without going into details (Charo & Pershant Sharma, 2015). The 'personal trigger' is availability of the information in eWOM which receiver wants to look for or in other words the degree of personal relevance that the eWOM holds for the consumer. Consumer wants to find the information that they want quickly and with little effort, and therefore, personal trigger influences eWOM adoption (Duan, Gu, & Whinston, 2008). One of the components of Personal trigger is consumer involvement, which is associated with ability to determine the degree of effortless information processing.

d.  **Receiver's Demographic Characteristics**: The Demographic attribute of receiver like age, gender, income, education etc influences eWOM effectiveness. Traditionally, each product tries to target different demographic profile which impact significantly in eWOM communication effectiveness (Saremi, 2014).

e.  **Receiver's Skepticism:** Receiver's skepticism is the tendency to disbelieve the information (Obermiller, 1998). This personal characteristic of receiver decides whether the processed information is relied or not. When a consumer has low level of skepticism they tend to rely more on eWOM information.

5.  **Effect of eWOM Adoption:** eWOM is a powerful mechanism to generate response for a product. The researchers have begun to explore the effect of eWOM on consumer response and market outcome in recent years (Godes & Mayzlin, 2004). eWOM communication stimulates the response if they produce information usefulness (Cheung & Thadani, 2012). The common response outcomes of eWOM communications are attitude (positive or negative), purchase intention and purchase (Cheung & Lai, 2005). Cheung (2005), attempted to establish and validate the relationship between attitude, purchase intentions and purchase. Their findings suggest that attitude significantly impact purchase intension (Charo & Pershant Sharma, 2015), while online purchase intention has positive impact on purchase. These relationships are also supported by theory of reasoned action (Fishbein & Ajzen, 1980). eWOM adoption is used for purchase of product (Cheung, Luo, Sia, & Chen, 2009). Researchers have brought to light that usefulness of information has positively effect on eWOM adoption (Cheung et. Al. 2005; Liu & Zhang. 2010).

The factors about source, message, medium and receivers of eWOM have discussed in detail framework to determine the effectiveness of eWOM communication. Business firms can take competitive advantage with understanding of these element and incorporate suitable strategy to drive desired results by conducting eWOM Marketing. The strategies to manage eWOM can be discussed in next segment below. When developing eWOM strategies, business firms must consider motivation of people to engage in eWOM communication. This can help companies to develop more customized online offerings, in terms of website navigation, product information, uses of web analytics and overall branding practices (Godes & Mayzlin, 2004).

## STRATEGIES TO MANAGE ELECTRONIC WORD OF MOUTH

The major part of online consumer behavior is eWOM which creates strong response for brand and product and drive return on investment (Chu & Kim, 2015). Keeping this fact in mind, business firms incorporate eWOM communication strategies to create new opportunities and speed up diffusion.Marketers cannot afford to ignore eWOM approaches in their business strategic plan. The main concern of eWOM is to establish credibility of recommendation. Further, companies should understand the response mechanism to unfavorable eWOM message. Few of them is discussed as below:

### Increase the Volume

eWOM presence and volume is associated with affirmative consumer behaviors. Asking a consumer to write review helps in building long term association with product and their purchase as whole (Goldsmith & Horowitz, 2006). Companies should invest substantial efforts in encouraging their customer for positive eWOM. The eWOM communication can be integrated part of Marketing communication activities of firms.

### Monitor and Respond On-Time

eWOM is one of the most popular sources of information used by consumer for getting relevant information about brand and product of their interest, thus it is important for companies to pay attention and manage eWOM effectively. The successful eWOM communication strategies include monitoring different online platforms and provide a quick response to eWOM communication for generating customer satisfaction. It has been observed that some companies do not provide opportunity to give eWOM due to fear of negative reviews (Abed et al., 2016). In order to decrease negative eWOM communication, the companies should allow customers to reach them through reviews and ratings in such a way that they can be responded promptly. While dealing with negative eWOM communication firms should answer with apologies and focus on factors that cause dissatisfaction and address these issues at the earliest (Wang et. al. 2013).

## Create a Standard Format to Provide eWOM by Genuine Reviewers

eWOM communication can effectively engage customers. Business organizations should ensure consumers' ability to participate actively in eWOM activities on their website or other online platform by providing the opportunities for customer review and rating. The 'spatial separation effect' means inability to touch, smell or feel the product while online purchase creates anxiety among consumer. eWOM communication can help in reduction of perceived risk and anxiety (Shareef et al., 2016). Researches have shown that there is positive relation between degree of detailed in review and their likeability to influence purchase decisions. Organizations can provide a standard format and ask for reviews related to those product aspects which may influence consumer behaviors. eWOM can enhance long-term profitability by more targeted information to customer (Mudamb & Schuff, 2010).

## Establish Author Credibility by Incorporating Reviewer's Rating System

Consumers like to be heard. They share their opinion and experiences about product with other consumer with different motives. Therefore, consumer opinions through eWOM should be regarded as one of the valuable assets that companies earn. eWOM generally comes from anonymous consumers, which gives the scope to get skeptical about credibility of eWOM when compare with traditional WOM. To improve trustworthiness in eWOM there is a need for a authors rating system. This mechanism can rate author of reviews based on their frequency of visit to a particular site, time engaged on that particular site, number of time writing reviews and rating of how helpful that review was for other consumer. Their expertise and knowledge about the product can be rated by expert reviews. As two ways communication system is already established theory, to talk about high influence of opinion leaders in WOM communication, this system tries to identify opinion leaders in online environment.

## Social Media Strategies

The Social media has changed traditional B2C and C2C communication by empowering consumers to communicate with each other. Social media engage customer on Internet and that's why brands and product incorporate social media strategies like viral marketing, buzz marketing and content marketing strategies into their e-business strategies (Bowen & Gordon, 2014). Social media monitoring and customer engagement on social Media will help to get more collaborative communication. Virtual communities with social networking sites can also be used to target niche segment of customer online.

eWOM efforts are generally very cost-effective and easy to actually reach to customers looking for specific products. E-WOM marketing is an important feature on the internet as it provides many different channels for consumers to share their experiences and exchange information (Trusov, Bucklin, & Pauwels, 2009). Further, the chapter provides directions for future research. The following case deliberated that managing WOM is very crucial for sustainability.

## Lemp Brewpub and Kitchen at Zomato.com

Most of the restaurants in Indian cities are listed on Zomato.com. Zomato has restaurant database and guide which allows a user to get relevant information. It is a common tendency of today's consumer to give and seek eWOM and therefore, Zomato allows registered users to review restaurants on scale of 1 to 5. In 2013, a group of friends decided to go to Lemp Brewpub & Kitchen, Gurgaon, India, after seeing a promotion of Hawaiian Brunch. After visiting the place they found that the said promotional branch could not be offered by restaurant, which led a heated argument between staff of restaurant and these customers. The local police got involved which give gave a ugly shape to this entire episode. Next day, a blog post written by these friends about their horrible experience at Lamp's got viral. They have uploaded photographs when the incident was happening and wrote in detail that how a Branch plan became nightmare experience for them. It is share on social media by multiple other consumers. It led to a dramatic drop down in user rating of Lemp Brewpub & Kitchen on Zomato.com. Multiple negative reviews and poor ratings were given which turn the average rating as low. The restaurant is struggling to recover from damage happened (Kapoor, 2016).

## FUTURE RESEARCH DIRECTIONS

Although there is a substantial amount of research devoted to WOM and eWOM, there are still considerable research gaps available. The current work attempts to identify what are the key elements in effective eWOM communication and how they are related to eWOM adoption. However, the relationship between those variables is not explored in existing study. Although a lot of research studies has been undertaken regarding credibility of eWom but none of the studies have been able to conclusively establish that factors responsible for trust influencing satisfaction. The relationship between customer trust of eWOM and product satisfaction can be further explored.

The quantitative analysis can further be taken to empirically validate the proposed propositions of eWOM communication. eWOM message has been researched many times by panel data analysis. The moderating effect of message characteristics can be evaluated in eWOM communication from receiver's point of view.

However, the greatest research need exists in identifying the right methodology for studying eWOM. There are various methods which can be applied to understand eWOM phenomenon but a standardized research technique is yet to be established in eWOM research. The complexity of eWOM communication should be reduced by active research contribution in the area. Further, the attention might be directed towards 'developing countries' where internet is still in growth stage to strategize the moves of firms. Such studies will make useful recommendations to policymakers of all stakeholders of Internet firms and many more.

## CONCLUSION

The Growth of Internet has changed the way business organizations have worked so far. Similarly, the growth of Internet technologies has been accountable for expansion of eWOM communication. eWOM is one of very important feature of consumer interaction. Even through eWOM communication have similarity from traditional offline WOM, the differences provide new possibilities of growth for consumer and business firms. Ignoring these differences might cost in losing customer and decreased brand preference. eWOM empower consumers with its high & speedy reachability, easy availability and sense of involvement which consumer gets. A favourable eWOM adoption usually results in positive attitude, increased purchase intention and satisfactory product consumption. This chapter has brought together diverse set of variables to provide complete understanding of eWOM effectiveness which is of high importance to all. The credibility of eWOM communication lies in characteristics of author and their eWOM message. One cannot underestimate the relation between source of eWOM message and its effectiveness on receivers. However, author and the message written could impact different receiver in different ways. To estimate the true effect of eWOM communication, each factor discussed in chapter needs to analyse and decided upon. The basic concept of eWOM and its current status of knowledge help in incorporating eWOM strategies. eWOM provide significant contribution in Digital economy practices. Therefore, monitoring and managing eWOM communication appropriately, business firms can understand their customer well, acquire and retain customers organically, maintain high brand value and possibility allocate necessary resources at right place. Consumers on the other hand with get benefited by using their power to voice their like and dislikes which will lead to empower consumerism in today's time.

# REFERENCES

Anderson, C. (2004). *The Long Tail*. San Francisco, CA: Wired.

Andrew, T., & Stephen, J. G. (2012). The Effects of Traditional and Social Earned Media on Sales: A Study of a Microlending Marketplace. *JMR, Journal of Marketing Research, 49*(5), 624–639. doi:10.1509/jmr.09.0401

Arndt, J. (1967). Role of product-related conversations in the diffusion of a new product. *JMR, Journal of Marketing Research, 4*(3), 291–295. doi:10.2307/3149462

Balasubramanian Sridhar, M. (2001). The economic leverage of the virtual community. *International Journal of Electronic Commerce, 18*(6), 103–138.

Bayus, B. C. (1985). Harnessing the power of word-of-mouth. In V. Maha (Ed.), *Innovation Diffusion Models of New Product Acceptance*. Cambridge, MA: Ballinger.

Bjorling, W. (2015). *How to manage online review sites successfully* (Bachelor's thesis). Jankoping University.

Bowen & Gordon. (2014). *Computer-Mediated Marketing Strategies: Social Media and Online Brand Communities*. Hershey, PA: IGI Global.

Breazeale, M. (2009). word of mouse: An assessment of electronic word of mouth resaerch. *International Journal of Market Research, 51*(3), 297–318. doi:10.2501/S1470785309200566

Burcher, N. (2012). *Paid, Owned, Earned: Maximising Marketing Returns in a Socially Connected World*. Kogen Page.

Cacioppo, Petty, R. E., Feinstein, J. A., & Jarvis, W. B. G. (1996). Dispositional Differences in Cognitive Motivation: The Life and Times of Individuals Varying in Need for Cognition. *Psychological Bulletin, 119*(2), 197–253. doi:10.1037/0033-2909.119.2.197

Chaffey, D. (2010). Applying Organisational Capability Models to Assess the maturity of Digital-Marketing Goverance. *Journal of Marketing Management, 26*(3-4), 187–196. doi:10.1080/02672571003612192

Charo, N., & Pershant Sharma, S. S. (2015). Determining the Impact of Ewom on Brand image and Purchase Intention through adoption of online opinions. *International Journal of Humanities and Management Sciences, 3*(1).

Chen, H., Bang, N., Klaus, P., & Wu, M. (2015). Exploring Electronic Word-of-Mouth (eWOM) in The Consumer Purchase Decision-Making Process: The Case of Online Holidays – Evidence from United Kingdom (UK) Consumers. *Journal of Travel & Tourism Marketing, 32*(8), 953–970. doi:10.1080/10548408.2014.956165

Cheung, C. M., & Thadani, D. R. (2012). The impact of electronic word-of-mouth communication: A literature analysis and integrative model. *Decision Support Systems, 54*(1), 461–470. doi:10.1016/j.dss.2012.06.008

Cheung, M., Luo, C., Sia, C., & Chen, H. (2009). Credibility of electronic word-of-mouth: informational and normative determinants of online consumer recommendation. *International Journal of e-Commerce, 13*(4), 9-38.

Cheung, M. K. (2005). Literature derived reference models for the adoption of online shopping. *Information & Management, 42*(4), 543–559. doi:10.1016/S0378-7206(04)00051-5

Chevalier, J. A., & Mayzlin, D. (2006). The Effect of Word of Mouth on Sales: Online Book Reviews. *JMR, Journal of Marketing Research, 43*(3), 345–354. doi:10.1509/jmkr.43.3.345

Christine Ennew, A. K. (2000). Managing word of mouth communication: Empirical evidence from India. *International Journal of Bank Marketing, 18*.

Chu, S.-C., & Kim, Y. (2015). Determinants of consumer engagement in electronic word-of-mouth (eWOM) in social networking sites. *International Journal of Advertising, 30*(1), 47–75. doi:10.2501/IJA-30-1-047-075

Dellarocas, C. N., & Narayan, R. (2006). A Statistical measure of a population's propensity to engage in post-purchase online word of mouth. *Statistical Science, 21*(2), 277–285. doi:10.1214/088342306000000169

Dellarocas. (2003). The Digitization of Word of Mouth: Promise and Challenges of Online Feedback Mechanisms. *Management Science, 49*, 1407–1424.

Duan & Whinston. (2008). Do online reviews matter? An empirical investigation of Panel data. *Decision Support System, 45*(4).

Erin, M. (2009). Social ties and online word of mouth. *Internet Research, 19*(1), 42–59. doi:10.1108/10662240910927812

Erkan, I., & Evans, C. (2016). The influence of eWOM in social media on consumers' purchase intentions: An extended approach to information adoption. *Computers in Human Behavior, 61*, 47–55. doi:10.1016/j.chb.2016.03.003

Fernando, F., & Whitelock, J. (2007). International advertising strategy: The standardisation question in manager studies. *International Marketing Review, 24*(5), 591–605. doi:10.1108/02651330710828004

Fill, M., & Krizaj, D. (2016). ElectronicWordofMouthandItsCredibility inTourism:TheCaseofTripadvisor. *Academica Turistica, 9*(2), 107-112.

Fishbein, M., & Ajzen, I. (1980). *Understanding Attitudes and Predicting Social Behavior.* Englewood, NJ: Prentice-hall.

Fox, G., & Longart, P. (2016). Electronic word-of-mouth: Successful communication strategies for Restaurants. *Tourism and Hospitality Management, 22*(2), 211–223. doi:10.20867/thm.22.2.5

Godes, & Mayzlin, D. A. (2004). Using Online Conversations to Study Word-of-Mouth Communication. *Marketing Science, 23*(4), 545-559.

Goldsmith, R. E. (2006). Electronic Word-of-Mouth. In Encyclopedia of E-Commerce, E-Government and Mobile Commerce. Hershey, PA: Idea Group Publishing. doi:10.4018/978-1-59140-799-7.ch067

Goldsmith, R. E., & Horowitz, D. (2006). Measuring Motivations for Online Opinion Seeking. *Journal of Interactive Advertising, 6*(2), 2–14. doi:10.1080/15252019.2 006.10722114

Guillermo, A., & Villanueva, J. (2008). Electronic Word of Mouth: What Do We Know About This powerful marketing tool? *e-business Center PricewaterhouseCoopers & IESE,* 1-67.

Hennig-Thurau, T., Gwinner, K. P., Walsh, G., & Gremler, D. D. (2004). Electronic word-of-mouth via consumer-opinion platforms: What motivates consumers to articulate themselves on the Internet? *Journal of Interactive Marketing, 18*(1), 38–52. doi:10.1002/dir.10073

Hong, J., & Sternthal, B. (2010). The effects of consumer prior knowledge and processing strategies on judgments. *JMR, Journal of Marketing Research, 47*(2), 301–311. doi:10.1509/jmkr.47.2.301

Hong, J., & Sternthal, B. (2010). The Effects of Consumer Prior Knowledge and Processing Strategies on Judgments. *Jiewen Hong. Brian Sternthal, 47*(2), 301–311.

Huang, M. C., Cai, F., Tsang, A. S. L., & Zhou, N. (2011). Making your online voice loud: The critical role of WOM information. *European Journal of Marketing, 45*(7/8), 1277–1297. doi:10.1108/03090561111137714

Kapoor, P. S. G. S. (2016). Impact of Anonymity and Identity Deception on Social Media eWOM. In Social Media: The Good, the Bad, and the Ugly. Springer.

Katz, E. &. (1956). *Interpersonal Relations and Mass Communications: Studies in the Flow of Influence.* Columbia University.

Klein, J. G., & Ahluwalia, R. (2005). Negativity in the evaluation of political candidates. *Journal of Marketing, 69*(1), 131–142. doi:10.1509/jmkg.69.1.131.55509

Kotler, P., & Keller, K. (2014). *Marketing Management (15ᵗʰ ed.).* Prentice Hall.

Krishna, A., & Johar, G. V. (1996). Consumer perceptions of deals: Biasing effects of varying deal prices. *Journal of Experimental Psychology. Applied, 2*(3), 187–206. doi:10.1037/1076-898X.2.3.187

Kucuka, S. U., & Krishnamurthy, S. (2007). An analysis of consumer power on the Internet. *Technovation, 27*(1-2), 47–56. doi:10.1016/j.technovation.2006.05.002

Lee, J. P., Park, D.-H., & Han, I. (2008). The effect of negative online consumer reviews on product attitude: An information processing view. *Electronic Commerce Research and Applications, 7*(3), 341–352. doi:10.1016/j.elerap.2007.05.004

Lee, K.-T., & Koo, D.-M. (2012). Effects of attribute and valence of eWOM on message adoption: Moderating roles of subjective knowledge and regulatory focus. *Computer in Human Behavior, 28*, 1974–1984.

Litvin, S. G., Goldsmith, R. E., & Pan, B. (2008). Electronic word-of-mouth in hospitality and tourism management. *Tourism Management, 29*(3), 458–468. doi:10.1016/j.tourman.2007.05.011

Matos, C. A., & Vargas, C. A. (2008). Word-of-mouth communications in marketing: A meta-analytic review of the antecedents and moderators. *Journal of the Academy of Marketing Science, 36*(4), 578–596. doi:10.100711747-008-0121-1

Mayzlin, D., Yaniv Dover, Y., & Chevalier, J. (2013). Promotional Reviews: An Empirical Investigation of online review Manipulation. *The American Economic Review*, 1–40.

McLaughlin, C. M. (2012). *Preference of Homophily, credibility and word of mouth process* (PhD dissertation). Michigan State University.

Menkveld, B. (2013). *Exploring credibility in electronic word of mouth* (Master's thesis). University of Twente.

Mislove, A. M. M. (2007). Measurement and Analysis of Online Social Networks. In *7th ACM SIGCOMM conference on Internet measurement* (pp. 29-42). San Diego, CA: AMC. 10.1145/1298306.1298311

Molinillo, S., Jose, L., & Fernandez, A. (2016). Hotel Assessment through Social Media: The case of TripAdvisor. *Tourism & Management Studies, 12*(1), 15–24. doi:10.18089/tms.2016.12102

Morrison, A., Cheong, H., & McMillan, S. (2013). Posting, Lurking, and Networking: Behaviours and Characteristics of Consumers in the Context of User-Generated Content. *Journal of Interactive Advertising, 13*(2), 97–108. doi:10.1080/1525201 9.2013.826552

Mudamb, S. M., & Schuff, D. (2010). What makes a helpful online review? A study of customer reviews on Amazon.com. *Management Information Systems Quarterly, 34*(1), 185–200. doi:10.2307/20721420

Nahed Al-Haidari, J. (2014). The influence of electronic-word-of-mouth on consumer decision-making for beauty products in a Kuwaiti Women`s online community. *Journal of Contemporary Eastern Asia, 13*(2), 3-14.

Neumann, M. (2015). *What does the research tell us about word-of-mouth communication?-A literature review*. University of Rostock.

Nguyen, B. K., Chen, C., Klaus, P., & Wu, M. (2015). Exploring Electronic Word-of-Mouth (eWOM) in The Consumer Purchase Decision-Making Process: The Case of Online Holidays – Evidence from United Kingdom (UK) Consumers. *Journal of Travel & Tourism Marketing, 32*(8), 953–970. doi:10.1080/10548408.2014.956165

Nyilasy, G. (2006). Word of mouth: What we really know - and what we don't. In *Connected marketing* (pp. 161–184). London, UK: Butterworth-Heinemann.

Obermiller, C., & Spangenberg, E. R. (1998). On the Origin and Distinctness of Skepticism toward Advertising. *Marketing Letters, 11*(4), 311–322. doi:10.1023/A:1008181028040

Park, C., & Lee, T. M. (2009). ParkInformation direction, website reputation and eWOM effect: A moderating role of product type. *Journal of Business Research, 62*(1), 61–67. doi:10.1016/j.jbusres.2007.11.017

Sánchez, C. A. (2015, June 1). *ewomcharacteristics*. Retrieved Jan 10, 2018, from brandba.se: http://www.brandba.se/blog/ewomcharacteristics

Saremi, H. Q. (2014). *Effectiveness of electronic word of mouth recommendations* (PhD thesis). McMaster University.

Schütze, N. (2014). Electronic Word-of-Mouth Communication for Local Service Providers. *Technology Innovation Management Review*, *4*(4), 35-42. Retrieved from http://timreview.ca/article/783

Shenglin, B. (2017). Digital infrastructure: Overcoming Digital Divide in Emerging Economies. Zhejiang University Center for Internet and Financial Innovation: G20 Insight.

Trusov, M., Bucklin, R., & Pauwels, K. (2009). Effects of Word-of-Mouth Versus Traditional Marketing: Findings from an Internet Social Networking Site. *Journal of Marketing*, *73*(5), 1–24. doi:10.1509/jmkg.73.5.90

Wang, X. (2011). The Effect of Inconsistent Word-of-Mouth During the Service Encounter. *Journal of Services Marketing*, *25*(4), 252–259. doi:10.1108/08876041111143087

Wu, P. C., & Wang, Y.-C. (2011). The influences of electronic word-of-mouth message appeal and message source credibility on brand attitude. *Asia Pacific Journal of Marketing and Logistics*, *23*(4), 448–472. doi:10.1108/13555851111165020

Yayli, A., & Bayram. (2012). eWOM: The effects of online consumer reviews on purchasing decisions of electronic goods. *International Journal of Internet Marketing and Advertising*, 52-61.

Yin, D., Bond, S., & Zhang, H. (2014). Anxious or Angry? Effects of discrete emotions on the Perceived Helpfulness of Online Reviews. *Management Information Systems Quarterly*, *38*(2), 539–560. doi:10.25300/MISQ/2014/38.2.10

Zhang, T., Behzad, A. O., & Cihan, C. (2017). Generation Y's positive and negative eWOM: Use of social media and mobile technology. *International Journal of Contemporary Hospitality Management*, *29*(2), 732–761. doi:10.1108/IJCHM-10-2015-0611

## ADDITIONAL READING

Anderson, C. (2004). *The Long Tail*. San Francisco, California, USA: Wired.

Chen, C., Nguyen, B., Klaus, P., & Wu, M. (2015). Exploring Electronic Word-of-Mouth (eWOM) in The Consumer Purchase Decision-Making Process: The Case of Online Holidays – Evidence from United Kingdom (UK) Consumers. *Journal of Travel & Tourism Marketing*, *32*(8), 953–970. doi:10.1080/10548408.2014.956165

Fox, G., & Longart, P. (2016). Electronic word-of-mouth: Successful communication strategies for Restaurants. *Tourism and Hospitality Management*, *22*(2), 211–223. doi:10.20867/thm.22.2.5

Mayzlin, D., Yaniv Dover, Y., & Chevalier, J. (2013). Promotional Reviews: An Empirical Investigation of online review Manipulation. *The American Economic Review*, *13*, 1–40.

Molinillo, S., Jose, L., & Fernandez, A. (2016). Hotel Assessment through Social Media: The case of TripAdvisor. *Tourism & Management Studies*, *12*(1), 15–24. doi:10.18089/tms.2016.12102

Tadelis, S. (2016). Reputation and Feedback Systems in Online Platform Markets. *Annual Review of Economics*, *8*(1), 321–340. doi:10.1146/annurev-economics-080315-015325

Yolanda, Y. Y. (2011). Conceptualising electronic word of mouth activity: An input-process-output perspective. *Marketing Intelligence & Planning*, *29*(5), 488–516. doi:10.1108/02634501111153692

## KEY TERMS AND DEFINITIONS

**Customer Retention:** A company's planned activities in order to ensure that the customer comes back to repurchase from the company.

**eWOM:** Any positive or negative statement made by potential, actual, or former customers about a product or company, which is made available to a multitude of people and institutions via the internet.

**eWOM Adoption:** The effect of eWOM in purchase decision with influence on consumer attitude.

**Message Valence:** Positive or Negative information content in eWOM message.

**Need for Cognition:** Level of individual's innate desire to think about and process information.

**Source Credibility:** Consumers' perception about the trustworthiness of the author of eWOM recommendation.

**Tie Strength:** Level of intensity of a social relationship between the source of eWOM message and the consumer.

**WOM:** Consumer to consumer oral communication about brand or product which is non-commercial in nature.

# Chapter 4
# E-WOM as a New Paradigm in the Consumer Decision-Making Process

**Esra Güven**
*Celal Bayar University, Turkey*

**Volkan Yakin**
*Abant Izzet Baysal University, Turkey*

## ABSTRACT

*Consumer-to-consumer communications in online environments are of a vital importance to the consumer decision-making process. This process consists of five phases, each affected by eWOM communications deeply from the stimulation to the post-purchase behavior. Among all other factors having an impact on this process, the impact of eWOM has a distinguished role. As the technology grows and the consumers use internet and the reviews via internet, they become more and more attached to these reviews to make a purchase decision. In this chapter, the authors make a comprehensive explanation about the consumer decision-making process and explain the relationship of the decision-making phases with eWOM communications.*

## INTRODUCTION

Consumers today need to make numerous decisions and therefore deal with information loads increasing day by day. To be able to cope with this mental load, they develop some short cuts or certain habits. The introduction of online and internet platforms into our lives is causing the markets having been controlled by the marketers for

DOI: 10.4018/978-1-5225-5993-1.ch004

long years to pass on consumer hands. The consumers being able to reach all the information through online environments have started to dominate in the markets, and this has caused the marketers to go through their strategies they have used persistently. Especially the social media platforms by means of web 2.0 following web 1.0 can be said to have a great impact on this shift. Consumer generated online environments, one of the biggest advantage of emerging social media platforms, not only provide the consumers with reaching the information in a rapid and efficient way but also offer a flexibility in time and evaluation opportunities.

Used as shortcuts by the consumers, internet and information technologies provide the potential buyers with all information and data about the products or services. These technologies are the most basic supporters of the consumers trying to make a good decision about the product or services. Blogs, forums, consumer review websites and other social media platforms offer every kind of information required by the consumers. At that point, what the consumers should do is to be able to give the best purchase decision by means of all these comments and reviews on the websites.

Today, the eWOM messages written by experienced consumers on the websites and social media platforms influence the consumers searching for information about the products or services they want to purchase. The consumers in search of information are greatly interested in these online environments hosting a huge number of unbiased and experienced customers as well as opinions leaders and market mavens.

While defining the consumer decision process, Engel (1991) mentions the activities directly related with buying, consuming and putting them out of use, and the process before and after all these activities. This purchase process makes up of several phases generally known as 'determining the needs, search for information, evaluating the alternatives, purchase decision and post purchase behaviour (Hutter et al., 2013:343).

Bonebau (2009) mentions collective intelligence and says that this kind of intelligence helps consumers to make a better decision. The eWOM activities in online environments are the very reason of trying to make use of collective intelligence during the consumer decision-making process. eWOM messages are directly related with this whole process and they are of vital importance for the consumers in need of collective intelligence while trying to make the best decision.

This chapter aims at describing consumer-decision making process through an eWOM point of view. The chapter gives a full explanation of the phases in consumer decision-making process and emphasizes the impact of eWOM communications on each of these phases.

## BACKGROUND

It can easily be said that consuming behaviour is a decision-making behaviour. So consumers are the people who always walk on this decision road, and deciding about something has mostly been a challenging cognitive work. To be able to share this cognitive load, consumers have applied to different sources for help. The friends and the people around have always been an important support for decision-making process so far. But the consumers of today have a faster and a more effective power in their hands: internet and social media platforms.

One of the best aspects of social media is that it is a part of a feedback cycle and supports this cycle. By using this feedback cycle, how and where the communication about services or products are made in this system can be learnt. Some well-known and promising companies do research about this role of social media. Acquiring the data is just a small part of the equation. The bigger part is to focus on how these data can be used to make the brand reach its goals in consumer-brand interaction. Simply, a social feedback cycle feeds on the consumption experiences of the some consumers ready to share information for other potential ones. This feedback is of vital importance for the marketers, and when it is neglected, an entropy process will be likely to start in the near future.

Thanks to the new internet and information technology, consumers today can easily have an access to the data and information about new products and services. What is important at that point is to be able make the right purchase-decision among all these rich varieties and diversities of products and services (Bechina & Husta, 2011:83). Both forums, blogs, consumer review websites and brands' own websites can offer any kind of information about the market required by the consumers. The only thing to do now is to be able give the best decision in the light of all these online information sources. A research by Guven (2014) found out that eWOM messages are the supporters of the advertisements and emphasized the need to create a synergy between these two communication models.

Consumer decision making process is generally regarded as a cognitive process. Consumers, typically, realize the need, the desire and the way to satisfy these needs and desires by means of the advertisement messages of a new brand, and they apply to their minds to evaluate the claims in these mesages. When they couldn't find the sufficient data in their minds to evaluate these messages, they start searching for more information from outside such as people around or some other people having information about the products (Baker & Hart, 2008:119). In such cases the needed information can be obtained sometimes from the friends or sometimes the mavens they trust about the products.

Often facing with several alternatives changing fast because of the new technologies and competition pressure, consumers need to have a significant amount of information from different sources (ads, online platforms, salesmen, friends and etc..). Furthermore they usually can not have a certain information about how all these products will perform, and they often experience dilemmas about which to choose between the price or the safety during a car purchase (Bettman et al.,1991:50).

Nowadays, the decisions of consumers can be significanty affected by the internet and social media platforms along with effects of traditional sources, and the eWOM communications in these platforms can have a great effect on the decisions of consumers. The individuals searching for information about the products and services pay a great attention to the online environments which host the messages of not only ordinary consumers but a lot of mavens and opinion leaders, as well. This heavy interest in the messages in these platforms make these environments an impact factor on the decision making process of consumers. The impartiality and unrequited sharing of these consumer reviews can increase the persuasiveness of the messages.

eWOM connects plenty of individual consumer to each other, and opens WOM network into all internet world not just into the consumer's own personal relationship. As more and more people use service and product information to make a purchase decision via eWOM networks, the credibility of online consumer reviews are getting more and more interesting. When consumers perceive the source as credible, they tend to rely on the reviews written. It is generally accepted as a reality that, there is no reason for a consumer not to adopt an online information once the source is thought reliable or credible (Cheung et al., 2009:9-10).

The multidimensional nature of consumer decision-making process bring several research questions together. How the consumers develop themselves, how they use decison-making process, how the background information affects the process, how the consumers adapto to different environments and how they categorize the products are all the questions being tried to answer in different marketing research (Bettman et al., 1991:51). One of the most interesting findings in these research is that consumers are affected not by a single but by a series of different factors.

Consumer centered marketing needs a more comprehensive definition of consumer buying behaviour. Engel (1991:4) defines this behaviour as 'all the activities related with obtaining, consuming and putting out of usage of the products and services, and all the other actrivities before and after these activities'. So, while trying to understand the purchase behaviour, the pre and post purchase activities must be taken into account. At that point, prepurchase activities include defining the problem, searching for information and evaluating the alternatives while post purchase activities and post purchase evaluation cover any kind of attempts to reduce post purchase dissonance (Baker & Hart, 2008)

Casielles and his colleagues (2013) attempted a researched to find out the relative effect of positive and negative eWOM on purchase intention. According to the study, while positive WOM messages cause a positive change in purchase intention, negative ones lead negative change in this intention. Again, it has been found out that positive WOM have a a bigger effect on purchase intention than negative WOM's. An important point here is the articulating power of the reviewer. A high articulating power can have a higher effect on purchase intention about the brand (Casielles et al.,2013:54).

## eWOM in the Decision-Making Process of Consumers

From this point of view, it can be said that consumer decision-making process consists of several phases. This process generally starts with defining the needs and searching for information before the purchase and extends to the evaluating the alternatives, purschase decision and finally to the post purchase period (Hutter et al., 2013:343).

The internet, one of the greatest oppurtunities of the developed technology, has caused a change in the longlasting habits in marketing field as in all other fields. Online social interaction platforms introduced into our lives by internet and especially web 2.0 technology are increasingly taking more and more part in marketing and consumption. Today it is commonly seen that the consumers in the decision-making process are heavily involved in the consumer communications called as eWOM in online platforms. One of the most significant phenomena resulted from this type of communication is regarded as 'collective intellegence'. Bonebau (2009:16) states that collective intelligence can help the consumers make better purchase decision, and that purchase decision can be divided into two parts as producing potential solutions and evaluations of these solutions. In these both parts, collective intelligence can affect the process in different ways.

When it comes to consumer decision making process, Fill (2009) mentions three types of purchase decision: extensive problem solving, limited problem solving and routinized reactions.

In the first type, consumers need to make a decision about the product types with high costs like house or cars about which they have not got enough experience and familiarity. In these types of decisions, consumers exhibit a great deal of information search behaviour from outer world, and also spend more time to reach a solution to satisfy themselves. Marketing communications are known to be highly effective in this first process.

In the second type of decision making, limited problem solving, consumers provide most of the information they need from internal sources (experience, memory, or etc..), but, though limited, they apply to the outer sources as well to update the internal information they own. This type of decision making needs marketers to give advertisement messages emphasizing the originality and additional characteristics of the products or services.

In routinized reaction behaviour, the products consumed by the consumers lots of times in their daily lives are the points to mention. The information search about these kinds of products is an internal search just in the lowest level. The reason for that is the massive experience they have about the products (Fill, 2009: 169).

Consumer purchase behaviour can be modelled as a cognitive process in the forms of thought, evaluation, and decision. These information process activities are believed to reflect the internal aspect of consumer choices. The basic accumulation of information coming from an environment such as friends and acquaintances or marketing messages can have an important role in the information search required for the inputs of this process (Baker & Hart, 2008:122). Especially the information sourcing from the close relationships can build a strong information background by means of the tie strength existing between the parts, and then the marketing efforts of the brand can help this information extend to a far more effective level.

To be able to understand the points to motivate the consumers can help the marketers design websites with a high effect power on the consumers in need of information in certain products or services. To be able to understand how the consumers evaluate the content of eWOM messages can play an important role in benefiting from the messages. And again, to be able to understand the strength of eWOM in the consumer decision-making process can be helpful to the marketers about how eWOM messages can be used better and more effectively. For example, marketers can aim at reaching the consumers with a high possibility of sharing reviews within online environments as this type of consumers are the ones functioning as opinion leaders. Besides that, marketers can apply to the effect power of eWOM messages as a motivator in the challenging behaviours such as losing weight and doing exercise (Schindler & Bickart, 2004:58). As seen here, eWOM can have an extraordinary role on the consumers as a motivator. Such a role can heavily be attributed to the perception that online review messages are impartial messages to trust more than other marketing messages.

When we look at the relationship between eWOM and purchase from the aspect of the phases in the decision-making process, the consumer to consumer communication in online platforms is believed to be effective in all phases of consumer decision-making process. For example, the product awareness created through eWOM communications sets forth the difference between the existing situation and ideal one, and thus makes it easy to define the problem. eWOM also sets forth the criteria to apply during the evaluation of alternatives, helps the consumer with where to buy a product and can reduce the cognitive dissonance experienced in the post purchase period (Schindler and Bickart, 2004:41). Associating eWOM with only one aspect of decisionmaking process means neglecting its content and effect power. So, it must be known that eWOM communication has important role in all phases of consumer decision-making process.

Consumer decision-making process is a cognitive process during which the individuals choose an behaviour or an activity among a series of product and service alternatives. While explaining the process, the prominent researchers about the relationship between WOM and decision-making process, Schindler and Bickart (2004) mentions four phases as problem recognition, consideration set, decision termination or alternative evaluation and postdecision processes. These authors starts the process with problem recognition and in this phase they attempt to explain the contribution of eWOM to determine the potential benefits of the purchase.

In the second phase of their process, there is a consideration set in which eWOM helps the consumers determine the alternatives in their mind. The consumers define some criteria to evaluate the alternatives in the fourth phase and these criteria are mostly obtained from eWOM messages in online platforms. In the final part of Schindler and Bickart's decision-making process stands postdecision behaviours. In this last phase, eWOM helps consumers attempt to confirm what they have purchased, or get guidance on how to consume the service or product. Putting Schindler and Bickart's point of view into the center and supporting it with a general literature review, we will try to make detailed explanation of this process and its relationship with ewom phase by phase. The purchase decision consists of;

1. Stimulation
2. Problem recognition and awareness
3. Information search
4. Evaluation of alternatives and purchase
5. Post decision processes

The decision making process about whether to buy or not are closely related with the quality of the information gathered and the relationship level with the subject. The amount of the information consumers need depends not only on the scope and the need but the financial factor as well (Bechina & Husta, 2011:83).

## Stimulation

Lamb (1992) adds a first phase before the four-known ones: Stimulation. We all get thirsty following a tiring exercise or wish to have a car following a TV commercial. Likewise, psychological thirst and commercials can have a stimulating effect on consumers. The stimulant here is any input unit into any of the sense organs. This stimulant can be either internal or external. The internal stimulants account for the usual needs like hunger. People learn to react to the internal stimulants through the experiences and also to satisfy their needs. External stimulants, on the other hand, can be the color of a car or a car brand mentioned by a friend or a commercial on TV. The reaction manners of the consumers to the external stimulant can change depending on the content, shape, complexity and the amount of the information. Humans actively perceive only a small amount among the billions of stimulants around. The challenge for the marketers here is to be able to put their messages among the stimulants actively perceived by the customers (Lamb et al.,1992:103).

Some groups of consumers using socail media platforms not for searching information but for just having a look at what it is are sometimes affected by the messages they read in these platforms, in other words, they are stimulated by these messages. When exposed to these stimulation, a lot of consumers can be actively involved in the purchase process though they have had no plan to buy someting before. The dynamism, attractiveness, availability and richness in maven and experts advices of these online platforms make them more effective, and this effect can exhibit itself in all phases of decision-making process. So It would be wrong to limit the relationship of eWOM messages and purchase just with the people searching for information.

Because of this richness in online environments, firms need to start the new product campaigns through eWOM in order to create more eWOM communications and to take advantage of eWOM communications. While doing that, firms should be in contact with the bloggers, existing customers, and other consumers, and they should encourage these people to spread information in favor of their brand. An important point here is that eWOM communication should be started before the introduction of the product into the market.

There are three methods to do that;

1.  Companies can ask the consumers about the planned product and encourage them to help the product develop. Brand's online groups or social network pages are the ideal platforms to put such an initiative into effect.
2.  Companies can provide required information with the consumers through e-mails, videos or blogs.
3.  Companies send the new product firstly to the opinion leaders to make them try and then give advice to other potential customers via eWOM messages.

Such a strategy will cause an awareness about the introduction of the product and thus accelerate the adoption process. To sum up, companies must find ways to make the consumers involved in the process, and start a communication flow before a commercial activity about the product (Lopez & Sicilia, 2012:1104). At that point, it should be reminded again that one of the best ways to empower the effect of an advertisement or commerical is to use the eWOM messages before, together and also after the advertisement activities.

## Problem Recognition and Awareness

Consumers are exposed to message bombardment from many different sources such as advertisements, political groups or acquaintances trying to persuade them to buy a certain product or service. These thousands of messages are in a fierce competition with each other to attract the potential customers. Supposing that all these messages attracted the people, the human nervous system wouldn't bear this burden. So, most of the messages coming from different sources are filtered by perception systems, and some of these messages cannot have an effect on decision making process. Only when ad message in this process achieves in passing through this filter and gains meanings effective in subconcious of consumers, can the consumer recognize the problem or the need (Baker & Hart, 2008:122).

When the consumer is exposed to a stimulant, this stimulant can trigger the need reconition phase. An individual experiences need recognition phase when he or she feels an imbalance between the conditions he has something at hand and the conditions he desires to have. The desired condition the individual to reach reflects the need or wish. A need means anything a person depends on to continue a balanced life, and these needs form the basis of all behaviours (Lamb et al., 1992:104). It must be known that the 'need' here is not limited to the minimum conditions enough for life, and covers a bigger area ranging from the basic needs to the unusual emotional expectancies.

Problem or need recognition phase is a step triggerred by the first phase known as stimulation. The trigger here can sometimes be an internal simulant, or an external stimulant can be effective here. Deciding to buy a new car while talking to a friend, for example, can be regarded as a need triggered by an external stimulant (Kotler & Armstrong, 2008:146).

Need recognition is a clear and understandable phase in which the consumer perceive the need or the problem and get motivated to solve this problem. Consumers can get motivated by some parameters such as price, status, safety or like that. Their motivations can sometimes be complicated, and this complexity can partly be explained through Maslow 's hierarchy of needs (Copley, 2009:65).

Though they can not create needs, marketers can create a desire which shows itself when an individual has an unsatisfied need and decides to buy a product to satisfy this need. A desire is not necessarily to be for a certain product, but instead, it can be for a special characteristics of a product. For example, the elderlies go for the products which mean comfort, trust, practicality and traditional values. The marketers doing business in different countries and culture are in the position of determining the different needs of different consumers. As an example, Tang, a brand of orange juice, can sell twice as much in Puerto Rico as the ones in the USA. A research by Craft Greneral Foods, the producer of Tang, has showed that Puerto Ricons prefer Tang just because they like sweeter and cheaper products (Lamb et al., 1992:105).

When it comes to defining the different demands and wishes of consumers, the skill to be able to analyse the online consumers messages or eWOM will come to the fore. An analysis including the directions and empasis points of the messages, the characteristics of the reviewers and effect sizes are regarded as a crucial for marketers. Recruiting the professionals having an ability to make this analysis is equally important. This kind of individuals can be involved in the eWOM communications of the consumers sometimes as a consumer and sometimes as maven or opinion leaders. By this way, the reviews or consumer messages will have a higher possibility to be analysed, and the strategies based on these analyses will help the company or the brand become more advantagous compared to their competitors. The consumer demand, wish or complaints and even the words used in the reviews will be able help the brand acquire a critical point of view about their existing products and services, or the products or services to be produced in the future. An important point to take into consideration here is that markets are directed by the consumers not by marketers as in the past. The most abstract platforms such directions are clearly felt in are the online platforms by which the consumer spread their eWOM messages.

Consumers recognize their unsatisfied needs in a variety of ways. One of these ways is the situations in which the consumer cannot get satisfied with the performance of the product at hand, and another situation is the one in which the product being used are about to come to an end. Apart from these two situations, consumers can recognize their unsatisfied needs in the situations in which they meet or hear something about the products or services. These kinds of desires are usually created by the promotion activities like advertisements or so on (Lamb et al., 1992:105).

Once a consumer starts to talk about the advantage of existing or potential product, the problem or need recognition phase will get activated. The consumers reviewing about their product or service experiences and especially about the advantages of these products in online environments can provide other consumers with their existing needs and thus recognize their problems. When it comes to the effect of eWOM during the need recognition phase, the role of positive eWOM messages will be realized once more, because there are always some consumers in need of this product but not so strong to move into a purchase process. The positive reviews at that point will cause the consumers to activate such a process.

To take advantage of this process, marketers must be able to determine what kind of needs the consumers have, how these needs can be revealed and what the causes are for these needs (Kotler & Armstrong, 2008:147). So, one of the best methods to be able to reach these data is the analysis of online consumer review websites in which a rich eWOM communications occur. It mustn't be neglected that marketing is an activity not only towards the consumers with clear purchase intentions but towards the consumers unaware of his or her needs.

## Information Search

Recognizing a problem or a need doesn't mean that decision-making process will go on. Only when the need is important for the consumer or it is believed that solution is possible, can the process go further. If the sufficient amount of involvement is achieved, the consumer will exhibit an information search behaviour (Baker & Hart, 2008:122).

After recognizing the need, the need for further information search can change depending on the cost-benefit perceptions of the consumers. The perceived benefit here can be considered to get the highest satisfaction in purchase decision by finding the the best price or model. And the perceived cost here is the time spent for information search, the cost incurred, and the psychological cost of information processing. In this cost-benefit analysis, when the benefit outweighes the cost, the search will go on; but otherwise, the search will come to an end (Lamb et al., 1992:106).

When the motive evoking the customer is strong enough, and when the product to satisfy this motive is available, a purchase likelihood of the consumer will emerge. But on the other hand, when this motive is not strong enough, the need will be kept in the memory or further information search will be exhibited (Kotler & Armstrong, 2008:147). Even if the motives are stored in the memory and don't result in a purchase decision, it must be taken into consideration that there is always a likelihood for these motives to reveal later together with new and further information or stimulants.

In information search, consumers don't take all the existing products in the market into account. Instead, they take some certain brands in their minds under review and use their purchase decision for one of these products. This information search is done sometimes through internal, sometimes external and some other times in both types. While in internal search, the existing information in the minds resulted from the past experiences is used, in external one, both the sources in control of marketers and the some others sources out of control can be used (Lamb et al., 1992:106). To tell the truth. The most effective sources are personal sources, which are not under control of marketers, because while other commercial sources dominated by the marketers just *give information* to the consumers, personal sources are the ones *assessing or evaluating* the product in favor of the consumers (Kotler & Armstrong, 2008:148). So eWOM messages obtained by personal sources are crucial for the potential buyers. An important point here is that whereas commercial sources tend to give information in favor of the brand, personal sources focus on the benefit in favor of the consumers. So these type of sources are regarded to be far more effective than other commercial sources controlled by the marketers.

How the consumers gather information from external sources and how they use this information are two important questions for the marketers to develop new strategies. This period called as the perceptive process of consumer by Belch (2001) is a process in which consumers perceive, prefer, arrange and comment (Copley, 2009:66).

The decision-making process phase in which we can see the effect of eWOM communications most clearly is information search phase, because the consumers in online environments can offer alternative opinions and advices to the consideration set of the potential consumers. These potential consumers searching for information, in other words demanding part of the eWOM communication, are affected profoundly from the reviews of other consumers and enrich the information in their minds through the information they get from the consumer reviews. It is a well-known fact that a consumer reading about the reviews and messages about products will become strongly equipped for the other phases of the decisonmaking process.

## Evaluation of Alternatives and Purchase

After gathering sufficient amount of information about the the product or service planned to purchase and determining the alternatives in their minds, consumers are ready for the purchase decision. At that point, consumer is known to use a series of criteria by using all these information from internal and external sources. One of the ways consumer use to reduce the alternatives in their minds is to determine a feature they want most and elect the products which don't have this feature. Another method with this is to determine an upper and lower limit in their minds and to elect the products out of these limits. For example a consumer who plans to pay between 100 and 200 dollars will elect the products upper and lower than these limits (Lamb et al.,1992:108).

After the consumers knock out some products, which don't match the criteria in their minds, there will stay a group of alternatives called *evoked set* or *consideration set*. Marketers at that point must try to be able to put their products among this group or evoked set. The repetation of advertisement again and again are just a struggle to enter into this set in the minds of consumers (Copley, 2009:66). It is known that unless an extraordinary effect occurs, consumers make a preference among this consideration set, because being in front of eyes via advertisements aims at being or staying in this set.

In some cases, consumers are so careful and rational in evaluating the alternatives, but in some other cases, they behave just instinctively (Kotler & Armstrong, 2008:148). Some factors not expected by consumers can also affect these evaluations. Family intervention, sudden rises in prices can be mentioned as some of these factors (Lamb et al.,1992:108).

The information coming from other consumers as eWOM messages about how to range the alternatives are important factors in evaluating the alternatives, and again eWOM can increase the satisfaction by offering supportive information and helping with the consumption problems (Schindler & Bickart, 2004:57).

Whether during the composition of an consideration set or during the ranging of these alternatives according to their priority and putting of this alternative to the forefront in purchase decision, eWOM messages by opinion leaders especially in blogs, or in other social media platforms can play an important role. The phase of evaluating alternatives requires a higher level of information which focuses directly on the goal and the benefit. The consumer in this phase, though he or she is satisfied with the information at hand so far, will need the opinions of unbiased people especially about the products with high prices. The impact of eWOM communication here will show itself once more.

## Post Decision Processes

Not all purchase decisions result in buying; consumer can the leave this process in any of the phases. Another important point here is that not all purchase decisions follow all these phases, but following all the phases consecutively is a typical situation for the consumers who are involved in making comprehensive purchase decision (Lamb et al., 1992:103). After the evaluating phase, the consumer decides to buy one of the alternatives or gives up buying. When the consumer decides to buy, he will hope some benefits from this decision. The level of the purchased products to meet these benefits will determine whether the consumer will be satisfied or not (Lamb et al.,1992:108).

Decision-making process of the consumers will not be completed when the purchase has taken place. From the marketing point of view, perhabs the most essential aim of this process, the beliefs or opinions about whether to buy the same brand again is of great importance. The cognitive dissonance likely to be experienced in this last phase has got an important role to determine the next purchases of the same products. Some advertisements are designed especially for the needs of the consumers who have recently purchased a product and experience the cognitive dissonance phase (Baker and Hart, 2008:124). Unless treated, this post purchase dissonance can increase more and more and thus affects the satisfaction behaviour of the consumer. The aim of these advertisements is to make the consumers believe that they have purchased the right product, and to sweep the dissonance before turning into dissatisfaction.

The feedback in this phase will affect the evaluations and preferences to repeat the purchase. The positive feedback especially in this last phase will strenghten the attitude towards the product and keep the product in the consideration set of the consumers. But negative feedbacks will lead negative eWOM messages and cause the product to be removed from the consideration set (Copley, 2009:67).

The the post-purchase dissonance and reducing this dissonance are the essential topics of eWOM literature. The consumers experiencing post-purchase dissonance need to reach other consumers having similar ideas and mentioning the advantages of the purchased products. The best way to reach these consumers are social media platforms. The consumers who want to use these effective platforms tend to apply to the eWOM messages to support the purchase decision in their mind by reading the positive reviews of similar consumers.

On the other hand, it is known that the unsatisfied consumers are a potential negative eWOM spreader in online platforms. So, the management of negative eWOM messages will be effective again at that point. Both the causing factors of damaging eWOM messages about companies and the results of these kind of negative contented messages must be taken into consideration. The findings obtained from these two ends should be used to manage the eWOM communications among consumers.

## SOLUTIONS AND RECOMMENDATIONS

The two sides of the online platforms are the experienced consumers such as opinion leaders, satisfied or unsatisfied consumers and the followers who search for information for all phases of decision-making process. For the formers ones, online platforms are a kind of megaphones to express themselves about the services or products they have used. They use these platforms to show their positive or negative reactions. As for the latter group, these platforms are the best sources to satisfy their information needs and so they are ready to listen what this megaphone says.

The consumers who are not satisfied with the products or services usually give their first reactions to the brand or the company by making a complaint. But when they have realised that the brand or the company ignores their complaints, the second and damaging way starts for the brand: making complaints to the other potential consumers especially on the net.

The marketers today has an opportunity to help the consumer affirm and confirm their purchase decision by using eWOM messages in online environments, because the consumers of our day meet their affirmation and confirmation needs via internet and the reviews on internet platforms.

So, knowing that the only way to control eWOM process is to satisfy the consumers and listen to what the says about the services they offer, the companies and brands should be aware of the potential damage of an unsatisfied consumer. They must learn to listen all the consumers no matter what they say, positive or negative about the services or products.

It must be taken into consideration by the marketers that positive eWOM messages are the supporter of promotion activities. To be able to create and spread positive WOM about the brand, marketers should be involved in WOM platforms, especially in the online environment which has a bigger potential to affect the consumers. Opinion leaders and social media celebrities, at that point, should be identified and used for the aims of the brand. What is important here ise that marketers should act in an ethical way and unethical behaviours or actions must be avoided. The negative eWOM messages are the very dynamites to destroy all the promotions trying to persuade the consumer to buy. So, marketers should create online platforms to help the consumers express their complaints about the brand. It must be taken into consideration that the unsatisfied consumers are the potential loyal consumers of the brands only when their complaints are resolved.

Realizing that eWOM messages are directly involved in all the phases of consumer decision-making process, marketers must need to produce strategies related with eWOM communication special for each individual phases of this decision-making process. A analyst team can be used for eWOM communications in online environments. These people are reqired to be deeply in these communications as both an observer and a channeler. It must be known that to be a good channeler depends on being a conscientious observer. The more they are careful with the eWOM messages or even the words in these messages, the more successful projects and decisions they will make about the future. An important job of this analyst team should find out what the consumers ask each other about the brands and what kind of answers they get for these questions. This team should be used to create stories about the brand and to spread these stories among current and also potential customers. The marketing strategies of the brands or the companies must be integrated with these analyses and applications.

## FUTURE RESEARCH DIRECTIONS

Consumer decision-making process is a complex and interactive process which needs to be analysed in more detail. Each phase of this complex process from the stimulation to the post purchase behaviours is directly related with eWOM communications. So the researchers can do a more detailed research about the relationships between all the individual phases of this process and they can try to produce strategies for the marketers to use for each phase.

The role of opinion leaders and mavens in this process are another important point to focus on. How they behave in online environments, how they direct the consumers and even how the marketers can use these people in favor of their brand goals are all the potential research fields for the future researchers.

Again, when it comes to eWOM and the interactions between consumers, some urgent concepts come to the fore: tie strength, homophily, trust and so on. These concepts are the ones directly related with the eWOM communications and their effects on consumers trying to make a purchase decision. Future researchers can deal with these concepts to able to identify and determine the effect of eWOM on consumers. The power of eWOM valence (positive and negative) is another point to be able to study on. There have been few studies about the effect of valence on purchase decision. So, new studies are needed to make an exact distingusment between these to opposite effects.

The effects of diferent social meda platforms on purchase decision is also a potentail research field. Guven's (2014) research is a comprehensive one on eWOM communications in online platforms. The researcher made a deep research about the effect differences between platforms. New and more comprehensive studies are needed on this field. So the researchers can attempt to find out the power of eWOM communications through different online platforms.

## CONCLUSION

To sum up, individuals today prefer socializing via social media platforms such as blogs, consumer review websites and social networks, thus shaping their purchase decisions. In these platforms, consumers are involved in this process sometimes as an opinion leader or sometimes as a follower, and spread positive or negative messages about the products or services. In other words social media, an indispensable part of millions of people's lives, and the interactions in these platforms are sometimes positive and sometimes negative.

The marketers and the businessmen need to take advantage of these online interactions. So it is a must for the marketers to analyse the eWOM communications and interactions in online platforms. What is needed at that point is to be able to understand the role of eWOM communications in consumer decision making process.

## REFERENCES

Baker, M. J., & Hart, S. J. (Eds.). (2008). *The marketing book*. Routledge.

Bechina, A. A., & Husta, E. (2011). The Role of Social Networking Tools on Purchasing Decision Making Process. *Proceedings of the International Conference on Intellectual Capital*, 81-87.

Belch, B. (2003). *Advertising and promotion an integrated marketing communications perspective (6th ed.)*. McGraw-Hill/Irwin.

Bettman, J. R., Johnson, E. J., & Payne, J. W. (1991). Consumer decision making. Handbook of Consumer Behavior, 50-84.

Bonabeau, E. (2009). Decisions 2.0: The power of collective intelligence. *MIT Sloan Management Review*, *50*(2), 45–52.

Cheung, M. Y., Luo, C., Sia, C. L., & Chen, H. (2009). Credibility of Electronic Word-of-Mouth: Informational and Normative Determinants of On-line Consumer Recommendations. *International Journal of Electronic Commerce*, *13*(4), 9–38. doi:10.2753/JEC1086-4415130402

Copley, P. (2004). *Marketing Communications Management concepts and theories, cases and practices*. Elsevier Butterworth Heinemann.

Engel, J. F., Blackwell, R. D., & Miniard, P. W. (2005). *Consumer Behaviour*. Thompson South Western Company.

Fill, C. (2009). Marketing Communications. Interactivity. In *Communities and Content* (5th ed.). Prentice Hall, Financial Times.

Güven, E. (2014). *Sosyal Medyadaki Ağızdan Ağıza Pazarlama Faaliyetlerinin Satınalma Kararları Üzerine Etkileri* (Dissertation thesis). Manisa Celal Bayar University.

Hutter, K., Hautz, J., Dennhardt, S., & Füller, J. (2013). The impact of user interactions in social media on brand awareness and purchase intention: The case of MINI on Facebook. *Journal of Product and Brand Management*, *22*(5/6), 342–351. doi:10.1108/JPBM-05-2013-0299

Kotler, P., & Keller, L. (2008). *Marketing Management* (13th ed.). Prentice Hall Publishing.

Lamb, C. W., Hair, J. F., & McDaniel, C. D. (1992). *Principles of marketing*. Thomson South-Western.

Lopez, M., & Sicilia, M. (2012). How WOM marketing contributes to new product adoption Testing competitive communication strategies. *European Journal of Marketing*, *47*(7), 1089–1114. doi:10.1108/03090561311324228

Schindler, R. M., Bickart, B. (2004). Published word of mouth: Referable, consumer-generated information on the Internet. *Online consumer psychology: Understanding and influencing consumer behavior in the virtual world, 2*, 35-61.

## KEY TERMS AND DEFINITIONS

**Cognitive Dissonance:** The mental stress or discomfort about the purchased services or products experienced by consumers in the post-purchase process.

**Consideration Set:** A set of assumptions, methods, or notations held by one or more consumers or groups of consumers.

**Decision-Making Process:** The basic decision process used by consumers to make a purchase or not.

**eWOM:** Any positive or negative statement made by potential, actual, or former customers about a product or company that is made available to a multitude of people and institutions via the internet.

**Opinion Leader:** Influential members of a community, group, or society to whom others turn for advice, opinions, and views.

**Social Media:** Computer-mediated tools that allow people and companies to create, share, or exchange information, ideas, and pictures/videos in virtual communities and networks.

**Valence:** The directions of consumer reviews as positive or negative.

# Chapter 5

# Investigating the Factors for Predictive Marketing Implementation in Algerian Organizations

**Soraya Sedkaoui**

*Djilali Bounaama University, Algeria & Montpellier University, France & SRY Consulting, France*

## ABSTRACT

*This chapter examines and identifies the factors that influence the implementation of predictive marketing in Algeria enterprises. A structured questionnaire was used to collect data from 30 respondents comprised of CEOs of selected enterprises. Some analytical methods were applied to analyze the data and evaluate the point of view of the enterprises with regard to the adoption and implementation of predictive marketing techniques. The major findings of the study indicated that the adoption of predictive marketing requires the relevant tools and software to extract knowledge "data mining." In addition, the existence of start-up (for analytics) and the level of development of e-commerce and digital marketing in Algeria will undoubtedly encourage the use of these techniques. This chapter also provides some suggestions for further research.*

DOI: 10.4018/978-1-5225-5993-1.ch005

# INTRODUCTION

The Internet and the Web has attracted considerable attention and research from both academics and practitioners. Numerous studies anticipated a "marketing revolution" (Hoffman & Novak, 1997; Keeny & Marshall, 2000) as businesses changed their modes of operation and customers adapted to novel and different ways of purchasing goods and services. With the advent of digital technology and smart devices, a large amount of digital data is being generated every day. Individuals are putting more and more publicly available data on the web. Thus, not only the quantity of digitally stored data is much larger, but the type of data is also tremendously diversified, due to various new technologies (Sedkaoui & Monino, 2016).

Customer databases have grown significantly larger over the last decade. Many companies collect information on their customers and their respective behavior. Thanks to technology advent which enables companies to produce a granular record of every touchpoint consumers make in their purchase journey. However, firms still depend on aggregate measures to guide their marketing investments in multiple channels (display, paid search, referral, e-mail …). If they want to predict how customers will respond in the future, there is one place to turn "predictive analytics". Organizations enabled with analytical tools can incorporate better strategies to use their resources in more efficient way (Ngai et al., 2009).

Predictive analytics comprise collection of statistical and empirical models with the goal of creating empirical predictions and further assessing the quality of those predictions in practice. These techniques are applicable in both theory building and theory testing approaches. Predictive analytics methods help to analyze and understand customer behaviors and acquire and retain customers and also maximize customer value. Thus it facilitates decisions making and supports development of businesses strategies. The notion of "big data" and the potential of producing actionable information from the existing databases are the main drivers of predictive analytics application (Halper, 2011).

Big data is often obtained by aggregating different sources of very different nature of data. We may have to deal simultaneously with numerical, categorical data, but also with text, preference data, browsing histories, historical purchase on e-commerce websites, social media data, analyzed by using methods of natural language processing, being fused with sales data to determine the effect of advertising on consumer sentiment about a product and behaviors of purchase. Indeed, marketing strategy, supported by the predictive analysis techniques is a project that is not limited to define ideas but especially to translate them into action and to control its state of evolution for better understand customer behavior.

The application of predictive analytics in Algerian enterprises is an emerging trend. Despite the transition from a planned economy to a market economy, many experts and researchers believe that the practice of Marketing companies is still weak and affecting their competitiveness. Moreover, these companies are also exposed to the universe of big data. Data is therefore collected and analyzed to support efficient business processes and to create significant additional value. This leads us to question the reasons for Algerian enterprises' delay in adopting predictive marketing tools and the factors likely to influence them to adapt predictive analytics in their marketing strategies.

Many researches have been examined in understanding analytics benefits. However, few studies, especially in Algeria, have examined this theme. It is on this premise that this study wants to examine the factors influencing adoption and implementation of predictive tools with special reference to the Algerian enterprises. This makes the present research one of the first studies analyzing this point. This paper seeks to investigate the issues relating to the adoption of predictive analytics methods for marketing purposes by enterprises. In particular it focuses on the factors that affect a need for such methods in Algerian enterprises. It builds primarily on existing based research and develops a conceptual framework to understand why organizations do or do not adopt predictive marketing.

A framework for predictive marketing factors in Algerian organizations was adopted and questionnaire was designed to collect the needed information to achieve our research objective. The paper begins with a brief overview of approaches to the adoption of predictive marketing analytics to establish the current theoretical context for work in this area. The conceptual framework is then presented. Following that, the quantitative methodology employed is then reviewed and the results discussed. The paper concludes with a discussion of the implications of the findings and directions for future research.

## BASIC CONCEPTS AND RESEARCH BACKGROUND

### Marketing Challenges and Big Data Age

One consequence of technological advances in electronic commerce is the generation of "massive quantities of data produced by and about individuals, things and their interactions" (Boyd & Crawford 2012). Beyond those interactions, large volumes of data are created through Internet searches, social networks, GPS systems, and stock market transactions. In these circumstances, it is clear that marketing is particularly concerned by the advent of the big data, due to its function within the company. Although big data is considered a new form of capital in today's marketplace (Mayer-Schönberger & Cukier, 2013; Satell, 2014), many firms fail to exploit its benefits (Mithas, Lee, Earley, & Murugesan, 2013).

Big data gets global attention and can be best described using the three Vs: volume, variety and velocity. These three dimensions often are employed to describe the phenomenon. Each dimension presents both challenges for data management and opportunities to advance decision-making (Sedkaoui, 2017). This 3 V's provide a challenge associated with working with big data. The volume put the accent on the storage, memory and computes capacity of a computing system and requires access to a computing cloud. Velocity stresses the rate at which data can be absorbed and meaningful answers produced. The variety makes it difficult to develop algorithms and tools that can address that large variety of input data.

So, there are still many difficulties and challenges in the use of big data technologies. The biggest challenge of the zetabytes age will not be storing all that data, it will be figuring out how to make sense of it. For marketing in particular, an old debate on prediction vs. explanation has become louder as big data has increased pressures for integrating conventional data management methods and governance processes. With the move from traditional marketing to digital marketing, marketing function has never been more challenging. Following these changes and the increasing inefficiency of traditional marketing practices, a new form of marketing has emerged: "predictive marketing".

Marketing constantly relies on customer data to develop winning strategies. It analyzes, exploits data about current or potential customers and company information and, as we have mentioned, the size of these data increases exponentially. To better understand, anticipate and satisfy the needs of their clients, marketers must make the most of this data, usually unstructured, in order to transform them into directly exploitable information on customers. Marketers must respond by using, leveraging, and applying data: customer's data, prospects data, data warehouses, internal and external data, etc. All of these data insights can be leveraged to create a competitive advantage.

## Analytics and the Transformation of Marketing

Companies face everyday problems related to uncertainty in organizational planning activities: accurate and timely knowledge means improved business performance. Traditional methods of customer analysis, like segmentation and market research, provide static knowledge about customers, which may become unreliable in time. Moreover, recent research into IT adoption and use has been motivated by the desire to predict factors, which can lead to successful application in a marketing context (El-Gohary, 2010; Lynn, Lipp, Akgün, & Cortez, 2002).

A competitive advantage can be gained by adopting a data mining approach whereby predictive analytics of customer behavior are learned from historical data. Companies may need to alter organization and business processes to act on the insights from big data (Viaene, 2013). As described by Erevelles et al. (2015), physical capital, human capital, and organizational capital resources moderate the process of transforming consumer activities into a sustainable competitive advantage at different stages.

The application of predictive analytics in marketing process is expedited by IT tools. For marketing, the challenge thus is not to keep sticking to traditional ways of researching but to seek new ways. It is only through such ways that we would achieve fuller understandings of how people, products and processes interact with one another. The ability to draw customer data and bring them rapidly into operational decision making is transforming the discipline of marketing. There are huge benefits for companies and marketers alike to get started with predictive marketing sooner rather than later.

Predictive marketing combines predictive and prescriptive analytics to predict what will happen and how to make it happen. Predictive marketing is a new way of thinking about customer relationships, powered by new technologies in big data and machine learning, which we collectively call predictive analytics. Marketers better pay attention to predictive analytics. The adoption of predictive marketing (Artun & Levin, 2015) is accelerating among companies large and small because: (a) customers are demanding more meaningful relationships with brands, (b) early adopters show that predictive marketing delivers enormous value, and (c) new technologies are available to make predictive marketing easy.

## Factors Influencing Adoption of Marketing and Analytics Methods

There is a huge career opportunity that comes from being an early adopter of new methodologies and technologies, predictive marketing and predictive analytics included. Research has unearthed voluminous perceived benefits of predictive marketing and benefits associated with the employment of analytics methods and in enterprises operational milieu. Predictive marketing has the potential to cover a number of specific strategies to help grow customer value: postpurchase campaigns, replenishment campaigns, repeat purchase programs, new product introductions, and customer appreciation campaigns. It offers feasible and pragmatic solutions for organizations to address the challenges in this dynamic environment.

Different sources of literature have acknowledged the challenges of predictive analytics adoption and its diffusion and applications in marketing field. The existing literature has categorized factors impeding adoption of marketing approaches by enterprises into internal and external barriers. A number of researchers highlight firm size, firm characteristic, product, sector, access to marketing, policy changes and economic conditions as factor that influence the extent of adoption and exploitation of marketing (Giovanni & Mario 2003; Shiels et al 2003; McConville 2008).

As mentioned above, the adoption of technology for support predictive marketing is then essential for the survival of the enterprise. There are a growing number of studies in the literature related to the adoption of technology for marketing by businesses (Durkin et al., 2013; Kim et al., 2011; Simmons et al., 2011; Jones et al., 2014). ICT investments are considered barriers too, in addition to cultural deficiencies, lack of cooperation, lack of relevancy of adoption to the organization and design of e-commerce (Luccehetti & Sterlaccini 2004; McConville, 2008). Legal and regulatory issues, weak strategies, lack of research and development, excessive and reliance on foreign technology are viewed as a challenge to adoption of e-marketing and analytics applications (Matambalya & Wolf 2001).

## CONCEPTUAL FRAMEWORK AND RESEARCH HYPOTHESES

The main objective of this study is to investigate the factors influencing the adoption of analytics methods in order to support marketing approach within the Algerian enterprises. Based on the literature discussed above, and the benefits of analytics methods on marketing function, research model illustrated in Figure 1 asserts that the attention to adopt analytics tools for marketing structure in selected enterprises depends on: internal business context, external business context, organizational culture and training, and ICT investment and the use of technology. The proposed constructs and hypotheses are supported by prior studies in marketing, big data and predictive analytics literature.

### Internal Business Context (Size, Resource Availability, Marketing Structure, Partnership, Skills)

The internal environments play a role among the reasons for adoption or non-adoption of analytics tools by Algerian enterprises. Sizes and resources determine the usage or non-usage of computers in the various businesses. Firm size is related to the ability of enterprises to provide certain resources, both financial and human resources. The larger the size of business means the greater its ability to provide certain resources, and the more likely the adoption of technology and analytics tools. Firm size in this study was measured by using two indicators: the number of employees and total assets.

Academics and business practitioners increasingly recognize the importance of organizational structure in marketing (Lee et al, 2015). Many researchers examined the effects of different organizational structure design elements on marketing outcomes remains fragmented and scarce. This statement opens up to look into what the adherents of the structural perspective think about effectiveness and according to them it is the organization structure that creates effectiveness within an organization (Eriksson et al., 2005).

Also, in today's hyper-competitive business environment, firms must constantly update and reconfigure resources by responding to changes in the external environment to develop a sustainable competitive advantage (Kozlenkova et al., 2014; Lin & Wu, 2014). A firm's ability to respond to change (dynamic capability) incorporates skills and knowledge embedded within the organization to alter existing resources and create new value (Day, 2014). A firm using novel consumer insight extracted from big data to understand unmet consumer needs enhances dynamic capability. Owner innovativeness, owner IT experience and analytics ability are identified as determinant factors that can influence enterprises in adopting predictive marketing.

As Baptista (2000) points out, the corporate status of a company might play a role in affecting the adoption of a new technology. The independence of an enterprise might be involved with higher flexibility in deciding whether or not to adopt a new technology and analytics tools. However, enterprises that belong to a group of firms generally have more financial resources than others and thus might be less risk-averse in adopting analytics tools.

Therefore, based on the above, it is expected that:

**H1:** *Firm size influences positively the adoption of predictive marketing*
**H2:** *Resource Availability influences positively the adoption of predictive marketing*
**H3:** *Existence of marketing function structure affects predictive marketing adoption*
**H4:** *Partnership and belonging to a group of firms influences predictive marketing adoption*
**H5:** *Employees with skills and IT ability affect the adoption of predictive marketing*

*Figure 1. Research model*

# External Business Context (E-Commerce Development, Expertise Start-Ups, Competition)

The external business context refers to external factors which influence the use of predictive marketing and analytics tools. The Algerian economy is based primarily on oil sector resources. Despite the rich natural environment, the economy has not prospered as most organizations do not operate smoothly and efficiently given to the lack in infrastructures required. Findings of this study identified telecommunication infrastructural as one of the barriers hindering the adoption of e-commerce in Algeria. In most part of selected enterprises author noticed low connections of the internet services. Broadband connectivity is a key component in ICT development, adoption and use.

Technology readiness is one of the organizational contexts proposed in this study as a determinant factor that influences enterprises in adopting predictive marketing. Technology readiness refers to what extent the technology infrastructure, relevant systems and technical skills in business can support e-commerce and the use of analytics tolls. Technology readiness consists of both technology infrastructure and IT human resources (Zhu & Kraemer, 2005) and both are really needed if the company wants to make e-business an integral part of the value chain (Tiago & Maria, 2010). Hence, the greater the technology readiness of an organization the more likely the organization adopts IT technology, and vice versa.

In addition, the adoption level of e-commerce might be reflected by the lack of training in e-commerce related technologies and there was some need for customizing technology, from abroad, for the Arab region (Warf & Vincent, 2007). Also, existing of service providers (start-up for in the field of data analytics) can be an external support that influences predictive analytics adoption for supporting marketing functions. In principle, an independent software firm could offer a service of customizing existing software also for proprietary embedded operating systems, and such firms indeed exist.

When competitors start to use e-commerce technology, firms will be shoved into adopting digital marketing more widely to obtain competitive advantages. The competitor pressure refers to the extent of pressure from competitors within the industry as felt by the firm (Zhu & Kraemer, 2005). When competitors start to use e-commerce technology, firms will be shoved into adopting e-commerce technology more widely to obtain competitive advantages. Thus, the higher the level of competition within the industry, the more likely it is that greater analytics methods use will be achieved required. For example, Target is utilizing exclusive predictive data to substantially enhance its adaptive capability to influence the customer's purchases for baby items capturing sales before competitors and initiating a long-term customer relationship.

These explanations lead to the following hypotheses:

**H6:** *The development of e-commerce and digital marketing in Algeria influences the adoption of predictive marketing*

**H7:** *Existence of expertise startups in the field (providers) influences the adoption of predictive marketing*

**H8:** *Competitor pressure influences the adoption of predictive marketing*

## Organizational Culture and Training

In addition to internal and external contexts explained above, in this study organizational culture and training are also considered as determinant factors of predictive marketing adoption by enterprises in developing countries. It is evident from related literatures that predictive marketing have gained ground in the developed countries but same is new in developing countries due to their cultural inclinations. Predictive marketing approach will be easily accepted in an organization if it is tune in with the prevailing values of that organization, can meet the needs of organization and accords with organization culture. In addition to the size, skills ... the culture obtained within the organization are among the draw backs of predictive marketing adoption among Algerian enterprises.

This is because mostly in businesses a strategic decision is highly dependent on the manager/owner. Cloete et al (2002) revealed that the e-commerce adoption by SMEs extensively depends on the acceptance of e-commerce technology by the owner of business. This is reasonable, because structurally SMEs tend to centralize, hence the manager have an important role in any business decision making (Nguyen & Waring, 2013). It must be a matter of great disappointment to enterprises that many of component of typical marketing analytics are rarely used by practicing marketing managers. Indeed, even experienced marketing managers with marketing qualifications often fail to apply the techniques of marketing. Adaptive and dynamic capabilities, enhanced by insight from Big Data, lead to value creation (Tellis et al., 2009; Wei & Lau, 2010).

As a technology innovation, predictive marketing also has risk, especially if it is applied in small business and even more in developing countries. Hence, the more innovative the enterprises owner, the more likely they have an intention to adopt a predictive analytics application. Therefore, increasing Algerian enterprises awareness, of the benefits of the adoption of predictive marketing, ought to affect positively the adoption of e-commerce. Increasing awareness could be achieved through providing better education and more training. Introducing predictive marketing requires that decision-makers and marketing specialists acquire new skills. While admitting their lack of skills and knowledge in embracing the data mining field as a new tools for marketing activities, most of the enterprises believed that training of managers and employees in predictive marketing analytics could considerably contribute to their marketing success and they could achieve further benefits. Overall, Big Data can raise more questions than answers (Weber & Henderson, 2014). Enterprises must devise new ways of analyzing big data, creating actionable insights and implementing new marketing activities. Without such innovative, creative thinking, firms would incur difficulty in utilizing big data to facilitate adaptive capabilities and broaden the scope of marketing activities that may facilitate radical innovation; however, in a hypercompetitive business environment, any new marketing activities eventually will be imitated (D'Aveni et al., 2010).

With the proliferation of new technologies, channels, and consumption approaches, the understanding of contemporary consumer behavior is becoming more complex. Simultaneously, advances in technology allow marketers to capture rich consumption data with greater volume, velocity, and variety. Often, these rich and newly available sources of information (big data) enable marketers to realize new gaps or areas of ignorance in marketers' understanding of consumer behavior (Firestein, 2012). As the richness of data increases, marketers are better able to recognize new gaps and advance their understanding of consumer behavior. Firms with greater awareness of information needs will uncover more hidden consumer insights from Big Data that facilitate adaptive capabilities than firms with little awareness of information needs.

Therefore, it is reasonable to hypothesize that:

**H9:** *Absence of manager strategic vision (internal culture or commitment of managers) about the importance of predictive tools influences the adoption of the predictive marketing*

**H10:** *More or less accurate knowledge of big data and data mining affects the adoption of the predictive marketing*

**H11:** *Training staff on big data and data mining influences predictive marketing adoption*

**H12:** *The lack of information influences the adoption and application of predictive marketing*

## Technological Context and ICT Investment

The technological context refers to those aspects such as ICT intensity and investment, complexity of predictive marketing tools (use, data security...) and cost that influence the adoption of predictive marketing. High cost of infrastructure and its implementation has been cited to impede predictive marketing adoption relating to buying ICT equipment for implementation, setting-up, training employees and consultancy fees, creation and maintenance of website and other infrastructures

(Mutula, 2017). An important aspect which is important in the context of using analytics methods and tools is the enterprise's openness to ICT. Managers know that the relative advantages of predictive marketing adoption raise the probability of allocating some resources: managerial, financial and technological resources.

Then, intensity of ICT tools refers to what extent marketing is appropriate with technology infrastructure, culture, value, and work practices that already exist in the enterprise. ICT including the web is believed to be the most cost efficient tool that can aid companies to gain bigger markets and be able to compete with their larger counterparts in attracting customers to their products and services (Tan et al., 2009). Cost is also considered, in this study, as a factor that influences Algerian businesses in their adopting predictive marketing. Usually, the less expensive the cost of a certain technology the more likely it will be quickly adopted and implemented in an organization (Premkumar & Roberts, 1999).

Predictive analytics methods varying with the level of technological complexity. Also, big data has put a great challenge on the current statistical methodology and computational tools. With growing size typically comes a growing complexity of data structures, of the patterns in the data, and of the models needed to account for the patterns. The difficulty of transforming big data into value or knowledge is related to its complexity, the essence of which is broadly captured by the three Vs: Volume, Variety and Velocity are used to define the term big data. Each of these dimensions presents both challenges for data management and opportunities to advance decision-making (Sedkaoui, 2017).

Data analysis, when it is not preceded by the word 'Big', refers to the development and sharing of useful and effective models. For the most part, it uses a variety of methods from different research fields, like statistics, data mining, visual analysis, etc. It caters to a wide range of applications, including data summarization, classification, prediction, correlation, etc. In the 1970s and 1980s, computers could process information in batch processing, but its operations were constrained and too costly. Only large firms could hope to analyze data with them. They started to work on data organization by designing database management systems (DBMSs), in particular of relational databases. Data processing and analysis, in the present day, are brought together under the notion of 'Business Intelligence', due especially to computers' increased processing capabilities (Shroff, 2013).

Hence, it is expected that:

**H13:** *ICT investment influences the adoption and application of predictive marketing*
**H14:** *The cost of the necessary IT tools support the adoption of predictive marketing*
**H15:** *The use of tools for the management of customer databases facilitate the application of predictive methods*

**H16:** *The complexity of predictive marketing tools influences the adoption of this approach*

## RESEARCH METHODS

Although there is a body of literature vis-à-vis enterprises factors in adopting predictive marketing, studies into the adoption and successful implementation of predictive marketing in Algeria is comparatively rare. Since enterprise are often acknowledged as the engine of national economic growth, it is relevant to investigate why they have not taken up the many opportunities of predictive marketing considering the rapid growth of analytics tools in the developed countries. A survey method using a google forms was employed. This was chosen in due to its advantages, namely: cheaper, faster, and easier than other methods. The questionnaire was developed by reference to previous studies.

## Questionnaire Development

In order to address the objectives of the study and to provide more insights into the points discussed above, an empirical investigation was deployed, and data obtained from a convenience sample of 30 Algerian enterprises. The investigation focused on enterprises from different sectors and located in different areas of the country (see appendix 1). Moreover, our sample falls to 30 enterprises that found an interest in the survey. A survey was employed in this study to investigate the factors affecting adoption of predictive marketing. The study employed questionnaire as instruments of data collection.

The questionnaire is developed according to the objectives of the study and analyzes the relationship between certain components of the company environment and the attitudes of its managers towards the adoption of predictive marketing tools. A total of sixteen factors of analytics tools and predictive marketing were combed from the related literature studies. From the conceptual framework (Figure 1), these factors were grouped into four categories by the help of professionals and experts. A questionnaire contains provide information on 2 topics that informs us about various aspects of the company and the state of predictive marketing within selected enterprises.

The instrument was designed to include a two-part questionnaire as presented in Appendix 2. Accordingly, the first part is basic information. This part of questionnaire was used to collect information about respondents' characteristics including gender, age and occupation. The second part was developed based on the constructs of information about the condition of the marketing function within enterprises before moving to a set of questions vis-à-vis predictive marketing and big data which is presented as an opportunity for development of the marketing function and has undoubtedly generated an increased need of customer databases analysis.

## Sample and Measurement of Variables

In fact, 30 enterprises responded to 33 questions (in the form of 22 questions about the predictive marketing, added to 11 presentation issues). Participants were tasked to select their most significant factors with regards to predictive marketing adoption in their enterprises. The questionnaire comprises of sixteen factors, grouped under 4 headings with a 5 point Likert-type scale which ranges from "1- Strongly Agree" to "5- Strongly Disagree" was adopted in the questionnaire administration. For other factors, the answers to the questions are coded from 1 to 3.

Before conducting the main survey, we performed a pre-test to validate the questionnaire. The pre-test involved 5 respondents whom were asked to comment on the length of the instrument, the format, and the wording of the scales. Therefore, the content validity of the instrument has been confirmed. The data collected was tested, analyzed and interpreted using STATISTICA version 12. Analysis of data was done using descriptive statistics specifically mean and standard deviation, t student test correlation analysis and multiple regression analysis. Cronbach's alpha (a measure of internal consistency or how closely related a set of items are) was also used to assess the inter-item reliability for each variable.

*Table 1. Construct reliabilities*

| Variable | Alpha Cronbach |
|---|---|
| Part1 | 0,754059 |
| Part2 | 0,751024 |
| Resource Availability | 0,699317 |
| Skills | 0,668164 |
| Startup | 0,688295 |
| e-commerce development | 0,698522 |
| Concurrence | 0,713825 |
| Lack of Information | 0,744457 |
| Cost | 0,698593 |
| Complexity tools | 0,705221 |
| Training | 0,726688 |

As reported in Table 1, Cronbach's alpha scores were over 0.735, suggesting that the items have a relatively high degree of internal consistency (note that a reliability coefficient of 0.70 or higher is considered "acceptable" in most social science research (Hair et al., 2010). These alpha scores are acceptable for an exploratory analysis, indicating that the factors within each variable are inter-related.

## Sample and Profile of Selected Enterprises

This study conducted online survey to overcome time and place constraints, thus helping our study to reach respondents more easily than using other survey methods (interviews: personal and telephone and other self-administered survey). Empirical data were collected by conducting a survey on an Algerian electronic directory which contains contact information. An email is then sent to 220 enterprises to invite them to fill out the questionnaire. This email stated the purpose of this study and provided a hyperlink to the survey form. This online survey was conducted for 2 month, resulting in a sample size of 30 enterprises for an overall response rate of 13.63%.

Concerning the profile of the surveyed enterprises in this study, all of them are interested in development of marketing function services. As mentioned above, we have selected several types of variables: Size, sector and marketing function. In the following, we will try to analyze each variable to better understand the nature of these enterprises and identify their characteristics.

## Size

The size is defined by the number of employees in the enterprises and the amount of turnover. Moreover, they are often cautious and do not disclose their turnover. This index is often considered a very personal data that can provide certain information to competitors. It is for this reason that the questionnaire proposed three modalities: Less than 50 million Algerian dinars (AD), between 50 and 200 million (AD) and more than 200 Million (AD). This ranking has been allocated according to the definition of SMEs in Algeria. Similarly, for the number of employees that has been categorized in five intervals. The results of the analysis are presented in Figure 2.

Regarding turnover, 50% of respondents had turnover in excess of 200 million (AD), 27% had turnover between 50 and 200 AD and 23% received less than 50 AD. Similarly, for respondents, the overwhelming majority had an employed workforce between 50 and 499 employees (46.67%). It should be noted that companies with fewer than 10 employees and between 10 and 49 employees represent respectively 20% and 13.33% of the response rate. The remaining two categories represent 13.33% (for 500-999 employees' category) and 6.67% (for more than 1,000 employees' category).

*Figure 2. Surveyed enterprises by size*

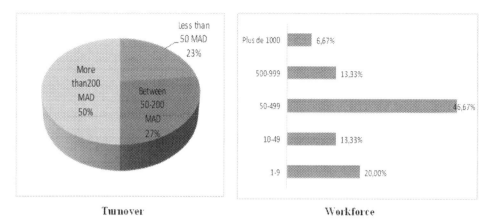

## Business Sector

The thirty enterprises selected were engaged in the different types of businesses as shown in Figure 3.

Figure 3 indicates that the sample came from different industry sectors; Commercial sector came first with 23.33% followed by Agribusiness and ICT sector with 13.33% for each sector, then, Services sector with 10%. Of the 30 surveyed enterprises 6 enterprises provide from various sectors such as: Telecommunication, Health, Construction, Automotive, industry and habitat. Our sample also includes professional training companies with 6.67%. This rate is the same for tourist and hydraulics sectors.

*Figure 3. Selected enterprises by business sector*

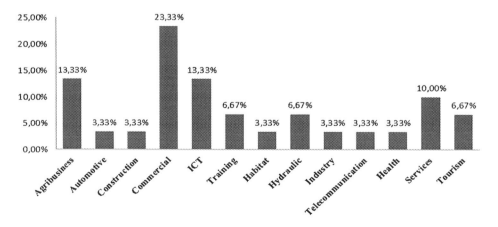

From the investigation of this study it can be seen that, among the 30 companies surveyed, four companies is part of a group, and 14 are subsidiaries of a group while other companies have not specified their status.

## Marketing Function Activities

In order to determine the importance placed on the marketing function and assess the experience with predictive marketing adoption and implementation by sampled enterprises, we asked a question about the existence of a specialized structure of the marketing. The results are presented in the Table 2.

It seemed that majority of sampled enterprise have a specialized structure for the practice of marketing (70%); eight other enterprises reported not having structure for marketing anointing (26.67%), and only one enterprise declared that the project is in progress. It's important to notice that among enterprises which draw attention to marketing function are companies in from Commercial, Agribusiness, Services and Tourism sector. This can be justified with regard to the importance of this function in their activity.

Enterprises that reported having an internal marketing structure should identify its main activities. As presented in questionnaire, five categories of responses were proposed in addition to one other category (to be specified). The results are presented as shown in Figure 4.

Figure 4 shows that the interest in marketing within the sampled enterprises is motivated mainly by: conducting market studies (20.97%), followed by new product launches (19.35%) and then for the development of sales forecasts (17.74%). It is also noted that 16.13% of enterprises have chosen all categories of possible answers. The lowest response rates are for the development of the Marketing Mix (9.68%) and formulation and implementation of the marketing strategy (8.06%). It should also be noted that 1.61% of these enterprises left this heading unanswered. However, 6.45% proposed other activities namely: the organization of events, e-marketing and the protection of new product.

*Table 2. Existence of marketing structure*

| Question | Number | % | Mean | St Dev |
|---|---|---|---|---|
| Yes | 21 | 70% | | |
| No | 8 | 26.67% | | |
| Ongoing | 1 | 3.33% | 1.8 | 0.5508 |
| Total | 30 | 100% | | |

*Figure 4. The main activities of the marketing structure*

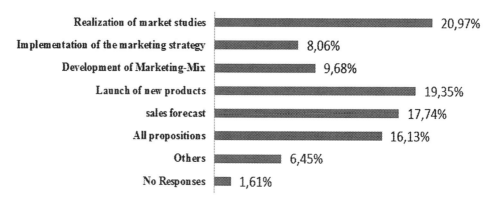

## RESULTS AND DISCUSSION

Understanding analytics power driven change in marketing is very crucial to Algerian enterprises, as it involves new customers, new brands, new markets and even new business models. This section presents the results data analysis and discusses it accordingly in relation to the hypotheses and with the aim of achieving the objectives stated. Through this section, we wish to highlight the behavior of companies with regard to the concept of predictive marketing and issues of big data, and analyzing the factors influencing the adoption of predictive marketing. This will cover the elements that correspond to the main axes on which our survey questionnaire was developed.

## Analytic Tools and the Perception of Big Data Universe

Algerian businesses can't longer afford to ignore the power of analytics in a voluminous data environment if they wish to retain their competitive advantage in a rapidly changing business environment. They need to know the benefits of more efficient use of their data, from improved process efficiencies to strategic decision-making and accurate predictions or the creation of new business models. But some questions arise: Do Algerian companies take advantage of these assets? And what is their situation with regard to this universe?

To answer these questions, the author analyzes the companies' knowledge of big data practices and analytics tools, as well as the technological, organizational and commercial contexts. The results obtained are summarized in the Table 3:

*Table 3. IT intensity and the use of software*

| Category | No | | Yes | | No Response | | Total |
|---|---|---|---|---|---|---|---|
| | N<sup>br</sup> | % | N<sup>br</sup> | % | N<sup>br</sup> | % | |
| High | 1 | 7.14% | 12 | 85.71% | 1 | 7,14% | 14 |
| Medium | 3 | 21.43% | 11 | 78.57% | 0 | 0% | 14 |
| Low | 1 | 50% | 1 | 50.% | 0 | 0% | 2 |
| Total | 5 | - | 24 | - | 1 | - | 30 |

It's important to have an idea about the ICT tools that companies own and use, I order to identify the level (low, medium and high) of the various applications of these tools. The results in the Table 3 show that enterprises reporting high levels of ICT. 85.71% of them use client database management software. Similarly, 78.47% of enterprises with an average level of ICT tools and applications also use this type of tools. This proves the interest of these companies in analyzing their customer behavior.

But this does not hide the reality of IT environment in Algeria, indices reflect the poor level of e-commerce adoption services and connectivity problems.

Regarding customer behavior analysis a question was devoted to know if these enterprises analyze and exploit customer data to better understand their behavior. The appendix 3 summarizes the results. It's found that a large majority of companies (80% of all enterprises surveyed) that appeal to their customer data for a purpose of a better understanding. On the other hand, only 10% of companies do not give importance to this type of analysis. The other companies (10%) didn't answer this question.

By eliminating these enterprises, we have 27 enterprises (responding "yes" or "no" to this question). Then, in the next step, author wanted to know if they issuing loyalty cards to their customers. The aim of this step is to investigate whether club card loyalty have a report with the use of database management systems (DBMSs) to understanding their customers behavior.

Enterprises recognize that satisfying and retaining consumers by building relationships is one of the most sustainable competitive advantages. Although the use of loyalty cards is popular, but only five enterprises deliver loyalty cards to their customers (20.83%), while 45.83% of enterprises that use management databases and analyze customer behavior don't use this type of loyalty strategy. Appendix 4 reflected also that 20.83% mentioned that they will adopt this kind of tools soon

For many businesses loyalty cards as a source of big data presents significant challenges. The marketing power of big data and data mining is recognized by Tesco PLC, with loyalty card data from their Club card representing the buying behavior of

17 million shoppers (approx. 40% of UK households). Then, are selected enterprises what aware of the benefits of the big data and data mining? What about the perception of these terms? The answer to this question is summarized in the Figure 5.

Figure 5 shows that the concept of 'big data' is unfamiliar since less than 44% reported knowing it. As against more than 56% have any idea despite its importance to the universal scale especially with the digitalization of customer data processing tools. Similarly to the term 'data mining', the results indicate that only 37% of enterprises have heard about this concept, while 43% unfortunately not familiar with it although their importance in the customer behavior analysis.

## Predictive Marketing and Marketing Function

In the literature review we have shown what predictive marketing is and what it can bring in the current context. However, Algerian enterprises don't have a global perspective with regard to this practice, so it's difficult to draw a profile of its applications. The analysis of the factors of the strategic character attributed to predictive marketing in these enterprises thus seems essential.

53.33% of enterprise confirmed that they are ready to adopt predictive marketing techniques, with an average of 2.16, compared with only 10% who said no. Another question was posed to these companies about the effect of predictive marketing on the marketing function and 70% agree that this concept will revolutionize their marketing strategies.

For some (external) factors some descriptive statistics (see appendix 5) have been calculated to measure items. The results indicate that the mean of the items varies between 3.5 and 4.27, which shows that the perceptions of the sample tested

*Figure 5. The perception of big data and data mining within enterprises*

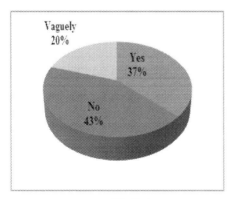

**Big Data**

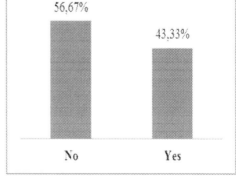

**Data Mining**

*Table 4. Predictive marketing Adoption and its effect on marketing function*

| Question | Yes | No | No Idea | Total | Mean | St Dev |
|---|---|---|---|---|---|---|
| Are you ready to adopt predictive marketing? | 53.33% | 10% | 36.67% | 100% | 2.27 | 0.0396 |
| MP will revolutionize the marketing function? | 70% | 6.67% | 23.33% | 100% | 2.16 | 0.5306 |

are positive. We conclude the growing interest and awareness of these enterprises within the important and strategic role of predictive marketing tools in the universe of the big data.

It should also be noted that another heading was introduced, namely the category "Others" to give enterprises the opportunity to cite certain points that could not be included in our survey. Only three enterprises have completed this section by proposition bellow:

- Mortality rates and risk reserve calculations for more loyalty, service delivery and compensation.
- Training offers in the field.
- Lack of marketing approach related to predictive marketing in the field health insurance in Algeria.

After analyzing the current situation of the marketing function and the big data perception within the 30 surveyed enterprises. It is now time to analyze the assumptions of our research and study the factors behind a positive (or negative) attitude of companies towards predictive marketing and its tools. For this, in the following part of this study we will look at the analysis of research hypotheses.

## Hypotheses Results

The analysis tools used for the testing and interpretation of the hypotheses are: t-test, correlation and regression analysis techniques. In this study the sixteen factors grouped into four categories (as described in section 3) are identified as determinant factors that influence Algerian enterprises in adopting predictive marketing.

### Internal Context

Table 5 shows descriptive analysis and t-test results of the statements that measure enterprise's internal context. The results indicate that selected enterprises were somehow satisfied with their internal context (size, resources, skills ...) to implement

*Table 5. Descriptive analysis and t-test analysis of selected enterprises regarding internal context*

| Items | | Mean | St Dev | t Value | Sig |
|---|---|---|---|---|---|
| Size | Nbr of employees | 2.73 | 1.14 | -1.9518 | 0.0557 |
| | Turnover | 2.27 | 0.8276 | 0.0000 | 1.0000 |
| Resources | | 4.27 | 0.7396 | -11.201 | 0.0000 |
| Marketing structure | | 1.8 | 0.5508 | 3.0278 | 0.0036 |
| Belonging group | | 2.47 | 0.8603 | -1.0218 | 0.3111 |
| Skills | | 1.77 | 0.7738 | 2.7277 | 0.0084 |

a predictive marketing strategy. Respondents are convinced, in some ways, of its potential role. However, based on the t-test analysis, it is found that it's only two internal factors that have a significant effect on predictive marketing adoption.

It concerns the existence of a marketing structure and the availability of skills in the field of big data and data mining with IT ability, which revealed respectively a t-value 3.0278 and 2.7277 with statistical significance less than 0.05. Based on the decision rule for hypotheses testing these results can support the third and the fifth hypothesis of the study (H3, H5), which states that: "Existence of marketing structure and skills affect the selected enterprises to implement and adopt predictive marketing". Moreover, the level of significance greater than 0.05 for Size, Resource and Belonging group can't support hypotheses H1, H2 and H4.

## External Context

The authors found Pearson's correlation coefficients between the variables associated with questions answered on the Likert scale such as external factors. As shown in appendix 6, the Pearson's r for the correlation between each factor and predictive marketing adoption was positive. This means that as one variable increases in value, the second variable also increases in value. Similarly, as one variable decreases in value, the second variable also decreases in value. The values of r were rather medium; there isn't a strong relationship between the variables. The strongest correlation is with the existence of startups (with proven expertise in the field) 0.521. The significance (2-tailed) values are less than 0.05. Therefore, we can conclude that there was a statistically significant correlation between each factor and adoption of marketing predictive.

In order to better analyze these factors to show which influences more the adoption of predictive marketing, a multiple regression analysis was carried out. The Table 6 presents the results.

Based on the multiple regression analysis, two variables have a positive and significant correlation with marketing predictive adoption. This result indicates that the level of e-commerce development in Algeria and the existence of star-ups analytics are recognized by Algerian enterprises as factors that influence them in adopting of predictive marketing, while competitors does not. Hence, H6 and H7 are fully supported, while H8 is not supported.

## Organizational Culture and Training

Concerning the third category of factors group and regarding to the correlation coefficient values, the analysis reveals that Algerian enterprises were likely to have a clear strategic vision to guide predictive marketing adoption. Appendix 6 shows that only two factors are moderately correlated with the enterprise's behavior towards predictive marketing. The first comes between manager vision and attitude toward predictive marketing with 0,380 and the second correlation is with the lack of information with 0,452.

The data presented in Table 7 show the results of the multiple regression analysis, which was used to learn more about the relationships between predictive marketing adoption and managerial factors.

This analysis indicates that only H9 are accepted based on the strong association among the variable ($p<0.05$). The other hypotheses (H10, H11, H12) are rejected because the relationships between the variables are weak ($p>0.05$).

## Technological Context

Table 8 shows the t-test results of the statements that measure enterprise's technological contexts. The analysis reveals that these enterprises were likely to have some limitations in their IT tools to address their information needs regarding their adoption of the predictive marketing.

*Table 6. Multiple regression analysis results*

| Variable | B | St Dev b | t | Sig |
|---|---|---|---|---|
| Constant | 0,903511 | 0,537238 | 1,68177 | 0,105065 |
| E-commerce Development | 0,397790 | 0,146603 | 2,71338 | 0,011884 |
| Start-up | 0,431829 | 0,117282 | 3,68198 | 0,001116 |
| Competitors | 0,035556 | 0,090661 | 0,39219 | 0,698241 |
| R = 0.78099 | $R^2 = 0.6099$ $R^2aj = 0.5475$ | F = 9.7734 | Sig = 0.000067 | df= 4,25 |

*Table 7. Multiple regression analysis regarding managerial factors*

| Variable | B | St Dev b | T | Sig |
|---|---|---|---|---|
| Constant | 1,963944 | 1,002392 | 1,95926 | 0,062875 |
| Manager vision | 0,230161 | 0,096695 | 2,38028 | 0,026390 |
| Known / Big data | -0,040254 | 0,249432 | -0,16138 | 0,873265 |
| Lack of information | -0,125071 | 0,101316 | -1,23447 | 0,230053 |
| Training | 0,078042 | 0,149268 | 0,52283 | 0,606318 |
| R = 0.6514 | $R^2$ = 0.4243 $R^2$aj =0.2412 | F = 2.3173 | Sig = 0.0623 | df= 7, 22 |

*Table 8. T-test regarding IT context*

| Items | T Value | Sig |
|---|---|---|
| ICT Investment | -0,81885 | 0,416222 |
| Cost | -4,72138 | 0,000015 |
| DBMS tools | **2,83386** | **0,006317** |
| Complexity | -5,99277 | 0,000000 |

According to the results analysis indicated in table, only one factor support the implementation and adoption of predictive marketing within Algerian enterprises (signification less than 0.05). We state that these enterprises need to improve their customer databases with respect of the use of management analysis tools. Therefore, H15 in this study is fully supported; however H13, H14 and H16 are rejected. These results are confirmed by Figure 6.

*Figure 6. Technological variables related to predictive marketing adoption*

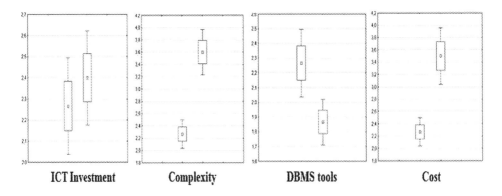

# CONCLUSION

Clearly, analytics has the potential to impact nearly every area of marketing in the big data universe. Firms that do not develop the resources and capabilities to effectively use big data will be challenged to develop sustainable competitive advantage. This study contributes to and extends our understanding of the predictive analytics techniques as means for marketing. To better enable companies to leverage predictive analytics tools, this paper introduces a theoretical framework that explores how predictive marketing leads to enterprise's competitive advantage in the area of big data.

The empirical investigation can be seen that the adoption of predictive marketing by enterprises in Algeria is affected by several factors which are: existence of marketing structure and availability of kills, manager vision, providers in the field of data mining and big data analytics, usage of databases management tools and information about the benefits of this practice. However, more government policies and support may be required to provide an enabling environment for development e-commerce.

It appears that the predictive marketing concept is still in its infancy stage in the Algerian businesses as most managers were likely to view it as mere implementation of IT to better manage customer relationships. Possibly, inadequate investment in ICT, coupled with little understanding of the big data analytics benefits, insufficient marketing database, and poor IT skills, could have been behind this delay in Algeria.

Although the research rests upon an empirical investigation, the study should in no way be seen as to offer conclusive findings, as it focuses on a subject to constant changes due to technological advances, databases size and changing consumer behaviors. It is hereby recommended that for Algerian companies to embrace analytics techniques for their business operations, technological infrastructures should be put in place by the government.

Thus, predictive marketing appears to be a fruitful area of research far into the future. This study has identified several potentially interesting questions for further research that would enrich our understanding of predictive marketing adoption and help to improve its practice in Algeria.

Regarding big data value and analytics power, studies reflect that these techniques will be a competitive necessity, so Algerian enterprises need to start to adapt to the trends in order to survive in the dynamic and digitalized markets. Having undertaken this colossal task it is important that more empirical studies are undertaken about internal culture and ICT investment settings to further understand more reasons for which businesses adopt (or not) predictive marketing and big data analytics in Algeria. It is also hoped that this research will serve as a foundational benchmark for further studies of marketing functions development trends.

## ACKNOWLEDGMENT

The author would like to thank to gratefully and sincerely Mr. Abdelhalim Mekbel (English Trainer at Anadarko company) for the endless English corrections (thank you very much for reading this manuscript), which taught me a lot and helped improve all my writings. The author expresses sincere gratitude to Mr. Ameur (Consultant). Also without the enthusiastic participation of CEOs of 30 enterprises this study would never have come into being. Thank you to all of you!

## REFERENCES

Artun, O., & Levin, D. (2015). *Predictive Marketing: Easy Ways Every Marketer Can Use Customer Analytics and Big Data*. Wiley. doi:10.1002/9781119175803

Baptista, R. (2000). Do innovations diffuse faster within georgraphical clusters? *International Journal of Industrial Organization, 18*(3), 515–535. doi:10.1016/S0167-7187(99)00045-4

Boyd, D., & Crawford, K. (2012). Critical Questions for Big Data. *Information Communication and Society, 15*(5), 662–679. doi:10.1080/1369118X.2012.678878

Cloete, E., Courtney, S., & Fintz, J. (2002). Small Businesses' Acceptance and Adoption of e-Commerce in the Western Cape Province of South Africa. *The Electronic Journal on Information Systems in Developing Countries, 10*.

D'Aveni, R. A., Dagnino, G. B., & Smith, K. G. (2010). The age of temporary advantage. *Strategic Management Journal, 31*(13), 1371–1385. doi:10.1002mj.897

Day, G. S. (2014). An outside-in approach to resource-based theories. *Journal of the Academy of Marketing Science, 42*(1), 27–28. doi:10.100711747-013-0348-3

Durkin, M., McGowan, P., & McKeown, N. (2013). Exploring social media adoption in small to medium-sized enterprises in Ireland. *Journal of Small Business and Enterprise Development, 20*(4), 716–734. doi:10.1108/JSBED-08-2012-0094

El-Gohary, H. (2010). Expanding TAM and IDT to understand the adoption of e-Marketing by small business enterprises. *International Journal of Customer Relationship Marketing and Management, 1*(3), 56–75. doi:10.4018/jcrmm.2010070105

Erevelles, S., Horton, V., & Fukawa, N. (2007). Imagination in marketing. *Marketing Management Journal, 17*(2), 109–119.

Eriksson, K., Kerem, K., & Nilsson, D. (2005). Customer acceptance of internet banking in Estonia. *International Journal of Bank Marketing, 23*(2), 200–216. doi:10.1108/02652320510584412

Firestein, S. (2012). *Ignorance: How it drives science*. New York: Oxford University Press.

Giovanni, F., & Mario, A. (2003). Small Company Attitude towards ICT Based Solutions: Some Key Elements to Improve IT. *Journal of Educational Technology & Society, 6*(1), 45–49.

Hair, J. F., Black, W. C., Babin, B. J., & Anderson, R. E. (2010). *Multivariate Data Analysis* (7th ed.). Upper Saddle River, NJ: Prentice Hall.

Halper, F. (2011). The top five trends in predictive analytics. *Information & Management, 21*(6), 16–18.

Hoffman, D. L., & Novak, T. P. (1997). A New Marketing Paradigm for Electronic Commerce. *The Information Society, 13*(1), 43–54. doi:10.1080/019722497129278

Jones, P., Simmons, G., Packham, G., Beynon-Davies, P., & Pickernell, D. (2014). An exploration of the attitudes and strategic responses of sole proprietor micro-enterprises in adopting information and communication technology. *International Small Business Journal, 32*(3), 285–306. doi:10.1177/0266242612461802

Keeny, D., & Marshall, J. F. (2000, November). Contextual Marketing: The Real Business on the Internet. *Harvard Business Review*, 119–125. PMID:11184966

Kim, H., Lee, I., & Lee, C. (2011). Building Web 2.0 enterprises: A study of small and medium enterprises in the United States. *International Small Business Journal, 31*(2), 156–174. doi:10.1177/0266242611409785

Kozlenkova, I. V., Samaha, S. A., & Palmatier, R. W. (2014). Resourcebased theory in marketing. *Journal of the Academy of Marketing Science, 42*(1), 1–21. doi:10.100711747-013-0336-7

Lee, J. Y., Kozlenkova, I. V., & Palmatier, R. W. (2015). Structural marketing: Using organizational structure to achieve marketing objectives. *Journal of the Academy of Marketing Science, 43*(1), 73–99. doi:10.100711747-014-0402-9

Lin, Y., & Wu, L. Y. (2014). Exploring the role of dynamic capabilities in firm performance under the resource-based view framework. *Journal of Business Research, 67*(3), 407–413. doi:10.1016/j.jbusres.2012.12.019

Luccehetti, R., & Sterlaccini, A. (2004). The Adoption of ICT among SMEs: Evidence from an Itallian Survey. *Small Business Economics, 23*(2), 15–168.

Lynn, G. S., Lipp, S. M., Akgün, A. E., & Cortez, A. Jr. (2002). Factors impacting the adoption and effectiveness of the world wide web in marketing. *Industrial Marketing Management, 31*(1), 35–49. doi:10.1016/S0019-8501(00)00104-8

Matambalya, F., & Wolf, S. (2001). *The Role of ICT for the Performance of SMEs in East Africa: Empirical Evidence from Kenya and Tanzania. ZEF – Discussion Papers on Development Policy No. 42.* Bonn: Center for Development Research.

Mayer-Schönberger, V., & Cukier, K. (2013). *Big data: A revolution that will transform how we live, work, and think.* New York: Houghton Mifflin Harcourt.

McConville, A. (2008). *Impact of ICT on SMEs in the South East. Prepared for South East of England Development Agency.* Birmingham, UK: SEEDA.

Mithas, S., Lee, M. R., Earley, S., Murugesan, S., & Djavanshir, R. (2013). Leveraging big data and business analytics. *IT Professional, 15*(6), 18–20. doi:10.1109/MITP.2013.95

Mutula, S. M., & Van Brakel, P. (2007). E-readiness of SMEs in the ICT sector in Botswana with respect to information access. *The Electronic Library, 24*(3), 402–417. doi:10.1108/02640470610671240

Ngai, E. W. T., Xiu, L., & Chau, D. C. K. (2009). Application of data mining techniques in customer relationship management: A literature review and classification. *Expert Systems with Applications, 36*(2), 2592–2602. doi:10.1016/j.eswa.2008.02.021

Nguyen, T. H., & Waring, T. S. (2013). The adoption of customer relationship management (CRM) technology in SMEs: An empirical study. *Journal of Small Business and Enterprise Development, 20*(4), 824–848. doi:10.1108/JSBED-01-2012-0013

Premkumar, G., & Roberts, M. (1999). Adoption of new information technologies in rural small businesses. *Omega, 27*(4), 467–484. doi:10.1016/S0305-0483(98)00071-1

Satell, G. (2014). Five things managers should know about the big data economy. *Forbes.*

Sedkaoui, S. (2017). The Internet, Data Analytics and Big Data. In Internet Economics: Models, Mechanisms and Management (pp. 144-166). Gottinger, H.W: eBook Bentham science.

Sedkaoui, S., & Monino, J. L. (2016). *Big data, Open Data and Data Development.* New York: ISTE-Wiley.

Shiels, H., McIvor, R., & O'Reilly, D. (2003). Understanding the Implications of ICT Adoption: Insights from SMEs. *Journal of Logistics Information Management, 16*(5), 312–326. doi:10.1108/09576050310499318

Shroff, G. (2013). *The Intelligent Web, Search, Smart Algorithms and Big Data.* Oxford, UK: Oxford Univ. Press.

Simmons, G., Armstrong, G., & Durkin, M. (2011). An exploration of small business website optimization: Enablers, influencers and an assessment approach. *International Small Business Journal, 29*(5), 534–561. doi:10.1177/0266242610369945

Tan, K. S., Chong, S. C., Lin, B., & Eze, U. C. (2009). Internet-based ICT adoption: Evidence from Malaysian SMEs. *Industrial Management & Data Systems, 109*(2), 224–244. doi:10.1108/02635570910930118

Tellis, G. J., Prabhu, J. C., & Chandy, R. K. (2009). Radical innovation across nations: The preeminence of corporate culture. *Journal of Marketing, 73*(1), 3–23. doi:10.1509/jmkg.73.1.3

Tiago, O., & Maria, F. M. (2010). Understanding e-business adoption across industries in European countries. *Industrial Management & Data Systems, 110*(9), 1337–1354. doi:10.1108/02635571011087428

Viaene, S. (2013). Data scientists aren't domain experts. *IT Professional, 15*(6), 12–17. doi:10.1109/MITP.2013.93

Warf, B., & Vincent, P. (2007). Multiple Geographies of the Arab Internet. *Royal Geographical Society, 39*(1), 83–96.

Weber, L., & Henderson, L. L. (2014). *The digital marketer: Ten new skills you must learn to stay relevant and customer-centric.* Hoboken, NJ: John Wiley & Sons.

Wei, L. Q., & Lau, C. M. (2010). High performance work systems and performance: The role of adaptive capability. *Human Relations, 63*(10), 1487–1511. doi:10.1177/0018726709359720

Zhu, K., & Kraemer, K. L. (2005). Post-adoption variations in usage and value of e-business by organizations: Cross-country evidence from the retail industry. *Information Systems Research, 16*(1), 61–84. doi:10.1287/isre.1050.0045

## KEY TERMS AND DEFINITIONS

**Analytics:** Emerged as a catch-all term for a variety of different business intelligence (BI)- and application-related initiatives. For some, it is the process of analyzing information from a particular domain, such as website analytics. For others, it is applying the breadth of BI capabilities to a specific content area (e.g., sales, service, supply chain and so on). In particular, BI vendors use the "analytics" moniker to differentiate their products from the competition. Increasingly, "analytics" is used to describe statistical and mathematical data analysis that clusters, segments, scores, and predicts what scenarios are most likely to happen. Whatever the use cases, "analytics" has moved deeper into the business vernacular. Analytics has garnered a burgeoning interest from business and IT professionals looking to exploit huge mounds of internally generated and externally available data.

**Big Data:** The term big data is used when the amount of data that an organization has to manage reaches a critical volume that requires new technological approaches in terms of storage, processing, and usage. Volume, velocity, and variety are usually the three criteria used to qualify a database as "big data."

**Customer Relationship Management (CRM):** A business strategy that optimizes revenue and profitability while promoting customer satisfaction and loyalty. CRM technologies enable strategy, and identify and manage customer relationships, in person or virtually. CRM software provides functionality to companies in four segments: sales, marketing, customer service, and digital commerce.

**Data Analysis:** This is a class of statistical methods that makes it possible to process a very large volume of data and identify the most interesting aspects of its structure. Some methods help to extract relations between different sets of data, and thus, draw statistical information that makes it possible describe the most important information contained in the data in the most succinct manner possible. Other techniques make it possible to group data in order to identify its common denominators clearly, and thereby understand them better.

**Data Mining:** This practice consists of extracting information from data as the objective of drawing knowledge from large quantities of data through automatic or semi-automatic methods. Data mining uses algorithms drawn from disciplines as diverse as statistics, artificial intelligence, and computer science in order to develop models from data; that is, in order to find interesting structures or recurrent themes according to criteria determined beforehand, and to extract the largest possible amount of knowledge useful to companies. It groups together all technologies capable of analyzing database information in order to find useful information and possible significant and useful relationships within the data.

**Marketing:** The management process through which goods and services move from concept to the customer. It includes the coordination of four elements called the 4 Ps of marketing: (1) identification, selection, and development of a product; (2) determination of its price; (3) selection of a distribution channel to reach the customer's place; and (4) development and implementation of a promotional strategy.

**Predictive Marketing:** Predictive marketing is a marketing technique that involves using data analytics to determine which marketing strategies and actions have the highest probability of succeeding. It has a place in the marketing technology (MarTech) landscape, as companies make use of general business data, marketing and sales activity data, and mathematical algorithms to match patterns and determine the best-fit criteria for their next marketing actions. Companies that utilize this strategy strive to make data-driven decisions to yield better results.

## APPENDIX 1: DISTRIBUTION OF
## SURVEYED ENTERPRISES (%)

*Figure 7.*

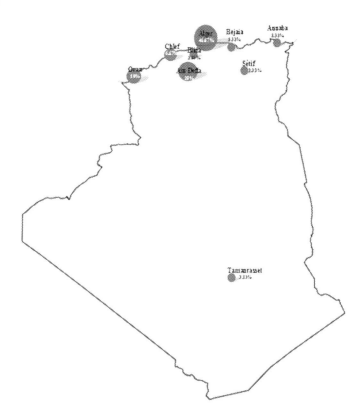

# APPENDIX 2: QUESTIONNAIRE ITEMS

*Table 9.*

| Constructs | | | | | |
|---|---|---|---|---|---|
| *About Enterprise:*<br>Name & Location<br>Status (Group …)<br>Business sector<br>Staff (1-9, 10-49, 50-499, 500-999, Plus de 1000)<br>Turnover (< 50MAD, <50 and 200>, > 200MAD …)<br>Web site | | | | | |
| *About Marketing activities and predictive marketing*<br>Existence of Marketing structure (yes, no, ongoing)<br>Principal activities: (Realization of market studies, forecasting …)<br>IT investment: (High, medium, low)<br>Loyalty cards delivered (yes, no, soon)<br>DBMS use (yes, no)<br>Use DBMS to understanding customer behavior (yes, no)<br>Perception of Big data (yes, no, vaguely)<br>Perception of data mining (yes, no)<br>Are you ready to adopt predictive marketing? (yes, no, no idea)<br>PM will revolutionize the marketing function? (yes, no, no idea)<br>The following factors are likely to motivate you to adopt the tools of Predictive Marketing: | | | | | |
| | **1** | **2** | **3** | **4** | **5** |
| Availability of information | ❑ | ❑ | ❑ | ❑ | ❑ |
| Cost of IT and analytics tools | ❑ | ❑ | ❑ | ❑ | ❑ |
| Complexity of tools and PM | ❑ | ❑ | ❑ | ❑ | ❑ |
| Lack of Training | ❑ | ❑ | ❑ | ❑ | ❑ |
| Resources availability | ❑ | ❑ | ❑ | ❑ | ❑ |
| Skills in IT and data mining | ❑ | ❑ | ❑ | ❑ | ❑ |
| Startups analytics (providers) | ❑ | ❑ | ❑ | ❑ | ❑ |
| Development of e-commerce | ❑ | ❑ | ❑ | ❑ | ❑ |
| Competitors | ❑ | ❑ | ❑ | ❑ | ❑ |
| Other factors | ……………………….. | | | | |

## APPENDIX 3: % OF ENTERPRISES ANALYZE CUSTOMER DATABASES

*Figure 8.*

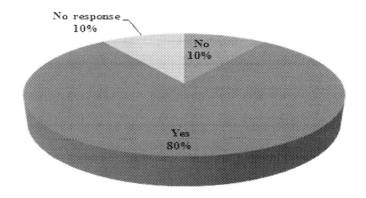

## APPENDIX 4: LOYALTY CARDS DELIVERED

*Table 10.*

| Management Database | Yes | | No | | Soon | | No Response | | Total |
|---|---|---|---|---|---|---|---|---|---|
| | Eff | % | Eff | % | Eff | % | Eff | % | |
| Yes | 5 | 20.83 | 11 | 45.83 | 5 | 20.83 | 3 | 12.5 | 24 |
| No | 1 | 33.33 | 2 | 66.67 | - | - | - | - | 3 |
| Total | 6 | - | 13 | - | 5 | 18.51 | 3 | - | 27 |

## APPENDIX 5: MEANS AND ST-DEV

*Table 11.*

| Items | Mean | St Dev |
|---|---|---|
| Resource | 4.27 | 0.739680 |
| Skills | 3.9 | 1.155198 |
| Start-up | 3.5 | 1.137147 |
| E-commerce Dev | 3.9 | 1.124952 |
| Competitors | 3.7 | 0.952311 |
| Information | 3.97 | 1.159171 |
| Cost | 3.5 | 1.279817 |
| Complexity | 3.6 | 1.037238 |
| Training | 4.033 | 0.808717 |

## APPENDIX 6: PEARSON'S CORRELATION COEFFICIENTS

*Table 12.*

| Variable | Coeff Correlation |
|---|---|
| MP adoption | 1 |
| Start-up | 0.521450 |
| E-commerce Dev | 0.517519 |
| Competitors | 0.305669 |
| Training | -0.017775 |
| Manager vision | 0.380751 |
| Big data Known | -0.287924 |
| Information | 0.452638 |

Chapter 6

# Managerial Perspectives on Willingness to Pay for Green Marketing:
## An Interpretative Phenomenological Analysis

**Michael Sony**
*Namibia University of Science and Technology, Namibia*

## ABSTRACT

*Green marketing meets the present needs of the consumer and business, while also preserving or enhancing the ability of the future generations to meet their needs. The chapter deals with customers' willingness to pay for green marketing initiatives. The chapter explores the managerial perspective using a qualitative inquiry using interpretative phenomenology approach. The customers are willing to pay for green initiatives provided 1) the green initiative does not cost a lot of inconvenience, 2) hotel has a good image, 3) customer profile environmental consciousness moderated the relationship between the customer profile and willingness to pay. Recommendations on how to implement the green strategy in hotels are discussed. The direction of future research sections important research areas in green marketing for an academic contribution.*

DOI: 10.4018/978-1-5225-5993-1.ch006

# INTRODUCTION

Business activities are a part of the social fabric of society. Therefore, the survival and development of business activity are depended on the environment in which it operates. The business environment includes the ecological environment. Thus, it is our duty to protect the ecological environment so that economic activities are carried on without harming the environment. Economic well- being is not the only reason for preserving the environment, but it can also impact the existence of mankind. Thus, protecting the ecology is the societal obligations of both the individual and business. Marketing discipline being an important cog in business activities plays an important role in linking ecology with economic activities. It is well documented in Marketing literature that the strategic importance of two factors 1) customer retention and 2) long-term customer relationship. Both these are used to achieve the marketing performance. The concept of ecological sustainability which is the convergence of marketing thought process to coexist with economic activities. Such an important thought process calls for consideration of environmental issues in business domain, especially Marketing. The concept of Green marketing credited to the work of Lazer in the year 1969, wherein he addressed the issue of, the societal dimension of marketing(Lazer, 1969). It is here, where in he addressed three important issues 1) the constraint of environmental resources, 2) environmental impacts of conventional marketing and 3) greening of the different aspects of traditional marketing. In modern times, the key challenge for mankind is to find more sustainable and equitable ways to produce, consume and live. Sustainability was once a vision of the future shared by an environmentally-orientated few. However, with the publication of the Brundtland Report 'Our Common Future' in 1987 brought the issue into the mainstream (Brundtland, 1987).

The Brundtland Report and the subsequent discovery of the environment by marketing practitioners and academics were the important factors for the renewed interest of Green Marketing in early 2000. For marketing field to trigger this philosophy, the challenge was twofold. The first challenge was in the short term. The ecological and social issues had become significant external influences on companies and the markets within which they operate. In other words, ecology and society cast influence on the manner companies operated. Therefore, the companies are having to react to these new threats. In addition, marketer has to respond to changing customer needs, new regulations and a new social consciousness. This also reflects the increasing concern about the socio-environmental impacts of business. The second challenge was in the longer term. It is that the pursuit of sustainability that will demand fundamental changes to the management paradigm which ramparts marketing and the other business functions. It was in these years we saw much research and many product launches, campaigns, conferences, books etc on this subject. Green marketing is defined by Kotler and Armstrong as Marketing that meets the present needs of the consumer and business, while also preserving or enhancing the ability of the future generations to meet their needs (Kotler & Armstrong, 2010). Another prominent author Charter defined, green marketing as a holistic and responsible management process that identifies, anticipates, satisfies and fulfills stakeholder requirements, for a reasonable reward, that does not adversely affect human or natural environment wellbeing (Charter, 2017). Polonsky and Rosenberger stated that green marketing is a holistic, integrated approach that continually re-evaluates how firms can achieve the corporate objective and meet consumer needs while minimizing long-term ecological harm (Polonsky & Rosenberger III, 2001). Studying these definitions, it is understood that there is not a universal concept of green marketing. However, we can find a common thread in these definitions. The underlying thread points out that green marketing is the organizational commitment in which focus on to produce the products and services friendly with ecological environment. Accordingly, making marketing activities in an environmentally responsible manner. Green marketing was also known by different names. It was known as "environmental marketing", "eco-marketing", "sustainable marketing" or "marketing for green products". The benefits of green marketing can create a sustainable competitive advantage. Increase in the profit and revenue; decrease the energy consumption; optimizing of material flows; reduce the pollution and waste; cost saving for firms are some of the reported benefits of Green Marketing (Prothero, 1998). Modern businesses are facing numerous challenges to sustain as well as to be competitive in the Market. Some firms have ethically used Green Marketing. But, others have used false promises and misleading advertisements to make their products look green. These actions have damaged both the customer and investor trust in green claims of the business. It is reported that many companies claim to be committed to green marketing in their marketing communications. Studies have shown that their aim is to capture a sizable share of the large and growing market of environmentally conscious consumers. Current studies have also shown that even young and old consumers are willing to pay for the Green Products. For practicing green marketing, the companies do the following (i) using packaging and raw materials that are recyclable, reusable, photo degradable and/or biodegradable, (ii) pollution-free production processes, (iii) aerosol-free raw materials, (iv) pesticide-free farming, (v) antichemical methods of food preservation, (vi) less bulky packaging that uses less of the raw material (vii) natural, as against synthetic fertilizer etc(Esty & Winston, 2009). While all these are essential to responding to consumer environments, which are the technical aspect of green marketing. It is equally important the ethical aspect of green marketing. Green marketing should not only be concerned with the environment, but also with people in the environment which focusses on several ethical aspects of Green Marketing. By reviewing the previous studies in this filed transpires that the academic knowledge of Green Marketing has grown over the last many years. Several aspects of Green marketing have gained the serious attention of the academics and practitioners. Studies have shown that over the years Green Marketing philosophy has impacted the business philosophy. It has also resulted in the business strategy being devised by the corporates to harness this potential fullest. It is evident from the research that this has resulted in the business unit's corporate reputation and market performance. What is more interesting to note is that it has evolved from responding to trade, market and regulatory pressures to enlightened self-interest of companies and the philosophy of environmental responsibility. Researchers have stated that such a paradigmatic shift enables the companies to change marketing boundaries. In addition, the Green Marketing has further ensured the survival, stability, and success in the markets the companies operate. Thus, Green Marketing has successfully traveled a Journey from its ideological beginning to the market competition. Hotels across the globe are also embracing green marketing. 71% of consumers said that they are going to indulge in the selection of green alternatives while it comes to choosing hotels(Rahman, Park, & Chi, 2015). However, with the increasing awareness among consumers about green behavior, there are also concerns expressed about the hotels charging extra costs for green motives but are not engaging in. The employees as well as customers in hotels are engaged in environmental management process. In spite of all the awareness about green marketing, some hoteliers hold the view that guest are not willing to pay for green practices (Tang & Lam, 2017). Most of the studies were conducted from the consumers end as to whether they are willing to pay for green practices (Manaktola & Jauhari, 2007; Tang & Lam, 2017) to name a few. This chapter intends to capture the hoteliers view about the customer willingness to pay for green practices in Hotels. This study will thus reduce the social desirable responding customer side study might have suffered because the willingness to pay for social phenomenon is a socially desirable issue. This chapter on green marketing will first introduce the topic of Green Marketing, followed by a section on the background theory of Green Marketing. A separate section of Green marketing initiatives in Hotel Industry will be followed by focus of the chapter and solution and recommendations. At last future research direction is given and conclusion.

## BACKGROUND

Green marketing is defined by Kotler and Armstrong as Marketing that meets the present needs of the consumer and business, while also preserving or enhancing the ability of the future generations to meet their needs. The basic differences between the Green Marketing and Traditional Market (Van Nguyen & Nguyen, 2016) is depicted in Table 1. The environment and stakeholder form the main differences

*Table 1. Difference of green marketing with traditional marketing*

| Differences | Traditional Marketing | Green Marketing |
|---|---|---|
| Parties Involved | Organization & customer | Organization, customer and environment |
| Objectives | Customer satisfaction Organization achieve its objectives | Customer satisfaction Organization achieve its objectives Reduce the ecological impact caused |
| Responsibility | Economic responsibility | Social responsibility |
| Spectrum of marketing decisions | Manufacture to product usage | The total value chain from raw material to post product use |
| Concern for Environment | To satisfy legal framework | Designing by taking environment into consideration |
| Response towards green groups | Confrontation or passive attitude | Collaboration and transparency |

between traditional and green marketing. In traditional Marketing, the long-term goals are Customer satisfaction and of course company's profit. In Green Marketing, the focus is not only on understanding the commercial exchange relationship, however, it also stresses on knowing about an organization's relationship with society. Thus, the Green marketing helps the organization achieve their strategized objectives and meet the needs of stakeholders that too by minimizing the impact on the natural environment.

## The Rise and Fall of Green Marketing

Despite the early beginning of Green Marketing in the 1970s, it was only in the late 1980s green marketing emerged as a topic of interest. The early studies on green marketing was on the rapid increase in green consumerism. There were also studies on the dramatic shift of consumption towards greener products. There were great number of studies in this area. Primarily on 1) identifying heightened environmental awareness 2) a growing consumer interest in green products, and 3) pronounced willingness to pay for green features in a product. The global boycott of CFC-based aerosols and other similar products were responsible for many successes of publications in this area. The corporate was also bustling with these green activities, after the early market research findings. A survey found that 92 per cent of European multinationals claimed to have changed their products in response to green concerns (Vandermerwe & Oliff, 1990). Around 85 per cent multinationals claimed to have changed their production systems. In the US, Green product introductions doubled to 11.4 per cent of all new household products between 1989 and 1990. Besides it continued to grow 13.4 per cent in 1991. In the advertisement sector, the green print ads grew by 430 per cent, and that of green TV ads by 367 per cent, between 1989 and 1990. Body Shop, Ecover, Volvo, 3M, and even McDonalds stories became most cited in the green business publications as an anecdotal evidence to illustrate how and why green marketing initiatives could pay. In spite of this optimistic scenario, by mid-1990's, the new market research evidence began to emerge, which showed only a slight increase in Green Consumerism. Besides, it also brought to light a fact that there is a gap between the concern about environment and actual purchase for green products. The tall claims of Green products were on a decline. However, in some sectors the growth story was encouraging like food, tourism, and financial services. There were many reasons cited for its failure in other sectors, however, the most important market research evidence in the decline of green marketing was the alarming suspicion being displayed by consumers about green products, their green claims by the companies. The corner of marketing is built around trust between customer and Organization. If there is distrust in these relationships than in the long terms the bonding will suffer. The reason for this distrust could be due to the types of activities of Green Marketing the companies have relied upon. However, organizations realised their follies and many improved the Green Marketing campaigns lead to reviving the topic in the 2000's.

## Benefits and Challenges in Green Marketing

The major benefits of green marketing are creating a sustainable competitive advantage for the organization. This leads to increase in the profit and revenue, decrease the energy consumption, optimizing of material flows, reduce the pollution and waste, cost saving for firms. The various challenges faced by the firms indulging in green marketing are the credibility of promises and advertisements to make their products look green in the eyes of consumers, non-green products having superior features compared to green products, the high cost of green marketing initiatives, investors, and customers not valuing green claims.

## GREEN MARKETING FUNCTIONS

With the advent of green marketing, the issues related to variables like Products, Promotion, Retailing, and Distribution will undergo some change. Besides other issues like Branding, Positioning and International Marketing will also undergo some transformation.

## Products

The product is the core of the green marketing function. The main green design strategies are Source reduction and better waste management. Reducing pollution at the source is the source reduction strategy. The product design strategy at the source is weight reduction, material substitution, and product life extension. In better waste management techniques of product design recycling and reclamation of materials are given great importance. Techniques in this category include some techniques like designing products for disassembly, recyclability, remanufacturing composting and incineration. However, the green product design techniques call for innovation. The green product design can be related to less resource consumption, using substitutes for harmful ingredients, recyclability and reusability. The non-product offerings can also be used for green marketing like offering incentives to consumers engaged in product recovery activities, adding emotional benefits and logical benefits.

## Promotion

In promotion function of green marketing, the objective is regarding green advertisement and using communication tools. The green advertisements relate to advertising message and message credibility. The advertising nature of green tools has been changing over the years. As earlier discussed the credibility of these advertisements has been a great issue. The promotion aspect of marketing function should indulge in dynamics of advertisements strategies of green products. Besides, there should be more transparency in the claims for promoting credibility. Certification from appropriate authorities about to the claim in advertisement adds to more credibility. Another aspect of promotion is using communication tools. Use of well-designed websites, sustainability reports, eco-labelling and environmental certifications adds value to the process of communication. Eco-labels are one of the most important tools of communication. It is used to as a means of spreading environmental knowledge, making awareness about green products and helps in credibility of the claims by an independent party.

## Retailing and Distribution

Green marketing has brought in sustainability issues in retailing. It also has brought retailers' shift towards sustainability practices. In retailing, the sustainability practices would include practices like fair trade, ethical sourcing, and reduced resource consumption. Besides, it would also include green atmospherics as a tool for service environment evaluations, green product assortment and promotion in retail stores and choice editing as retailer's tool for sustainable consumption. Another issue which should be considered here is the issue of reverse logistics. Product recovery practices like aftermarket practices, recovery and waste collection strategies forms an important aspect of reverse logistics. In addition to these marketing function, there are other issues in Green Marketing like branding, positioning and international marketing.

# GREEN MARKETING STRATEGIES

Green marketing uses the traditional marketing functions for considering the environmental benefits in the development, promotion, distribution and/or pricing of products and services. Green marketing is a differentiation strategy, considering superior product attributes, for firms to achieve competitive advantage. The assumption here is environmental attributes will allow the business to charge a higher price for the product. This will enable us to capture greater market share. It is also assumed here that environmental attribute increases costs of production and these costs will be outweighed by charging the higher price. If environmental attributes reduce costs of production, the company may incur a double benefit. Though it is felt that the market for green products is relatively small. In reality, it could be relatively broad. To understand this, it is pertinent to understand how value is created by offering green products to the customer. The strategies typically fall into five categories. They are 1) pure-green play, 2) marketing green status and image 3) selling functional value 4) targeting commercial markets and the holistic brand.

## Green Marketing Initiatives in Hotels

The hotel industries immediately recognized the need from green marketing initiatives and have been in the forefront. The Hilton hotels "we care" program has been an important green marketing initiative in the Hotel Industry. There are also many case studies in which hotels have contributed to 1) reduced energy use 2) reduced water consumption 3)CO2 emission per guest 4) reduced greenhouse gas emissions etc (Rahman et al., 2015). Despite all these activities green marketing initiatives have not reached full potential in Hotels. There could be many reasons for it. Increasing competition calls for cost cutting strategies which do not support green initiatives. Another reason, some stringent green initiatives may reduce the convenience of guests, which will result in customer switching(Baker, Davis, & Weaver, 2014). In addition, many studies have reported customers are not willing to pay for green products (Hinnen, Hille, & Wittmer, 2017). In hotel industry, the customer willingness to pay for green initiatives will vary depending on the type of hotels. In other words, depending upon on the type of hotels, customer may or may not pay for the green initiatives.(Kang, Stein, Heo, & Lee, 2012). In addition, customers willingness to pay differs according to the type of green practice followed by the Hotel. Previous studies were either self-reported type or experimental in nature. Self-reported studies are bound to suffer from socially desirable responding (Paulhus, 1984b). In addition, experimental studies could also induce artificial awareness, by which responses may be in a desirable manner(Morris, 2008). Thus, this study will intend to revisit the willingness to pay for green initiatives in Hotel from Managers perspective.

## FOCUS OF THE CHAPTER

The previous studies on green marketing show its importance, usefulness and industry acceptance of green marketing. However, there are studies which show that green marketing is just a passing fad (Dimara, Manganari, & Skuras, 2015; Kortam, 2017; Prothero, 1998). In hotel industries, the majority of the customers were not willing to pay for green practices (Dimara et al., 2015). However, further studies in a different setting show that in a study using hypothetical scenarios proves that most customers are willing to pay for green practices(Namkung & Jang, 2017). The conflicting studies shows the need for further understanding the importance of green marketing in Hotel Industry. In addition, the previous studies were either self-reported customer research or experimental studies. Among the many issues reported in self-reported studies, an important issue is social desirable responding(Paulhus, 1984a). Experimental studies also suffer from various biases (Morris, 2008). The conflicting nature of responses for customer willingness to pay needs to revisit from a different perspective. Many studies have reported that though there is awareness among the customers as regards to environmental problems, however, this does translate into the customer willingness to pay(Dimara et al., 2015). Thus, the main issue that would be of prime concern in this chapter is customers are willing to pay for green practices. The authors decided to take the views of managers who are working in hotels in India, to understand whether customers are willing to pay for green practices in Hotel. This chapter will thus add to the academic body of knowledge of green marketing, which will clarify whether customers are willing to pay for Green Practices. Besides, being a qualitative study, it will enable further building of knowledge in this area.

### Objective

The study was designed to explore the lived experience of managers who are working at hotels where green practices are promoted. The primary aim of the study was to add to the knowledge and understanding of this complex phenomenon of customers whether they are willing to pay for green practices in hotels.

## Methodology

The research question directed the researchers to design a study that explored the lived experience of managers working in hotels that promote green practices in hotels. Since the managers interact with customers during the work. In a hotel service, they are the main cog in the service encounter. Hence, to avoid the bias of previous research where in customers were asked about whether they are willing to pay for green practices, this research wanted to ask the views of managers. The results of this study will thus contribute to the growing body of study where-in one can understand whether green practices are being valued by the customers. Being a lived-in experience, an interpretative phenomenological research approach was used for this study. As the study involves both analyzing and interpreting the phenomena, the Interpretive phenomenological approach is used. In addition, a second reason for choosing the IPA was because it views the analytic outcome as resulting from an interaction between participant's accounts and the researcher's frameworks of meaning which will help better understanding of this complex phenomenon of whether customers are willing to pay for green practices in hotels

## Selection of Participants

The participants were recruited through a personal contact using the snowballing method. The potential participants were first approached for a casual discussion and the nature of the research with its agenda was explicitly expressed. The main criterion for participant's inclusion was participants themselves describing them to be working in the hotel. Besides they should be willing to talk in depth about their experiences with working with customers. The samples in IPA studies are usually small. This enables a detailed and very time-consuming case-by-case analysis. Besides, there are studies conducted using IPA, for example one, four, nine and fifteen. Though the large sample size is possible but are less common (Pietkiewicz & Smith, 2014; Michael Sony, Mekoth, & Therisa, 2018) . In this study we wanted an in-depth analysis, hence we choose a sample size for 28. Twenty-eight participants took part in this study: 13 females and 15 male participants with an age range from 24 to 48. Participants' mean age was 38.9 years (SD 5.2). All had a religious upbringing and belonged to Hindu (69.2%), Christian (19.2%) and Muslim (11.6%) faiths. Participants signed a consent form and their names were changed to protect confidentiality. All were Indians, thirteen (50.0%) was graduate in hotel management, six (23.07%) had a post graduate degree in hotel management, three (11.53%) had a diploma in Hotel management and four (15.4%) had 12th Standard qualification + general degree. During the interviews, in order to remove this bias, the first author attempted as far as possible to remain led by the participant. So that to avoid imposing his own beliefs and ideas on the interview process. This included encouraging the participants in the study to explicate the concepts in detail that seemed clear from the viewpoint of the first author to ensure that assumptions were not being made. Number of studies have advocated this methodology (Cassar & Shinebourne, 2012; M Sony & Mekoth, 2014; Michael Sony et al., 2018)

## Interviews

The IPA methodology provides flexible guidelines to be adopted by researchers as per the aims of the research (Larkin & Thompson, 2012). Semi-structured interviews were conducted by the first author with consenting employees at their homes to collect the data. Primarily questions focused on the experiences of the participants as regards to customer willingness to pay for green practices. Subsequently, as a probing methodology specific green practices were asked where customers would be willing to pay. To enable analysis, the interviews were tape recorded. Besides, the participants feelings and observations were also noted. The participants were given Pseudo names to enable anonymity of respondents. The participants were shown the transcripts, to confirm that transcript confirmed to what they had to tell.

## Plan of Data Analysis

The analysis of the data was conducted in several stages. In the first stage written description and the transcript of the first participant were read many times to become immersed in the data and to get theoretical sensitivity. Care was taken during reading to take notes or comments which appear significant or interesting were recorded in the transcript. In the second stage, the written description and transcript transformed into initial notes were classified into emerging themes or concepts. However, care was taken not to lose the connection between the participant's own words and the researcher's interpretations. The third stage consisted of examining the emerging themes during the second phase and trying to cluster them together based on the conceptual similarities. The emerging clusters were given a descriptive label which was selectively chosen to convey the conceptual nature of the themes for each cluster. The written description and the transcript were checked to ensure that the connection with what the participant has said was maintained as the clusters of themes starts emerging. In the final stage, a tabulation of themes was undertaken and the same is reproduced in figure 1. The table depicts the structure of major themes and subthemes. This process was repeated for every respondent. An audit of the first author's thematic analysis was meticulously conducted by the second author independently, to ensure that the themes identified were warrantable and wherever difference arose, through discussions it was solved. The Table 2 shows the themes and sub -themes emerged in this study.

## SOLUTIONS AND RECOMMENDATIONS

Three super ordinate themes were identified in the analysis: Type of Green Practices, Green Brand Image & Customer Attributes. A summary of the results is given in table 1, describes the Master and the Subthemes that were constructed from the participants' accounts. Sometimes participants struggled to talk about their superstitious experiences and the respondents felt anxious in trying to express what they mean by superstition. This was observed in the way participants behaved and hesitated with their words and the anxiety was implicitly in seen by the researcher. Despite this unease the researcher chose not to put words in the mouth and however participants were put at ease. Thereafter, somehow participants were able to find a way to talk about their supernatural orientation / superstition. The language by the respondents used ranged from more traditional religious vocabulary to pseudo-scientific terminology However, the theme that featured in all accounts of participants and it provided the underlying thematic texture with its connection. In order to further improve the quality of the analysis it was thought to adhere to the criteria of trustworthiness in qualitative research. The important aspects to be considered for trust worthiness are 1) credibility, 2) transferability, 3) dependability, and 4) confirmability (Larkin & Thompson, 2012). Credibility is the defined as the degree of subjective relevance of the interpretations of the participants accounts and the degree of truthfulness of the data This was enhanced by inviting the participants to

*Table 2. Master and sub themes for customers willingness to pay*

| Master Themes | Sub Theme |
|---|---|
| Type of Green Practices | Low on Customer Convenience |
| | High on Customer Convenience |
| Green Brand Image | Low green Brand Image |
| | High Green brand Image |
| Customer Attributes | Socio-economical |
| | Education |
| | Type of Customer |
| | Environmental Awareness |

review the transcripts and the ideographic descriptions transcribed of the interviews. In addition, this also minimized selective perception and reactive effects which may creep in during the interviews. The issue of transferability which is the possibility of applying interpretations to similar phenomena was done by collecting extensive composite textural and structural descriptions of the respondent's accounts. For addressing the issue of Dependability, the level of similarity between the data, researcher's interpretations, and actual occurrences in the research setting, was promoted by preparing, revising and documenting changes in the interview guide or plan and the subsequent plan. The issue of confirmability and the goal to provide a variety of relevant explanations to the studied phenomenon without bias was undertaken. The bracketing phase which consisted of documenting an epoche of the phenomenon by the researcher before undertaking the analyses of the data was resorted to arresting this issue.

## Type of Green Practices

Previous studies have stated that according to customers the top three green practices were towel / linen reuse, adjustable thermostat in room and water efficient low flow toilets and showerheads. (Tripeadvisor, 2012). The managers of the hotel expressed that customer willingness to pay for green practices depend on the type of green practices which are further linked to customer convenience. Customers are willing to pay for green practices where customer convenience is not affected e.g. reusing water or recycling, composting or energy efficient appliances or solar panels or electric car charging stations or green roofing etc. Manager 1 remarked that " The all hullabaloo about going green etc is good. But when it comes to paying money, customers, prefer to pay for the practices which does not impact the convenience of customers" Manager 7 was of the view that " I have seen guys who don't mind paying for going green, but, when it comes to their comfort no body compromises". Manager 12 was of the view that "Customers will not pay more if you are planning for a green practice which will make their stay uncomfortable. Customers will pay for items like if Hotel has energy efficient appliance etc"

Green practices which cause high inconvenience for customers like having energy efficient lighting system, reusing towels or linens or energy efficient low flow showers are sometimes perceived negatively and customer are not willing to pay more. Manager 3 stated that " Once I was dealing with a customer who said that you say that it is a water efficient toilet, but I don't agree with it. I feel you guys are making money there also by saving water and you want to charge me in the name of Green". Manager 5 said that "most customers complain to him that CFL bulbs are not that bright, you guys are cutting cost and telling us you saving environment. It is difficult to convince them these things are to save environment"

This study thus highlights the importance of the degree of customer convenience and the willingness to pay for green practices. The importance of service quality in hotels are more important than green practices (Manaktola & Jauhari, 2007) .

The Figure 1 shows the relationship between customer inconvenience and willingness to pay. In other words, customers won't sacrifice the service quality and pay for the green service. Hence it imperative to depict the relationship between the type of green practice and willingness to pay. The type of green practice is classified based on the degree of inconvenience that green practice will cause to the customer. Thus, the following propositions are made

**P1:** Customer are willing to pay more for the green practices which cause low inconvenience to customers.

**P2:** Customers are willing to pay less for the green practices which cause high inconvenience to customers.

## Green Brand Image of The Hotel

Green brand image of the hotel is the perceived green image of the hotel in the eyes of customer. Previous study has shown that green brand image is positively associated with green satisfaction (Chen, 2010). In this study, respondents expressed that if the perceived green brand image of the hotel is high, the customers are willing to pay for green practices. Manager 2 expressed that "If the social media rating is very high about the green practices in Hotel, the customers are willing to pay more. We have shown our presence on the social media. We try to transparent to them about the green practices. We get good reviews from most of the customers. So, I did not have much problems with customers, when I charge more for our green initiatives"

*Figure 1. Customer inconvenience and willingness to pay*

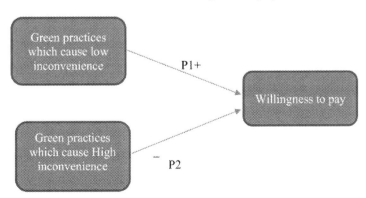

Manager 6 stated that "We try to maintain our hotel as environmentally friendly. Our website speaks of it clearly. Customers who have been our patrons have seen that we mean what we say. In the market, we have a good image about what we do. My customers don't mind paying more. Because they know they are getting a good value for money."

Some respondents who have recently begun with green initiatives opinioned the importance of Green image of the hotel in the customer eyes. Manager 17 "See it is always going to be difficult to convince customer unless a good image of the Hotel is built in the customer eyes. I won't pay more to stay in a hotel which is not known for its green initiatives. The previous customers review, and the image of the Hotel speaks a lot when it comes to someone actually wanting to pay more for such initiatives".

The Figure 2 shows the relationship between green brand image of the hotel and Willingness to pay. The importance of green brand image is very important in the perspectives of the customer (Namkung & Jang, 2017). Thus, if the green brand image is high customers are willing to pay more. If the green brand image is less than customers will not be willing to pay more. From the above, the following propositions are generated

**P3:** Customers are willing to pay less if the Green Brand image of the Hotel is low
**P4:** Customers are willing to pay more if the Green Brand image of the Hotel is high

## Customer Attributes

Another important theme that came across is the customer attribute. The customer attributes like socio economic status, education, type of customer & Environmental awareness. The respondents expressed the importance of Socio economic status.

*Figure 2. Green brand image of hotel and willingness to pay*

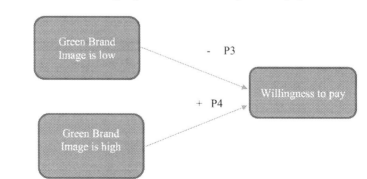

Manager 4 "If the customer is economically well off, then I don't think they have any problem to pay for green initiatives"

Manager 7 "Well to do customers from high social status usually pay for Green initiatives in Hotels. They usually do not complain that cost of staying in green hotels are too high etc"

Some respondents also stated that educational status of customers play a role in their willingness to pay for green practices. Manger 19 expressed that "Educated lot usually understand the importance of paying more to save the environment". Another important aspect that surfaced during the study is type of customer also plays a role. The business class customers are willing to pay more for green initiatives in hotel compared to leisure class. Manager 23 "Corporate customers don't have any problem and are willing to pay more for green initiatives". Manager 25 " We usually cater to people who come to Goa for holidays. They usually have a problem and are sometimes not willing to pay for such green stuff. Some say that it will offset their budgets, even though they are concerned about the environment".

Respondents also expressed that if the customer are environmentally conscious than they are willing to pay more. Manager 17 "It is important that customers understand about the environmental problem. If they understand the problem, than usually they are willing to pay more such green things". Manager 22 "Customers who know the importance of environment is willing to pay more for hotels with green initiatives. Convincing such people are a bit easier than people who are unaware of environmental issues." The Figure 3 shows the relationship between Socio-economic status, Environmental Consciousness and willingness to pay. The following propositions are

**P5:** Customers whose socio-economic status is high and Environmental Consciousness are high are willing to pay for green initiatives.

*Figure 3. Relationship between Socio-economic status, Environmental Consciousness and willingness to pay*

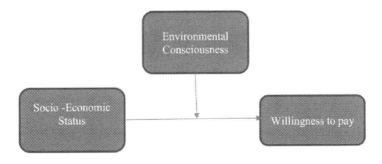

**P6:** Customers whose socio-economic status is low and Environmental Consciousness are high are willing to pay for green initiatives.

**P7:** Customers whose socio-economic status is high and Environmental Consciousness are low are not willing to pay for green initiatives.

**P8:** Customers whose socio-economic status is low and Environmental Consciousness are low are not willing to pay for green initiatives

The Figure 4 shows the relationship between Socio-economic status, Environmental Consciousness and willingness to pay. The proposition on education status and willingness to pay for green initiatives

**P9:** Customers whose educational status is high and Environmental Consciousness are high are willing to pay for green initiatives.

**P10:** Customers whose educational status is low and Environmental Consciousness are high are willing to pay for green initiatives.

**P11:** Customers whose educational status is high and Environmental Consciousness are low are not willing to pay for green initiatives.

**P12:** Customers whose educational status is low and Environmental Consciousness are low are not willing to pay for green initiatives

The Figure 5 shows the relationship between Type of Customer, Environmental Consciousness and willingness to pay. The proposition on type of customer and willingness to pay for green initiatives

**P13:** Business customers whose Environmental Consciousness are high are willing to pay for green initiatives.

**P14:** Leisure customers whose Environmental Consciousness are high are willing to pay for green initiatives.

*Figure 4. Relationship between educational status, environmental consciousness and willingness to pay*

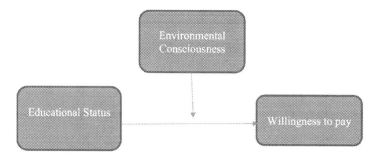

*Figure 5. Relationship between Type of Customer, Environmental Consciousness and willingness to pay*

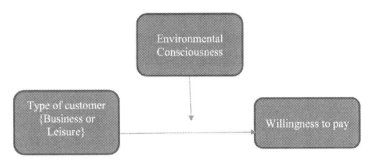

**P15:** Business customers whose Environmental Consciousness are low are not willing to pay for green initiatives.

**P16:** Leisure customers whose environmental Consciousness are low are not willing to pay for green initiatives

## Recommendation

This research has shown that customers are willing to pay more for the green practices which cause low inconvenience to customers. Hoteliers should keep in mind the convenience of the customer while indulging in green practices. The personal needs of comfort are very important for a human being, especially if one is residing in a hotel. If the green initiatives do not cause any major inconvenience to either body or mind, one can expect customer to pay for it. In addition, various green practices could be ranked based on the degree of inconvenience to human body. This will help the hoteliers to choose the green practices as per strategic initiatives of the Hotels.

Another important factor that came across this research is that customers are not willing to pay if the Green Brand image of the Hotel is low. It is a very important finding as far as the hotels are concerned. If the Hotels indulge in improving the green brand image, then the customers are willing to pay for it. Therefore, advertising plays a major role. It is recommended that if the hotel is willing to do indulge in green initiatives, then, they should display it. Such kind of display will improve the chances of building a green brand image. Various brand image building strategies should be used to position the hotel. If the hotel is catering to leisure travelers, customer willingness to pay will be depended upon the environmental consciousness of the customer. Hence, it is recommended that hotels in leisure travel segment should systematically venture out in green initiatives. The first phase would be indulging in green initiatives which cause less body and mind discomfort. Evaluate the output of the strategy initiatives and subsequently venture into green initiatives which cause medium body and mind discomfort. A thorough evaluation of this strategy should be done only then it is recommended for leisure hotels to venture into the green initiatives which may cause body or mind discomfort. The socio-economic status of customers also play an important role in customers willing to pay for green initiatives. An economically disadvantaged customer, though he may have good environmental consciousness, but he circumstances may not permit him to pay more. Thus, hotels in low budget segment may opt for green initiatives, which are cost effective. A small incremental price may not discourage customer who though economically disadvantaged, but willing to pay a small increment for the green initiatives.

## FUTURE RESEARCH DIRECTION

The future studies of green marketing should evaluate the willingness of customers to pay for green initiatives in different sectors. An across the sector analysis of factors which impact the customer willingness to pay will result in further enriching the theory on which customers are willing to pay. The studies should move in different cultural settings. The cultural fabric of the society may play a major role in green initiatives of its members as the impact on the initiatives. Studies should also explore out to study the dyad between the customers and hoteliers in a setting. Such studies will also help to clarify whether the customer is willing to pay for green initiatives. Customer perception of green activities may be ranked in terms of the degree of inconvenience the green practice may cause to the customer. It is important, because a specialist in green initiatives may feel a practice may be least inconvenient, but it is the customer who view it as most important. Future studies should also clarify how to strongly build a green brand image for hotels in both leisure and business segments. Such studies will act as guide for implementation of the green marketing initiatives. Customer analytics and green marketing should also receive attention. Because the amount of customer data which is at disposal, green customer analytics studies will help green marketing theory to be further enriched. Though there are some studies of green and lean, however, there are only few studies on lean green practices in Hotels. Studies should also explore the impact of social media on hotel green strategy.

## CONCLUSION

There has been a huge hue and cry about Green marketing in academic and Business communities. Does this increased level of awareness contribute to customer willingness to pay? The main purpose of this chapter was to explore the managerial perspective on the customer willingness to pay for green marketing. The chapter began with a brief discussion on the green marketing and followed by discussion on customers willingness to pay. The focus of the chapter was on customer willingness to pay in Hotels from managerial perspective using Interpretative phenomenological analysis. The customers are willing to pay provided the green initiative does not cost a lot of inconvenience. Besides, brand image of the Hotel also plays a Major role. The business customers are willing to pay more leisure customers. However, environmental awareness plays a moderating role in this relationship. The customer socio-economic status also plays a role in willingness to pay. However, environmental consciousness also plays a role in this relationship. Even education plays a role in willingness to pay, also moderated by willingness to pay. Green Marketing is here to stay and if practiced strategically the customer are willing to pay. Thus, industries in general can adopt green marketing and derive economic and social benefit from it.

# REFERENCES

Baker, M. A., Davis, E. A., & Weaver, P. A. (2014). Eco-friendly attitudes, barriers to participation, and differences in behavior at green hotels. *Cornell Hospitality Quarterly*, *55*(1), 89–99. doi:10.1177/1938965513504483

Brundtland, G. H. (1987). *Report of the World Commission on environment and development:" our common future*. United Nations.

Cassar, S., & Shinebourne, P. (2012). What does spirituality mean to you? An Interpretative Phenomenological Analysis of the experience of spirituality. *Existential Analysis*, *23*(1), 133–149.

Charter, M. (2017). *Greener marketing: A responsible approach to business.* Routledge.

Chen, Y.-S. (2010). The drivers of green brand equity: Green brand image, green satisfaction, and green trust. *Journal of Business Ethics*, *93*(2), 307–319. doi:10.100710551-009-0223-9

Dimara, E., Manganari, E., & Skuras, D. (2015). Consumers' willingness to pay premium for green hotels: Fact or Fad? *Proceedings International Marketing Trends Conference 2015*.

Esty, D., & Winston, A. (2009). *Green to gold: How smart companies use environmental strategy to innovate, create value, and build competitive advantage.* John Wiley & Sons.

Hinnen, G., Hille, S. L., & Wittmer, A. (2017). Willingness to Pay for Green Products in Air Travel: Ready for Take-Off? *Business Strategy and the Environment, 26*(2), 197–208. doi:10.1002/bse.1909

Kang, K. H., Stein, L., Heo, C. Y., & Lee, S. (2012). Consumers' willingness to pay for green initiatives of the hotel industry. *International Journal of Hospitality Management, 31*(2), 564–572. doi:10.1016/j.ijhm.2011.08.001

Kortam, W. (2017). *Sustainability Marketing: A Marketing Revolution or A Research Fad*. Academic Press.

Kotler, P., & Armstrong, G. (2010). *Principles of marketing*. Pearson education.

Larkin, M., & Thompson, A. (2012). Interpretative phenomenological analysis. *Qualitative Research Methods in Mental Health and Psychotherapy: A Guide for Students and Practitioners*, 99–116.

Lazer, W. (1969). Marketing's changing social relationships. *Journal of Marketing, 33*(1), 3–9. doi:10.2307/1248739

Manaktola, K., & Jauhari, V. (2007). Exploring consumer attitude and behaviour towards green practices in the lodging industry in India. *International Journal of Contemporary Hospitality Management, 19*(5), 364–377. doi:10.1108/09596110710757534

Morris, S. B. (2008). Book Review: Hunter, JE, & Schmidt, FL (2004). Methods of Meta-Analysis: Correcting Error and Bias in Research Findings. Thousand Oaks, CA: Sage. *Organizational Research Methods, 11*(1), 184–187. doi:10.1177/1094428106295494

Namkung, Y., & Jang, S. (2017). Are consumers willing to pay more for green practices at restaurants? *Journal of Hospitality & Tourism Research (Washington, D.C.), 41*(3), 329–356. doi:10.1177/1096348014525632

Paulhus, D. L. (1984a). *Balanced Inventory of Social Desirable Responding. PsycTESTS Dataset*. APA. doi:10.1037/t58985-000

Paulhus, D. L. (1984b). Two-component models of socially desirable responding. *Journal of Personality and Social Psychology, 46*(3), 598–609. doi:10.1037/0022-3514.46.3.598

Pietkiewicz, I., & Smith, J. A. (2014). A practical guide to using interpretative phenomenological analysis in qualitative research psychology. *Psychological Journal, 20*(1), 7–14.

Polonsky, M. J., & Rosenberger, P. J. III. (2001). Reevaluating green marketing: A strategic approach. *Business Horizons*, *44*(5), 21–30. doi:10.1016/S0007-6813(01)80057-4

Prothero, A. (1998). *Green Marketing: The'Fad'That Won't Slip Slide Away*. Taylor & Francis.

Rahman, I., Park, J., & Chi, C. G. (2015). Consequences of "greenwashing" Consumers' reactions to hotels' green initiatives. *International Journal of Contemporary Hospitality Management*, *27*(6), 1054–1081. doi:10.1108/IJCHM-04-2014-0202

Sony, M., & Mekoth, N. (2014). The dimensions of frontline employee adaptability in power sector: A grounded theory approach. *International Journal of Energy Sector*. Retrieved from http://www.emeraldinsight.com/doi/abs/10.1108/IJESM-03-2013-0008

Sony, M., Mekoth, N., & Therisa, K. K. (2018). Understanding nature of empathy through the lens of service encounter: A phenomenological study on FLE's. *International Journal of Productivity and Quality Management*, *23*(1), 55–73. doi:10.1504/IJPQM.2018.088608

Tang, C. M. F., & Lam, D. (2017). The role of extraversion and agreeableness traits on Gen Y's attitudes and willingness to pay for green hotels. *International Journal of Contemporary Hospitality Management*, *29*(1), 607–623. doi:10.1108/IJCHM-02-2016-0048

Tripeadvisor. (2012). *TripAdvisor Survey Reveals Travelers Growing Greener*. Author.

Van Nguyen, T. T., & Nguyen, T. D. (2016). Green Marketing Strategy-A New Trend for Businesses in Vietnam. In *Green Technology and Sustainable Development (GTSD), International Conference on* (pp. 116–119). IEEE. 10.1109/GTSD.2016.36

Vandermerwe, S., & Oliff, M. D. (1990). Customers drive corporations. *Long Range Planning*, *23*(6), 10–16. doi:10.1016/0024-6301(90)90096-M

## ADDITIONAL READING

Coddington, W. (1993). *Environmental marketing: positive strategies for reaching the green consumer*. McGraw-Hill Companies.

Dangelico, R. M., & Vocalelli, D. (2017). "Green Marketing": An analysis of definitions, strategy steps, and tools through a systematic review of the literature. *Journal of Cleaner Production*, *165*, 1263–1279. doi:10.1016/j.jclepro.2017.07.184

Papadas, K. K., Avlonitis, G. J., & Carrigan, M. (2017). Green marketing orientation: Conceptualization, scale development and validation. *Journal of Business Research*, *80*, 236–246. doi:10.1016/j.jbusres.2017.05.024

Peattie, K., & Charter, M. (2003). Green marketing. *The marketing book, 5*, 726-755.

Peattie, K., & Crane, A. (2005). Green marketing: Legend, myth, farce or prophesy? *Qualitative Market Research*, *8*(4), 357–370. doi:10.1108/13522750510619733

# Chapter 7
# Marketing and Technologies Platforms in Smart F-Store

**José Duarte Santos**
*Polytechnic of Porto, Portugal*

**Fernando Luís Almeida**
*University of Porto, Portugal*

## ABSTRACT

*Social networks, originally built as channels for personal interaction, are being used in the commercial market as a support for product sales. The use of applications integrated in social networks appears as an opportunity to explore by companies. Facestore emerged in 2013 as the first e-commerce solution integrated in social networks, allowing the creation of online stores within Facebook, without the customer having to leave the social network interface. Operations like looking into the catalog, choosing the product, and paying the transaction is carried out without the customer need to open a new website. The use of Facestore offers direct and indirect benefits on the different areas of an organization. At the direct level, there are changes in processes in terms of customer service and marketing and sales. However, its use also potentiates indirect benefits in other organizational areas, such as operations, finance, administration and information technologies support, human resources, and research and development.*

DOI: 10.4018/978-1-5225-5993-1.ch007

## INTRODUCTION

In 2016, worldwide revenue of e-commerce is amounted to almost 1,859 billion USD, and it is expected to reach 4 Trillion USD by 2020 (Statista, 2017a; Lui, 2017). Consequently, with the evolution of e-commerce and social media, it is expected that social commerce platforms will have a big boom in upcoming years.

This work focuses on a specific form of social commerce: the virtual stores of Facebook. This social network, with more than 2 trillion active users in September 2017, was the first social network to incorporate the concept of store social commerce (Statista, 2017b). As a first step, we analyze the evolution and different perspectives of social commerce as, for example, communities, social selling, social cashback, presence of virtual stores on social networks, and also how to incorporate in the company's strategy. We intend also to look for the main motivations that may be at the origin of the decision by companies in joining the social commerce. Then, we make a short presentation of the Facebook's role in marketing and we examine the contribution that f-commerce can provide to improve sales and customer relationships, especially in terms of customer retention strategies, the creation of value and the construction of brand loyalty.

There are a number of good practices which tend to contribute to the success of a virtual store on Facebook and we concern to identify and seek to contribute in this way, to increase the probability of success of the companies that choose to include a f-store on their business strategy. We give a special emphasis to the role of marketing in the characterization of buyer personas, content management, in the creation of exclusive offers, and other initiatives that monetize the features of Facebook. Therefore, there is also the concern of presenting previously Facebook features that marketing can enhance and integrate with the f-store.

The technology cannot also be overlooked in the implementation of a f-store and, therefore, based on the identification of the most important features of the f-store platforms, such as analytical component, sending newsletters, analysis of the experience of each user, and back-office. Additionally, we show the relationship of each feature with the functional areas of organizational responsibility, looking to reflect how organizational structure models can contribute to the success of the f-store.

## LITERATURE REVISION

### The Evolution and Different Perspectives of Social Commerce

Wang (2009) uses the expression "social shopping", which is the combination of shopping in Internet and social networking activities. Sharma and Crossler (2014) also use de word "shopping", when they state that social commerce combines the online shopping experience with the power of online social networks, which allow companies to increase the value of the business and also provides customer value. There are multiple social commerce definitions and, in table below, we present some of them in chronological order.

The social commerce, introduced by Yahoo in 2005, can be seen as an evolution of e-commerce, which is supported on two pillars: web 2.0 technologies and social media (Han & Trimi, 2017). To Turban, Bolloju and Liang (2010) there are two elements that influence the social commerce: marketing and social behavior. However, this addition is only a strengthening of what currently exists in social media for a company, since the fundamental concept of marketing is based on the principles of looking to analyze the online and offline consumer behavior.

*Table 1. Social commerce definitions*

| Definition | Author |
|---|---|
| Social commerce is about utilizing web-based social communities by e-commerce companies, focusing on the impact of social influence which shapes the interaction among consumers | Kim and Srivastava (2007) |
| Social commerce is the application of social media to shape business and transforms a market for goods and services into a user-driven marketplace. | Wigand, Benjamin and Wigand (2008) |
| Social commerce can be defined as word of mouth application to e-commerce, and it is the marriage of a retailer's products and the interaction of shoppers with content. | Dennison, Bourdage-Braun, and Chetuparambil (2009) |
| Social commerce is an emerging category of e-commerce, based on social media platform like social network services and services through the platforms. | Marsden (2010) |
| Social commerce can be considered a subset of e-commerce that involves using social media to assist in e-commerce transactions and activities. It also supports social interactions and user content contributions. In essence, it is a combination of commercial and social activities. | Liang and Turban (2012) |
| Social commerce is a form of commerce mediated by social media involving the convergence between online and offline environments. | Wang and Zhang (2012) |
| Social commerce refers to exchange-related activities that occur in, or are influenced by, an individual's social network in computer-mediated social environments, where the activities correspond to the need recognition, pre-purchase, purchase, and post-purchase stages of a focal exchange. | Yadav, Valck, Henning-Thurau, Hoffman and Spann (2013) |
| Social commerce is not just a simple fusion between e-commerce and social networking technology, its integration with commerce activities, and its mechanisms for promoting social interaction and trust. | Zhou, Zhang and Zimmermann (2013) |
| Social commerce as the online buying and selling activities initiated via social media, which entails business transactions through either social media or other e-commerce sites. | Ng (2014) |

Source: authors

While the e-commerce relies on products, s-commerce is more people-oriented, focusing on the information generated by them and between them (Huang & Benyoucef, 2013). Considered the four stages in the decision-making process (need recognition, pre-purchase activities, purchase decision, post-purchase activities), the s-commerce is present in all phases. In the first stage, with external stimuli that the consumer can obtain, for example, in creating an "whishlist"; in the second phase, in obtaining information, for example, through testimonials; in the third phase when the consumer makes an acquisition, for example, in a store on Facebook; finally, for example, when the customer recommends the product to others. Therefore, social commerce can provide value perception to customers across the purchasing decision process (Yadav et al, 2013).

Social commerce can be also viewed as a subset of social business. In this case, the organization uses social media in intensive mode in most or all set of its operations and departments, for example, human resources. So, social business is broader, and doesn't only incorporate marketing activities (Turban, Strauss & Lai, 2016).

Huang and Benyoucef (2013) propose a social commerce design model based in four layers:

- **Individual:** Personal profile, context profile and activity profile;
- **Conversation:** Social content presentation, topic focus, notification, content creation and information sharing;
- **Community:** Community support, connection and relationship maintenance;
- **Commerce:** Group purchase, social proof, authority, reciprocity, participation, social ads and applications, business functions and payment mechanisms.

In all four layers the same authors define common features:

- **Information Quality:** Relevancy, accuracy, completeness and update;
- **System Quality:** Security, accessibility, precise operation and computation, participant control, transparency;
- **Service Quality:** Responsiveness and following up services;
- **Usability:** Ease of use, navigation, error recovery, valid links, help functions and consistency;
- **Playfulness:** Enjoyment, attractive and appearance.

## Social Commerce Categories

Constantinides and Fountain (2008), Marsden (2010) and Indvik (2013) identified different categories of social commerce. The analysis of these studies allows us to propose the following categories:

1.  **Evaluations and Reviews:** This category can be divided into four subcategories:
    a.  **Evaluations and Reviews of Customers:** opinions of real customers, whether integrated with an e-commerce site or a site of reviews (Normally connected to comparison sites);
    b.  **Evaluations and Reviews of Experts:** The sight of persons or entities that are considered authority in certain area and possess social influence;
    c.  **Sponsored Reviews:** Reviews paid for customers, experts, influencers, or celebrities. They make favorable comments and contribute to the dissemination of a particular product or service;
    d.  **Testimonials From Customers:** They are less structured approvals, usually made in e-commerce sites or social networks.
2.  **Recommendations and References:** Unlike evaluations and comments, recommendations and references are not visible to all. These custom actions can be defined for each product/services, respectively:
    a.  **Social Bookmarking:** "Wishlists", "picklist", "giftlists" or galleries of stored products, business, and tips. They include, essentially, lists, links, and saved albums that can be shared with third parties and even searched for these. There are sites incorporating this feature, where consumers can go keeping their products like it for review or purchase later. May also be shared with friends, family or other interested through link or email;
    b.  **Reference Programs:** Programs and/or compensation campaigns for clients that reference and suggest new customers. Typically are suggested close people, like friends, family, or worker colleagues;
    c.  **Social Recommendations:** Personal custom shopping recommendations based on social similarities, and shopping research, tracing how profiles interact with other consumers. Several sites have been doing this in real time so that clients feel prestigious with the recognition of their tastes and, therefore, they are interested to purchase new products.
3.  **Blogs:** Online platforms on a specific subject or organization, mostly with text content, but sometimes combined with images, audio and video podcasts;
4.  **Social Networks:** Users or enterprises build and customize their pages, making it accessible to other users, and through which they can communicate, promote products, ideas, create and exchange content, experiences;
5.  **Communities:** Thematic sites that present contents ready to be used and shared by participants. Virtual communities are made by a group of individuals who work with common interests or goals, which may be a brand, a product or a theme;
6.  **Forums:** Online platforms whose principal objectives are the exchange and sharing of ideas/information on any given topics. The forums linked to

e-commerce platforms are based on the discovery, selection, and reference products, providing a moderate environment around a topic, task or category;

7. **Aggregators of Content:** Include websites that allow the dissemination of various contents, articles and publications on the Internet from a multitude of sources in one place;

8. **Price Comparers:** As its name indicates, there are platforms that allow users to query and compare several products from the various stores where they are sold, allowing the consumer to have greater market awareness and save time and money on acquisition;

9. **Participatory Commerce:** Become involved directly in the production process through voting, funding and collaboratively designing products, or conception de ideas to incorporate;

10. **Social Cashback:** The consumer gets a "reward" by encouraging his/her network of contacts and acquire at the same store or the same well;

11. **Social Shopping:**
    a. **Social Shopping Portals:** Allow people to buy online at many stores using a series of e-commerce tools. Usually combined with reviews, comments, recommendations, references, and comparators of price;
    b. **Peer-to-Peer Sales Platforms:** Community-based marketplaces, or bazaars, where persons can communicate, promote and sell directly to other individuals. Some enterprises use this platform not only to sell, but essentially to promote the products;
    c. **Group Gifting:** Allows people to buy a gift online together with other people;
    d. **Group Buying:** Products and services offered at a reduced rate if enough buyers agree to make the purchase. The purchase is carried out by various consumers, with great discounts;
    e. **Discount Clubs:** Usually offer smaller discounts for collective buying sites. On the other hand, tends to be larger product exclusivity;
    f. **Social Network-Driven Sales (Facebook, Pinterest, Twitter):** Sales driven by referrals from established social networks, or take place on the networks themselves (for example, through a "shop" tab on Facebook).

## Facebook's Role in Marketing

Companies are increasingly interested to communicate with their consumers on social networks and Facebook is referred to as a powerful tool for marketing activities and a way for companies to reach more broadly the target audience. The fact that Facebook provide unlimited forms of users generate content, or express their opinion on something, makes that the online activity of them has great impact on companies.

144

To predict and manage this interaction, it is imperative to understand the motivations of people and motivations of their engagement, being for that necessary to attract the attention of users, building communities that subsequently go fostering greater brand loyalty through communication strategies implemented (Kanade, 2016).

A Fan Page is a page created especially for brands and companies. Unlike a common and personal account, it is a space that brings together fans instead of friends, where brands can create a community loyal to the company, as well as strengthen the online presence and the opinion that others have of it. In this sense, a Fan Page serves as an online platform for business, without resorting to a website, with the core functionality to notify people about upcoming events, provide the hours of operation and contact information, news, and even view photos, videos, text and other content related to the company. These pages also allow users to maintain conversations with customers and followers, which represent a new form of the company to find out more about what they look for and expect from products sold (Haydon, 2015).

Fan Pages facilitate also the communication between the client and the company itself, exposing their experiences with the products sold, waiting for part of a rapid response organization, this uses in order to try to maintain, recover or rebuild customer trust (Thakor, 2016). Abdillah (2016) looked for the motivational factors of the individuals to become involved with Fan Pages, having concluded that four factors stand out: (i) identification with the brand; (ii) interactivity; (iii) informational content; and (iv) valence. These elements overlap the brand popularity attribute, which is often considered as the most relevant element. Additionally, Halaszovich and Nel (2017) consider that Fan Pages are an enabler for the establishment of customer-brand engagement.

Facebook is mainly used by companies for five main actions: make new customer prospection; increase customer databases; create tools to communicate with consumers; creating contacts; e-commerce management, aiming at all of this increased engagement, as well as the influence and promotion of involvement between the current and potential consumers (Smith & Treadway, 2010).

## The F-Commerce

To Joshi and Dumbre, (2017) f-Commerce is a specialized form of e-commerce like the m-commerce. The f-Commerce is a capability offered by Facebook to the users to take contact with products or services which the enterprise wants to sell. It's a form to retail products, but does not replace the e-commerce through websites. It's another channel that takes advantage of Facebook's facility to target audience through the uses of Facebook FanPage and advertising. In Facebook, the brand can perform a refined segmentation to ads according to the position that the person holds in the company, age, interests, age, gender, location and more diverse possibilities.

Therefore, we may conclude that Facebook is a platform that helps to promote and facilitate the sales transactions.

Organizations can adopt the f-commerce in three ways (Marsden, 2011):

- **On Facebook (F-Store):** Social commerce on Facebook Store is a win-win situation for businesses as well for customers. In Facebook, the business creates a space that promotes the purchase and improves brand loyalty. To the customer, it's an opportunity to buy products with less effort compare to the necessity to go to the site of e-commerce. The use of Facebook is often triggered by the need of socialization and content sharing, where users can interact and participate in the various Facebook pages. Consequently, the presence of a store can take advantage of engagement that the user has with the brand;
- **On-Site (Integrating Facebook Into E-Commerce Site):** It's possible to make login with Facebook credentials, which turn easier to sign and start conversions. It's fast, convenient (especially when we need to log in multiple devices) and safe. This way also provides social validation by displaying the Facebook profile photos of people who have connected with the Facebook page of the enterprise, using for example the Facebook Open Graph technology;
- **In-Store (Integrating Facebook Into the In-Store Experience):** The organization must develop interactions at the store to encourage the customer to take an action, to promote the brand (for example, tag the location to their post), to share the experience at the store in Facebook, when the customer is encouraged to publish, for example, a selfie or make a movie about an object and assign a designated hashtag.

In f-store, it's possible to identify three kinds of stores (Díaz, 2013):

- **Storefront:** The most basic and static version, where it's presented a catalog of products or services within the Facebook page. Is not available for sale of products, but in each product is possible include a link that allows direct the user to the same product in e-commerce site;
- **Facebook Store:** An evolution of the Storefront enabling the full purchase process, including payment, without the client having to leave Facebook. Allow users to integrate a product catalog or service, as well as incorporate the tools needed to perform the purchase, such as the choice of transport to receive the merchandise;
- **Smart Facebook Store:** These are more complex stores that seek to establish a loyalty relationship with the Fan. There are, therefore, stores hosted on Facebook that not only integrate the entire purchase process, but offer a

personalized shopping experience based on the profile of each user. The technology is capable of analyzing or behaving of each user and can offer products according to customer profile.

Marsden (2011) considers respectively that smart stores can be decomposed into three types of stores: (i) faux-stores, (ii) fan-stores, and (iii) full-stores. In faux-store, users can browse the products, but can't buy them; in fan-stores, users can buy some products for a limited time; and in full-stores all products can be purchased without restriction.

Kang and Johnson (2015) consider that there is still margin for Facebook's social shopping services to evolve. They also advocate the use of pop-up f-stores, that is, stores which aim to sell a new product or products of limited series over a single period of time.

Facebook was not developed with the goal of making the selling of products, but rather to promote the socialization of people. The use of a third-party application to integrate with Facebook is possible, but this approach causes more difficulties in design and configurations. On the other hand, the user can choose the desired layout and apply it to the f-store. In this approach, the choice of layout and configuration is further reduced and simplified and, therefore, the process of creating a virtual store becomes faster.

## METHODOLOGY

The methodology is divided into three phases as depicted in Figure 1. In the preliminary phase, we realized an extensive literature review on the evolution of social commerce and we analyzed the growing importance of facebook's role in marketing. Then, in the contextual phase, we performed a research on the Facestore platform to identify a set of features and characteristics that we can typically find in online stores integrated in social networks. In a last step, we explored the relation between each Facestore feature with the functional areas of organizational responsibility.

The study adopts a qualitative approach, which allows us to understand and explore the impact of Facestore on organizations. We adopted a field research method to explore several implementations of the f-store. For each of them, we extract information about the implementation models, activity sector and available features, and we perform a triangulation of these functionalities with the functional areas of these companies. According to Queirós, Faria and Almeida (2017) argue that field research method is an appropriate approach to understand people's behavior and experiences. Additionally, Jamshed (2014) considers that field research method allows in-depth exploration on a given experiment considering multiple dimensions.

*Figure 1. Research methodology*
Source: authors.

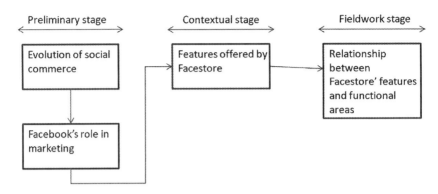

This approach is particularly indicated in a scenario where it is intended to explore the impact of adopting a technological tool in several dimensions of the companies.

## ANALYSIS AND DISCUSSION OF RESULTS

### Facestore Features and Characteristics

Facestore is an innovative e-commerce platform that allows any company to open an online store and sell their products or services directly on social networks such as Facebook, Instagram or Pinterest. The store can be accessed in a desktop or mobile environment. Each mobile version of the store is associated with a QR code, thus, allowing its access through smartphones and tablets. Facestore also lets its clients to sell through their own websites, blogs or domains, providing online stores for various business areas and an integrated back-office system for managing all multi-channel activity. The structure of the online store, as well as the definition of payment methods supported, is installed in a simplified way, without the need of technical knowledge.

Facestore provides online store templates for various business areas and offers an intuitive back-office system that enables easy management and tracking of all online store activity with access to sales reports, customer management, payments, products, inventory, orders, visitor statistics, marketing campaigns, and other resources. Templates are made using HTML, CSS, AJAX and JavaScript technologies. It is also possible to manage multiple stores in the same client's account, and each store can be installed on several Facebook pages.

The products are available on the Facebook website and the whole sales process, from choosing products to payment and ordering, is carried out without leaving Facebook. The application is free for up to ten products. From there the price plan is gradual, from an initial plan of 100 products to 5000 products. Payment can be made monthly or annually, and in the latter case there are associated discounts. One of the potentialities of the application is the integration with several methods of payment and also the automatic calculation of the costs of sending the orders.

Facestore allows the creation of "flash offers". A "flash offer" is a special promotion that only lasts for a limited period of time, and it is possible to define which products will be included in a "flash offer". It is also possible to offer discounts for fans, typically users who have clicked "like" on the page. This encourages more customers to visit the online store, and share it with their group of friends.

Facestore can be integrated directly into the Facebook page of the company, but also in its own domain. Several stores offer both versions to the user, in addition to a mobile version. Facestore offers a SSL certificate, free of charge, for all stores hosted in own domains. It is also relevant to mention the integration of Facestore with a wide range of Apps. In this regard, we highlight the use of Mailchimp for newsletter delivery, Invoice Express and Sage One for invoice generation and delivery, IfThen Software to generate payment references, and Google Analytics for statistical analysis of website access.

## Facestore and Its Relationship With Functional Areas

The functional areas of a company represent a set of company's processes, which together turn possible the achievement of business objectives. They include functions and activities directly and indirectly involved in the process of transforming resources into products and placing them on the market. Galbraith (2014) considers the existence of seven functional areas: (i) operations; (ii) finance; (iii) customer services; (iv) administration and IT support; (v) marketing and sales; (vi) human resources; and (vii) research and development.

The functional area of operations, also known as production, includes the structuring of the layout and production system within the company that ensures the supply of the products and services defined by the marketing area. Operations include the activities necessary for the transformation of supplies into goods and services. This process of transformation must necessarily add value to the inputs, where the finished product is perceived as useful and desired by the customer.

The Facestore application does not directly change the production model established by the company, but indirectly it can provide elements that contribute for its optimization. The reception of online orders contributes to a better management of inventory and inventory, which will allow a more rational use of company resources.

Additionally, the ecommerce paradigm contributes also for a better articulation with partners. We can have a Just-In-Time (JIT) production process, which has been successfully implemented in manufacturing, but can also be extended to service industries (Aradhye & Kallurkar, 2014). According to Kootanaee, Babu and Talari (2013) this paradigm has resulted in increases in quality, productivity and efficiency, in addition to contributing to the reduction of costs and waste.

Finance area is responsible for all the processes related to the planning of financial resources, fundraising and accounting. Treasury management is one of the fundamental tasks of this functional area and encompasses the management of liquidity, payments and charges.

This is an organizational area of the company that does not undergo significant changes with the introduction of Facestore, except in the accounting area. At this level, the possibility of incorporating Invoice Express and Sage One apps into the billing process is recommended. The choice of the app must take into account the area of activity of the company. It is important to ensure that the software chosen by the company has the desired functionality. The billing software must be certified by the local taxing authority. Integrating the billing process with Facestore allows company to streamline and simplify the online sales process.

Customer service is a key area in the current society. Having an efficient customer service support is essential to ensure the success of a business, being one of the most decisive factors to attract and retain customers. The main purpose of a customer service policy is to satisfy the wishes of the customers. During the sales process, doubts about product specificities, delivery time, payment method, among others, are common. Therefore, offering a communication channel with the consumer ensures that he feels more comfortable and secure with the purchase.

Customer service has experienced significant changes with the introduction of Facestore. In a traditional store model, customer support is provided through a telephone helpline or by email. The integration of Facestore in Facebook makes it possible to take advantage of the synchronous communication mechanisms offered by this social network. Facebook has now a number of options available that allow administrators to more easily manage the private and public interactions that are recorded on their pages. Retailers' pages can display the average time, calculated by Facebook, which indicates how slow they are to respond to messages. Options range from a response within minutes, within hours, or within a day. Another relevant option is the indication of the state "absent" that indicates that the company is unavailable at that moment to respond to the messages, and these are not accounted for in the response rates of companies determined by the social network. The retailer can also send automatic messages informing when they expect to respond to the customer or where they can find more information. Finally, the retailer has in his inbox of private conversations initiated with consumers, the previous interactions with them, the information that each client has available in his profile, recent orders, and service preferences, or others considered relevant.

Administration and IT support area is responsible for offering a set of processes, methods and technologies that allows the daily operation of the business. The constant evolution of technology and the increasing requirement of the market for efficiency, originate that companies seek to have better information systems. The goal of IT support is to ensure the correct operation of the technology for the daily operation. Chi and Sun (2015) argue that technology cannot be seen as a mere cost, but it must be a competitive differential of the company.

At this level, we establish that there are not any significant changes in the component of administration and IT support. The inclusion of Facestore does not cause changes in the company's technological structure. Facestore guarantees technical support if some technical arises in the online store. All plans offer a helpdesk for questions and paid plans also include telephone support, available from Monday to Friday from 10am to 6pm.

Marketing and sales are two functional areas of the company that often work independently. While they share the same general goals, in terms of boosting sales and increasing revenue, they have different visions of how to achieve those goals. In most cases, this division is not something planned, and is simply the result of how the company is organized or structured. The result is that the sales force has little or no involvement in product development and marketing campaigns. In this regard, it is desirable that both functional areas can be properly aligned. Involving sales with marketing processes can increase the success of the business's campaigns.

The integration of Facestore in social networks revolutionizes the role of company marketing. Through the use of the Facebook in conjunction with Google Analytics, it becomes possible to understand the target consumer's demands. The segmentation process, with which we define our target audience, reaches a new dimension. Access to statistics allows companies to monitor user behavior, taking into account their interaction with the various components of the store. For example, it is possible to collect information about active users during the selected time period, type of interaction (e.g., number of comments, likes, views), demographics of users, etc. Furthermore, it is still possible to include a wide range of marketing campaigns that include the buyer's participation in online marketing, such as the gathering of opinions and suggestions about new products. Fundamental in the whole process is the creation of engaging conversations and communities, in which flourish confidence over time.

It is also possible to link Facestore to a CRM tool, where data is stored centrally, making it accessible to all members of the organization. This enables employees of the company to communicate more easily with the market and their customers. Other benefits of this approach can be explored, such as:

- Better customer service, since the CRM system stores detailed information about each customer, such as order history, correspondence, survey responses, email marketing. In smaller companies, Facestore can be used as the main point of contact with the customer, but other means of communication such as postal mail, e-mail, phone calls, etc. may necessarily co-exist. It is, therefore, important to centrally record all these occurrences. Having this information accessible can significantly improve the speed and quality of customer service;
- Improves customer satisfaction, because customers become more valued by the company. The interaction with the client, and using his preferred method of contact, allows to establish a more optimized and consistent communication process;
- Greater profit, because having a more effective communication allows the interactions with the client to be optimized. For example, it becomes possible to define customized campaigns of the products that the customer searches, without having to leave Facebook. Using the same environment, the client can quickly make a purchase, without having to go to the institutional website of the company;
- Cost reduction, since the marketing activities developed by the company are more coordinated. This will also help eliminate wasted resources.

The management of human resources is in the current macroeconomic scenario fundamental to the sustainability of every business. The implementation of appropriate human resources processes will have a direct impact on employee satisfaction and motivation, productivity, creativity and innovation. Aslam, Aslam, Ali and Habib (2013) state that due to globalization and to the increasingly complex and uncertain environment, it becomes even more important to align the company's business strategy with its human resources.

The use of Facestore does not imply itself a restructuring or requalification of human resources. However, it is recognized the importance that digital marketing takes in the context of an online store. It is expected, therefore, that human resources will be able to implement digital marketing policies to attract new customers, create relationships and develop a brand identity.

Finally, research and development (R&D) functional area includes creative activities or work performed in a systematic way to increase human knowledge. This knowledge can later be applied to the creation or improvement of new products / services.

The existence of an online store integrated in Facebook enables R&D activities to reach a new dimension, particularly through customer participation in the innovation process. Several studies have suggested co-innovation strategies processes through the participation of customers in the process of designing new products, in order to reduce uncertainties, and to have a product more adjusted to the customer's desires (Goel & Singhal, 2015; Zhihong, Duffield & Wilson, 2015). This strategy intends to increase the chances of commercial success of new products/services.

It is also important to highlight that the large amount of information that social networks turn possible to collect on the consumption pattern of the clients makes possible to improve the user experience and helps sales growth. Through Facebook we can collect information on customer satisfaction, needs and desires, and also cross this information with internal data of the company. Use of Big Data turns this scenario feasible, by allowing an analysis of a large volume of heterogeneous information in a timely and inexpensive manner.

## FUTURE RESEARCH DIRECTIONS

Increasingly more companies are offering virtual stores to their customers. Without leaving a social network, the user can make purchases of their favorite brands and goods. Promoters of social networks expect that companies use their pages not only to inform customers, but also to sell directly to them. One area of research is to analyze the features that these stores must have to offer a good user experience. It is also important to define the criteria that establish what can be a good online shopping experience.

The rules defined by the social networks of not charging any commission to the companies that implant their virtual stores are also a paradigm that in the future can change. For example, there are proposals that point to the social network starts to charge a percentage for each sale (Turban, Whiteside, King & Outland, 2017). Other business models may also emerge. At this level, it is important to explore business models that can be sustained by store promoters, social networks and customers.

The security of online transactions on social networks is another area that needs further investigation. With the proliferation of online stores, consumers have a wide range of shopping options, but the security of some of them is quite questionable (Kumar, Saravanakumar & Deepa, 2016; Zhang, Trusvov, Stephen, & Jamal, 2017). Therefore, it is important to offer security mechanisms to the client so that he can distinguish these situations.

Finally, it is important to analyze the impact of the use of virtual stores online by each sector of activity. It is important to study if this impact is identical for all sectors of activity, or if there are more propitious areas to the acceptance of this type of platforms.

## CONCLUSION

Social networks are currently the world's largest information exchange tool, allowing a rapid and simple instantaneous interaction between geographically dispersed users. They offer a platform of excellence for interaction among users. Several e-commerce solutions have emerged through a virtual store, in which it becomes very important the integration of the store with the main social networks, in order to reach the largest possible number of people and, thus, increase the profitability of their business. Selling on social networks offers several advantages, as it allows the company to have a faster and measurable return with a smaller investment. However, integrating a store into a social network is not merely a technological process. It also involves defining a policy of communication and relationship with the client adapted to the characteristics and potential of the social network. It is important to recognize that users of social networks trust the credibility of information posted by other users, that is, the customer may increasingly influence other customers through their opinion and experience. Therefore it is very important to create a strategy focused on interacting, engaging and always responding to the brand's public.

Facestore is an innovative e-commerce platform that allows any company to open an online store and sell its products or services directly on social networks and through devices such as smartphones and tablets. Facestore can be used by any company or individual that intends to sell online. The partnerships established by Facestore with key partners of the e-commence ecosystem, such as payment gateways, postal services, ERP and CRM solutions allow clients to integrate and optimize the processes of logistics, billing, payments and digital campaigns.

Facestore allows companies to take advantage of the potential of online e-commerce solutions and social networks. Communication with the customer becomes more fast and personalized taking advantage of the synchronous communication mechanisms offered by Facebook. In the same way, marketing companies become more effective, enabling a more precise and targeted segmentation process. This situation turns possible to better understand consumer behavior and better measure the success of each marketing campaign.

## REFERENCES

Abdillah, W. (2016). Motivation for Individuals' Involvement with Fan Pages. *Journal of Indonesian Economy and Business*, *31*(2), 220–234. doi:10.22146/jieb.15292

Aradhye, A., & Kallurkar, S. (2014). A Case Study of Just-In-Time System in Service Industry. *Procedia Engineering*, *97*, 2232–2237. doi:10.1016/j.proeng.2014.12.467

Aslam, H., Aslam, M., Ali, N., & Habib, B. (2013). Importance of Human Resource Management in 21$^{st}$ Century: A Theoretical Perspective. *International Journal of Human Resource Studies*, *3*(3), 87–96. doi:10.5296/ijhrs.v3i3.6255

Chi, J., & Sun, L. (2015). IT and Competitive Advantage: A Study from Micro Perspective. *Modern Economy*, *6*(03), 404–410. doi:10.4236/me.2015.63038

Constantinides, E., & Fountain, S. J. (2008). Web 2.0: Conceptual foundations and marketing issues. *Journal of Direct. Data and Digital Marketing Practice*, *9*(3), 231–244. doi:10.1057/palgrave.dddmp.4350098

Dennison, G., Bourdage-Braun, S., & Chetuparambil, M. (2009). *Social commerce defined*. IBM Corporation. Retrieved December 15, 2017, from https://digitalintelligencetoday.com/documents/IBM2009.pdf

Díaz, D. (2013). *F-commerce (III): modelos de tienda en Facebook*. Retrieved December 26, 2017, from https://www.educadictos.com/f-commerce-iii-modelos-de-tienda-en-facebook/

Galbraith, J. (2014). *Design Organizations: Strategy, Structure, and Process at the Business Unit and Enterprise Levels*. Jossey-Bass.

Goel, A., & Singhal, P. (2015). *Product Innovation through Knowledge Management and Social Media Strategies*. Hershey, PA: IGI Global.

Halaszovich, T., & Nel, J. (2017). Customer–brand engagement and Facebook fan-page "Like"-intention. *Journal of Product and Brand Management*, *26*(2), 120–134. doi:10.1108/JPBM-02-2016-1102

Han, H., & Trimi, S. (2017). Social Commerce Design: A Framework and Application. *Journal of Theoretical and Applied Electronic Commerce Research*, *12*(3), 50–68. doi:10.4067/S0718-18762017000300005

Haydon, J. (2015). *Facebook Marketing for Dummies*. John Wiley & Sons.

Huang, Z., & Benyoucef, M. (2013). From e-commerce to social commerce: A close look at design features. *Electronic Commerce Research and Applications*, *12*(4), 246–259. doi:10.1016/j.elerap.2012.12.003

Indivik, L. (2013). *The 7 Species of Social Commerce*. Retrieved January 2, 2018, from http://mashable.com/2013/05/10/social-commerce-definition/#O2pecz7FrEqj

Jamshed, S. (2014). Qualitative research method-interviewing and observation. *Journal of Basic and Clinical Pharmacy*, *5*(4), 87–88. doi:10.4103/0976-0105.141942 PMID:25316987

Joshi, J. M., & Dumbre, G. M. (2017). Basic Concept of E-Commerce. *International Research Journal of Multidisciplinary Studies*, *3*(3), 1–5.

Kanade, D. S. (2016). Engage your customers with contests: An overview. *Papirex - Indian Journal Research*, *5*(3), 150-152.

Kang, J.-Y., & Johnson, K. K. (2015). F-Commerce platform for apparel online social shopping: Testing a Mowen's 3M model. *International Journal of Information Management*, *35*(6), 691–701. doi:10.1016/j.ijinfomgt.2015.07.004

Kim, Y., & Srivastava, J. (2007, August). Impact of social influence in e-commerce decision making. In *Proceedings of the Ninth International Conference on Electronic Commerce* (pp. 293-302). ACM. 10.1145/1282100.1282157

Kootanaee, A., Babu, K., & Talari, H. (2013). Just-in-Time Manufacturing System: From Introduction to Implement. *International Journal of Economics, Business and Finance*, *1*(2), 7–25.

Kumar, S., Saravanakumar, K., & Deepa, K. (2016). On Privacy and Security in Social Media – A Comprehensive Study. *Procedia Computer Science*, *78*, 114–119. doi:10.1016/j.procs.2016.02.019

Liang, T.-P., & Turban, E. (2012). Social Commerce: A Research Framework for Social Commerce. *International Journal of Electronic Commerce*, *16*(2), 5–13. doi:10.2753/JEC1086-4415160201

Lui, H. (2017). *Global Ecommerce Markets Will Reach $4 Trillion By 2020. Are You In?* Retrieved January 6, 2018, from https://www.shopify.com/enterprise/global-ecommerce-markets

Marsden, P. (2010). *Social Commerce: Monetizing Social Media*. SYZYGY Group. Retrieved December 15, 2017, from https://digitalintelligencetoday.com/documents/Syzygy_2010.pdf

Marsden, P. (2011). *F-Commerce Selling on Facebook: The Opportunity for Consumer Brands*. SYZYGY Group. Retrieved December 15, 2017, from https://digitalintelligencetoday.com/documents/Syzygy_2011.pdf

Ng, C. (2014). Intention to purchase on social commerce websites across cultures: A cross-regional study. *Information & Management*, *50*(8), 609–620. doi:10.1016/j.im.2013.08.002

Queirós, A., Faria, D., & Almeida, F. (2017). Strengths and Limitation of Qualitative and Quantitative Research Methods. *European Journal of Education Studies*, *3*(9), 369–387.

Sharma, S., & Crossler, R. (2014). Intention to Engage in *Social commerce*: uses and gratifications approach. *Proceeding of the XX Americas Conference on Information Systems*. Retrieved December 26, 2017, from http://aisel.aisnet.org/cgi/viewcontent.cgi?article=1695&context=amcis2014

Smith, M., & Treadway, C. (2010). *Facebook Marketing: An hour a day*. Wiley Publishing, Inc.

Statista. (2017a). *Retail e-commerce sales worldwide from 2014 to 2021 (in billion U.S. dollars)*. Retrieved January 6, 2018, from https://www.statista.com/statistics/379046/worldwide-retail-e-commerce-sales/

Statista. (2017b). *Most famous social network sites worldwide as of September 2017, ranked by number of active users (in millions)*. Retrieved January 6, 2018, from https://www.statista.com/statistics/272014/global-social-networks-ranked-by-number-of-users/

Thakor, D. C. (2016). The Social CRM - New Age of Business Strategy for the Organization: An Explorative Study. *Indian Journal Of Applied Research*, 6(2), 195–197.

Turban, E., Bolloju, N., & Liang, T. (2010). Social commerce: An e-commerce perspective. *Proceedings of the International Conference on Electronic Commerce: Roadmap for the Future of Electronic Business*, 33-42.

Turban, E., Strauss, J., & Lai, L. (2016). *Social Commerce: marketing, technology and management*. Springer. doi:10.1007/978-3-319-17028-2

Turban, E., Whiteside, J., King, D., & Outland, J. (2017). *Introduction to Electronic Commerce and Social Commerce*. Springer. doi:10.1007/978-3-319-50091-1

Wang, C. (2009). Linking shopping and social networking: Approaches to social shopping. *Proceedings of the 15th Americas Conference on Information Systems (AMCIS)*.

Wang, C., & Zhang, P. (2012). The Evolution of Social Commerce: An Examination from the People, Business, Technology, and Information Perspective. *Communications of the AIS*, *31*(5), 105–127.

Wigand, R. T., Benjamin, R. I., & Birkland, J. L. (2008, August). Web 2.0 and beyond: implications for electronic commerce. In *Proceedings of the 10th International Conference on Electronic Commerce* (p. 7). ACM. 10.1145/1409540.1409550

Yadav, M., Valck, K., Henning-Thurau, T., Hoffman, D., & Spann, M. (2013). Social Commerce: A Contingency Framework for Assessing Marketing Potential. *Journal of Interactive Marketing*, *27*(4), 311–323. doi:10.1016/j.intmar.2013.09.001

Zhang, Y., Trusvov, M., Stephen, A., & Jamal, Z. (2017). Online Shopping and Social Media: Friends or Foes? *Journal of Marketing*, *81*(6), 24–41.

Zhihong, L., Duffield, C., & Wilson, D. (2015). Research on the Driving Factors of Customer Participation in Service Innovation in a Virtual Brand Community. *International Journal of Innovation Science*, *7*(4), 299–309. doi:10.1108/IJIS-07-04-2015-B006

Zhou, L., Zhang, P., & Zimmermann, H.-D. (2013). Social commerce research: An integrated view. *Electronic Commerce Research and Applications*, *12*, 61–68.

Zhou, L., Zhang, P., & Zimmermann, H.-D. (2013). Social commerce research: An integrated view. *Electronic Commerce Research and Applications*, *12*(2), 61–68. doi:10.1016/j.elerap.2013.02.003

## KEY TERMS AND DEFINITIONS

**Asynchronous Javascript and XML (AJAX):** Set of techniques for programming and web development that uses technologies such as Javascript and XML to load information asynchronously.

**Big Data:** Very large sets of data that can only be stored, used, and analyzed with the help of technological tools and methods.

**Cascade Style Sheets (CSS):** Language used to define the presentation of web pages built with markup language, such as hypertext markup language (HTML).

**Customer Relationship Management (CRM):** Approach that places the customer as the main focus of business processes, with the purpose of perceiving and anticipating their needs.

**Enterprise Resource Planning (ERP):** Enterprise management software that seeks to automate the daily routines of company management, automating the productive, financial, and administration processes.

**HTML:** Markup language used to build web pages. HTML files can be rendered and accessed from web browsers.

**JavaScript:** Client-side programming language, which is processed by the browser itself. By using JavaScript, we can create more interactive interfaces with users.

**QR Code:** Barcode that is used by various industries. It can also be easily read by a smartphone, which allows the forward of the customer to the company's website.

**SSL Certificate:** Technology created to bring more security in the exchange of information between a visitor and the server that hosts the site. The purpose of an SSL certificate is to prevent malicious people from capturing sensitive information.

**User Experience:** The quality of experience a person has when interacting with a specific design.

# Chapter 8
# Value–Added Crowdsourcing:
## Digital Catalysts for Creative Contests

**Nadia Steils**
*University of Lille, France*

**Salwa Hanine**
*Université Côte d'Azur, France*

## ABSTRACT

*This chapter investigates the role of digital tools in the value co-creation process of creative contests. Based on a multidisciplinary literature and a discourse analysis of existing creative and innovation contests, the authors identify four categories of tools that affect the value co-creation process: proactive and reactive, trial-and-error, and social learning tools. A synthesizing framework presents how the integration of these tools is beneficial to the exchange of resources between the different stakeholders of creative crowdsourcing. The authors further identify practical tools (i.e., instructive and promoting, creativity supporting, collaborative, and evaluating tools), which intervene in the three phases of crowdsourcing activities (i.e., before, during, and after).*

## INTRODUCTION

Crowdsourcing is a problem-solving model that takes advantage of the Internet (Brabham, 2013). Jeff Howe, who first coined the concept in 2006, describes it as the act of taking a job, traditionally performed by a designated agent (usually an employee), and outsourcing it to an undefined, generally large group of people in the form of an open call (Howe, 2006). Crowdsourcing is typically characterized

DOI: 10.4018/978-1-5225-5993-1.ch008

by a proactive crowd, an outsourced task and an empowering online environment (Djelassi & Decoopman, 2013). Among the most popular and most promising types of crowdsourcing is creative crowdsourincg, often organized in the form of creative contests (e.g., idea or design competitions) (Terwiesch & Xu, 2008). Contests are used for both, problem-solving and decision-making tasks, in a variety of industries. They help reducing market failure rates of new products and services, accelerating the innovation process, reducing traditional outsourcing costs, and strengthening the relationship between brands and customers (Brabham, 2013; Hanine & Steils, 2018). Even though the principle of outsourcing a task to a group of people is not fundamentally new, the digital environment lifts the usage and usefulness of crowdsourcing to a whole new level.

The rise of crowdsourcing has been nurtured by technological and digital improvements, but also by consumers' increasing empowerment (Loi, Rosati & Manca, 2008; Wathieu et al., 2002). People have long been willing to participate in companies' creative and innovative challenges (Thomke & Von Hippel, 2002). With the advent of technological opportunities, Internet users are now not only willing (Roth, Brabham & Lemoine, 2015), but also capable of participating in corporate problem resolution (Frey, Lühtje & Haag, 2011; Jeppesen & Lakhani, 2010; Poetz & Schreier, 2012).

Technological advancements enable the emergence of a value ecosystem in which organisms (i.e., individuals, companies or networks) interact (Thrift, 2006). Crowdsourcing refers to a form of value co-creation, which is defined as a joint process in which value is created reciprocally for each of the actors (Füller, 2010). These actors are engaged in a value-creating process by interacting and exchanging resources of different nature (Leclerq et al., 2016; Schaffers et al., 2011).

This chapter describes how the Internet acts as a catalyst for value co-creation in creative crowdsourcing. First, the authors identify the digital components that lead to the rise of crowdsourcing in the scientific literature. Second, based on this literature and a discourse analysis of existing creative and innovation contests, the authors identify the technological stakes that affect the value co-creation process in crowdsourcing activities. Finally, overlaps between the exchange of resources and technological tools are described and illustrated in a synthesizing framework.

## Exchanging Resources in the Value Co-Creation Process

Consumers are increasingly empowered and want to play a greater and more active role in the idea generation process (Loi, Rosati & Manca, 2008; Wathieu et al., 2002). The emergence of new terminologies like "prosumers" or "collaborative consumers" describes the increasing involvement of consumers in co-creating activities (Payne, Storbacka & Frow, 2008). Wider choice, better information and an enhanced corpus of rights characterize empowered consumers (Loi, Rosati & Manca, 2008). More specifically, consumers have now greater access to information about products, tools, applications and services. They acquire greater expertise in involving product or service categories and have an increased influence on the dissemination of product and service evaluations through online and offline word-of-mouth. The scientific literature has shown the benefits of improving customer empowerment and thus the need to provide accurate information and tools from the company's side.

Value co-creation describes a process in which resources are exchanged and value mutually created (Grönroos, 2008). This definition implies that stakeholders have to both, provide and receive resources. They give away resources that are valuable to the receiver, and integrate resources to create new value. Among the conditions of value co-creation, resources thus need to be exchanged between involved actors (i.e., individuals, organizations or networks). For participants, resources reflect time and effort investment, and their creativity. For organizers of crowdsourcing initiatives, a platform composed of dialogue and feed-back enabling technologies provides the necessary resources to contribute to the ideation process. In other words, interaction and thus interaction-enabling technologies are part of the keys of successful value co-creation.

For instance, *Dell Ideastorm* is a platform, launched by Dell in 2007, to enoucrage value co-creation. According to *Dell*, the purpose of this initiative is to "gauge which ideas are most important and most relevant" to the public (Bayus, 2013). A four-step process is offered to any customer willing to participate in the *Ideastorm* project. First, the crowd can post ideas for *Dell* products and services (e.g., "creating backlit keyboards"). Second and third, the community can view all posted ideas and then vote for preferred idea(s). They can also comment suggested ideas and make improvement suggestions. Finally, *Dell* promises to implement the best ideas. For instance, as the backlit keyboard idea received 3603 votes from the community, the company decided to launch the production and marketing of this idea.

In this crowdsourcing example, how is value co-created? As defined earlier, value co-creation implies an exchange of resources on the one hand, and the mutual creation of value on the other hand (Grönroos, 2008). From participants' side, resources related to time investment, creativity, ideas and social capital is provided. From the company's side, an engaging and interaction platform including a voting system is developed and available to any visitor of their website. The exchange of resources allows the creation of value for both stakeholders. Participants benefit from the engaging experience and the recognition from the company, while the latter receives ideas, inspiration and knowledge about consumers' needs. The experience creates tighter social bonds and brings both actors closer together (Füller, 2010).

# DIGITAL TOOLS IN CREATIVE CROWDSOURCING

## Insights From the Scientific Literature

Both, practitioners and researchers recognize and value consumers' innovative and creative potential by integrating their contributions using crowdsourcing activities (Poetz & Schreier, 2012). Creative crowdsourcing represents a collaborative approach in which companies benefit from the intelligence and creativity of a crowd of participants online (Bullinger et al., 2010). Social media and the constant development of digital interaction tools facilitate a company's access to creative participants. Thereby, companies are able to collect and use knowledge and ideas coming from a large group of people all over the world (Afuah & Tucci, 2012). Nowadays, a growing number of crowdsourcing contests are flourishing online concerning both product or service design and general problem solving. They encourage win-win relationships involving consumers, and thereby aim to favor value co-creation (Fuller, 2010). Creative contests may differ depending on their structure. Companies can decide running their own competitions or using mediating platforms. Contests may take the form of a single competition or a permanent tournament with different stages. They can allow individual or group participation and are carried out during a limited period of time (Bullinger et al., 2010).

For instance, *eYeka* is an online crowdsourcing marketplace, where the community can be solicited to submit designs or ideas for different purposes (e.g., websites, book covers or logos). Founded in 2006, *eYeka* now counts more than 1200 contests, 125 000 submitted ideas and a community of over 380 000 creators. Companies benefit from mediating platforms in two ways. First, they may receive hundreds of designs and ideas for more than half of the prize they would have paid using traditional outsourcing solutions. Second, these platforms offer integrated tools that facilitate company-participant interaction and improve their engagement (e.g., voting system, badge attributions).

In other words, technological platforms and tools connect the crowdsourcing organizer to the crowd on a crowdmarket (Chu & Kennedy, 2011). They represent a novel way of accessing solutions to corporate problems and innovative ideas. The advancements in the field of collaborative technologies have eased the access to user-generated innovations and are appreciated by participants (Antikainen, Mäkipää & Ahonen, 2010). Piller and Walcher (2006) perceive the Internet as the main driver of a broad integration of user input in new product development.

According to previous research, the process of crowdsourcing includes two tasks for a company; a description of the problem and a provision of adequate tools to complete the task (Shneiderman, 2007). Another task that can be added in creative crowdsourcing is the evaluation of submitted contributions. When planning these crowdsourcing activities, companies have to face two challenges. First, it is difficult for companies to provide the right description and tools if they do not know what to expect from a crowdsourcing activity. Another challenge refers to the difficulty of anticipating the outcome of a crowdsourcing campaign. Boundary spanning has been suggested as a solution in the literature. Crowdsourcing organizers can opt for high or low boundary spanning. Based on extent crowdsourcing activities high boundary spanning seems to go along with higher technological requirements. On the one hand, Bullinger and colleagues (2010) define *proactive boundary spanning* as the active monitoring and reviewing of the flow of action, namely submissions, comments and other feedback. On the other hand, *reactive boundary spanning* refers to the passive reception of feedback or reviews. Since companies can provide or use tools to facilitate the ideation process during the phases of creative contests, the authors distinguish proactive from reactive tools in the upcoming synthesizing framework.

## Insights From a Complementary Document Analysis

To complete the understanding from this multidisciplinary literature (i.e., innovation, marketing, information systems), the authors conducted a document analysis based on secondary data from three French creative contest platforms, namely Studyka.com, Eyeka.com and Creads.fr. The document analysis aimed to identify phases of creative contests and technological tools that are used to support participation and the development of creative contributions. The corpus was composed of 54 briefs (i.e., companies' instructions regarding a specific task that needs to be carried out) from Studyka.com (552 pages), 12 briefs from Eyeka.com (94 pages) and 56 briefs from Creads.fr (103 pages). The sample was composed of all briefs available at the time of the study. Confidential projects, which were only available to advanced graphic designers, were excluded. Known and unknown brands, who ordered the challenges, came from various backgrounds and contexts (e.g., Microsoft, Philips, Renault). The final corpus was composed of 749 pages of brand instructions, containing information about the challenge and available tools. Following the recommendations of qualitative research principles, the authors used open coding to identify the phases of creative crowdsourcing and describe the tools that were used to accompany participants in each of the steps of the idea generation process.

Based on the literature and the content analysis of these briefs, the authors suggest that creative crowdsourcing is composed of three major phases during which the company can intervene to improve the ideation process: (1) the promotion of the project and the provision of adequate instructions, (2) the conduct of the contest, and (3) the evaluation of submitted contributions. During the crowdsourcing campaign (phase 2), the authors suggest that providing user-friendly technologies improves the innovation process in two ways: (a) providing tools that improve or guide consumers in the creative process and (b) providing technologies that help participants to collaborate with other participants, the company or external opinion holders (cf. Table 1).

Various tools and toolkits have been listed in the literature when studying creative crowdsourcing (e.g., design tools, wikis, social networks). Based on the literature and the brief analysis, the four types of tools are outlined below. The authors describe how they intervene in the three phases of creative contest campaigns.

## Promoting and Instructive Tools

Crowdsourcing instructions about the topic and task specificity provide participants with the necessary resources to complete a task (Steils & Hanine, 2016). Instructions may be more or less constrained, providing individuals with different degrees of liberty regarding the expected outcome (Dahl & Moreau, 2007). The scientific literature explains that giving very specific and constrained instructions leads to outcome uniformness, but is beneficial for novice participants to activate relevant concepts they would not have thought of without any guidelines. Task instructions, and more precisely, the way the problem statement is crafted, plays a decisive role on the creativity of participants in online idea generation. By selecting the right problems and adequately formulating them, companies are able to define the

*Table 1. Intervening technological tools in the creative crowdsourcing process*

| | CREATIVE CONTEST | | | |
|---|---|---|---|---|
| | Before | During | | |
| | 1) Promoting and instructive tools | 2a) Creativity supporting tools | 2b) Collaborative tools | 3) Evaluation tools |
| Definition and use | Written or animated instructions about the task providing participants with the necessary resources to complete a task | User-friendly tools, that enable users to create their own prototypes through trial and error | Tools enabling feedback and dialogue among participants, with the company or with external opinion holders. | Tools allowing contribution evaluation by peers, and their recognition |
| Tools | Instructions, video, social networks, FAQ, templates for deliverables | Innovation toolkits (e.g., editing tools) | Forum, chat, e-mail, social networks, comment and reaction tools | Voting systems, badge-attributing systems |
| Example | PepsiCo Go | Microsoft challenge | Creads.fr | MyStarbucksIdea |

boundaries of the solution space without necessary prescribing specific paths to reach a solution (Bullinger et al., 2010).

Based on specific observations, instructions can be accompanied by templates for deliverables. As mentioned before, one of the challenges of crowdsourcing activities, is the evaluation of hundreds of creative contributions. In order to facilitate post-crowdsourcing evaluation, the authors observe that some companies provide templates to generate format uniformness and facilitate their processing in the pre-selection step. Instructions are generally in written format, and often include a presentation video. Videos have shown to reduce the odds of campaign failure and are increasingly used as a part of companies' instructions. They are also used as a promotional tool that can easily be spread through social media. Besides videos, social networks are the most widely used promotional tool for creative competitions. Most contests create specific Facebook and Twitter accounts to promote their creative challenges, but also to keep participants and non-participants updated about the advancement of the contest and winning contributions.

As an example, *PepsiCo* launches every year the *PepsiCo Go* challenge. Its aim is to discover the new generation of young people, who initiate the next global consumer trends. Participants who develop the best idea join the *PepsiCo* innovation program. The top three finalists also win high-tech items. To conduct their challenge successfully, *PepsiCo* uses the mediating plateform *Studyka* to disseminate relevant instructions and promote their project. Instructions are presented in form of written guidelines and accompanied by a promoting video showing the organization and the success of their past contests. Participants subscribe to the contest using integrated forms on the platform. To guide participants in their creative process, participating groups are accompanied by mentors. For the finalist groups, the company organizes two days of pitches and business case presentations to help participants understanding the industry, the business and the challenges, and thus to improve their final project.

## Creativity Supporting Tools

According to previous research, creativity supporting tools, such as toolkits, contain a range of user-friendly tools, including those to test a design, that enable users to create their own prototypes through trial and error. They have five objectives (Von Hippel, 2001):

1.  Consumers are able to carry out complete cycles of trial-and-error learning;
2.  Consumers are offered a guiding "solution space";
3.  Consumers are able to operate their solutions with their customary design language and skills (user-friendly);

4.  Toolkits often contain libraries of commonly used modules that can be incorporated, which helps users to focus their efforts on truly new design elements;
5.  Increasing the odds of producible solutions with less revision required by the companies' engineers.

The iterative improvement until satisfaction is encouraged with appropriate toolkits (Von Hippel, 2001). They help empowering participants and shifting the locus towards the user. Toolkits fulfill participants' desire for creativity and personal expression. By lowering effort and cost, they support innovation and problem-solving activities. Technological advancement help toolkit designers to improve the user-friendliness of such tools and to make the co-creation process accessible to a greater number of participants, who originally were hindered by their lack of technological competences to adequately put into practice their creative ideas and challenge their creative minds (Franke & Piller, 2004; Shneiderman, 2007; Von Hippel, 2001; Von Hippel & Katz, 2002).

Piller and Walcher (2006) distinguish two types of toolkits: solution information tools and tools that help accessing needed information. The first type of tool provides a purposive platform for communication and interaction, and thereby encourages feed-back and learning by doing. The second type of tools offers participants with the opportunity to design their idea within a solution space imposed by the company. These tools ensure feasibility and real-life application of suggested contributions.

As an example, a *hackathon* refers to an event where a group of volunteers come together to collaboratively do computer programming over several days. It is a creative process frequently used in the field of digital innovation. *Microsoft* regularly organizes *hackatons* to improve their innovation process. A recent example refers to the *Microsoft Chatbot Contest*, in which *Microsoft* encouraged the crowd to develop new experiences for the television audience using chatbot (i.e., conversational agent) technologies. To support the crowd in their idea development, *Microsoft* made a series of user-friendly tools freely available to the participating crowd. They allowed the creation of a chatbot in an hour and could even be used by novice participants. More precisely, three tools were offered during the contest period. First, *LUIS* provided pre-constructed *BOT* models and assisted participants in the development of more specialized models. Second, *BOT Framework* allowed participants to build and connect their *BOT* with the aim of interacting with users wherever they are (e.g., SMS, Skype, Slack, Office 365). Finally, *Azure* hosted their Chatbot online and included a range of integrated tools and services to improve participants' solution.

## Collaborative Tools

One of the major advantages of innovation toolkits, according to Von Hippel (2001), is that they enable trial-and-error learning, which significantly improves the quality of provided solutions. In a recent paper of Steils and Hanine (2016), it is shown that trial-and-error learning is not the only important learning approach that generates quality and value in crowdsourcing activities. Social learning provides participants with the opportunity to add value through collaboration. Collaborative tools accelerate the innovation process and allow the collaboration between numerous Internet users. The interactions take place on a platform of engagement, where each actor shares his own resources, integrates the resources proposed by other actors, and potentially develops new resources through a learning process (Leclerq et al., 2016). Collaborative tools not only improve creativity and efficiency, but also innovativeness (Antikainen, Mäkipää & Ahonen, 2010; Chu and Kennedy, 2011. Participants can collaborate with other competitors, with external opinion holders (e.g., family, experts) or with the company. Contests with low cooperative orientation also require less communication mechanisms (Bullinger et al., 2010).

For instance, mediating platforms include a range of collaborative tools, which ease the innovation process and make it socially more engaging. *Creads* is a French crowdsourcing platform, founded in 2008, which connects creative freelancers with demands from companies of different industries. Tasks mainly include the development of graphic design, videos or creative writing. *Creads* offers diverse collaborative tools for different purposes to support the crowdsourcing process. When browsing the different creative challenges, an integrated chat allows interested participants to interact with members of the crowdsourcing platform to receive further information or ask questions on a variety of topics. During the contest, the creative step of submitting ideas is followed by a voting period. The platform allows Internet users to view all submitted ideas, to vote and comment each submission. This interaction allows participants to not only understand the company's preference and final choice, but also to receive feed-back from the designer community on their work. *Creads* also organizes one-to-one projects, where only one designer works for a company and can continuously interact with the client asynchronously (e.g., through e-mails) or synchronously (e.g., using instant messaging).

## Evaluation Tools

Evaluation includes methods and tools to determine or influence the ranking of submitted contributions. Contributions may be evaluated by a jury, through peer review, self-assessment or mixed. Many contests select winning contributions based on an expert jury's evaluation that require no further technologies. Peer review includes voting systems and technologies that provide badges to reward most popular ideas, most creative ideas, etc.

For instance, *My Starbucks Idea* is a platform similar to the *Dell Ideastorm* platform, which allows the crowd to suggest, view and vote for ideas. Its aim is to improve customers' *Starbucks* experience. Examples of submitted and implemented ideas include free Wifi, happy hours, mobile payment and many new flavors (e.g., mocha coconut frappucino, hazelnut machiatto, pumkin spice latte). Integrating a voting system to vote for the best ideas, helps consumers not only co-creating value by suggesting new ideas, but also by evaluating and voting for their favorite submissions. Voting also facilitates the evaluation for companies and ensures market validation. However, there is a risk of not receiving sufficient ideas that are sufficiently innovative or feasible. Companies therefore have to control for the quality of ideas and justify their final choice.

## VALUE-ADDING CROWDSOURCING TECHNOLOGIES

### Framework

The literature suggests that value co-creation implies an exchange of resources between participants and organizers of crowdsourcing activities (e.g., Grönroos, 2008). Companies provide an engaging platform, task instructions, supporting tools and an expert evaluation of contributions in exchange for creativity, time and effort investment from participants. To support and improve the exchange of these resources, different technological tools come into play. In the following paragraphs, the authors present a synthesizing framework, which is based on insights coming from the scientific literature and from the document analysis.

Participants' investment and creativity are supported by learning tools. In line with previous research, trial-and-error and social learning both improve participants' creativity (Steils & Hanine, 2016). First, receiving feed-back (e.g., through voting, ranking or comments) helps accelerating the trial-and-error learning process and improving the quality of contributions. Moreover, innovation toolkits are designed in a way to allow for trial-and-error learning (Von Hippel, 2001). Second, collaborative tools help improving social learning, and thus the creativity of the outcome. Collaborative tools such as forums, chats or (a)synchronous messaging allow for the effective and rapid exchange of information.

Companies are involved in the provision of task instructions, an engaging platforms and evaluation tools. As outlined in Table 1, different tools are available and currently used to fulfill this mission. The authors make a distinction between proactive and reactive tools. Proactive tools include technologies that can be prepared and made available in advance to ensure the smooth running of the campaign. Reactive tools encompass tools that help companies to react to participants' actions (e.g., commenting or evaluating). They include all dialogue-enabling technologies. Figure 1 summarizes the exchange of value-adding resources and technological stakes involved in creative crowdsourcing.

In order to give more weight and demonstrate the practical applicability of the model suggested in Figure 1, the authors demonstrate the components of this framework through a practical example.

## Context

The National Union of French Furnishing Industries was founded in 1960. Its mission is to represent, defend and promote French furniture manufacturing companies. As a social partner, they collaborate with public authorities and take part in negotiations between employers' organizations and employee unions.

In 2017, they organized a national challenge with the aim of reinventing companies' workspaces. Participants were instructed to challenge furniture managers regarding their future products and services using a "blue ocean strategy" (i.e., systematic approach to making the competition irrelevant using principles and tools to create and capture their own "blue oceans"). Participant groups had to be composed of 2 to 5 individuals, including three mandatory profiles: 1 commercial/marketing, 1 designer/architect and 1 engineer/technology specialist.

The contest was organized in five steps.

*Figure 1. Digital tools as catalysts for value co-creation in crowdsourcing activities*

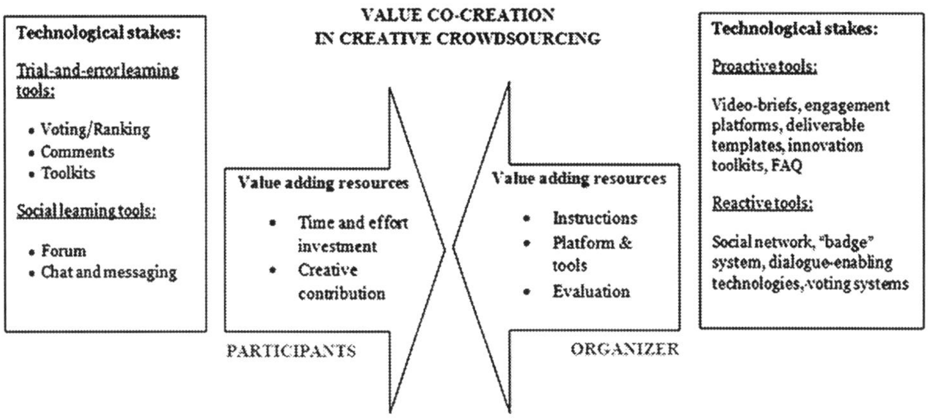

First, participants had to develop a strategic canvas comparing different offers on the market. To assist participants in this step, the organizer provided them with a webinar they could watch online and a deliverable template with an example of the organization's expectation regarding content and format of participants' submission.

Second, in the exploration phase, participants had to conduct 5 to 11 interviews with customers and non-customers of office space planning and design. Sector coaches assisted groups in setting meetings with interviewees. 21 coaches guided participant groups in their work. They included ergonomists, researchers, specialists in furnishing or blue ocean strategies, start-up coaches, etc. A second webinar was organized to guide participants in the construction and conduct of these exploratory interviews.

Third, participants were introduced to the blue ocean strategy and had to explore different solutions. During this seminar, an interactive webinar, in which they could directly interact with their sector coaches in real time, was offered. With the help of their coaches, best ideas were selected and submitted on the platform.

Fourth, another interactive webinar guided participant groups in the development of their selected strategy, with the help of their coaches.

Fifth and finally, the three best ideas were invited to prototype using toolkits made available by partners of the organizing committee and in collaboration with designers, architects and ergonomics. A final webinar presented the available tools (e.g., fab labs).

Social media networks with special accounts (a.o., Twitter, Facebook) were created to keep participants and non-participants updated on the challenge and provided relevant information.

## Participant Resources and Value

In the developed framework, the authors suggest that participants create value and are supported by technological tools that improve their investment and contribution. In the above described context, participants invested a considerable amount of time and effort to provide a creative and innovative contribution. From April to June, participant groups had to develop a detailed project and five intermediary deliverables. Not only did they have to balance creativity and feasibility using their own research and imagination, but they also had to include their coaches' input to improve their project. This collaboration and the available resources (e.g., webinars) improved the final output to a great extent when compared with traditional challenges where little guidance is offered.

Both types of learning strategies were thus highly present, namely trial-and-error learning and social learning. First, since constant feedback on their ideas was provided through coaches' feed-back and the pre-selection phases, participants' projects were constantly questioned and challenged. This form of direct feed-back helped participant groups to learn from their mistakes and improve their ideas continuously. Moreover, the fab lab they could use during the prototyping phase of the idea development included an experimentation lab using virtual reality. Their project could thereby be tested in "close-to-real" conditions. Design elements could be added or removed in a trial-and-error learning fashion. Participants thus benefited from instruction and creativity supporting tools to improve their project. Second, social learning (i.e., learning from others) was supported by allowing participants to learn from each other and from external persons. On the one hand, since challenge participation was organized in groups, the diversity of profiles (e.g., architects, marketing) encouraged divergent thinking and required greater collaboration and reflection to consider the different aspects and stakes in the development of their idea. Social learning was further encouraged through the presence of coaches and the organizing committee. Collaborative tools such as social media, interactive webinars and chats facilitated social learning and thus contributed to improved deliverables.

## Company Resources and Value

From the company's perspective most value was created through the provision of detailed instructions (e.g., webinars), an interactive platform, namely *Studyka*, and their coaching and evaluation of pre-selected ideas and final submissions. To do so, this challenge clearly shows the necessary investment of organizing companies before, during and after the competition. While proactive tools are mainly used in the pre- and post-contest phases, reactive tools add value during the competition. To guide participants and thereby ensure greater quality of submitted contributions, the organizing committee provided detailed instructions in form of webinars, downloadable guidelines, deliverable templates for each of the five steps and innovation toolkits in form of high-tech material in their experimental laboratories.

During the contest, the organizer offered a high degree of interaction by attributing responsible coaches to each group of participants. Moreover, they used reactive tools to facilitate the information exchange between participants, coaches and organizers. Besides social media, instant messaging and asynchronous messaging allowed participants to constantly contact their coaches or organizers. Table 2 illustrates how available tools acted as catalysts in the value co-creation process.

*Table 2. Application of the suggested framework*

| PARTICIPANTS | | ORGANIZER | |
|---|---|---|---|
| Value adding resources<br>• Contribution to the challenge<br>• Time and effort investment | | Value adding resources<br>• Instructions & evaluation<br>• Platform & tools | |
| **Trial-and-error learning tools** | **Social learning tools** | **Proactive tools** | **Reactive tools** |
| Feed-back, experimentation lab | Synchronous and asynchronous communication tools | Instructions, webinars, downloadable guidelines, deliverable templates, innovation toolkits | Social media, instant messaging, asynchronous messaging |

# CONCLUSION

Analyzing digital tools in crowdsourcing activities provides new and relevant insights on the importance and diversity of available tools. While previous research mainly considered one tool at a time, this chapter contributes to the crowdsourcing literature by offering a synthesizing framework of available tools and shows how they act as catalysts in the co-creation of value. Even though previous authors have highlighted the importance of the exchange of resources in value co-creation, scarcely have they identified the way these resources are exchanged and how companies and mediating platforms can intervene in the facilitation of value co-creation.

Although the scientific community has long considered crowdsourcing as a form of value co-creation, practically, managers often perceived its mere economic benefit and used it as a low-cost innovation strategy. This chapter concludes that to contribute to successful crowdsourcing activities, the input of all stakeholders is needed. In this sense, participants can only provide the quality and quantity of contributions expected from the company if the latter correctly assists them in this innovation process by providing an engaging and interactive environment. Mediating platforms ease the crowdsourcing organization to a great extent by providing guidance in designing proactive tools such as written or video briefs. While some platforms offer free e-books on how to develop relevant instructions, others offer their guidance and direct feed-back on companies' instructions. Such proactive tools are in general the first contact point between participants and companies. They include all material and tools available to any Internet user on the challenge's website. Investing effort in user-friendly tools and carefully designing unambiguous instructions represent thus two of the major determinants of participants' decision of integrating the challenge and their willingness and level of engagement. They shape the image the company's wishes to convey.

In contrast with proactive tools, reactive tools, including dialogue-enabling technologies, are less under the control of the crowdsourcing organizer in advance and highly depend on the comment, contribution or generally speaking the information the organization has to react to. Their effective use greatly depends on the organizer's social skills. However, their importance is as high as the use of proactive tools. Participants expect and appreciate exchanging and being in contact with the organizers. They especially expect some type of feed-back on their submitted contributions. Reactive tools help reducing the common risks of crowdsourcing activities, such as participant frustration because of a lack of transparency or communication form the company, and thus have to carefully be prepared in advance (e.g., designating a responsible community manager).

Besides these tools, which help directly improving the innovation process, companies can also indirectly influence the quality and quantity of submitted ideas by making use of learning tools. The latter help participants learning from experience (trial-and-error) or learning from others (social) to improve the quality of their contribution. Again, if companies collaborate with mediating platforms, many of these tools are integrated in the platform and simply available on demand (e.g., commenting ideas, instant messaging). Other tools can be additionally be integrated in the innovation process (e.g., toolkits).

In any case, integrating tools does not only consist in the decision to making them available to individual or group participants, but also requires a careful management of these tools before and especially during the creative contest. For instance, companies have to be ready to assist participants in the use of toolkits if necessary or to react to comments or questions in a timely manner. To ease its management, a responsible manager should be appointed. The company also has to make sure that it possesses the necessary competences to accomplish its mission properly. This way, organizers of creative crowdsourcing increase the value derived from digital tools and activate their catalyst power in the co-creation of value.

# REFERENCES

Afuah, A., & Tucci, C. L. (2012). Crowdsourcing as a Solution to Distant Search. *Academy of Management Review*, *37*(3), 355–375. doi:10.5465/amr.2010.0146

Antikainen, M., Mäkipää, M., & Ahonen, M. (2010). Motivating and supporting collaboration in open innovation. *European Journal of Innovation Management*, *13*(1), 100–119. doi:10.1108/14601061011013258

Bayus, B. (2013). Crowdsourcing New Product Ideas over Time: An Analysis of the Dell IdeaStorm Community. *Management Science*, *59*(1), 226–244. doi:10.1287/mnsc.1120.1599

Bullinger, A. C., Neyer, A.-K., Rass, M., & Moeslein, K. M. (2010). Community-based innovation contests: Where competition meets cooperation. *Creativity and Innovation Management*, *19*(3), 290–303. doi:10.1111/j.1467-8691.2010.00565.x

Chu, S. K. W., & Kennedy, D. M. (2011). Using online collaborative tools for groups to co-construct knowledge. *Online Information Review*, *35*(4), 581–597. doi:10.1108/14684521111161945

Dahl, D. W., & Moreau, C. P. (2007). Thinking inside the box: Why consumers enjoy constrained creative experiences. *JMR, Journal of Marketing Research*, *44*(3), 357–369. doi:10.1509/jmkr.44.3.357

Djelassi, S., & Decoopman, I. (2013). Customers' participation in product development through crowdsourcing: Issues and implications. *Industrial Marketing Management*, *42*(5), 683–692. doi:10.1016/j.indmarman.2013.05.006

Franke, N., & Piller, F. (2003). Key research issues in user interaction with configuration toolkits in a mass customization system. *International Journal of Technology Management*, *26*(5/6), 578–599. doi:10.1504/IJTM.2003.003424

Franke, N., & Piller, F. (2004). Toolkits for user innovation and design: An exploration of user interaction and value creation. *Journal of Product Innovation Management*, *21*, 401–415. doi:10.1111/j.0737-6782.2004.00094.x

Frey, K., Lühtje, C., & Haag, S. (2011). Whom Should Firms Attract to Open Innovation Platforms? The Role of Knowledge Diversity and Motivation. *Long Range Planning*, *44*(5-6), 397–420. doi:10.1016/j.lrp.2011.09.006

Füller, J. (2010). Refining Virtual Co-Creation from a Consumer Perspective. *California Management Review*, *52*(2), 98–122. doi:10.1525/cmr.2010.52.2.98

Grönroos, C. (2008). Service logic revisited: Who creates value? And who co-creates? *European Business Review*, *20*(4), 298–314. doi:10.1108/09555340810886585

Howe, J. (2006). The rise of crowdsourcing. *Wired Magazine*, *14*(6), 1–4.

Hoyer, W. D., Chandy, R., Dorotic, M., Krafft, M., & Singh, S. S. (2010). Consumer cocreation in new product development. *Journal of Service Research*, *13*(3), 283–296. doi:10.1177/1094670510375604

Jeppesen, L. B., & Lakhani, K. R. (2010). Marginality and Problem-Solving Effectiveness in Broadcast Search. *Organization Science*, *21*(5), 1016–1033. doi:10.1287/orsc.1090.0491

Leclerq, T., Hammedi, W., & Poncin, I. (2016). Ten years of cocreation: An integrative review [English Edition]. *Recherche et Applications en Marketing*, *31*(3), 26–60. doi:10.1177/2051570716650172

Nardo, M., Loi, M., Rosati, R. & Manca, A. (2011). The Consumer Empowerment Index – A measure of skills, awareness and engagement of European Consumers. *JRC Scientific and Technological Reports*, 1 – 232.

Payne, A. F., Storbacka, K., & Frow, P. (2008). Managing the co-creation of value. *Journal of the Academy of Marketing*, *36*(1), 83–96. doi:10.100711747-007-0070-0

Piller, F. T., & Walcher, D. (2006). Toolkits for idea competitions: A novel method to integrate users in new product development. *R & D Management*, *36*(3), 307–318. doi:10.1111/j.1467-9310.2006.00432.x

Poetz, M. K., & Schreier, M. (2012). The value of crowdsourcing: Can users really compete with professionals in generating new product ideas? *Journal of Product Innovation Management*, *29*(2), 245–256. doi:10.1111/j.1540-5885.2011.00893.x

Roth, Y., Brabham, D.C., & Lemoine, J.F. (2015). Recruiting Individuals to a Crowdsourcing Community: Applying Motivational Categories to an Ad Copy Test. *Advances in Crowdsourcing*, 15-31.

Salwa, H., & Steils, N. (2018). Crowdsourcing: A Double-Edged Sword Outsourcing Strategy. In M. Franco (Ed.), Positive and Negative Aspects of Outsourcing. InTech.

Schaffers, H., Komninos, N., Pallot, M., Trousse, B., Nilsson, M., & Oliveria, A. (2011). Smart Cities and the Future Internet: Towards Cooperation Frameworks for Open Innovation. In *The future Internet* (pp. 431–446). Berlin: Springer. doi:10.1007/978-3-642-20898-0_31

Shneiderman, B. (2007). Creativity support tools: Accelerating discovery and innovation. *Communications of the ACM*, *50*(12), 20–32. doi:10.1145/1323688.1323689

Steils, N., & Hanine, S. (2016). Creative contests: Knowledge generation and underlying learning dynamics for idea generation. *Journal of Marketing Management*, *32*(17-18), 1647–1669. doi:10.1080/0267257X.2016.1251956

Terwiesch, C., & Xu, Y. (2008). Innovation Contests, Open Innovation, and Multiagent Problem Solving. *Management Science*, *45*(9), 1529–1543. doi:10.1287/mnsc.1080.0884

Thomke, S., & von Hippel, E. (2002). Customers as innovators: A new way to create value. *Harvard Business Review*, *80*(4), 74–81. PMID:12024760

Thrift, N. (2006). Re-inventing invention: New tendencies in capitalist commodification. *Economy and Society*, *35*(2), 279–306. doi:10.1080/03085140600635755

Von Hippel, E. (2001). User toolkits for innovation. *Journal of Product Innovation*, *18*(4), 247–257. doi:10.1016/S0737-6782(01)00090-X

Von Hippel, E., & Katz, R. (2002). Shifting innovation to users via toolkits. *Management Science*, *48*(7), 821–833. doi:10.1287/mnsc.48.7.821.2817

Wathieu, L., Brenner, L., Carmon, Z., Chattopadhyay, A., Drolet, A., Gourville, J., ... Wu, G. (2002). Consumer Control and Empowerment: A Primer. *Marketing Letters*, *13*(3), 295–303. doi:10.1023/A:1020311914022

## ADDITIONAL READING

Brabham, C. B. (2013). *Crowdsourcing*. The MIT Press Essential Knowledge Series.

Chu, S. K. W., & Kennedy, D. M. (2011). Using online collaborative tools for groups to co-construct knowledge. *Online Information Review*, *35*(4), 581–597. doi:10.1108/14684521111161945

Franke, N., & Piller, F. (2004). Toolkits for user innovation and design: An exploration of user interaction and value creation. *Journal of Product Innovation Management*, *21*, 401–415. doi:10.1111/j.0737-6782.2004.00094.x

Howe, J. (2006). The rise of crowdsourcing. *Wired Magazine*, *14*(6), 1–4.

Von Hippel, E. (2001). User toolkits for innovation. *Journal of Product Innovation*, *18*(4), 247–257. doi:10.1016/S0737-6782(01)00090-X

## KEY TERMS AND DEFINITIONS

**Creative Crowdsourcing:** Collaborative approach in which companies benefit from the intelligence and creativity of a crowd of participants online.

**Crowdsourcing:** Crowdsourcing is the act of taking a job traditionally performed by a designated agent (usually an employee) and outsourcing it to an undefined, generally large group of people in the form of an open call.

**Digital Tools:** Tools characterized by electronic and especially computerized technologies.

**Proactive Tools:** Technologies that can be prepared and made available in advance to ensure the smooth running of the crowdsourcing campaign.

**Reactive Tools:** Reactive tools encompass tools that help companies to react to participants' actions (e.g., commenting or evaluating). They include all dialogue-enabling technologies.

**Social Learning:** Theory according to which acquisition of social competence happens exclusively or primarily as a function of observing, retaining and replicating behavior observed in one's environment of other people.

**Trial-and-Error Learning:** Method of problem solving learning which is characterized by repeated, varied attempts which are continued until success or until the agent stops trying.

**Value Co-Creation:** Joint process in which value is created reciprocally for each of the actors. These actors are engaged in a value-creating process by interacting and exchanging resources of different nature.

# Chapter 9
# The Dynamics of Resistance to Brand Switching in the Smartphones Industry

**Dominic Appiah**
*Arden University, UK*

**Wilson Ozuem**
*University of Gloucestershire, UK*

## ABSTRACT

*The impact of identity on brand loyalty has taken precedence as an area of focus in recent marketing research. This has taken place in an era defined by technological revolution, which has created market disruptions, and there are implications for customer-brand relationships. Nonetheless, existing research has failed to acknowledge the impact of socio-psychological attributes and functional utility maximization. Knowledge that illuminates how firms can reposition themselves to sustain brand loyalty when disruptions occur in today's complex and globalized business environment is also required. This study will present an empirical investigation into the phenomenon of brand switching behavior among consumers in a specific competitive market, the smartphone industry. It explores how resistance could be built from an identity theory perspective, as emphasis has historically been placed on the functional utility of products at the expense of social meanings. This study provides consideration for market disruptions in the smartphone industry and confirms that the literature does not capture other non-utilitarian factors such as socio-psychological benefits, hence there are underlying factors that motivate consumers to continue buying brands they buy.*

DOI: 10.4018/978-1-5225-5993-1.ch009

# INTRODUCTION AND BACKGROUND

Marketing research based on identity theory focuses on how individual consumers behave in agreement with the most salient identity (i.e. the highest in the hierarchy), because it provides the most meaning for the self (Arnett, German & Hunt, 2003; Reed, 2002; Farhana, 2014). This stream of research also frames the customer–brand relationship in the light of what is 'me' and what is 'not me' (Kleine, Kleine & Allen, 1995). Drawing on Bhattacharya, Rao and Glynn (1995), Da Siveira, Lages and Simoes (2013) and Wang and Yieh, (2016), this study posits that customers who identify with a brand are likely to be loyal to the brand, but all brand-loyal customers need not identify with the brand. This view necessitates a detailed analysis of two main aspects of brand loyalty literature to ascertain which perspective is preferred in a competitive market in order to establish and consolidate consumer loyalty.

The chapter examines two major limitations in brand loyalty. The first is that the sustainability of brand loyalty predictors refers to resisting both time and market disruptions (Lam, Arheane & Schillewaert, 2010). However, the brand loyalty literature has mainly focused on how brands perform under normal market conditions (Keller & Lehmann, 2006; Ozuem, Thomas & Lancaster, 2016). Yet as the business environment grows more complex, globalised and innovative, market disruptions become more prevalent. The second limitation in brand loyalty is that the perceived value of a brand is conceptualised and operationalised as a functional utilitarian value. As is prevalent in the brand loyalty literature, this does not capture other non-utilitarian factors, such as socio-psychological benefits, that might motivate customers to continue buying what they buy (e.g. Richins, 1994; Sweeney & Soutar, 2001; Hsu & Liou, 2017). This study proposes that customers identify with brands to satisfy one or more self-definitional needs (Lam et al., 2013; Ahearne, Bhattacharya & Gruen, 2005; Bhattacharya & Sanker, 2003).

This chapter seeks to examine consumer identification with brands in the Smartphone industry. This industry was specifically chosen as the product category for this study because it represents a context in which brand switching is most likely to occur due to multiple alternatives and short inter-purchase frequencies (Campo, Gijsbrechts & Nisol, 2000; Goldsmith, 2000; Jung, Hung & Ho, 2017). Notably, the market for Smartphones is probably the most dynamic of any product category, considering the degree and rate of change in technology (Azize, Hakan & Cemal, 2013; Cecere, Corroche & Battaglia, 2015).

## Overview of the Smartphone Industry

There has been a huge increase in the number of Smartphone users recently as it is widely used as a communication tool that connects users through voice calls, text messages, emails and social networking sites for entertainments (Wang, Xiang & Fesenmaier, 2014; Kim & Tussyadiah, 2015; Tan, Hsiao, Tseng & Chang, 2017). The Smartphone is a multi-functional device which apart from its telephone functionalities has a wide range of applications such as email, Internet, calendar, notepads and in-built cameras (Norazah, 2013; Wang et al., 2014; Jeong, Kim, Yum & Hwang, 2016). The Smartphone is a significant shift from the traditional mobile phone and a major difference between the two is that various applications can be added after the purchase of the Smartphone device, whereas the same cannot be said of the mobile phone. Hence Smartphones are considered radically innovative products due their additional features which are similar to computers.

The evolution of the Smartphone has impacted significantly on consumer behaviour and choice. Mobile phone technology was initially used only for communication purposes but has recently advanced to include additional features that have created a greater market and altered the purchase behaviour of the consumers (Slawsby et al., 2003; Dwivedi, 2015). In this modern era of technological advancement, users of mobile phones expect other features such as media support, Internet connectivity and special applications (Jones, 2002; Hansen, 2003; Norazah, 2013; Jeong et al., 2016; Tan et al., 2017).

There is the need to emphasise that recently, Smartphones have attracted the attention of all age groups from teenagers to the older generation, and special features in terms of both hardware and software have largely contributed to the impact on customer choice and purchase intentions (Tussyadiah, 2015), enabling manufacturers to innovate new services that have created a competitive environment.

The dramatic growth in the usage of Smartphones has attracted researchers and academics (Park & Yang, 2006; Wang et al., 2014; Kim et al., 2016; Jeong et al., 2016; Tan et al., 2017), and special features in Smartphones have created greater perception and expectations (Aaker, 1997; Dickinson, Ghali, Cherret, Speed, Davis & Norgate, 2014; Wang et al., 2014; Tan et al., 2017). The significant component of the Smartphone that drives demand and helps manufacturers maintain a strong influence in the Smartphone market is the operating system (OS). There are major software operating systems such as iOS (Apple), Android (Google), Windows (Microsoft), Symbian (Nokia), and RIM (Blackberry). Innovations in hardware and software have triggered enormous growth in the Smartphone market, since the multi-functional operations in these devices generate the trust in technology that consumers expect. Trust in Smartphone devices and their features ultimately adds brand recognition and this is the primary factor that affects intentions to purchase (Nah et al., 2003; Tussyadiah, 2015).

The Smartphone market has experienced strong growth in recent years mainly due to technological advancement in the industry (Kim et al., 2016; Tan et al., 2017; Jeong et al., 2016). A MarketLine (2017) report confirmed an impressive volume of 1,349.6 million sales of Smartphone units in 2016, which according to the report represents 92.7 per cent of the market's overall volume in the mobile phone industry as compared to ordinary mobile devices with a sales volume of 106.3 million units, which constituted 7.3 per cent of the market total in the same year.

The current global Smartphone market continues to be dominated by a small number of large technology firms such as Apple, Samsung and Huawei. Apple's Smartphone market share continues to grow across the globe, after consumers increasingly turn their backs on competing Android devices. It realised $215,639 million in revenue in 2016. Samsung, in particular, has seen its market share dropping across the world, retaining revenues of $172,840 million in the year 2015, a decrease of 2.7 per cent compared to fiscal 2014. Huawei's consumer business segment develops, manufactures and sells a range of Smartphone devices, with the company recording $59,453 million revenue in 2015 (MarketLine, 2017).

In spite of the significant growth in the industry (Kim, Nam, Oh & Kan, 2016), the Smartphone market is changing with severe threats facing the industry (Felix, 2015; Tan et al., 2017). Manufacturers with high demand leverage their competitive advantage to enable them to maintain their position in the market and a positive brand image, to explore new revenue streams and most importantly achieve a sustainable product differentiation to drive sales (Gartner, 2016; Jeong et al., 2016).

## Theoretical Context

Although brands themselves are not new, and have operated as a force in the organisation of production (Lury, 2004), the term 'brand' has only come to prominence in recent times (Quinton, 2013; Mitchell, Hutchinson, Quinn & Gilmore, 2015). Davies and Ward (2005) posit that there is little that remains unbranded in some respect, and even those that seek to create goods devoid of the obvious visual trappings of 'brand' do so by constructing a specific and clear set of values around their products. Hence they insist that branding has become one of the most important aspects of business practice regardless of sector or product (Leckie, Nyadzayo & Johnson, 2016).

Brand names may communicate unique functional attributes, subjective virtues surrounding the brand and other information that consumers may have accumulated over a period of time. These accumulated ideas are said to influence consumers' perception of brands and the reality of what brands mean to them (Arnold, 1992; Ebrahim, Ghoneim, Irani & Fan, 2016).

Such perceived reality is not based on the functional attributes of a brand alone (Farhana, 2014; Leckie et al., 2016). Indeed, brand attributes are selected based on a consideration of their utilitarian functions (Lam et al., 2013) and this is beyond the 'technical' skills of consumers. Rather, everything people associate with a brand, both intrinsic and extrinsic, contributes to what consumers purchase. While the product is the intrinsic element of the brand, it represents the basic element in a whole article to which the consumer attaches value (Brodie, Ilic, Juric & Hollebeek, 2013; Hollebeek, Glynn & Brodie, 2014). This subjective belief held by customers represents the essence at the heart of a brand.

This is exemplified in terms of the 'psychological values' brought to bear on enhancing the functional benefit of a brand beyond its utility capacity (Lam et al., 2013). Such psychological value is embodied in the complex variety of 'soft' attributes and other associations that determine the desirability of purchasing a particular brand instead of its alternatives. These subjective attributes embody the values over and above the basic product that a brand provides to consumers.

Brands are sometimes seen in terms of their identities and brand names along with their long-term communication elements. They are also regarded as 'added value' that can enhance the intrinsic value of products (Farquhar, 1989; Leckie, 2016; O'Kaffe, Ozuem & Lancaster, 2016). De Chernatony and McDonald (1992) opined that the added value that a brand provides differentiates it from a commodity. In the same vein, Doyle (1994) and Quinton (2013) define a brand as a successful integration of an effective product, distinctive identity and added value. The definition of brand as added value has its origin in economics where added value refers to the difference between the cost of an offering and the actual price it can attract in sales.

In a marketing context, it refers to subjective attributes such as those built around names, symbols, colours, slogans, tag lines and other devices created to link a product to the market (O'Kaffe et al., 2016)

The above definition resonates with the historical role of branding as an identification of ownership. What seems implicit in the ownership is that it fits very well with production-era marketing for which the above definition is perfectly suited. It also provides a simple definition that aggregates the various elements that make up a branded item. However, it is important to look deeper into the meaning of a brand as the basis for creating continual value for the consumer (Appiah & Ozuem, 2017).

Murphy (1992) used Gestalt theory to explain the complex nature of the brand. According to Murphy (ibid.), while a brand is made up of different constituents of both tangible and intangible elements, it is not simply the sum of its individual parts that makes it distinct. Therefore, 'any attempt to analyse the whole by breaking it down to its molecular components' (Murphy, 1992, p. 2) will not adequately capture the concept. A brand thus acts as a gestalt in that it is a concept that is more than the sum of its parts; parts that may have developed out of numerous scraps of information that it has established in the minds of consumers.

In order to establish a different pattern of beliefs and values that consumers internalise as a gestalt (Solomon, 2002), a brand needs to offer credible, coherent and attractive value propositions over time (Lam et al., 2013).

In keeping with the notion that a brand embodies many parts, Keller (2008) defines the brand as a product, then, but one that adds other dimensions to differentiate it in some way from other products designed to satisfy the same needs. In terms of the gestalt analogy made by Murphy (1992), one can argue that these differentiation and satisfaction dimensions are also part of what makes a brand. Yet this does not explain the whole concept, because the uniqueness of physical composition (product) and presentation are not sufficient to offer as a strong concept of brand.

It was observed that brands tend to create uniqueness through perceptions in the mind of the consumer, and that there is no other brand quite like a successful brand (Keller, 2008; Quinton, 2013). If the differentiation of a physical product does not represent the whole brand, what explanations can one have for the concept of brand? Brand has been rightly defined as a product or service that a particular firm is offering to customers in the marketplace which is differentiated by its name, presentation and the uniqueness of its compositions. However, it is erroneous to assume that is sufficient alone to explain the essence of a brand.

With increasing technological and manufacturing sophistication, many brands competing in the same product category can be produced to a virtually identical specification. Furthermore, they can be produced at exactly the same cost. This in turn can create parity among brands in the same product category. With the possibility of such conditions, one cannot assume that uniqueness of composition and presentation makes a brand. This by itself suggests that there are many other factors that come together to explain a brand.

No single definition can satisfactorily explain the concept of brand. Kapferer (2001) observed that the inability to come up with a singular definition reflects the complexity that is inherent in any attempt to define a concept, which in reality may mean different things to many people. Kapferer (2001, p. 3) explains further that:

*It is as if any definition that came to mind would not be complete. Some people talk about the name by which a product is known, others about added value, image, expectation, values, still others about the differentiating mark of the product and consumer badge. In fact they are all right in their own way; a brand is all of these things simultaneously.*

In light of the complexity of this discussion, one could agree with Kapferer (2001) that the reality of the modern brand makes it impossible to assert that a singular definition can capture all types of brands in their guises. One may not be able to reduce all of a brand's parts to only one encompassing definition. Building on the issues discussed above, a specific definition of brand is offered to reflect the particular approach of the research reported in this study. Hence, a brand is defined in terms of its perceptual, intangible elements, as much as its tangible aspects. This chapter takes orientation from Murphy's (1990, p. 4) definition of brand as:

*a blend of attributes, both tangible and intangible, which are relevant and appealing, and which meaningfully and appropriately distinguish one brand's uniqueness from another.*

In light of the above discussion, there is no singular acceptable conceptual definition of a brand. It is worth noting that this definitional problem is not peculiar to brand. Conclusions could be drawn to the effect that definitions adopted by researchers, particularly in the social sciences, are generally more often than not controversial in nature (Kerlinger & Lee, 2000). Therefore, an examination of the meaning of brand in this chapter will be based upon its ability to be many things to many people. However, for the purposes of the current study, a brand must convey authority, cohesion and confidence and it must prompt recognition in the mind of the consumer.

## Brand Loyalty

It is important that companies build strong brands. A strong and healthy brand is instrumental in creating a sustainable competitive advantage (Aaker, 1995; Bhattacharya & Lordish, 2000; Liu, Li, Mizerski & Soh, 2012). The transition to a relationship marketing paradigm places brand loyalty as a central indicator of customer relational strength (Oliver, 1999; O'Keeffe, Ozuem et al., 2016; Ozuem, Thomas & Lancaster, 2016; Giovanisa & Athanasopouloub, 2018). Brand loyalty has traditionally been conceived of as a behavioural construct relating to intentions towards repeat purchases (Nam, Ekinci & Whyatt, 2011).

Brand loyalty is a 'deeply held commitment to rebuy or re-patronise a preferred product or service consistently in the future, causing repetitive same-brand or same-brand-set purchasing, despite situational influence and marketing efforts having the potential to cause switching behaviour' (Oliver, 1999, p. 34).

Dimitriades (2006) shares this view and suggests it is widely accepted that satisfied consumers are less sensitive to price change, less influenced by competitor attacks, and more loyal to the firm for longer than dissatisfied customers.

In line with all the above definitions, loyalty to a brand is expressed due to a positive attitude, which makes a consumer repeatedly demand goods or services of a particular brand, or a limited number of brands within a suitably defined period of time (Dwivedi, 2015; Liu, Li, Mizerski & Soh, 2012; O'Keeffe et al., 2016). Consistent with this view, Leckie, Nyadzayo & Johnson (2016) share the opinion that consumers may possess a strong attitude, which may have a strong effect on their behaviour towards a particular brand. They refer to this phenomenon as brand insistence, and further describe brand insistence in terms of recognition, preference and insistence.

## Behavioural and Attitudinal Loyalty

Despite the large number of studies on brand loyalty, much of the research over the past three decades investigates consumer loyalty from two perspectives and so, broadly, there are two schools of thought underlining the definition of brand loyalty. These are behavioural loyalty and attitudinal loyalty (Dick & Basu, 1994; Ozuem, Patel, Howell & Lancaster, 2017)

The first marketing studies perceived customer loyalty in a behavioural way, measuring the concept as a behaviour involving repeat purchases of a particular product or service. This behaviour was evaluated either by the sequence in which goods and services are purchased, as a proportion of purchases, as an act of recommendation, as the scale of the relationship, its scope, or as a measure of several of these criteria combined (Hallowell, 1996; Homburg & Giering, 2001; Yi, 1990). Nam et al. (2011) confirmed the above-mentioned perception by stating that loyalty has traditionally been conceived of as a behavioural construct relating to intentions towards repeat purchase. Put simply, Nam et al. (2011) refer to behavioural loyalty as the frequency of repeat purchases, and repeat purchases may to a certain degree capture a consumer's loyalty towards his or her brand of interest.

Kuusik and Varblane (2009) identify three sub-segmented reasons for behaviourally loyal customers: those that are (i) forced to be loyal (e.g. by monopoly or high exit costs), (ii) loyal due to inertia, and (iii) functionally loyal. Oliver (1999) attaches the concept of inert loyalty to routine purchases, so a sense of satisfaction is not experienced and it becomes a task. From a marketing perspective, this would suggest that as long as there are no specific 'triggers' to compel behaviourally loyal customers to change providers, they will remain passively loyal (Roos, 1999). According to Liu, Wu and Hung (2007), even when presented with more attractive alternatives, consumers who have high inertia will be reluctant to change and this behaviour can be linked to a consumer's familiarity and a perception that frequenting a familiar service vendor requires less effort. They state that consumer inertia has greater influence on repeat purchase intentions, and they recommend that managers make efforts to develop consumer consumption inertia.

Day (1969) criticised this one-dimensional view as behaviourally centred, and therefore not particularly useful to distinguish true loyalty from 'spurious loyalty'. Since then, many researchers have recognised the need to add an attitudinal component to the behavioural one (Berné, Mu'gica & Yague, 2001; Dick, Mu'gica & Basu, 1994; Jacoby & Kyner, 1973; Oliver, 1997). Similarly, Day's criticism above was embraced by Uncles and Laurent (1997) who argued that by classifying these behavioural observations as a form of loyalty, there is a tendency to overlook customers who are emotionally attached to products and services. This can lead to overestimations of loyalty customer bases and the stability of portfolios (Crouch, Perdue, Timmermans & Uysal, 2004). Significantly, Dick and Basu (1994) contend that a favourable attitude and repeat purchase was ideal to define loyalty, by viewing loyalty as an attitude-behaviour relationship in their framework.

Attitudinal loyalty, on the other hand, can be defined as capturing the emotional and cognitive components of brand loyalty (Kumar & Shah, 2004; Ozuem, Thomas & Lancaster, 2016). Oliver (1999) aligns his description with this belief by defining loyalty as a deeply held commitment to rebuy or re-patronise preferred products or services consistently in future, despite situational influences and marketing efforts having the potential to cause switching behaviour. Brand commitment, therefore, is the pledging or binding of a person to his or her brand choice within a product class (Leckie et al., 2016). Chaudhuri and Holbrook (2001) treat brand commitment as synonymous with attitudinal loyalty. The issue of commitment is discussed in more detail in the next chapter.

Attitudinal loyalty represents a more long-term and emotional commitment to an organisation or brand (Bennett & Rundle-Thiele, 2002; Shankar et al., 2003; Ozuem et al., 2016), which is why attitudinal loyalty is referred to as 'emotional loyalty' and is regarded as being 'much stronger and longer lasting' (Hofmeyr & Rice, 2000). The idea has been compared with marriage (Albert & Merunka, 2013).

Consistent with the above, attitudinal loyalty refers to the psychological commitment that a consumer makes in the purchase act, such as intentions to purchase and recommend without necessarily taking repeat purchase behaviour into account (Jacoby, 1971; Ozuem et al., 2017). Jacoby and Kyner (1973) defended Jacoby's (1971) definition of brand loyalty. Their definition was expressed as a set of six necessary and collectively sufficient conditions. According to these authors, brand loyalty is: (1) biased (i.e. non-random), (2) a behavioural response (i.e. purchase), (3) expressed over time, (4) undertaken by some decision-making unit, (5) fulfilled with respect to one or more alternative brands out of a set of such brands, and (6) a function of psychological (decision-making, evaluative) processes. They stated that it is the evaluation process (the sixth condition) that makes an individual develop a commitment towards a brand. It is this notion of commitment, they argued, that provides an essential basis for differentiating brand loyalty from other forms of repeat purchasing behaviour.

Attitudinal loyalty is preferred to behavioural loyalty (Day, 1969; Dick & Basu, 1994; Appiah & Ozuem, 2017) for the following reasons. A behaviourally loyal customer may be spuriously loyal, that is, they might stay loyal to a brand, organisation or service provider until a better alternative in the marketplace is available (Dick &

Basu, 1994; Appiah, 2014). An attitudinally loyal customer, on the other hand, has some attachment or commitment to an organisation, service or brand, and is not easily swayed by a slightly more attractive alternative. Attitudinal loyalty not only indicates higher repurchase intent, but also resistance to counter-persuasion and adverse expert opinion. It is an indicator of a willingness to pay a price premium and to recommend the service provider or brand to others.

From the reasons established above, this study adopts the idea of attitudinal loyalty towards a brand or service provider and defines brand loyalty as the consumer's intention to visit or willingness to recommend a particular brand regardless of price change. The choice of attitudinal loyalty is emphasised by Shankar et al. (2003) who viewed attitudinal loyalty as similar to the type of affective or cognitive loyalty proposed by Oliver (1999). This represents a higher order or a long-term commitment of a customer to an organisation or brand, which cannot be inferred by merely observing customer repeat purchase behaviour (Lam et al., 2013; Appiah & Ozuem, 2017).

## Innovations and Market Disruptions

The ultimate causes of brand switching are market disruptions. Market disruptions are key happenings in a market which more often than not impede customer–brand relationships (Fournier, 1998; Stern, Thompson & Arnould, 1998; Christensen, 2013; Jung et al, 2017). Disruption is therefore a state where markets cease to operate in their usual routine, characteristically by steep and huge market declines.

This research focuses on disruptions that occur within product markets. As noted by McGrath (2011), the concept of 'market disruption' that occurs in a product market directly harkens to research in two significant areas (technology and innovation), which in recent time have attracted significant attention and development by firms placed in the Smartphone industry. Disruptions displace and alter how we think, behave, transact business, learn and go about our daily undertakings. This is echoed by Christensen (2013), who states that disruptions displace existing markets, industries and technology that develops something unique, more efficient and more worthwhile.

The theory of disruptive innovation introduced by Christensen (2013) provides clarification for the displacement of industry giants by lesser competitors, opening a channel for new entrants (Bower & Christensen, 1995; Christensen, 2013; Giovanisa & Athanasopouloub, 2018). Disruptive innovation creates a new market, apart from disrupting existing ones. The term is used in business and technology literature to describe innovations that improve products or services in ways that markets do not expect; first by generating a different set of consumers in the new market (Ozuem, Howell & Lancaster, 2008; Christensen, 2013; Giovanisa & Athanasopouloub, 2018), and later by lowering prices in the existing market.

According to McGrath (2011), the concept's explanatory power is derived from the belief that industry incumbents and new entrants rely on technological trajectories. Industry front-runners tend to lay more emphasis on and invest in sustaining innovations that constantly improve their leading products and increase their overall performance in attributes that are perceived as being important for their existing customer base. Over time, the performance increase achieved through sustaining innovations begins to overshoot the needs of the best customers who pay the most, whereas the new entrants' disruptive products become good enough to meet the needs of the dominant incumbents' customers.

Christensen (2013) identified a number of industries in which the pattern of disruption closely fits with his theory. These include retail, computers, hospitals and automobiles but there has been little research into how these disruptions impact upon and affect the perceived value of brands in disruptive times. There are different factors and determinants which affect consumers in switching from one product to another. The next section looks at two main switching behaviours for the purpose of this study.

## Brand Switching and Resistance

The function of identity, loyalty literature and its causal effects on brand switching proponents (BSP) in the context of Smartphone purchases is considered in this section. Contextually, the Smartphone was utilised as a relevant product category for this study mainly because it represents an industry where brand switching is most likely to occur due to the multiple alternatives and short inter-purchase frequency that define the setting for innovative disruptions (Campo et al., 2000; Goldsmith, 2000; Jung et al., 2017).

Switching is likely to happen at any time a customer is motivated to review available alternatives of the same product within the same marketplace due to a variation in competitive activity (Seiders & Tigert, 1997; Jung et al., 2017). Similarly, Hogan and Armstrong (2001) posited that brand switching is the process of substituting a more preferred product for an incumbent one from the same category in order to attain satisfaction. Sathish et al. (2011) indicated that brand switching is a consumer behaviour that depicts differences centred on consumers' satisfaction levels. Hence, brand switching is the process of being loyal to one product or service for a period of time but deciding to swap to another, due to dissatisfaction or a change in preferences. They further suggest that even if a consumer is loyal to a selected brand but subsequently establishes dissatisfaction, he/she may switch to a competing brand. Therefore, brand managers must consistently evaluate and redirect resources and capabilities into a product to ensure a strong position.

Losing a consumer is a serious setback for a firm as it has severe financial implications and also affects its market position, since reinvesting resources in attracting new consumers can create huge costs in advertising and promotions. Product characteristics are likely to affect exploratory tendencies such as BSPs and innovation in product contexts with a large number of alternatives and a short inter-purchase frequency (Jung et al., 2017). These characteristics include perceived risk, brand loyalty, perceived brand differentiation/similarity, hedonism (or pleasure) and strength of preference (Van Trijp et al., 1996). When consumers are extremely engaged with a product, their tendency to switch is likely to be lower (Sloot et al., 2005).

Consumers with high involvement with a product have 'a narrow latitude acceptance' (Sherif & Sherif, 1967; Giovanisa & Athanasopouloub, 2018). They remain doubtful about being persuaded toward other alternatives. On the same issue, Sloot et al. (2005) agree that loyal consumers are less likely to switch to another brand. Usually activities to persuade consumers to switch may be demonstrated in the form of sales promotions, typically as offers and discounts, that most often encourage switching across various product categories (Kahn & Louie, 1990).

Perceived risk is an indicator that consumers are worried about potential losses resulting from their purchases (Mitchell, 1999; Jung et al., 2017). High perceived risk results in avoidance tendencies and behaviours (e.g. commitment to a brand, repeat purchase behaviour) as consumers are 'more often motivated to avoid mistakes than to maximise utility in purchasing' (Mitchell, 1999, p. 163). Yet perceived similarity amongst brands in the product category reflects a high tendency of consumers possibly to switch.

Hedonism encourages switching within specific categories of products (Van Trijp et al., 1996). Hedonism is related to enjoyment or pleasure that a consumer derives from a selected product (Griffin et al., 2000), as consumers are innately inspired by products that provide (hedonic) feelings (Hirschman & Holbrook, 1982; Giovanisa & Athanasopouloub, 2018). They are consequently expected to trigger repeat purchase intentions or to elicit switching tendencies (Van Trijp et al., 1996).

## Brand Switching as Functional Utility Maximisation

Switching occurs when a customer is motivated to review their available alternatives in the marketplace due to a change in competitive activities in the market (Seiders & Tigerts, 1997; Appiah & Ozuem, 2017). Economists view consumer choices as a means to achieve maximisation of functional utility (Appiah, 2014; McFadden, 1986). In addition, a common practice among marketing researchers is to model consumer brand switching as choices based on product attributes and the marketing mix (Guadagni & Little, 1983).

However, according to the original text on multi-attribute utility theory (Lancaster, 1966), consumer utility includes not only a brand's functional, but also its socio-psychological, attributes. Furthermore, McFadden (1986, p. 284), contends that it is necessary to incorporate psychometric data in choice models because these factors also shape the utility function.

Following existing models of brand choice, 'relative perceived value' is defined as the extent to which the utilitarian value of the functional benefits of a branded offering exceeds those of another alternative in the same product category (Lam et al., 2010; 2013). When customers experience difficulty in generating positive information about their choice, they may infer that the amount of positive information is rather limited and may reverse their attitude towards the chosen brand (Wänke, Bohner & Jurkowitsch, 1997; Jung et al., 2017). With its relevance to functional utility, relative perceived value influences switching behaviour as functional utility maximisation. In line with recent developments in choice modelling, social identity theory suggests that brand switching also serves socio-psychological purposes besides functional utility maximisation (Rao et al., 2000; Tajfel & Turner, 1979). This theory posits that people derive their identity from affiliations with social groups. They value such membership and distinguish themselves from those who do not share such affiliations, forming the in-group and the out-group. According to Lam et al. (2010), when a social identity is threatened, that is, negatively perceived, in-group members will likely respond by resorting to three basic strategies: social mobility, social creativity, and social change. Social mobility refers to a person's attempt to leave or dissociate him/herself from the group, and moving from a lower-status group to a higher status one is an example (ibid.). Social creativity describes a person's attempt to 'seek positive distinctiveness for the in-group by redefining or altering the elements of the comparative situation' (Tajfel & Turner, 1979, p. 43). For example, a business school that does not compare favourably with other schools in overall evaluation may seek out specific dimensions of comparison that grant it superiority over these other schools (Elsbach & Kramer, 1996).

Finally, social change refers to direct competition with the out-group to retrieve higher status. In the marketing context, social change can be initiated either by competitors or by customers who identify with a brand. Market disruptions that are externally caused by competitors (e.g. radically innovative brands) can be viewed as attempts to initiate social change between competitors to vie for favour amongst customers. When a radically new brand is introduced, some customers may perceive it as having a more attractive identity than the incumbent's identity.

From the customer's point of view, brand identifiers sometimes proactively generate negative word-of-mouth about brands that they do not identify with, especially after they are exposed to comparative advertising. From the identity theory perspective, the researcher proposes that customers may switch to a new brand for self-enhancement purposes to maximise socio-psychological utility (e.g. symbolic benefits) rather than functional utility (i.e. functional benefits). In support of the social mobility argument, Rao, Davis and Ward (2000) insist that firms migrate from the National Association of Securities Dealers Automated Quotations (NASDAQ) stock market to the New York Stock Exchange (NYSE) to preserve a positive identity.

## CONCLUSION AND MANAGERIAL IMPLICATIONS

In the marketing context, the narrative analysis of marketing relationships by Stern, Thomson and Arnold (1998) implies that customers may switch to a brand they used to dislike by revising their view of the brand's identity and reference group. Research into cultural assimilation also reports that immigrants swap their cultural identities in consumption as they assimilate into the mainstream culture (Oswald, 1999). Similarly, Chaplin and Roedder (2005) suggest that as children mature into adolescents, their self-concept becomes more sophisticated and so do their connections with brands. When the boundary between the in-group and the out-group is impermeable and changing group membership is not realistic, social mobility is not a viable strategy to cope with identity threats. For example, people rarely change their political affiliation, as social identity theory suggests that under such circumstances people will engage in social creativity (Tajfel & Turner, 1979). Tajfel and Turner (1979, p. 43) posit that social creativity can take multiple forms, such as (1) comparing the in-group with the out-group based on some new dimensions, (2) changing the values assigned to the attributes of the group such that previously negative comparisons are now cast in a positive light, and (3) avoiding using the high-status out-group as a comparative frame of reference. In other words, social creativity is a form of identity-based comparison that is based on in-group biases, and defined as a strong belief in the superiority of the group with which a person identifies. It is a form of prejudice against the non-identified group. Brewer (1979) posits that such in-group biases are both cognitive and motivational because these biases motivate in-group members (e.g. brand identifiers) to attend only to elements that the in-group will evaluate more positively than the out-group.

Managerial implications based on findings from this study indicate that innovative brands, such as Smartphones, are susceptible to disruption in their initial stages. This drives huge interest that may interrupt consumer–brand relationships, yet with time this interest may become fragile (Fournier, 1998). Brand managers must allocate investment to build stronger customer–brand identification/relationship at the maturity stage of the product life cycle to resist switching during disruptions. First, in order to extend the maturity stage of a brand, brand managers should invest in activities that enhance consumers' perceived quality and self–brand congruity. Smartphone manufacturers must commit investment to symbolic drivers such as self–brand congruity at maturity stages of the brand life cycle rather than instrumental drivers such as quality (functional utility). This strategy is effective as brand loyalty and resilience to market disruptions are sustained.

## REFERENCES

Aaker, D. A. (1991). *Managing Brand Equity*. New York: The Free Press.

Aaker, D. A. (1995). *Building Strong Brands*. New York: The Free Press.

Aaker, D. A. (1996). Measuring Brand Equity across Products and Markets. *California Management Review*, *38*(3), 102–120. doi:10.2307/41165845

Aaker, D. A. (1996). *Building Strong Brands*. New York: The Free Press.

Aaker, D. A. (2009). *Managing Brand Equity*. Simon and Schuster.

Aaker, J. (1997). Dimensions of Brand Personality. *JMR, Journal of Marketing Research*, *34*(3), 347–356. doi:10.2307/3151897

Agarwal, M. K., & Rao, V. R. (1996). An empirical comparison of consumer-based measures of brand equity. *Marketing Letters*, *7*(3), 237–247. doi:10.1007/BF00435740

Aggarwal, P. (2004). The Effects of Brand Relationship Norms on Consumer Attitudes and Behaviour. *The Journal of Consumer Research*, *31*(1), 87–101. doi:10.1086/383426

Ahearne, M., Bhattacharya, C. B., & Gruen, T. (2005). Antecedents and Consequences of Customer–Company identification: Expanding the Role of Relationship Marketing. *The Journal of Applied Psychology*, *90*(3), 574–585. doi:10.1037/0021-9010.90.3.574 PMID:15910151

Ailawadi, K. L., Scott, A. N., & Karen, G. (2001). Pursuing the Value Conscious Consumer: Store Brands Versus National Brand Promotions. *Journal of Marketing*, *65*(1), 71–89. doi:10.1509/jmkg.65.1.71.18132

Albert, N., & Merunka, D. (2013). The Role of Brand Love in Consumer-Brand Relationships. *Journal of Consumer Marketing*, *30*(3), 258–266. doi:10.1108/07363761311328928

Appiah, D. (2014). *Building Brand Loyalty: Identity Theory Perspective. Seventh International Scientific Conference*. Institute of Economic Research, Prishtine, Albania.

Appiah, D., & Ozuem, W. (2017). Issues and the Importance of Branding, Brand Personality and Symbolic Meaning of Brands to the Consumer. In Global Information Diffusion and Management in Contemporary Society. IGI Global.

Appiah, D., Ozuem, W., & Howell, E. K. (2016). Towards a Sustainable Brand Loyalty*: Attitudinal Loyalty Perspective. Eighteenth Annual International Conference*. Global Business and Technology Association.

Appiah, D., Ozuem, W., & Howell, K. E. (2017). *Brand Switching in the Smartphone Industry: A Preliminary Study. Global Business and Technology Association Conference*, Vienna, Austria.

Arnett, D. B., German, S. D., & Hunt, S. D. (2003). The Identity salience Model of Relationship Marketing success: The case of Non-profit Marketing. *Journal of Marketing*, *67*(4), 89–105. doi:10.1509/jmkg.67.2.89.18614

Arnold, D. (1992). *The handbook of brand management*. Century Business. The Economist Books.

Aron, A., Aron, E. N., & Smollan, D. (1992). Inclusion of Other in the Self–Scale and the Structure of Interpersonal Closeness. *Journal of Personality and Social Psychology*, *63*(4), 596–61. doi:10.1037/0022-3514.63.4.596

Ashok, K., Dillon, W. R., & Yuan, S. (2002). Extending Discrete Choice Models to Incorporate Attitudinal and Other Latent Variables. *JMR, Journal of Marketing Research*, *39*(2), 31–46. doi:10.1509/jmkr.39.1.31.18937

Azize, S., Hakan, K., & Cemal, Z. (2013). Creating Commitment, Trust and Satisfaction for a Brand: What is the Role of Switching Costs in Mobile Phone Market? *Procedia: Social and Behavioral Sciences*, *99*, 496–502. doi:10.1016/j.sbspro.2013.10.518

Barnes, S. J., & Scornavacca, E. (2004). Mobile Marketing: The Role of Permission and Acceptance. *International Journal of Mobile Communications*, *2*(2), 128–139. doi:10.1504/IJMC.2004.004663

Batra, R., Lehmann, D. R., & Singh, D. (1993). The Brand Personality Component of Brand Goodwill: Some Antecedents and Consequences. In Brand Equity and Advertising. Hillsdale: Lawrence Erlbaum Associates.

Belk, R. W. (1988). Possessions and the Extended Self. *The Journal of Consumer Research, 15*(9), 139–168. doi:10.1086/209154

Berne´, C., Mu'gica, J. M., & Yague, M. J. (2001). The Effect of Variety-Seeking on Customer Retention in Services. *Journal of Retailing and Consumer Services, 8*(6), 335–345. doi:10.1016/S0969-6989(01)00002-9

Berry, L. L. (2000). Cultivating Service Brand Equity. *Journal of the Academy of Marketing Science, 28*(1), 128–137. doi:10.1177/0092070300281012

Bharadwaj, G. B., Tuli, R. K., & Bonfrer, A. (2011). The Impact of Brand Equity on Shareholder Wealth. *Journal of Marketing, 75*(9), 88–104. doi:10.1509/jmkg.75.5.88

Bhat, S., & Srinivas, K. R. (1998). Symbolic And Functional Positioning Of Brands. *Journal of Consumer Marketing, 15*(1), 32–43. doi:10.1108/07363769810202664

Bhattacharya, C. B., & Lordish, L. (2000). *Towards a System for Monitoring Brand Health from Store Scanner Data.* MSI working Paper, Report No. 00-111.

Bhattacharya, C. B., Rao, H., & Glynn, M. A. (1995). Understanding the bond of identification: An investigation of its correlates among art museum. *Journal of Marketing, 59*(4), 46. doi:10.2307/1252327

Bhattacharya, C. B., & Sanker, S. (2003). Consumer-Company Identification: A Framework for Understanding Consumers' Relationship with Companies. *Journal of Marketing, 67*(4), 76–88. doi:10.1509/jmkg.67.2.76.18609

Biel A. L, (1993). Converting Image into Equity. In *Brand Equity and Advertising: Advertising's Role in Building Strong Brands.* Hillsdale: Lawrence Erlbaum Associates.

Bower, J. L., & Christensen, C. M. (1995). Disruptive Technologies: Catching the Wave. *Harvard Business Review,* (2-3), 43-53.

Brakus, J. J., Bernd, H. S., & Shi, Z. (2008). Experiential Attribute and Consumer Judgments. In *Handbook on Brand and Experience Management.* Cheltenham, UK: Edward Elgar Publisher. doi:10.4337/9781848446151.00022

Brakus, J. J., Bernd, H. S., & Zarantonello, L. (2009). Brand Experience: What Is It? How Is It Measured? Does It Affect Loyalty? *Journal of Marketing, 73*(3), 52–68. doi:10.1509/jmkg.73.3.52

Brewer, M. B. (1979). In group Bias in the Minimal Intergroup Situation: A Cognitive–Motivational Analysis. *Psychological Bulletin, 86*(2), 307–324. doi:10.1037/0033-2909.86.2.307

Brodie, R. J., Ilic, A., Juric, B., & Hollebeek, L. (2013). Consumer Engagement in a Virtual Brand Community: An exploratory Analysis. *Journal of Business Research*, *66*(1), 105–114. doi:10.1016/j.jbusres.2011.07.029

Campo, K., Gijsbrechts, E., & Nisol, P. (2000). Towards understanding consumer Response to Stock outs. *Journal of Retailing*, *76*(2), 219–242. doi:10.1016/S0022-4359(00)00026-9

Carpenter, G. S., Glazer, R., & Nakamoto, K. (1997). *Reading on Market-Driving Strategies: Towards a New Theory of Competitive Advantage*. Addison Wesley.

Cecere, G., Corrocher, N., & Battaglia, R. D. (2015). Innovation and Competition in the Smartphone Industry: Is there a Dominant Design? *Journal of Telecommunications Policy,* (39), 162-175.

Chaplin, L. N., & Roedder, D. J. (2005). The Development of Self-Brand Connections in Children and Adolescents. *The Journal of Consumer Research*, *32*(1), 119–129. doi:10.1086/426622

Chaudhuri, A., & Holbrook, M. B. (2001). The Chain of Effects From Brand Trust And Brand Affect To Brand Performance: The Role Of Brand Loyalty. *Journal of Marketing*, *65*(2), 81–93. doi:10.1509/jmkg.65.2.81.18255

Chernev, A., Hamilton, R., & Gal, D. (2011). Competing for Consumer Identity: Limits to Self-Expression and the Perils of Lifestyle Branding. *Journal of Marketing*, *75*(3), 66–82. doi:10.1509/jmkg.75.3.66

Christensen, C. M. (2013). *The Innovators Dilema: When New Technologies Cause Great Firms to Fail*. Boston: Harvard Business School Press.

Cobb-Walgren, C. J., Ruble, C. A., & Donthu, N. (1995). Brand Equity, Brand Preference, and Purchase Intent. *Journal of Advertising*, *24*(3), 2540. doi:10.1080/00913367.1995.10673481

Crouch, G. I., Perdue, R. R., Timmermans, H. J. P., & Uysal, M. (2004). *Consumer Psychology of Tourism, Hospitality and Leisure*. Oxon, UK: CABI. doi:10.1079/9780851997490.0000

Da Silveira, C., Lages, C., & Simões, C. (2013). Reconceptualizing brand identity in a dynamic environment. *Journal of Business Research*, *66*(1), 28–36. doi:10.1016/j.jbusres.2011.07.020

Davies, J. B., & Ward, P. (2005). Exploring the Connections between Visual Merchandising and Retail Branding. An Application of Facet Theory. *International Journal of Retail & Distribution Management, 33*(7), 505–513. doi:10.1108/09590550510605578

Day, G. S. (1969). A Two-Dimensional Concept of Brand Loyalty. *Journal of Advertising Research, 9*, 29–35.

de Chernatony, L., & Dall'Olmo Riley, F. (1998). Defining Brand: Beyond the Literature with Expert Opinion. *Journal of Marketing Management, 14*(5), 417–443. doi:10.1362/026725798784867798

de Chernatony, L., & MacDonnald, M. (1992). *Creating Powerful Brands*. Oxford, UK: Heinermann and Butterworth.

de Chernatony, L., & McWilliam, G. (1990). Appreciating Brands as Assets through using a Two-Dimensional Model. *International Journal of Advertising, 9*(2), 111–119. doi:10.1080/02650487.1990.11107137

Dell Rio, A. B., Vazquez, R., & Iglesias, V. (2001). The Effects of Brand Associations on Consumer Response. *Journal of Consumer Marketing, 18*(5), 410–425. doi:10.1108/07363760110398808

Dick, A., & Basu, K. (1994). Customer Loyalty: Towards an Integrated Conceptual Framework. *Journal of the Academy of Marketing Science, 22*(2), 99–113. doi:10.1177/0092070394222001

Dickinson, J. E., Ghali, K., Cherrett, T., Speed, C., Davies, N., & Norgate, S. (2014). Tourism and the smartphone app: Capabilities, emerging practice and scope in the travel domain. *Current Issues in Tourism, 17*(1), 84–101. doi:10.1080/13683500.2012.718323

Dimitriades, Z. S. (2006). Customer Satisfaction, Loyalty and commitment in service organisations: Some evidence from Greece. *Management Research News, 29*(12), 782–800. doi:10.1108/01409170610717817

Dion, D., & Arnould, E. (2016). Persona-fied Brands: Managing Branded Persons through Persona. *Journal of Marketing Management, 32*(1-2), 121–148. doi:10.1080/0267257X.2015.1096818

Dolich, I. J. (1969). Congruence Relationships between Self Images and Product Brands. *JMR, Journal of Marketing Research, 6*(1), 80–84. doi:10.2307/3150001

Doyle, P. (1994). *Marketing Management and Strategy*. Englewood Cliffs, NJ: Prentice-Hall.

Dwivedi, A. (2015). A higher-order model of consumer brand engagement and its impact on loyalty intentions. *Journal of Retailing and Consumer Services, 24*, 100–109. doi:10.1016/j.jretconser.2015.02.007

Ebrahim, R., Ghoneim, A., Irani, Z., & Fan, Y. (2016). A Brand Preference and Repurchase Intention Model: The Role of Consumer Experience. *Journal of Marketing Management, 32*(13-14), 13–14, 1230–1259. doi:10.1080/0267257X.2016.1150322

Ebrahim, R., Ghoneim, A., Irani, Z., & Fan, Y. (2016). A brand preference and repurchase intention model: The role of consumer experience. *Journal of Marketing Management, 32*(13-14), 13–14, 1230–1259. doi:10.1080/0267257X.2016.1150322

Edell, J. A., & Burke, M. C. (1987). The power of feelings in understanding advertising effects. *The Journal of Consumer Research, 14*(3), 421–433. doi:10.1086/209124

Elliott, R., & Wattanasuwan, K. (1998). Brand as Symbolic Resources for the Construction of Identity. *International Journal of Advertising, 17*(2), 131–144. doi:10.1080/02650487.1998.11104712

Elsbach, K. D., & Kramer, M. K. (1996). Members' Responses to Organizational Identity Threats: Encountering and Countering the Business Week Rankings. *Administrative Science Quarterly, 41*(3), 442–76.

Escalas, J. E. (2004). Narrative Processing: Building Consumer Connections to Brands. *Journal of Consumer Psychology, 14*(1-2), 168–180. doi:10.120715327663jcp1401&2_19

Escalas, J. E., & Bettman, J. R. (2003). You Are What You Eat: The Influence of Reference Groups on Consumers' Connections to Brands. *Journal of Consumer Psychology, 13*(3), 339–348. doi:10.1207/S15327663JCP1303_14

Escalas, J. E., & Bettman, J. R. (2005). SelfConstrual, Reference Groups, and Brand Meaning. *The Journal of Consumer Research, 32*(12), 378–389. doi:10.1086/497549

Farhana, M. (2014). Implication of Brand Identity Facets on Marketing Communication of Lifestyle Magazine: Case Study of a Swedish Brand. *Journal of Applied Economics and Business Research., 4*(1), 23–24.

Farquhar, P. H. (1989). Managing brand equity. *Marketing Research., 1*(3), 24–33.

Felix, R. (2015). *The state of the Global Smartphone Market. Statista Infographics.* Retrieved from: https://www.statista.com/charts/2512/smartphone-market-share

Fournier, S. (1998). Consumers and Their Brands: Developing Relationship Theory in Consumer Research. *The Journal of Consumer Research*, *24*(3), 343–373. doi:10.1086/209515

Gartner. (2016). *Worldwide Smartphone grew 9.7 percent in Fourth Quarter of 2015*. Retrieved from: http://www.Gartner.com/newsroom

Giovanisa, A. N., & Athanasopouloub, P. (2018). Consumer-Brand Relationships and Brand Loyalty in Technology-Mediated Services. *Journal of Retailing and Consumer Services*, *40*(1), 287–294. doi:10.1016/j.jretconser.2017.03.003

Goldsmith, R. E. (2000). Characteristics of the Heavy User of Fashionable Clothing. *Journal of Marketing Theory and Practice*, *8*(4), 21–28. doi:10.1080/10696679.2000.11501877

Gremler, D. D., & Brown, S. W. (1996). Service Loyalty; its Nature, Importance and Implications. In B. Edvardsson, S. W. Brown, R. Johnston, & E. Scheuing (Eds.), *QUIS V: Advancing Service Quality: A Global Perspective*. New York, NY: ISQA.

Griffin, M., Babin, B. J., & Modianos, D. (2000). Shopping Values of Russian Consumers: The Impact of Habituation in a Developing Economy. *Journal of Retailing*, *76*(1), 33–52. doi:10.1016/S0022-4359(99)00025-1

Guadagni, P. M., & Little, J. D. C. (1983). A Logit Model of Brand Choice Calibrated on Scanner Data: A Logit Model of Brand Choice Calibrated on Scanner Data. *Journal of Marine Science*, *2*(3), 203–238. doi:10.1287/mksc.2.3.203

Hallowell, R. (1996). The Relationships of Customer Satisfaction, Customer Loyalty, and Profitability: An Empirical Study. *International Journal of Service Industry Management*, *7*(4), 27–42. doi:10.1108/09564239610129931

Han, Y. J., Joseph, C. N., & Drèze, X. (2010). Signaling Status with Luxury Goods: The Role of Brand Prominence. *Journal of Marketing*, *74*(4), 15–30. doi:10.1509/jmkg.74.4.15

Hansen, L. (2003). Service Layer Essential for Future Success. *Ericsson Mobility World*. Available at: http://www.ericsson.com

Helgeson, J. G., & Supphellen, M. (2004). A Conceptual and Measurement Comparison of Self-Congruity and Brand Personality. *International Journal of Market Research*, *46*(2), 205–233. doi:10.1177/147078530404600201

Hirschman, E. C., & Holbrook, M. B. (1982). Hedonic consumption: Emerging Concepts, Methods and Propositions. *Journal of Marketing*, *46*(3), 92–101. doi:10.2307/1251707

Hofmeyr, J., & Rice, B. (2000). *Commitment-Led Marketing*. Chichester, UK: Wiley.

Hogan, E. J., & Armstrong, G. (2001). Toward a Resource Based Theory of Business Exchange Relationships: The Role of Relational Asset Value. *Journal of Business-To-Business Marketing*, *8*(4), 3–28. doi:10.1300/J033v08n04_02

Holbrook, M. B., & Corfman, K. P. (1985). Quality and Value in the Consumption Experience: Phaedrus Rides Again. In C. V. S. How, J. J. Merchandise, & J. C. Olson (Eds.), *Perceived Quality*. Lanham, MD: Lexington Books.

Holbrook, M. B., & Hirschman, E. C. (1982). The Experiential Aspects of Consumption: Consumer Fantasies, Feelings, and Fun. *The Journal of Consumer Research*, *9*(2), 132–140. doi:10.1086/208906

Hollebeek, L. D., Glynn, M. S., & Brodie, R. J. (2014). Consumer Brand Engagement in Social Media: Conceptualization, Scale Development and Validation. *Journal of Interactive Marketing*, *28*(2), 149–165. doi:10.1016/j.intmar.2013.12.002

Homburg, C., & Giering, A. (2001). Personal Characteristics as Moderators of the Relationship between Customer Satisfaction and Loyalty— an Empirical Analysis. *Journal of Psychology and Marketing*, *18*(1), 43–66. doi:10.1002/1520-6793(200101)18:1<43::AID-MAR3>3.0.CO;2-I

Hoyer, W. D., & MacInnis, D. J. (1997). *Consumer Behaviour*. Boston: Houghton Mifflin Publishers.

Hsu, L. C., & Liou, D. K. (2017). Maintaining Customer-Brand Relationships in the Mobile Industry: The Mediation Effects of Brand Relationship Benefits and Quality. *International Journal of Mobile Communications*, *15*(4), 388. doi:10.1504/IJMC.2017.084861

Hutton, J. G. (1997). A Study of Brand Equity in an Organisational-Buying Context. *Journal of Product and Brand Management*, *6*(6), 428–439. doi:10.1108/10610429710190478

Itami, H., & Roehl, W. T. (1987). Mobilizing Invisible. Assets, MA: Harvard University Press.

Jacoby, J. (1971). A Model of Multi-Brand Loyalty. *Journal of Advertising Research*, *11*(3), 25–31.

Jacoby, J., & Kyner, D. B. (1973). Brand Loyalty vs. Repeat Purchasing Behaviour. *JMR, Journal of Marketing Research*, *10*(1), 1–9. doi:10.2307/3149402

Jeong, S. H., Kim, H. J., Yum, J. Y., & Hwang, Y. R. (2016). What Type of Content are Smartphone Users Addicted to? SNS vs Games. *Journal of Computers in Human Behavior, 54,* 10–17. doi:10.1016/j.chb.2015.07.035

Jones, S. (2002). *3G Launch Strategies, Early Adopters, Why & How to make them yours.* Tarifica report.

Jung, J., Hun, H., & Oh, M. (2017). Travellers Switching Behaviour in the Airline Industry from the Perspective of the Push-Pull-Mooring Framework. *Journal of Torurism Management., 59,* 139–153. doi:10.1016/j.tourman.2016.07.018

Kahn, B. E., & Louie, T. A. (1990). Effects of Retraction of Price Promotions on Brand Choice Behaviour for Variety-Seeking and Last-purchase Loyal Consumers. *JMR, Journal of Marketing Research, 27*(3), 279–289. doi:10.2307/3172586

Kapferer, J. N. (2001). *Reinventing the Brand: Can Top Brands Survive the New Market Realitie?* London: Kogan Page.

Keller, K. L. (1993). Conceptualizing, Measuring and Managing Customer-based Brand Equity. *Journal of Marketing, 57*(1), 1–22. doi:10.2307/1252054

Keller, K. L. (2001). Building Customer-Based Brand Equity. *Journal of Marketing Management, 10*(2), 16–26.

Keller, K. L. (2008). *Strategic Brand Management: Building, Measuring, and Managing Brand Equity* (3rd ed.). Upper Saddle River, NJ: Pearson Education, Inc.

Keller, K. L., & Lehmann, D. R. (2006). Brands and Branding: Research Findings and Future Priorities. *Journal of Marine Science, 25*(6), 740–759. doi:10.1287/mksc.1050.0153

Kerlinger, F. N., & Lee, H. B. (2000). Foundations of Behavioural Research (4th ed.). Holt, NY: Harcourt College Publishers.

Kim, C. K., Han, D. C., & Park, S. B. (2001). The Effect of Brand Personality and Brand Identification on Brand Loyalty: Applying the Theory of Social Identification. *The Japanese Psychological Research, 43*(4), 195–206. doi:10.1111/1468-5884.00177

Kim, D., Nam, J. K., Oh, J. S., & Kang, M. C. (2016). A Latent Profile Analysis of the Interplay between PC and Smartphone in Problematic Internet Use. *Journal of Computers in Human Behavior, 56,* 360–368. doi:10.1016/j.chb.2015.11.009

Kleine, S. S., Kleine, R. E. III, & Allen, C. T. (1995). How is a Possession 'Me' or 'Not Me'? Characterizing Types and Antecedents of Material Possession Attachment. *The Journal of Consumer Research, 22*(12), 327–343. doi:10.1086/209454

Kottler, P., & Amtrong, G. (1994). *Principles of Marketing.* Prentice Hall.

Kressman, F., Sirgy, M. J., Hermmann, A., Hubber, F., Hubber, S., & Lee, D. J. (2006). Direct and Indirect Effects of Self-Image Congruence on Brand Loyalty. *Journal of Business Research, 59*(9), 955–964. doi:10.1016/j.jbusres.2006.06.001

Krohmer, H., Malär, L., & Nyffenegger, B. (2007). The Fit between Brand Personality and Consumer's Self: The Importance of Self-Congruence for Brand Performance. *AMA Winter Educators' Conference Proceedings.*

Kumar, V., & Shah, D. (2004). Building and Sustaining Profitable Customer Loyalty for 21st century. *Journal of Retailing, 80*(4), 317–330. doi:10.1016/j.jretai.2004.10.007

Kuusik, A., & Varblane, U. (2009). How to Avoid Customers Leaving: The Case of the Estonian Telecommunication Industry. *Baltic Journal of Management, 4*(1), 66–79. doi:10.1108/17465260910930458

Lam, S. K., Ahearn, M., Hu, Y., & Schillewaert, N. (2010). Resistance to Brand Switching When a Radically New Brand Is Introduced: A Social Identity Theory Perspective. *Journal of Marketing, 74*(6), 128–146. doi:10.1509/jmkg.74.6.128

Lam, S. K., Ahearne, M., Mullins, R., Hayati, B., & Schillewaert, N. (2013). Exploring the Dynamics of Antecedents to Consumer–Brand Identification with a New Brand. *Journal of the Academy of Marketing Science, 41*(2), 243–252. doi:10.100711747-012-0301-x

Lancaster, K. J. (1966). A New Approach to Consumer Theory. *Journal of Political Economy, 74*(2), 132–157. doi:10.1086/259131

Leckie, C., Munyaradzi, W. N., & Johnson, L. W. (2016). Antecedents of Consumer Brand Engagement and Brand Loyalty. *Journal of Marketing Management, 32*(5-6), 5–6, 558–578. doi:10.1080/0267257X.2015.1131735

Lee, J. W. (2009). Relationship between Consumer Personality and Brand Personality as Self-Concept: From the Case of Korean Automobile Brands. *Academy of Marketing Studies Journal, 13*(1), 25–44.

Ligas, M., & Cotte, J. (1999). The Process of Negotiating Brand Meaning: A Symbolic Interactionist Perspective. *Advances in Consumer Research. Association for Consumer Research (U. S.), 26*(1), 609–614.

Liu, F., Li, J., Mizerski, D., & Soh, H. (2012). Self-congruity, brand attitude, and brand loyalty: A study on luxury brands. *European Journal of Marketing, 46*(7/8), 922–937. doi:10.1108/03090561211230098

Liu, T. C., Wu, L. W., & Hung, C. T. (2007). The Effects of Inertia and Switching Barriers on Satisfaction-Retention Relationship: A Case of Financial Service Industries. *Journal of Management*, *24*, 671–687.

Lury, C. (2004). *Brands: The Logos of the Global Economy*. London, New York: Routledge.

Malär, L., Krohmer, H., Hoyer, W. D., & Nyffenegger, B. (2011). Emotional Brand Attachment and Brand Personality: The Relative Importance of the Actual and the Ideal Self. *Journal of Marketing*, *75*(4), 35–52. doi:10.1509/jmkg.75.4.35

Mano, H., & Oliver, R. L. (1993). Assessing the Dimensionality and Structure of the Consumption Experience: Evaluation, Feeling, and Satisfaction. *The Journal of Consumer Research*, *20*(3), 451–466. doi:10.1086/209361

Massoud, S., & Gupta, O. K. (2003). Consumer perception and attitude toward mobile communication. *International Journal of Mobile Communications*, *1*(4), 390–408. doi:10.1504/IJMC.2003.003993

McCracken, G. (1988). *The Long Interview*. London: Sage. doi:10.4135/9781412986229

McFadden, D. (1986). The Choice Theory Approach to Market Research. *Journal of Marine Science*, *5*(4), 275–297. doi:10.1287/mksc.5.4.275

McGrath, R. G. (2011, January). When your Business Model is in Trouble. *Harvard Business Review*, 96–98.

Meenaghan, T. (1995). The Role of Advertising in Brand Image Development. *Journal of Product and Brand Management*, *4*(4), 23–34. doi:10.1108/10610429510097672

Merz, M. A., Yi, H., & Vargo, S. L. (2009). The Evolving Brand Logic: A Service-Dominant Logic Perspective. *Journal of the Academy of Marketing Science*, *37*(3), 328–344. doi:10.100711747-009-0143-3

Mintel Group. (2017). *Smartphone Purchasing Process*. London: Author.

Mitchell, R., Hutchinson, K., Quinn, B., and Gilmore, A. (2015). A framework for SME retail branding. *Journal of Marketing Management*, *31*(17-18), 1818-1850

Mitchell, V.-W. (1999). Consumer Perceived Risk: Conceptualisations and Models. *European Journal of Marketing*, *33*(1/2), 163–195. doi:10.1108/03090569910249229

Mollerup, P. (1997). *Marks of Excellence: The History and Taxonomy of Trademarks*. London: Phaidon.

Moon, H., & Sprott, E. D. (2016). Ingredient Branding for a Luxury Brand: The Role of Brand and Product Fit. *Journal of Business Research*, *69*(4), 5768–5774. doi:10.1016/j.jbusres.2016.04.173

Muniz, A. M. Jnr, & O'Guinn, T. C. (2001). Brand Community. *The Journal of Consumer Research*, *27*(4), 412–432. doi:10.1086/319618

Murphy, J. (1990). *Brand Strategy*. Cambridge: Director Books.

Murphy, J. (1992). What is Branding? In J. Murphy (Ed.), *Branding, a key marketing tool* (pp. 1–12). London: Macmillan. doi:10.1007/978-1-349-12628-6_1

Nah, F. F.-H., Zhao, F., & Zhu, W. (2003). Factors influencing Users' Adoption of Mobile Computing. In J. Mariga (Ed.), *Managing E-commerce and Mobile Computing Technologies Book*. Hershey, PA: Idea Group Inc.

Nam, J., Ekinci, Y., & Whyatt, G. (2011). Brand Equity, Brand Loyalty and Consumer Satisfaction. *Annals of Tourism Research*, *38*(3), 1009–1030. doi:10.1016/j.annals.2011.01.015

Norazah, M. S. (2013). Students' dependence on smart phones: The influence of social needs, social influences and convenience. *Campus-Wide Information Systems*, *30*(2), 124–134. doi:10.1108/10650741311306309

O'Keeffe, A., Ozuem, W., & Lancaster, G. (2016). Leadership Marketing: An Exploratory Study. *Journal of Strategic Marketing*, *24*(5), 418–443. doi:10.1080/0965254X.2014.1001867

Oliver, R. (1980). A cognitive Model of The Antecedents and Consequences of Satisfaction Decisions. *JMR, Journal of Marketing Research*, *17*(4), 460–469. doi:10.2307/3150499

Oliver, R. L. (1997). *Satisfaction: A Behavioural Perspective on the Consumer*. New York: Irwin/McGraw-Hill.

Oliver, R. L. (1999). Whence Consumer Loyalty? *Journal of Marketing*, *63*(10), 33–44. doi:10.2307/1252099

Orth, U. R., & De Marchi, R. (2007). Understanding The Relationships Between Functional, Symbolic, And Experiential Brand Beliefs, Product Experiential Attributes, And Product Schema Advertising-Trial Interactions Revisited. *Journal of Marketing Theory and Practice*, *15*(3), 219–233. doi:10.2753/MTP1069-6679150303

Oswald, L. R. (1999). Culture Swapping: Consumption and the Ethnogenesis of Middle-Class Haitan Immigrants. *The Journal of Consumer Research, 25*(3), 303–318. doi:10.1086/209541

Ozuem, W., Howell, K. E., & Lancaster, G. (2008). Communicating in the New Interactive Marketplace. *European Journal of Marketing, 42*(9/10), 1059–1083. doi:10.1108/03090560810891145

Ozuem, W., Thomas, T., & Lancaster, G. (2016). The Influence of Customer Loyalty on Small Island Economies: An empirical and Exploratory Study. *Journal of Strategic Marketing, 24*(6), 447–469. doi:10.1080/0965254X.2015.1011205

Park, C. S., & Srinivasan, V. (1994). A Survey-Based Method for Measuring and Understanding Brand Equity and Its Extendibility. *JMR, Journal of Marketing Research, 31*(2), 271–288. doi:10.2307/3152199

Park, C. W., Eisingerich, A. B., & Park, J. W. (2013). Attachment– Aversion (AA) Model of Customer–Brand Relationships. *Journal of Consumer Psychology, 23*(2), 229–248. doi:10.1016/j.jcps.2013.01.002

Park, C. W., MacInnis, D. J., & Priester, J. R. (2009). Research Directions on Strong Brand Relationships. In D. J. MacInnis, C. W. Park, & J. R. Priester (Eds.), *Handbook of Brand Relationships*. Armonk, NY: M.E. Sharpe.

Park, C. W. B., Jaworski, J., & MacInnis, D. J. (1986). Strategic Brand Concept-Image Management. *Journal of Marketing, 50*(4), 135–145. doi:10.2307/1251291

Park, J. K., & Yang, S. (2006). The Moderating Role of Consumer Trust and Experiences: Value Driven Usage of Mobile Technology. *International Journal of Mobile Marketing, 1*(2), 24–32.

Park, R. E. (1959). Race and Culture. Glencoe, IL: The Free Press.

Peter, J., Paul, J., Olson, C., & Grunert, K. G. (1999). *Consumer Behaviour and Marketing Strategy* (European Edition). London: McGraw Hill.

Phau, I., & Kong, C. L. (2001). Brand Personality and Consumer Self Expression: Single or Dual Carriageway? *Journal of Brand Management, 8*(6), 428–444. doi:10.1057/palgrave.bm.2540042

Plummer, J. T. (1984). How Personality Makes a Difference. *Journal of Advertising Research, 24*(6), 27–31.

Quinton, S. (2013). The Community Brand Paradigm: A Response to Brand Management's Bilemma in the Digital Era. *Journal of Marketing Management, 29*(7-8), 7–8, 912–932. doi:10.1080/0267257X.2012.729072

Rao, H., Davis, F. G., & Ward, A. (2000). Embeddedness, Social Identity and Mobility: Why Firms Leave the NASDAQ and Join the New York Stock Exchange. *Administrative Science Quarterly, 45*(2), 268–292. doi:10.2307/2667072

Reed, A. I. I. (2002). Social Identity as a Useful Perspective for Self-Concept Based Consumer Research. *Journal of Psychology and Marketing, 19*(3), 235–266. doi:10.1002/mar.10011

Reicheld, F. (1996). *The Loyalty Effect: The Hidden Force behind Growth, Profits, and Lasting Value.* Boston: Harvard Business School Press.

Richins, M. L. (1994). Valuing Things: The Public and Private Meanings of Possessions. *The Journal of Consumer Research, 21*(10), 504–521. doi:10.1086/209414

Roos, I. (1999). Switching processes in customer relationships. *Journal of Service Research, 2*(1), 376–393. doi:10.1177/109467059921006

Roselius, T. (1971). Consumer Rankings of Risk Reduction Method. *Journal of Marketing, 35*(1), 55–61. doi:10.2307/1250565

Ruth, J. A. (2001). Promoting a Brand's Emotion Benefits: The Influence of Emotion Categorization Processes on Consumer Evaluations. *Journal of Consumer Psychology, 11*(2), 99–113. doi:10.1207/S15327663JCP1102_03

Sathish, M., Kumar, K. S., Naveen, K. J., & Jeevanantham, V. (2011). A Study on Consumer Switching Behaviour in Cellular Service Provider: A Study with reference to Chennai. *Far East Journal of Psychology and Business, 2*(2), 72.

Seiders, K., & Tigert, D. J. (1997). Impact of Market Entry and Competitive Structure on Store Switching/Store Loyalty. *International Review of Retail, Distribution and Consumer Research, 7*(3), 227–247. doi:10.1080/095939697343003

Shankar, V., Smith, A. K., & Rangaswamy, A. (2003). Customer Satisfaction and Loyalty in Online and Offline Environments. *International Journal of Research in Marketing, 20*(2), 153–175. doi:10.1016/S0167-8116(03)00016-8

Shapiro, L. M. (2010). *Severe Market Dissruption on 6th May, 2010: Congressional Testimony.* Collingdale, PA: Diane Publishing Co.

Sherif, C. W., & Sherif, M. (1967). *Attitude, Ego-involvement, and Change.* Westport, CT: Green Wood Press.

Sheth, J. N., Newman, B. I., & Gross, B. L. (1991). Why We Buy What We Buy: A Theory of Consumption Values. *Journal of Business Research, 22*(2), 159–170. doi:10.1016/0148-2963(91)90050-8

Shimp, T. A., & Madden, T. J. (1988). Consumer-Object Relations: A Conceptual Framework Based Analogously on Sternberg's Triangular Theory of Love. *Advances in Consumer Research. Association for Consumer Research (U. S.), 15*(1), 163–168.

Sirgy, J. M. (1982). Self-Concept in Consumer Behaviour: A Critical Review. *The Journal of Consumer Research, 9*(12), 287–300. doi:10.1086/208924

Sirgy, M. J., Grewal, D., & Mangleburg, T. (2000). Retail Environment, Self-Congruity, and Retail Patronage: An Integrative Model and a Research Agenda. *Journal of Business Research, 49*(2), 127–138. doi:10.1016/S0148-2963(99)00009-0

Slawsby, A., Leibovitch, A. M., & Giusto, R. (2003). *Worldwide Mobile Phone Forecast and Analysis, 2003-2007*. IDC Report, No. 29586.

Sloot, L. M., Verhoef, P. C., & Franses, P. H. (2005). The Impact of Brand Equity and the Hedonic Level of Products on Consumer Stock-Out Reactions. *Journal of Retailing, 81*(1), 15–34. doi:10.1016/j.jretai.2005.01.001

Solomon, M. R. (2002). The Role of Products as Social Stimuli: A Symbolic Interactionism Perspective. *The Journal of Consumer Research, 10*(10), 319–329.

Stern, B. B., Thompson, J. C., & Arnould, E. J. (1998). Narrative Analysis of a Marketing Relationship: The Consumer's Perspective. *Journal of Psychology and Marketing, 15*(3), 195–214. doi:10.1002/(SICI)1520-6793(199805)15:3<195::AID-MAR1>3.0.CO;2-5

Sung, Y., & Kim, J. (2010). Effects of Brand Personality on Brand Trust and Brand Affect. *Journal of Psychology and Marketing, 27*(7), 639–661. doi:10.1002/mar.20349

Swait, J., & Erdem, T. (2007). Brand Effects on Choice and Choice Set Formation under Uncertainty. *Journal of Marine Science, 26*(5), 679–697. doi:10.1287/mksc.1060.0260

Sweeney, J. C., & Soutar, G. N. (2001). Consumer Perceived Value: The Development of a Multiple Item Scale. *Journal of Retailing, 77*(2), 203–220. doi:10.1016/S0022-4359(01)00041-0

Tajfel, H., & Turner, J. C. (1979). The Social Identity Theory of Inter-Group Behaviour. In *Psychology of Intergroup Relations*. Chicago: Nelson-Hall.

Tan, W., Hsiao, Y., Tseng, S., & Chang, C. (2017). Smartphone Application Personality and its Relationship to Personalities of Smartphone Users and Social Capital Accrued through use of Smartphone Social Applications. *Journal of Telematics and Informatics*, *35*(1), 255–26. doi:10.1016/j.tele.2017.11.007

Thompson, D. V., Hamilton, R. W., & Rust, R. T. (2005). Feature Fatigue: When Product Capabilities become too much of a Good Thing. *JMR, Journal of Marketing Research*, *42*(4), 431–442. doi:10.1509/jmkr.2005.42.4.431

Tussyadiah, I. P. (2015). The Influence of Innovativeness on On-Site Smartphone Use among American. *Journal of Travel & Tourism Marketing*. doi:10.1080/1054 8408.2015.1068263

Uncles, M., & Laurent, G. (1997). Travelers: Implications for Context-based Push Marketing Editorial. *International Journal of Research in Marketing, 14*, 399-404.

Underwood, R. L., Klein, N. M., & Burke, R. R. (2001). Packaging Communication: Attentional Effects of Product Imagery. *Journal of Product and Brand Management*, *10*(7), 403–422. doi:10.1108/10610420110410531

Van Trijp, H. C. M., Hoyer, W. D., & Inman, J. J. (1996). Why Switch? Product Category-Level Explanations for True Variety-Seeking Behaviour. *JMR, Journal of Marketing Research*, *33*(3), 281–292. doi:10.2307/3152125

Wang, D., Park, S., & Fesenmaier, D. R. (2012). The Role of Smartphones in Mediating the Touristic Experience. *Journal of Travel Research*, *51*(4), 371–387. doi:10.1177/0047287511426341

Wang, D., Xiang, Z., & Fesenmaier, D. R. (2014). Adapting to the Mobile World: A Model of Smartphone Use. *Journal of Tourism Research*, *48*, 11–26.

Wanke, M., Bohner, G., & Jurkowitsch, A. (1997). There Are Many Reasons to Drive a BMW: Does Imagined Ease of Argument Generation Influence Attitudes? *The Journal of Consumer Research*, *24*(9), 170–177. doi:10.1086/209502

Wee, T. T. T. (2004). Extending Human Personality to Brands: The Stability Factor. *Journal of Brand Management*, *11*(4), 317–330. doi:10.1057/palgrave.bm.2540176

Westbrook, R. A. (1987). Product/Consumption Based Affective Responses and Post Purchase Processes. *JMR, Journal of Marketing Research*, *24*(3), 258–270. doi:10.2307/3151636

Yeh, C. H., Wang, Y. S., & Yieh, K. (2016). Predicting smartphone brand loyalty: Consumer value and consumer-brand identification perspectives. *International Journal of Information Management, 36*(3), 245–257. doi:10.1016/j.ijinfomgt.2015.11.013

Yi, Y. (1990). A Critical Review of Consumer Satisfaction. In V. Zeithaml (Ed.), American Marketing Association (pp. 68–123). Chicago: Academic Press.

Yoo, B., Donthu, N., & Lee, S. (2000). An Examination of Selected Marketing Mix Elements and Brand Equity. *Journal of the Academy of Marketing Science, 28*(2), 195–211. doi:10.1177/0092070300282002

Zhang, J., & Bloemer, J. M. M. (2008). The Impact of Value Congruence on Consumer-Service Brand Relationships. *Journal of Service Research, 11*(8), 161–178. doi:10.1177/1094670508322561

## KEY TERMS AND DEFINITIONS

**AMA:** American Marketing Association.
**BSP:** Brand switching proponents.
**NASDAQ:** National Association of Securities Dealers Automated Quotations.
**NYSE:** New York Stock Exchange.
**OS:** Operating system.

# Compilation of References

Aaker, D. A. (1991). *Managing Brand Equity*. New York: The Free Press.

Aaker, D. A. (1995). *Building Strong Brands*. New York: The Free Press.

Aaker, D. A. (1996). Measuring Brand Equity across Products and Markets. *California Management Review*, *38*(3), 102–120. doi:10.2307/41165845

Aaker, J. (1997). Dimensions of Brand Personality. *JMR, Journal of Marketing Research*, *34*(3), 347–356. doi:10.2307/3151897

Abdillah, W. (2016). Motivation for Individuals' Involvement with Fan Pages. *Journal of Indonesian Economy and Business*, *31*(2), 220–234. doi:10.22146/jieb.15292

Accenture. (2013). *Banking 2020: As the storm abates, North American banks Must Chart a New Course to Capture Emerging Oportunities*. Author.

Afuah, A., & Tucci, C. L. (2012). Crowdsourcing as a Solution to Distant Search. *Academy of Management Review*, *37*(3), 355–375. doi:10.5465/amr.2010.0146

Agarwal, M. K., & Rao, V. R. (1996). An empirical comparison of consumer-based measures of brand equity. *Marketing Letters*, *7*(3), 237–247. doi:10.1007/BF00435740

Aggarwal, P. (2004). The Effects of Brand Relationship Norms on Consumer Attitudes and Behaviour. *The Journal of Consumer Research*, *31*(1), 87–101. doi:10.1086/383426

Ahearne, M., Bhattacharya, C. B., & Gruen, T. (2005). Antecedents and Consequences of Customer–Company identification: Expanding the Role of Relationship Marketing. *The Journal of Applied Psychology*, *90*(3), 574–585. doi:10.1037/0021-9010.90.3.574 PMID:15910151

Ailawadi, K. L., Scott, A. N., & Karen, G. (2001). Pursuing the Value Conscious Consumer: Store Brands Versus National Brand Promotions. *Journal of Marketing*, *65*(1), 71–89. doi:10.1509/jmkg.65.1.71.18132

Albert, N., & Merunka, D. (2013). The Role of Brand Love in Consumer-Brand Relationships. *Journal of Consumer Marketing*, *30*(3), 258–266. doi:10.1108/07363761311328928

Al-Mommani, K., Al-Afifi, A., & Mahfuz, M. A. (2015). The Impact of Social Networks on Maximizing the Competitive Value of Micro, Small, and Medium Enterprises. *International Journal of Management Science and Business Administration*, *3*(1), 64–70. doi:10.18775/ijmsba.1849-5664-5419.2014.13.1005

Anderson, C. (2004). *The Long Tail*. San Francisco, CA: Wired.

Andrew, T., & Stephen, J. G. (2012). The Effects of Traditional and Social Earned Media on Sales: A Study of a Microlending Marketplace. *JMR, Journal of Marketing Research*, *49*(5), 624–639. doi:10.1509/jmr.09.0401

Andriole, J. S. (2010). Business impact of Web 2.0 Technologies. *Communications of the ACM*, *53*(12), 67–79. doi:10.1145/1859204.1859225

Antikainen, M., Mäkipää, M., & Ahonen, M. (2010). Motivating and supporting collaboration in open innovation. *European Journal of Innovation Management*, *13*(1), 100–119. doi:10.1108/14601061011013258

Appiah, D. (2014). *Building Brand Loyalty: Identity Theory Perspective. Seventh International Scientific Conference*. Institute of Economic Research, Prishtine, Albania.

Appiah, D., & Ozuem, W. (2017). Issues and the Importance of Branding, Brand Personality and Symbolic Meaning of Brands to the Consumer. In Global Information Diffusion and Management in Contemporary Society. IGI Global.

Appiah, D., Ozuem, W., & Howell, E. K. (2016). Towards a Sustainable Brand Loyalty: *Attitudinal Loyalty Perspective. Eighteenth Annual International Conference*. Global Business and Technology Association.

Appiah, D., Ozuem, W., & Howell, K. E. (2017). *Brand Switching in the Smartphone Industry: A Preliminary Study. Global Business and Technology Association Conference*, Vienna, Austria.

Aradhye, A., & Kallurkar, S. (2014). A Case Study of Just-In-Time System in Service Industry. *Procedia Engineering*, *97*, 2232–2237. doi:10.1016/j.proeng.2014.12.467

Arndt, J. (1967). Role of product-related conversations in the diffusion of a new product. *JMR, Journal of Marketing Research*, *4*(3), 291–295. doi:10.2307/3149462

Arnett, D. B., German, S. D., & Hunt, S. D. (2003). The Identity salience Model of Relationship Marketing success: The case of Non-profit Marketing. *Journal of Marketing*, *67*(4), 89–105. doi:10.1509/jmkg.67.2.89.18614

Arnold, D. (1992). *The handbook of brand management*. Century Business. The Economist Books.

Aron, A., Aron, E. N., & Smollan, D. (1992). Inclusion of Other in the Self–Scale and the Structure of Interpersonal Closeness. *Journal of Personality and Social Psychology*, *63*(4), 596–61. doi:10.1037/0022-3514.63.4.596

Artun, O., & Levin, D. (2015). *Predictive Marketing: Easy Ways Every Marketer Can Use Customer Analytics and Big Data*. Wiley. doi:10.1002/9781119175803

Ashok, K., Dillon, W. R., & Yuan, S. (2002). Extending Discrete Choice Models to Incorporate Attitudinal and Other Latent Variables. *JMR, Journal of Marketing Research*, *39*(2), 31–46. doi:10.1509/jmkr.39.1.31.18937

Aslam, H., Aslam, M., Ali, N., & Habib, B. (2013). Importance of Human Resource Management in 21st Century: A Theoretical Perspective. *International Journal of Human Resource Studies*, *3*(3), 87–96. doi:10.5296/ijhrs.v3i3.6255

Azize, S., Hakan, K., & Cemal, Z. (2013). Creating Commitment, Trust and Satisfaction for a Brand: What is the Role of Switching Costs in Mobile Phone Market? *Procedia: Social and Behavioral Sciences*, *99*, 496–502. doi:10.1016/j.sbspro.2013.10.518

Baker, M. A., Davis, E. A., & Weaver, P. A. (2014). Eco-friendly attitudes, barriers to participation, and differences in behavior at green hotels. *Cornell Hospitality Quarterly*, *55*(1), 89–99. doi:10.1177/1938965513504483

Baker, M. J., & Hart, S. J. (Eds.). (2008). *The marketing book*. Routledge.

Balasubramanian Sridhar, M. (2001). The economic leverage of the virtual community. *International Journal of Electronic Commerce*, *18*(6), 103–138.

Baptista, R. (2000). Do innovations diffuse faster within georgraphical clusters? *International Journal of Industrial Organization, 18*(3), 515–535. doi:10.1016/S0167-7187(99)00045-4

Barkan, T. (2008). *How to develop a successful "Social Network Strategy"*. Retrieved from: http://www.globalstrat.org/

Barlow, A. K. J., Siddiqui, N. Q., & Mannion, M. (2004). Development in information and communication tehnologies for retail marketing channels. *International Journal of Retail & Distribution Management, 32*(3), 157–163. doi:10.1108/09590550410524948

Barnes, S. J., & Scornavacca, E. (2004). Mobile Marketing: The Role of Permission and Acceptance. *International Journal of Mobile Communications, 2*(2), 128–139. doi:10.1504/IJMC.2004.004663

Batra, R., Lehmann, D. R., & Singh, D. (1993). The Brand Personality Component of Brand Goodwill: Some Antecedents and Consequences. In Brand Equity and Advertising. Hillsdale: Lawrence Erlbaum Associates.

Bayus, B. (2013). Crowdsourcing New Product Ideas over Time: An Analysis of the Dell IdeaStorm Community. *Management Science, 59*(1), 226–244. doi:10.1287/mnsc.1120.1599

Bayus, B. C. (1985). Harnessing the power of word-of-mouth. In V. Maha (Ed.), *Innovation Diffusion Models of New Product Acceptance*. Cambridge, MA: Ballinger.

Bechina, A. A., & Husta, E. (2011). The Role of Social Networking Tools on Purchasing Decision Making Process. *Proceedings of the International Conference on Intellectual Capital*, 81-87.

Belch, B. (2003). *Advertising and promotion an integrated marketing communications perspective (6th ed.)*. McGraw-Hill/Irwin.

Belk, R. W. (1988). Possessions and the Extended Self. *The Journal of Consumer Research, 15*(9), 139–168. doi:10.1086/209154

Bergeron, B. (2002). *Essentials of CRM: A guide to Customer Relationship management (Essential series)*. Wiley.

Berne´, C., Mu'gica, J. M., & Yague, M. J. (2001). The Effect of Variety-Seeking on Customer Retention in Services. *Journal of Retailing and Consumer Services*, *8*(6), 335–345. doi:10.1016/S0969-6989(01)00002-9

Berry, L. L. (2000). Cultivating Service Brand Equity. *Journal of the Academy of Marketing Science*, *28*(1), 128–137. doi:10.1177/0092070300281012

Bettman, J. R., Johnson, E. J., & Payne, J. W. (1991). Consumer decision making. Handbook of Consumer Behavior, 50-84.

Bharadwaj, G. B., Tuli, R. K., & Bonfrer, A. (2011). The Impact of Brand Equity on Shareholder Wealth. *Journal of Marketing*, *75*(9), 88–104. doi:10.1509/jmkg.75.5.88

Bhat, S., & Srinivas, K. R. (1998). Symbolic And Functional Positioning Of Brands. *Journal of Consumer Marketing*, *15*(1), 32–43. doi:10.1108/07363769810202664

Bhattacharya, C. B., & Lordish, L. (2000). *Towards a System for Monitoring Brand Health from Store Scanner Data*. MSI working Paper, Report No. 00-111.

Bhattacharya, C. B., Rao, H., & Glynn, M. A. (1995). Understanding the bond of identification: An investigation of its correlates among art museum. *Journal of Marketing*, *59*(4), 46. doi:10.2307/1252327

Bhattacharya, C. B., & Sanker, S. (2003). Consumer-Company Identification: A Framework for Understanding Consumers' Relationship with Companies. *Journal of Marketing*, *67*(4), 76–88. doi:10.1509/jmkg.67.2.76.18609

Biel A. L, (1993). Converting Image into Equity. In *Brand Equity and Advertising: Advertising's Role in Building Strong Brands*. Hillsdale: Lawrence Erlbaum Associates.

Bjorling, W. (2015). *How to manage online review sites successfully* (Bachelor's thesis). Jankoping University.

Bonabeau, E. (2009). Decisions 2.0: The power of collective intelligence. *MIT Sloan Management Review*, *50*(2), 45–52.

Bowen & Gordon. (2014). *Computer-Mediated Marketing Strategies: Social Media and Online Brand Communities*. Hershey, PA: IGI Global.

Bower, J. L., & Christensen, C. M. (1995). Disruptive Technologies: Catching the Wave. *Harvard Business Review*, (2-3), 43-53.

Boyd, D., & Crawford, K. (2012). Critical Questions for Big Data. *Information Communication and Society, 15*(5), 662–679. doi:10.1080/1369118X.2012.678878

Boyd, D., & Ellison, N. (2008). Social Network Sites: Definition, History, and Scholarship. *Journal of Computer-Mediated Communication, 13*(1), 210–230. doi:10.1111/j.1083-6101.2007.00393.x

Brabham, D. (2013). *Crowdsourcing.* Cambridge, MA: MIT Press.

Bradley, A. J. (2013). *A New Definition of Social Media,* Social Media: *Cultivate Collaboration and Innovation.* Retrieved from: http://blogs.gartner.com/anthony_bradley/2010/01/07/a-

Brakus, J. J., Bernd, H. S., & Shi, Z. (2008). Experiential Attribute and Consumer Judgments. In *Handbook on Brand and Experience Management.* Cheltenham, UK: Edward Elgar Publisher. doi:10.4337/9781848446151.00022

Brakus, J. J., Bernd, H. S., & Zarantonello, L. (2009). Brand Experience: What Is It? How Is It Measured? Does It Affect Loyalty? *Journal of Marketing, 73*(3), 52–68. doi:10.1509/jmkg.73.3.52

Breazeale, M. (2009). word of mouse: An assessment of electronic word of mouth resaerch. *International Journal of Market Research, 51*(3), 297–318. doi:10.2501/S1470785309200566

Brewer, M. B. (1979). In group Bias in the Minimal Intergroup Situation: A Cognitive–Motivational Analysis. *Psychological Bulletin, 86*(2), 307–324. doi:10.1037/0033-2909.86.2.307

Brodie, R. J., Ilic, A., Juric, B., & Hollebeek, L. (2013). Consumer Engagement in a Virtual Brand Community: An exploratory Analysis. *Journal of Business Research, 66*(1), 105–114. doi:10.1016/j.jbusres.2011.07.029

Brundtland, G. H. (1987). *Report of the World Commission on environment and development:" our common future.* United Nations.

Buchnowska, D. (2013). Social Business: A Conceptual Framework. *Informatyka Ekonomiczna Business Inforatics, 4*(30).

Bulankulama, S.W., Ali, K., & Herath, H.M. (2014). Utilization of social media in an organization and competitive advantages: Development of a conceptual framework. *International Journal of Economics, Commerce and Management, 3*(2).

Bullinger, A. C., Neyer, A.-K., Rass, M., & Moeslein, K. M. (2010). Community-based innovation contests: Where competition meets cooperation. *Creativity and Innovation Management, 19*(3), 290–303. doi:10.1111/j.1467-8691.2010.00565.x

Burcher, N. (2012). *Paid, Owned, Earned: Maximising Marketing Returns in a Socially Connected World.* Kogen Page.

Cacioppo, Petty, R. E., Feinstein, J. A., & Jarvis, W. B. G. (1996). Dispositional Differences in Cognitive Motivation: The Life and Times of Individuals Varying in Need for Cognition. *Psychological Bulletin, 119*(2), 197–253. doi:10.1037/0033-2909.119.2.197

Campo, K., Gijsbrechts, E., & Nisol, P. (2000). Towards understanding consumer Response to Stock outs. *Journal of Retailing, 76*(2), 219–242. doi:10.1016/S0022-4359(00)00026-9

Carpenter, G. S., Glazer, R., & Nakamoto, K. (1997). *Reading on Market-Driving Strategies: Towards a New Theory of Competitive Advantage.* Addison Wesley.

Carson, D., Cromie, S., McGowan, P., & Hill, J. (1995). *Marketing and Entrepreneurship in SMEs: An Innovative Approach.* Harlow: Prentice-Hall.

Cassar, S., & Shinebourne, P. (2012). What does spirituality mean to you? An Interpretative Phenomenological Analysis of the experience of spirituality. *Existential Analysis, 23*(1), 133–149.

Cecere, G., Corrocher, N., & Battaglia, R. D. (2015). Innovation and Competition in the Smartphone Industry: Is there a Dominant Design? *Journal of Telecommunications Policy,* (39), 162-175.

Chaffey, D. (2010). Applying Organisational Capability Models to Assess the maturity of Digital-Marketing Goverance. *Journal of Marketing Management, 26*(3-4), 187–196. doi:10.1080/02672571003612192

Chaplin, L. N., & Roedder, D. J. (2005). The Development of Self-Brand Connections in Children and Adolescents. *The Journal of Consumer Research, 32*(1), 119–129. doi:10.1086/426622

Charo, N., & Pershant Sharma, S. S. (2015). Determining the Impact of Ewom on Brand image and Purchase Intention through adoption of online opinions. *International Journal of Humanities and Management Sciences, 3*(1).

Charter, M. (2017). *Greener marketing: A responsible approach to business.* Routledge.

Chaudhuri, A., & Holbrook, M. B. (2001). The Chain of Effects From Brand Trust And Brand Affect To Brand Performance: The Role Of Brand Loyalty. *Journal of Marketing, 65*(2), 81–93. doi:10.1509/jmkg.65.2.81.18255

Chen, H., Bang, N., Klaus, P., & Wu, M. (2015). Exploring Electronic Word-of-Mouth (eWOM) in The Consumer Purchase Decision-Making Process: The Case of Online Holidays – Evidence from United Kingdom (UK) Consumers. *Journal of Travel & Tourism Marketing, 32*(8), 953–970. doi:10.1080/10548408.2014.956165

Chen, Y.-S. (2010). The drivers of green brand equity: Green brand image, green satisfaction, and green trust. *Journal of Business Ethics, 93*(2), 307–319. doi:10.100710551-009-0223-9

Chernev, A., Hamilton, R., & Gal, D. (2011). Competing for Consumer Identity: Limits to Self-Expression and the Perils of Lifestyle Branding. *Journal of Marketing, 75*(3), 66–82. doi:10.1509/jmkg.75.3.66

Cheung, M., Luo, C., Sia, C., & Chen, H. (2009). Credibility of electronic word-of-mouth: informational and normative determinants of online consumer recommendation. *International Journal of e-Commerce, 13*(4), 9-38.

Cheung, C. M., & Thadani, D. R. (2012). The impact of electronic word-of-mouth communication: A literature analysis and integrative model. *Decision Support Systems, 54*(1), 461–470. doi:10.1016/j.dss.2012.06.008

Cheung, M. K. (2005). Literature derived reference models for the adoption of online shopping. *Information & Management, 42*(4), 543–559. doi:10.1016/S0378-7206(04)00051-5

Cheung, M. Y., Luo, C., Sia, C. L., & Chen, H. (2009). Credibility of Electronic Word-of-Mouth: Informational and Normative Determinants of On-line Consumer Recommendations. *International Journal of Electronic Commerce, 13*(4), 9–38. doi:10.2753/JEC1086-4415130402

Chevalier, J. A., & Mayzlin, D. (2006). The Effect of Word of Mouth on Sales: Online Book Reviews. *JMR, Journal of Marketing Research, 43*(3), 345–354. doi:10.1509/jmkr.43.3.345

Chi, J., & Sun, L. (2015). IT and Competitive Advantage: A Study from Micro Perspective. *Modern Economy, 6*(03), 404–410. doi:10.4236/me.2015.63038

Christensen, C. M. (2013). *The Innovators Dilema: When New Technologies Cause Great Firms to Fail*. Boston: Harvard Business School Press.

Christine Ennew, A. K. (2000). Managing word of mouth communication: Empirical evidence from India. *International Journal of Bank Marketing, 18*.

Christopher, M. (1998). *Logistics and Supply Chain Management: Strategies for Reducing Cost and Improving Service* (2nd ed.). Harlow, UK: Prentice Hall.

Christopher, M. G. (1998). *Logistics and Supply Chain Management; strategies for reducing costs and improving services*. London: Pitman Publishing.

Chu, S. K. W., & Kennedy, D. M. (2011). Using online collaborative tools for groups to co-construct knowledge. *Online Information Review, 35*(4), 581–597. doi:10.1108/14684521111161945

Chu, S.-C., & Kim, Y. (2015). Determinants of consumer engagement in electronic word-of-mouth (eWOM) in social networking sites. *International Journal of Advertising, 30*(1), 47–75. doi:10.2501/IJA-30-1-047-075

Cloete, E., Courtney, S., & Fintz, J. (2002). Small Businesses' Acceptance and Adoption of e-Commerce in the Western Cape Province of South Africa. *The Electronic Journal on Information Systems in Developing Countries, 10*.

Cobb-Walgren, C. J., Ruble, C. A., & Donthu, N. (1995). Brand Equity, Brand Preference, and Purchase Intent. *Journal of Advertising, 24*(3), 2540. doi:10.1080/00913367.1995.10673481

Constantinides, E., & Fountain, S. J. (2008). Web 2.0: Conceptual foundations and marketing issues. *Journal of Direct. Data and Digital Marketing Practice, 9*(3), 231–244. doi:10.1057/palgrave.dddmp.4350098

Copley, P. (2004). *Marketing Communications Management concepts and theories, cases and practices*. Elsevier Butterworth Heinemann.

Crouch, G. I., Perdue, R. R., Timmermans, H. J. P., & Uysal, M. (2004). *Consumer Psychology of Tourism, Hospitality and Leisure*. Oxon, UK: CABI. doi:10.1079/9780851997490.0000

Crowe, M. (2011). New social media study: nearly 60 percent say LinkedIn is most important social network account. *Perfomics.* Retrieved from: https://www.performics.com/new-social-media-study-nearly-60-percent-say-linkedin-is-most-important-social-network-account

D'Aveni, R. A., Dagnino, G. B., & Smith, K. G. (2010). The age of temporary advantage. *Strategic Management Journal, 31*(13), 1371–1385. doi:10.1002mj.897

Da Silveira, C., Lages, C., & Simões, C. (2013). Reconceptualizing brand identity in a dynamic environment. *Journal of Business Research, 66*(1), 28–36. doi:10.1016/j.jbusres.2011.07.020

Dahl, D. W., & Moreau, C. P. (2007). Thinking inside the box: Why consumers enjoy constrained creative experiences. *JMR, Journal of Marketing Research, 44*(3), 357–369. doi:10.1509/jmkr.44.3.357

Davies, J. B., & Ward, P. (2005). Exploring the Connections between Visual Merchandising and Retail Branding. An Application of Facet Theory. *International Journal of Retail & Distribution Management, 33*(7), 505–513. doi:10.1108/09590550510605578

Day, G. S. (1969). A Two-Dimensional Concept of Brand Loyalty. *Journal of Advertising Research, 9,* 29–35.

Day, G. S. (2014). An outside-in approach to resource-based theories. *Journal of the Academy of Marketing Science, 42*(1), 27–28. doi:10.100711747-013-0348-3

de Chernatony, L., & Dall'Olmo Riley, F. (1998). Defining Brand: Beyond the Literature with Expert Opinion. *Journal of Marketing Management, 14*(5), 417–443. doi:10.1362/026725798784867798

de Chernatony, L., & MacDonnald, M. (1992). *Creating Powerful Brands.* Oxford, UK: Heinermann and Butterworth.

de Chernatony, L., & McWilliam, G. (1990). Appreciating Brands as Assets through using a Two-Dimensional Model. *International Journal of Advertising, 9*(2), 111–119. doi:10.1080/02650487.1990.11107137

Dell Rio, A. B., Vazquez, R., & Iglesias, V. (2001). The Effects of Brand Associations on Consumer Response. *Journal of Consumer Marketing, 18*(5), 410–425. doi:10.1108/07363760110398808

Dellarocas. (2003). The Digitization of Word of Mouth: Promise and Challenges of Online Feedback Mechanisms. *Management Science*, *49*, 1407–1424.

Dellarocas, C. N., & Narayan, R. (2006). A Statistical measure of a population's propensity to engage in post-purchase online word of mouth. *Statistical Science*, *21*(2), 277–285. doi:10.1214/088342306000000169

Dennison, G., Bourdage-Braun, S., & Chetuparambil, M. (2009). *Social commerce defined*. IBM Corporation. Retrieved December 15, 2017, from https://digitalintelligencetoday.com/documents/IBM2009.pdf

Díaz, D. (2013). *F-commerce (III): modelos de tienda en Facebook*. Retrieved December 26, 2017, from https://www.educadictos.com/f-commerce-iii-modelos-de-tienda-en-facebook/

Dick, A., & Basu, K. (1994). Customer Loyalty: Towards an Integrated Conceptual Framework. *Journal of the Academy of Marketing Science*, *22*(2), 99–113. doi:10.1177/0092070394222001

Dickinson, J. E., Ghali, K., Cherrett, T., Speed, C., Davies, N., & Norgate, S. (2014). Tourism and the smartphone app: Capabilities, emerging practice and scope in the travel domain. *Current Issues in Tourism*, *17*(1), 84–101. doi:10.1080/13683500.2012.718323

Dimara, E., Manganari, E., & Skuras, D. (2015). Consumers' willingness to pay premium for green hotels: Fact or Fad? *Proceedings International Marketing Trends Conference 2015*.

Dimitriades, Z. S. (2006). Customer Satisfaction, Loyalty and commitment in service organisations: Some evidence from Greece. *Management Research News*, *29*(12), 782–800. doi:10.1108/01409170610717817

Dion, D., & Arnould, E. (2016). Persona-fied Brands: Managing Branded Persons through Persona. *Journal of Marketing Management*, *32*(1-2), 121–148. doi:10.1080/0267257X.2015.1096818

Djelassi, S., & Decoopman, I. (2013). Customers' participation in product development through crowdsourcing: Issues and implications. *Industrial Marketing Management*, *42*(5), 683–692. doi:10.1016/j.indmarman.2013.05.006

Dolich, I. J. (1969). Congruence Relationships between Self Images and Product Brands. *JMR, Journal of Marketing Research*, 6(1), 80–84. doi:10.2307/3150001

Domazet, I. (2007). *Unapređenje konkurentnosti preduzeća primenom CRM strategijskog koncepta.* Ekonomski fakultet Beograd i Naučno društvo ekonomista Beograd.

Domazet, I. (2011). Improving the quality of human resources by implementation of internal marketing, u monografiji. In *The Role of Markets and Human Capital in the Unstable Environmenture.* Karta Graphic Publishing House.

Domazet, I. (2012). *Marketing komunikacije finansijskih organizacija.* Institut ekonomskih nauka.

Domazet, I. (2015). Nacionalni brend Srbije kao faktor unapređenja konkurentnosti zemlje. *Strukturne promene u Srbiji: dosadašnji rezultati i perspektive*, 482-496.

Domazet, I. (2016). Improving Competitiveness through National Branding. In Development, Competitiveness and Inequality in EU and Western Balkans. Sofia University.

Domazet, I., & Simović, V. (2014). *Mogućnosti i pretpostavke za razvoj IKT industrije u Srbiji, u Drašković B. Ur. Zbornik radova "Deindustrijalizacija u Srbiji: mogućnost revitalizacije industrijskog sektora".* Institut ekonomskih nauka.

Domazet, I., & Zubović, J. (2011). Database marketing based business development: the case of Serbian financial sector. In Contemporary issues in the integration processes of Western Balkan countries in the European Union. International Center for Promotion of Enterprises Ljubljana, Slovenia.

Domazet, I., Đokić, I., & Milovanov, O. (2017). The Influence of advertising media on brand awareness. Časopis Management, 22(23).

Domazet, I., Hanić, H., & Simeunović, I. (2012). Marketing communication efficiency and effectiveness of the media for various target group. *International Scientific Conference-Management 2012, Fakultet za industrijski menadžment*, 791-796.

Domazet, I., Zubović, J., & Jeločnik, M. (2010). Development of long-term relationship with clients in financial sector companies as a source of competitive advantage. Bulletin, 62(2), 1-11.

Domazet, I., Zubović, J., & Simeunović, I. (2012). Analiza procesa i faza razvoja efikasnih marketing komunikacija. *Ekonomika, 3*, 21-31.

Domazet, I., Stošić, I., & Hanić, A. (2016). New technologies aimed at improving the competitiveness of companies in the services sector. In *Europe and Asia: Economic Integration Prospects* (pp. 363–377). Nice, France: CEMAFI.

Doyle, P. (1994). *Marketing Management and Strategy*. Englewood Cliffs, NJ: Prentice-Hall.

Dreher, S. (2014). Social media and the world of work. *Corporate Communications, 19*(4), 344–356. doi:10.1108/CCIJ-10-2013-0087

Duan & Whinston. (2008). Do online reviews matter? An empirical investigation of Panel data. *Decision Support System, 45*(4).

Durkin, M., McGowan, P., & McKeown, N. (2013). Exploring social media adoption in small to medium-sized enterprises in Ireland. *Journal of Small Business and Enterprise Development, 20*(4), 716–734. doi:10.1108/JSBED-08-2012-0094

Dwivedi, A. (2015). A higher-order model of consumer brand engagement and its impact on loyalty intentions. *Journal of Retailing and Consumer Services, 24*, 100–109. doi:10.1016/j.jretconser.2015.02.007

Ebrahim, R., Ghoneim, A., Irani, Z., & Fan, Y. (2016). A Brand Preference and Repurchase Intention Model: The Role of Consumer Experience. *Journal of Marketing Management, 32*(13-14), 13–14, 1230–1259. doi:10.1080/0267257X.2016.1150322

Edell, J. A., & Burke, M. C. (1987). The power of feelings in understanding advertising effects. *The Journal of Consumer Research, 14*(3), 421–433. doi:10.1086/209124

Edosomwan, S., Prakasan, S. K., Kouame, D., Watson, J., & Seymour, T. (2011). The History of Social Media and its Impact on Business. *The Journal of Applied Management and Entrepreneurship, 16*(3).

Ehrlich, E., & Fanelli, D. (2004). *The Financial Services Marketing*. Princeton, NJ: Bloomberg Press.

El-Gohary, H. (2010). Expanding TAM and IDT to understand the adoption of e-Marketing by small business enterprises. *International Journal of Customer Relationship Marketing and Management, 1*(3), 56–75. doi:10.4018/jcrmm.2010070105

Ellaboudy, S. (2010). The global financial crisis: Economic impact on gcc countries and policy implications. *International Research Journal of Finance and Economics, 41*, 180–193.

Elliott, R., & Wattanasuwan, K. (1998). Brand as Symbolic Resources for the Construction of Identity. *International Journal of Advertising, 17*(2), 131–144. do i:10.1080/02650487.1998.11104712

Elsbach, K. D., & Kramer, M. K. (1996). Members' Responses to Organizational Identity Threats: Encountering and Countering the Business Week Rankings. *Administrative Science Quarterly, 41*(3), 442–76.

Engel, J. F., Blackwell, R. D., & Miniard, P. W. (2005). *Consumer Behaviour.* Thompson South Western Company.

Ennew, C., & Waite, N. (2007). *Financial services marketing.* Oxford, UK: Butterworth-Heinemann, Elsevier.

Erevelles, S., Horton, V., & Fukawa, N. (2007). Imagination in marketing. *Marketing Management Journal, 17*(2), 109–119.

Eriksson, K., & Mattsson, J. (1996). Organising for Market Segmentation in Banking: the Impact from Production Technology and Coherent Bank Norms. *The Service Industry Journal.* Retrieved from www.fsa. gov.uk/pubs/conhsumer-research/crpr47.pdf

Eriksson, K., Kerem, K., & Nilsson, D. (2005). Customer acceptance of internet banking in Estonia. *International Journal of Bank Marketing, 23*(2), 200–216. doi:10.1108/02652320510584412

Erin, M. (2009). Social ties and online word of mouth. *Internet Research, 19*(1), 42–59. doi:10.1108/10662240910927812

Erkan, I., & Evans, C. (2016). The influence of eWOM in social media on consumers' purchase intentions: An extended approach to information adoption. *Computers in Human Behavior, 61*, 47–55. doi:10.1016/j.chb.2016.03.003

Escalas, J. E. (2004). Narrative Processing: Building Consumer Connections to Brands. *Journal of Consumer Psychology, 14*(1-2), 168–180. doi:10.120715327663jcp1401&2_19

Escalas, J. E., & Bettman, J. R. (2003). You Are What You Eat: The Influence of Reference Groups on Consumers' Connections to Brands. *Journal of Consumer Psychology, 13*(3), 339–348. doi:10.1207/S15327663JCP1303_14

Escalas, J. E., & Bettman, J. R. (2005). SelfConstrual, Reference Groups, and Brand Meaning. *The Journal of Consumer Research, 32*(12), 378–389. doi:10.1086/497549

Esty, D., & Winston, A. (2009). *Green to gold: How smart companies use environmental strategy to innovate, create value, and build competitive advantage.* John Wiley & Sons.

Ewing, M.T. (2009). Integrated Marketing Communications Measurement and Evaluation. *Journal of Marketing Communications, 15*(2-3), 103-117.

Farhana, M. (2014). Implication of Brand Identity Facets on Marketing Communication of Lifestyle Magazine: Case Study of a Swedish Brand. *Journal of Applied Economics and Business Research., 4*(1), 23–24.

Farquhar, P. H. (1989). Managing brand equity. *Marketing Research., 1*(3), 24–33.

Felix, R. (2015). *The state of the Global Smartphone Market. Statista Infographics.* Retrieved from: https://www.statista.com/charts/2512/smartphone-market-share

Fernando, F., & Whitelock, J. (2007). International advertising strategy: The standardisation question in manager studies. *International Marketing Review, 24*(5), 591–605. doi:10.1108/02651330710828004

Fill, C. (2009). Marketing Communications. Interactivity. In *Communities and Content* (5th ed.). Prentice Hall, Financial Times.

Fill, M., & Krizaj, D. (2016). ElectronicWordofMouthandItsCredibility inTourism:TheCaseofTripadvisor. *Academica Turistica, 9*(2), 107-112.

Firestein, S. (2012). *Ignorance: How it drives science.* New York: Oxford University Press.

Fishbein, M., & Ajzen, I. (1980). *Understanding Attitudes and Predicting Social Behavior.* Englewood, NJ: Prentice-hall.

Fournier, S. (1998). Consumers and Their Brands: Developing Relationship Theory in Consumer Research. *The Journal of Consumer Research, 24*(3), 343–373. doi:10.1086/209515

Fox, G., & Longart, P. (2016). Electronic word-of-mouth: Successful communication strategies for Restaurants. *Tourism and Hospitality Management*, 22(2), 211–223. doi:10.20867/thm.22.2.5

Franke, N., & Piller, F. (2003). Key research issues in user interaction with configuration toolkits in a mass customization system. *International Journal of Technology Management*, 26(5/6), 578–599. doi:10.1504/IJTM.2003.003424

Franke, N., & Piller, F. (2004). Toolkits for user innovation and design: An exploration of user interaction and value creation. *Journal of Product Innovation Management*, 21, 401–415. doi:10.1111/j.0737-6782.2004.00094.x

Frey, K., Lühtje, C., & Haag, S. (2011). Whom Should Firms Attract to Open Innovation Platforms? The Role of Knowledge Diversity and Motivation. *Long Range Planning*, 44(5-6), 397–420. doi:10.1016/j.lrp.2011.09.006

Füller, J. (2010). Refining Virtual Co-Creation from a Consumer Perspective. *California Management Review*, 52(2), 98–122. doi:10.1525/cmr.2010.52.2.98

Galbraith, J. (2014). *Design Organizations: Strategy, Structure, and Process at the Business Unit and Enterprise Levels*. Jossey-Bass.

Gartner. (2016). *Worldwide Smartphone grew 9.7 percent in Fourth Quarter of 2015*. Retrieved from: http://www.Gartner.com/newsroom

Giovanisa, A. N., & Athanasopouloub, P. (2018). Consumer-Brand Relationships and Brand Loyalty in Technology-Mediated Services. *Journal of Retailing and Consumer Services*, 40(1), 287–294. doi:10.1016/j.jretconser.2017.03.003

Giovanni, F., & Mario, A. (2003). Small Company Attitude towards ICT Based Solutions: Some Key Elements to Improve IT. *Journal of Educational Technology & Society*, 6(1), 45–49.

Gnyawali, D. R., Fan, W., & Penner, J. (2010). Competitive Actions and Dynamics in the Digital Age: An Empirical Investigation of Social Networking Firms. *Information Systems Research*, 21(3), 594–613. doi:10.1287/isre.1100.0294

Godes, & Mayzlin, D. A. (2004). Using Online Conversations to Study Word-of-Mouth Communication. *Marketing Science*, 23(4), 545-559.

Goel, A., & Singhal, P. (2015). *Product Innovation through Knowledge Management and Social Media Strategies*. Hershey, PA: IGI Global.

Golden, M. (2011). *Social Media Strategies for Professionals and their Firms.* John Wiley & Sons Inc.

Goldsmith, R. E. (2006). Electronic Word-of-Mouth. In Encyclopedia of E-Commerce, E-Government and Mobile Commerce. Hershey, PA: Idea Group Publishing. doi:10.4018/978-1-59140-799-7.ch067

Goldsmith, R. E. (2000). Characteristics of the Heavy User of Fashionable Clothing. *Journal of Marketing Theory and Practice*, 8(4), 21–28. doi:10.1080/10696679.2000.11501877

Goldsmith, R. E., & Horowitz, D. (2006). Measuring Motivations for Online Opinion Seeking. *Journal of Interactive Advertising*, 6(2), 2–14. doi:10.1080/15252019.2006.10722114

Gremler, D. D., & Brown, S. W. (1996). Service Loyalty; its Nature, Importance and Implications. In B. Edvardsson, S. W. Brown, R. Johnston, & E. Scheuing (Eds.), *QUIS V: Advancing Service Quality: A Global Perspective*. New York, NY: ISQA.

Griffin, M., Babin, B. J., & Modianos, D. (2000). Shopping Values of Russian Consumers: The Impact of Habituation in a Developing Economy. *Journal of Retailing*, 76(1), 33–52. doi:10.1016/S0022-4359(99)00025-1

Gronroos, C. (1998). Marketing services: The case of a missing product. *Journal of Business and Industrial Marketing*, 13(4/5), 322–338. doi:10.1108/08858629810226645

Grönroos, C. (2008). Service logic revisited: Who creates value? And who co-creates? *European Business Review*, 20(4), 298–314. doi:10.1108/09555340810886585

Grove, S., Carlson, L., & Dorsch, M. J. (2002). Addresing Services' intangibility through integrated marketing communication. *Journal of Services Marketing*, 16(5). doi:10.1108/08876040210436876

Guadagni, P. M., & Little, J. D. C. (1983). A Logit Model of Brand Choice Calibrated on Scanner Data: A Logit Model of Brand Choice Calibrated on Scanner Data. *Journal of Marine Science*, 2(3), 203–238. doi:10.1287/mksc.2.3.203

Guillermo, A., & Villanueva, J. (2008). Electronic Word of Mouth: What Do We Know About This powerful marketing tool? *e-business Center PricewaterhouseCoopers & IESE*, 1-67.

Güven, E. (2014). *Sosyal Medyadaki Ağızdan Ağıza Pazarlama Faaliyetlerinin Satınalma Kararları Üzerine Etkileri* (Dissertation thesis). Manisa Celal Bayar University.

Hair, J. F., Black, W. C., Babin, B. J., & Anderson, R. E. (2010). *Multivariate Data Analysis* (7th ed.). Upper Saddle River, NJ: Prentice Hall.

Halaszovich, T., & Nel, J. (2017). Customer–brand engagement and Facebook fanpage "Like"-intention. *Journal of Product and Brand Management, 26*(2), 120–134. doi:10.1108/JPBM-02-2016-1102

Hallowell, R. (1996). The Relationships of Customer Satisfaction, Customer Loyalty, and Profitability: An Empirical Study. *International Journal of Service Industry Management, 7*(4), 27–42. doi:10.1108/09564239610129931

Halper, F. (2011). The top five trends in predictive analytics. *Information & Management, 21*(6), 16–18.

Han, H., & Trimi, S. (2017). Social Commerce Design: A Framework and Application. *Journal of Theoretical and Applied Electronic Commerce Research, 12*(3), 50–68. doi:10.4067/S0718-18762017000300005

Hanić, H., & Domazet, I. (2011). Managing Customer Relationship within Financial Organizations. Polish Journal of Management Studies, 4, 151-166.

Hanić, H., & Domazet, I. (2012). Strengthening Economic SubjectsInternal Capacities: Marketing Management and CRM. *Managing Structural Changes: Trends and Requirements*, 44-60.

Hanine, S., & Steils, N. (2018). *Crowdsourcing: A Double-Edged Sword Outsourcing Strategy*. Academic Press. . doi:10.5772/intechopen.74531

Hansen, L. (2003). Service Layer Essential for Future Success. *Ericsson Mobility World*. Available at: http://www.ericsson.com

Han, Y. J., Joseph, C. N., & Drèze, X. (2010). Signaling Status with Luxury Goods: The Role of Brand Prominence. *Journal of Marketing, 74*(4), 15–30. doi:10.1509/jmkg.74.4.15

Harvard Business Review Analytic Services. (2010). *The New Conversation: Taking Social Media from Talk to Action*. Harvard Business School Publishing.

Haydon, J. (2015). *Facebook Marketing for Dummies*. John Wiley & Sons.

Helgeson, J. G., & Supphellen, M. (2004). A Conceptual and Measurement Comparison of Self-Congruity and Brand Personality. *International Journal of Market Research*, *46*(2), 205–233. doi:10.1177/147078530404600201

Hennig-Thurau, T., Gwinner, K. P., Walsh, G., & Gremler, D. D. (2004). Electronic word-of-mouth via consumer-opinion platforms: What motivates consumers to articulate themselves on the Internet? *Journal of Interactive Marketing*, *18*(1), 38–52. doi:10.1002/dir.10073

Hill, P. (1997). On Goods and Services. *Review of Income and Wealth*, *23*(4), 13.

Hinnen, G., Hille, S. L., & Wittmer, A. (2017). Willingness to Pay for Green Products in Air Travel: Ready for Take-Off? *Business Strategy and the Environment*, *26*(2), 197–208. doi:10.1002/bse.1909

Hirschman, E. C., & Holbrook, M. B. (1982). Hedonic consumption: Emerging Concepts, Methods and Propositions. *Journal of Marketing*, *46*(3), 92–101. doi:10.2307/1251707

History Cooperative. (n.d.). Retrieved from: http://Historycooperative.org

Hoffman, D. L., & Novak, T. P. (1997). A New Marketing Paradigm for Electronic Commerce. *The Information Society*, *13*(1), 43–54. doi:10.1080/019722497129278

Hofmeyr, J., & Rice, B. (2000). *Commitment-Led Marketing*. Chichester, UK: Wiley.

Hogan, E. J., & Armstrong, G. (2001). Toward a Resource Based Theory of Business Exchange Relationships: The Role of Relational Asset Value. *Journal of Business-To-Business Marketing*, *8*(4), 3–28. doi:10.1300/J033v08n04_02

Holbrook, M. B., & Corfman, K. P. (1985). Quality and Value in the Consumption Experience: Phaedrus Rides Again. In C. V. S. How, J. J. Merchandise, & J. C. Olson (Eds.), *Perceived Quality*. Lanham, MD: Lexington Books.

Holbrook, M. B., & Hirschman, E. C. (1982). The Experiential Aspects of Consumption: Consumer Fantasies, Feelings, and Fun. *The Journal of Consumer Research*, *9*(2), 132–140. doi:10.1086/208906

Hollebeek, L. D., Glynn, M. S., & Brodie, R. J. (2014). Consumer Brand Engagement in Social Media: Conceptualization, Scale Development and Validation. *Journal of Interactive Marketing*, *28*(2), 149–165. doi:10.1016/j.intmar.2013.12.002

Homburg, C., & Giering, A. (2001). Personal Characteristics as Moderators of the Relationship between Customer Satisfaction and Loyalty— an Empirical Analysis. *Journal of Psychology and Marketing*, *18*(1), 43–66. doi:10.1002/1520-6793(200101)18:1<43::AID-MAR3>3.0.CO;2-I

Hong, J., & Sternthal, B. (2010). The Effects of Consumer Prior Knowledge and Processing Strategies on Judgments. *Jiewen Hong. Brian Sternthal*, *47*(2), 301–311.

Hong, J., & Sternthal, B. (2010). The effects of consumer prior knowledge and processing strategies on judgments. *JMR, Journal of Marketing Research*, *47*(2), 301–311. doi:10.1509/jmkr.47.2.301

Howe, J. (2006, June 6). *A Definition*. Retrieved from http://crowdsourcing.typepad.com/cs/2006/06/crowdsourcing_a.html

Howe, J. (2006). The rise of crowdsourcing. *Wired Magazine*, *14*(6), 1–4.

Howley, E. (2010). *Harness the power of social media: An Alternative Guide for Design & Construction Firms*. Zweigwhite.

Hoyer, W. D., Chandy, R., Dorotic, M., Krafft, M., & Singh, S. S. (2010). Consumer cocreation in new product development. *Journal of Service Research*, *13*(3), 283–296. doi:10.1177/1094670510375604

Hsu, L. C., & Liou, D. K. (2017). Maintaining Customer-Brand Relationships in the Mobile Industry: The Mediation Effects of Brand Relationship Benefits and Quality. *International Journal of Mobile Communications*, *15*(4), 388. doi:10.1504/IJMC.2017.084861

Huang, M. C., Cai, F., Tsang, A. S. L., & Zhou, N. (2011). Making your online voice loud: The critical role of WOM information. *European Journal of Marketing*, *45*(7/8), 1277–1297. doi:10.1108/03090561111137714

Huang, Z., & Benyoucef, M. (2013). From e-commerce to social commerce: A close look at design features. *Electronic Commerce Research and Applications*, *12*(4), 246–259. doi:10.1016/j.elerap.2012.12.003

Hutter, K., Hautz, J., Dennhardt, S., & Füller, J. (2013). The impact of user interactions in social media on brand awareness and purchase intention: The case of MINI on Facebook. *Journal of Product and Brand Management*, *22*(5/6), 342–351. doi:10.1108/JPBM-05-2013-0299

Hutton, J. G. (1997). A Study of Brand Equity in an Organisational-Buying Context. *Journal of Product and Brand Management*, 6(6), 428–439. doi:10.1108/10610429710190478

Indivik, L. (2013). *The 7 Species of Social Commerce*. Retrieved January 2, 2018, from http://mashable.com/2013/05/10/social-commerce-definition/#O2pecz7FrEqj

Itami, H., & Roehl, W. T. (1987). Mobilizing Invisible. Assets, MA: Harvard University Press.

Jacoby, J. (1971). A Model of Multi-Brand Loyalty. *Journal of Advertising Research*, 11(3), 25–31.

Jacoby, J., & Kyner, D. B. (1973). Brand Loyalty vs. Repeat Purchasing Behaviour. *JMR, Journal of Marketing Research*, 10(1), 1–9. doi:10.2307/3149402

Jamshed, S. (2014). Qualitative research method-interviewing and observation. *Journal of Basic and Clinical Pharmacy*, 5(4), 87–88. doi:10.4103/0976-0105.141942 PMID:25316987

Jeong, S. H., Kim, H. J., Yum, J. Y., & Hwang, Y. R. (2016). What Type of Content are Smartphone Users Addicted to? SNS vs Games. *Journal of Computers in Human Behavior*, 54, 10–17. doi:10.1016/j.chb.2015.07.035

Jeppesen, L. B., & Lakhani, K. R. (2010). Marginality and Problem-Solving Effectiveness in Broadcast Search. *Organization Science*, 21(5), 1016–1033. doi:10.1287/orsc.1090.0491

Jevremovic, M., Stavljanin, V., & Kostic-Stankovic, M. (2016). Istraživanje aktuelne i percepirane interaktivnosti veb sajta. *Info M*, 15(57), 42–47.

Jones, S. (2002). *3G Launch Strategies, Early Adopters, Why & How to make them yours*. Tarifica report.

Jones, P., Simmons, G., Packham, G., Beynon-Davies, P., & Pickernell, D. (2014). An exploration of the attitudes and strategic responses of sole proprietor micro-enterprises in adopting information and communication technology. *International Small Business Journal*, 32(3), 285–306. doi:10.1177/0266242612461802

Joshi, J. M., & Dumbre, G. M. (2017). Basic Concept of E-Commerce. *International Research Journal of Multidisciplinary Studies*, 3(3), 1–5.

Jung, J., Hun, H., & Oh, M. (2017). Travellers Switching Behaviour in the Airline Industry from the Perspective of the Push-Pull-Mooring Framework. *Journal of Torurism Management.*, *59*, 139–153. doi:10.1016/j.tourman.2016.07.018

Kahn, B. E., & Louie, T. A. (1990). Effects of Retraction of Price Promotions on Brand Choice Behaviour for Variety-Seeking and Last-purchase Loyal Consumers. *JMR, Journal of Marketing Research*, *27*(3), 279–289. doi:10.2307/3172586

Kanade, D. S. (2016). Engage your customers with contests: An overview. *Papirex - Indian Journal Research, 5*(3), 150-152.

Kancir, R. (2006). Marketing usluga, 2. izdanje Beogradska poslovna škola.

Kangis, P.Y. (2000). Service Quality and customer retentionin financial services. *Journal of Financial Services Marketing, 4*(4).

Kang, J.-Y., & Johnson, K. K. (2015). F-Commerce platform for apparel online social shopping: Testing a Mowen's 3M model. *International Journal of Information Management*, *35*(6), 691–701. doi:10.1016/j.ijinfomgt.2015.07.004

Kang, K. H., Stein, L., Heo, C. Y., & Lee, S. (2012). Consumers' willingness to pay for green initiatives of the hotel industry. *International Journal of Hospitality Management*, *31*(2), 564–572. doi:10.1016/j.ijhm.2011.08.001

Kapferer, J. N. (2001). *Reinventing the Brand: Can Top Brands Survive the New Market Realitie?* London: Kogan Page.

Kapoor, P. S. G. S. (2016). Impact of Anonymity and Identity Deception on Social Media eWOM. In Social Media: The Good, the Bad, and the Ugly. Springer.

Katz, E. &. (1956). *Interpersonal Relations and Mass Communications: Studies in the Flow of Influence.* Columbia University.

Keeny, D., & Marshall, J. F. (2000, November). Contextual Marketing: The Real Business on the Internet. *Harvard Business Review*, 119–125. PMID:11184966

Keller, K. L. (2001). Building Customer-Based Brand Equity. *Journal of Marketing Management, 10*(2), 16–26.

Keller, K. L. (1993). Conceptualizing, Measuring and Managing Customer-based Brand Equity. *Journal of Marketing*, *57*(1), 1–22. doi:10.2307/1252054

Keller, K. L. (2008). *Strategic Brand Management: Building, Measuring, and Managing Brand Equity* (3rd ed.). Upper Saddle River, NJ: Pearson Education, Inc.

Keller, K. L., & Lehmann, D. R. (2006). Brands and Branding: Research Findings and Future Priorities. *Journal of Marine Science*, *25*(6), 740–759. doi:10.1287/mksc.1050.0153

Kerlinger, F. N., & Lee, H. B. (2000). Foundations of Behavioural Research (4th ed.). Holt, NY: Harcourt College Publishers.

Kim, C. K., Han, D. C., & Park, S. B. (2001). The Effect of Brand Personality and Brand Identification on Brand Loyalty: Applying the Theory of Social Identification. *The Japanese Psychological Research*, *43*(4), 195–206. doi:10.1111/1468-5884.00177

Kim, D., Nam, J. K., Oh, J. S., & Kang, M. C. (2016). A Latent Profile Analysis of the Interplay between PC and Smartphone in Problematic Internet Use. *Journal of Computers in Human Behavior*, *56*, 360–368. doi:10.1016/j.chb.2015.11.009

Kim, H., Lee, I., & Lee, C. (2011). Building Web 2.0 enterprises: A study of small and medium enterprises in the United States. *International Small Business Journal*, *31*(2), 156–174. doi:10.1177/0266242611409785

Kim, Y., & Srivastava, J. (2007, August). Impact of social influence in e-commerce decision making. In *Proceedings of the Ninth International Conference on Electronic Commerce* (pp. 293-302). ACM. 10.1145/1282100.1282157

Kirtiş, A. K., & Karahan, F. (2011). To Be or Not to Be in Social Media Arena as the Most Cost-Efficient Marketing Strategy after the Global Recession. *Procedia: Social and Behavioral Sciences*, *24*, 260–268. doi:10.1016/j.sbspro.2011.09.083

Kleine, S. S., Kleine, R. E. III, & Allen, C. T. (1995). How is a Possession 'Me' or 'Not Me'? Characterizing Types and Antecedents of Material Possession Attachment. *The Journal of Consumer Research*, *22*(12), 327–343. doi:10.1086/209454

Klein, J. G., & Ahluwalia, R. (2005). Negativity in the evaluation of political candidates. *Journal of Marketing*, *69*(1), 131–142. doi:10.1509/jmkg.69.1.131.55509

Kootanaee, A., Babu, K., & Talari, H. (2013). Just-in-Time Manufacturing System: From Introduction to Implement. *International Journal of Economics, Business and Finance*, *1*(2), 7–25.

Kortam, W. (2017). *Sustainability Marketing: A Marketing Revolution or A Research Fad*. Academic Press.

Kotler, P. (2000). *Marketing Management Analysis, Planning, and Control* (5th ed.). Prentice-Hall.

Kotler, P., & Keller, K. (2014). *Marketing Management (15ᵗʰ ed.)*. Prentice Hall.

Kotler, P., & Keller, L. (2008). *Marketing Management* (13th ed.). Prentice Hall Publishing.

Kottler, P., & Amtrong, G. (1994). *Principles of Marketing*. Prentice Hall.

Kozlenkova, I. V., Samaha, S. A., & Palmatier, R. W. (2014). Resourcebased theory in marketing. *Journal of the Academy of Marketing Science*, *42*(1), 1–21. doi:10.100711747-013-0336-7

Kressman, F., Sirgy, M. J., Hermmann, A., Hubber, F., Hubber, S., & Lee, D. J. (2006). Direct and Indirect Effects of Self-Image Congruence on Brand Loyalty. *Journal of Business Research*, *59*(9), 955–964. doi:10.1016/j.jbusres.2006.06.001

Krishna, A., & Johar, G. V. (1996). Consumer perceptions of deals: Biasing effects of varying deal prices. *Journal of Experimental Psychology. Applied*, *2*(3), 187–206. doi:10.1037/1076-898X.2.3.187

Krohmer, H., Malär, L., & Nyffenegger, B. (2007). The Fit between Brand Personality and Consumer's Self: The Importance of Self-Congruence for Brand Performance. *AMA Winter Educators' Conference Proceedings*.

Kucuka, S. U., & Krishnamurthy, S. (2007). An analysis of consumer power on the Internet. *Technovation*, *27*(1-2), 47–56. doi:10.1016/j.technovation.2006.05.002

Kuenn, B. (2014). *10 Top Content Promotion Tools and Services*. Retrieved December 11, 2014 from http://www.verticalmeasures.com/content-marketing-2/10-topcontent-promotion-tools-and-services/

Kumar, S., Saravanakumar, K., & Deepa, K. (2016). On Privacy and Security in Social Media – A Comprehensive Study. *Procedia Computer Science*, *78*, 114–119. doi:10.1016/j.procs.2016.02.019

Kumar, V., & Shah, D. (2004). Building and Sustaining Profitable Customer Loyalty for 21st century. *Journal of Retailing*, *80*(4), 317–330. doi:10.1016/j.jretai.2004.10.007

Kuusik, A., & Varblane, U. (2009). How to Avoid Customers Leaving: The Case of the Estonian Telecommunication Industry. *Baltic Journal of Management*, *4*(1), 66–79. doi:10.1108/17465260910930458

Lamb, C. W., Hair, J. F., & McDaniel, C. D. (1992). *Principles of marketing*. Thomson South-Western.

Lam, S. K., Ahearne, M., Mullins, R., Hayati, B., & Schillewaert, N. (2013). Exploring the Dynamics of Antecedents to Consumer–Brand Identification with a New Brand. *Journal of the Academy of Marketing Science*, *41*(2), 243–252. doi:10.100711747-012-0301-x

Lam, S. K., Ahearn, M., Hu, Y., & Schillewaert, N. (2010). Resistance to Brand Switching When a Radically New Brand Is Introduced: A Social Identity Theory Perspective. *Journal of Marketing*, *74*(6), 128–146. doi:10.1509/jmkg.74.6.128

Lancaster, K. J. (1966). A New Approach to Consumer Theory. *Journal of Political Economy*, *74*(2), 132–157. doi:10.1086/259131

Larkin, M., & Thompson, A. (2012). Interpretative phenomenological analysis. *Qualitative Research Methods in Mental Health and Psychotherapy: A Guide for Students and Practitioners*, 99–116.

Lazer, W. (1969). Marketing's changing social relationships. *Journal of Marketing*, *33*(1), 3–9. doi:10.2307/1248739

Leckie, C., Munyaradzi, W. N., & Johnson, L. W. (2016). Antecedents of Consumer Brand Engagement and Brand Loyalty. *Journal of Marketing Management*, *32*(5-6), 5–6, 558–578. doi:10.1080/0267257X.2015.1131735

Leclerq, T., Hammedi, W., & Poncin, I. (2016). Ten years of cocreation: An integrative review [English Edition]. *Recherche et Applications en Marketing*, *31*(3), 26–60. doi:10.1177/2051570716650172

Lee, K.-T., & Koo, D.-M. (2012). Effects of attribute and valence of eWOM on message adoption: Moderating roles of subjective knowledge and regulatory focus. *Computer in Human Behavior*, *28*, 1974–1984.

Lee, J. P., Park, D.-H., & Han, I. (2008). The effect of negative online consumer reviews on product attitude: An information processing view. *Electronic Commerce Research and Applications*, *7*(3), 341–352. doi:10.1016/j.elerap.2007.05.004

Lee, J. W. (2009). Relationship between Consumer Personality and Brand Personality as Self-Concept: From the Case of Korean Automobile Brands. *Academy of Marketing Studies Journal*, *13*(1), 25–44.

Lee, J. Y., Kozlenkova, I. V., & Palmatier, R. W. (2015). Structural marketing: Using organizational structure to achieve marketing objectives. *Journal of the Academy of Marketing Science*, *43*(1), 73–99. doi:10.100711747-014-0402-9

Levison, J. C., & Rubin, C. (1996). *Guerrilla Marketing Online Weapons*. Hoghtom Mifflin Company.

Liang, T.-P., & Turban, E. (2012). Social Commerce: A Research Framework for Social Commerce. *International Journal of Electronic Commerce*, *16*(2), 5–13. doi:10.2753/JEC1086-4415160201

Ligas, M., & Cotte, J. (1999). The Process of Negotiating Brand Meaning: A Symbolic Interactionist Perspective. *Advances in Consumer Research. Association for Consumer Research (U. S.)*, *26*(1), 609–614.

Lin, Y., & Wu, L. Y. (2014). Exploring the role of dynamic capabilities in firm performance under the resource-based view framework. *Journal of Business Research*, *67*(3), 407–413. doi:10.1016/j.jbusres.2012.12.019

Litvin, S. G., Goldsmith, R. E., & Pan, B. (2008). Electronic word-of-mouth in hospitality and tourism management. *Tourism Management*, *29*(3), 458–468. doi:10.1016/j.tourman.2007.05.011

Liu, F., Li, J., Mizerski, D., & Soh, H. (2012). Self-congruity, brand attitude, and brand loyalty: A study on luxury brands. *European Journal of Marketing*, *46*(7/8), 922–937. doi:10.1108/03090561211230098

Liu, T. C., Wu, L. W., & Hung, C. T. (2007). The Effects of Inertia and Switching Barriers on Satisfaction-Retention Relationship: A Case of Financial Service Industries. *Journal of Management*, *24*, 671–687.

Ljubojević, Č. (1998). *Menadžment i marketing usluga*. Beograd: Želnid.

Lopez, M., & Sicilia, M. (2012). How WOM marketing contributes to new product adoption Testing competitive communication strategies. *European Journal of Marketing*, *47*(7), 1089–1114. doi:10.1108/03090561311324228

Lovelock, Ch., & Wirtz, J. (2004). *Services Marketing* (5th ed.). Pearson Education International.

Luccehetti, R., & Sterlaccini, A. (2004). The Adoption of ICT among SMEs: Evidence from an Itallian Survey. *Small Business Economics*, *23*(2), 15–168.

Lui, H. (2017). *Global Ecommerce Markets Will Reach $4 Trillion By 2020. Are You In?* Retrieved January 6, 2018, from https://www.shopify.com/enterprise/global-ecommerce-markets

Lury, C. (2004). *Brands: The Logos of the Global Economy*. London, New York: Routledge.

Lynn, G. S., Lipp, S. M., Akgün, A. E., & Cortez, A. Jr. (2002). Factors impacting the adoption and effectiveness of the world wide web in marketing. *Industrial Marketing Management*, *31*(1), 35–49. doi:10.1016/S0019-8501(00)00104-8

Malär, L., Krohmer, H., Hoyer, W. D., & Nyffenegger, B. (2011). Emotional Brand Attachment and Brand Personality: The Relative Importance of the Actual and the Ideal Self. *Journal of Marketing*, *75*(4), 35–52. doi:10.1509/jmkg.75.4.35

Manaktola, K., & Jauhari, V. (2007). Exploring consumer attitude and behaviour towards green practices in the lodging industry in India. *International Journal of Contemporary Hospitality Management*, *19*(5), 364–377. doi:10.1108/09596110710757534

Mano, H., & Oliver, R. L. (1993). Assessing the Dimensionality and Structure of the Consumption Experience: Evaluation, Feeling, and Satisfaction. *The Journal of Consumer Research*, *20*(3), 451–466. doi:10.1086/209361

Marinković, S., & Stanković, L. (2011). Institucionalna osnova zaštite korisnika finansijskih usluga u Srbiji. Marketing, 4(42), 257-266.

Marsden, P. (2010). *Social Commerce: Monetizing Social Media*. SYZYGY Group. Retrieved December 15, 2017, from https://digitalintelligencetoday.com/documents/Syzygy_2010.pdf

Marsden, P. (2011). *F-Commerce Selling on Facebook: The Opportunity for Consumer Brands*. SYZYGY Group. Retrieved December 15, 2017, from https://digitalintelligencetoday.com/documents/Syzygy_2011.pdf

Massoud, S., & Gupta, O. K. (2003). Consumer perception and attitude toward mobile communication. *International Journal of Mobile Communications, 1*(4), 390–408. doi:10.1504/IJMC.2003.003993

Matambalya, F., & Wolf, S. (2001). *The Role of ICT for the Performance of SMEs in East Africa: Empirical Evidence from Kenya and Tanzania. ZEF – Discussion Papers on Development Policy No. 42*. Bonn: Center for Development Research.

Matos, C. A., & Vargas, C. A. (2008). Word-of-mouth communications in marketing: A meta-analytic review of the antecedents and moderators. *Journal of the Academy of Marketing Science, 36*(4), 578–596. doi:10.100711747-008-0121-1

Mayer-Schönberger, V., & Cukier, K. (2013). *Big data: A revolution that will transform how we live, work, and think*. New York: Houghton Mifflin Harcourt.

Mayzlin, D., Yaniv Dover, Y., & Chevalier, J. (2013). Promotional Reviews: An Empirical Investigation of online review Manipulation. *The American Economic Review*, 1–40.

McConville, A. (2008). *Impact of ICT on SMEs in the South East. Prepared for South East of England Development Agency*. Birmingham, UK: SEEDA.

McCracken, G. (1988). *The Long Interview*. London: Sage. doi:10.4135/9781412986229

McFadden, D. (1986). The Choice Theory Approach to Market Research. *Journal of Marine Science, 5*(4), 275–297. doi:10.1287/mksc.5.4.275

McGrath, R. G. (2011, January). When your Business Model is in Trouble. *Harvard Business Review*, 96–98.

McLaughlin, C. M. (2012). *Preference of Homophily, credibility and word of mouth process* (PhD dissertation). Michigan State University.

Meenaghan, T. (1995). The Role of Advertising in Brand Image Development. *Journal of Product and Brand Management, 4*(4), 23–34. doi:10.1108/10610429510097672

Menkveld, B. (2013). *Exploring credibility in electronic word of mouth* (Master's thesis). University of Twente.

Merrill, T., Latham, K., Santalesa, R., & Navetta, D. (2011). *The Business Benefits May Be Enormous, But Can the Risks -- Reputational, Legal, Operational -- Be Mitigated?* ACE Limited.

Merz, M. A., Yi, H., & Vargo, S. L. (2009). The Evolving Brand Logic: A Service-Dominant Logic Perspective. *Journal of the Academy of Marketing Science*, *37*(3), 328–344. doi:10.100711747-009-0143-3

Milosavljević, M., & Mišković, V. (2011). *Elektronska trgovina*. Beograd: Univerzitet Singidunum.

Mintel Group. (2017). *Smartphone Purchasing Process*. London: Author.

Mirković, A. (2009). Društvene mreže – društveni fenomen. *Profit*, *16-17*, 12–13.

Mislove, A. M. M. (2007). Measurement and Analysis of Online Social Networks. In *7th ACM SIGCOMM conference on Internet measurement* (pp. 29-42). San Diego, CA: AMC. 10.1145/1298306.1298311

Mitchell, R., Hutchinson, K., Quinn, B., and Gilmore, A. (2015). A framework for SME retail branding. *Journal of Marketing Management*, *31*(17-18), 1818-1850

Mitchell, V.-W. (1999). Consumer Perceived Risk: Conceptualisations and Models. *European Journal of Marketing*, *33*(1/2), 163–195. doi:10.1108/03090569910249229

Mithas, S., Lee, M. R., Earley, S., Murugesan, S., & Djavanshir, R. (2013). Leveraging big data and business analytics. *IT Professional*, *15*(6), 18–20. doi:10.1109/MITP.2013.95

Mittal, B. (2002). Services Communications: from mindless tangibilization to meaningful messages. *Journal of Services Marketing, 16*(5), 424 – 431.

Molinillo, S., Jose, L., & Fernandez, A. (2016). Hotel Assessment through Social Media: The case of TripAdvisor. *Tourism & Management Studies*, *12*(1), 15–24. doi:10.18089/tms.2016.12102

Mollerup, P. (1997). *Marks of Excellence: The History and Taxonomy of Trademarks*. London: Phaidon.

Monino, J., Sedkaoui, S., & Monino, J. (2016). *Big Data, Open Data and Data Development*. London: ISTE. doi:10.1002/9781119285199

Moon, H., & Sprott, E. D. (2016). Ingredient Branding for a Luxury Brand: The Role of Brand and Product Fit. *Journal of Business Research*, *69*(4), 5768–5774. doi:10.1016/j.jbusres.2016.04.173

Morgan, R. M., & Hunt, S. D. (1994). The Commitment-Trust Theory of Relationship Marketing. *Journal of Marketing*, *58*(3), 20–38. doi:10.2307/1252308

Morrison, A., Cheong, H., & McMillan, S. (2013). Posting, Lurking, and Networking: Behaviours and Characteristics of Consumers in the Context of User-Generated Content. *Journal of Interactive Advertising*, *13*(2), 97–108. doi:10.1080/1525201 9.2013.826552

Morris, S. B. (2008). Book Review: Hunter, JE, & Schmidt, FL (2004). Methods of Meta-Analysis: Correcting Error and Bias in Research Findings. Thousand Oaks, CA: Sage. *Organizational Research Methods*, *11*(1), 184–187. doi:10.1177/1094428106295494

Mortimer, K. (2002). Integrated advertising theories with conceptual models of services advertising. *Journal of Services Marketing*, *16*(5), 21. doi:10.1108/08876040210436920

Mudamb, S. M., & Schuff, D. (2010). What makes a helpful online review? A study of customer reviews on Amazon.com. *Management Information Systems Quarterly*, *34*(1), 185–200. doi:10.2307/20721420

Muniz, A. M. Jnr, & O'Guinn, T. C. (2001). Brand Community. *The Journal of Consumer Research*, *27*(4), 412–432. doi:10.1086/319618

Murphy, J. (1990). *Brand Strategy*. Cambridge: Director Books.

Murphy, J. (1992). What is Branding? In J. Murphy (Ed.), *Branding, a key marketing tool* (pp. 1–12). London: Macmillan. doi:10.1007/978-1-349-12628-6_1

Mutula, S. M., & Van Brakel, P. (2007). E-readiness of SMEs in the ICT sector in Botswana with respect to information access. *The Electronic Library*, *24*(3), 402–417. doi:10.1108/02640470610671240

Nahed Al-Haidari, J. (2014). The influence of electronic-word-of-mouth on consumer decision-making for beauty products in a Kuwaiti Women`s online community. *Journal of Contemporary Eastern Asia*, *13*(2), 3-14.

Nah, F. F.-H., Zhao, F., & Zhu, W. (2003). Factors influencing Users' Adoption of Mobile Computing. In J. Mariga (Ed.), *Managing E-commerce and Mobile Computing Technologies Book*. Hershey, PA: Idea Group Inc.

Nam, J., Ekinci, Y., & Whyatt, G. (2011). Brand Equity, Brand Loyalty and Consumer Satisfaction. *Annals of Tourism Research*, *38*(3), 1009–1030. doi:10.1016/j.annals.2011.01.015

Namkung, Y., & Jang, S. (2017). Are consumers willing to pay more for green practices at restaurants? *Journal of Hospitality & Tourism Research (Washington, D.C.)*, *41*(3), 329–356. doi:10.1177/1096348014525632

Nardo, M., Loi, M., Rosati, R. & Manca, A. (2011). The Consumer Empowerment Index – A measure of skills, awareness and engagement of European Consumers. *JRC Scientific and Technological Reports*, 1 – 232.

Neumann, M. (2015). *What does the research tell us about word-of-mouth communication?-A literature review*. University of Rostock.

Ngai, E. W. T., Xiu, L., & Chau, D. C. K. (2009). Application of data mining techniques in customer relationship management: A literature review and classification. *Expert Systems with Applications*, *36*(2), 2592–2602. doi:10.1016/j.eswa.2008.02.021

Ngai, E., Moon, K., Lam, S., Chin, E., & Tao, S. (2015). Social media models, technologies, and applications. *Industrial Management & Data Systems*, *115*(5), 769–802. doi:10.1108/IMDS-03-2015-0075

Ng, C. (2014). Intention to purchase on social commerce websites across cultures: A cross-regional study. *Information & Management*, *50*(8), 609–620. doi:10.1016/j.im.2013.08.002

Nguyen, T. H., & Waring, T. S. (2013). The adoption of customer relationship management (CRM) technology in SMEs: An empirical study. *Journal of Small Business and Enterprise Development*, *20*(4), 824–848. doi:10.1108/JSBED-01-2012-0013

Norazah, M. S. (2013). Students' dependence on smart phones: The influence of social needs, social influences and convenience. *Campus-Wide Information Systems*, *30*(2), 124–134. doi:10.1108/10650741311306309

Nyilasy, G. (2006). Word of mouth: What we really know - and what we don't. In *Connected marketing* (pp. 161–184). London, UK: Butterworth-Heinemann.

O'Keeffe, A., Ozuem, W., & Lancaster, G. (2016). Leadership Marketing: An Exploratory Study. *Journal of Strategic Marketing*, *24*(5), 418–443. doi:10.1080/0965254X.2014.1001867

Obermiller, C., & Spangenberg, E. R. (1998). On the Origin and Distinctness of Skepticism toward Advertising. *Marketing Letters*, *11*(4), 311–322. doi:10.1023/A:1008181028040

Olanrewaju, T., Smaje, K., & Willmott, P. (2014). *The several traits of effective digital enterprises*. McKinsey Insights.

Oliver, R. (1980). A cognitive Model of The Antecedents and Consequences of Satisfaction Decisions. *JMR, Journal of Marketing Research*, *17*(4), 460–469. doi:10.2307/3150499

Oliver, R. L. (1997). *Satisfaction: A Behavioural Perspective on the Consumer*. New York: Irwin/McGraw-Hill.

Oliver, R. L. (1999). Whence Consumer Loyalty? *Journal of Marketing*, *63*(10), 33–44. doi:10.2307/1252099

Orth, U. R., & De Marchi, R. (2007). Understanding The Relationships Between Functional, Symbolic, And Experiential Brand Beliefs, Product Experiential Attributes, And Product Schema Advertising-Trial Interactions Revisited. *Journal of Marketing Theory and Practice*, *15*(3), 219–233. doi:10.2753/MTP1069-6679150303

Oswald, L. R. (1999). Culture Swapping: Consumption and the Ethnogenesis of Middle-Class Haitan Immigrants. *The Journal of Consumer Research*, *25*(3), 303–318. doi:10.1086/209541

Ozuem, W., Howell, K. E., & Lancaster, G. (2008). Communicating in the New Interactive Marketplace. *European Journal of Marketing*, *42*(9/10), 1059–1083. doi:10.1108/03090560810891145

Ozuem, W., Thomas, T., & Lancaster, G. (2016). The Influence of Customer Loyalty on Small Island Economies: An empirical and Exploratory Study. *Journal of Strategic Marketing*, *24*(6), 447–469. doi:10.1080/0965254X.2015.1011205

Park, R. E. (1959). Race and Culture. Glencoe, IL: The Free Press.

Park, C. S., & Srinivasan, V. (1994). A Survey-Based Method for Measuring and Understanding Brand Equity and Its Extendibility. *JMR, Journal of Marketing Research*, *31*(2), 271–288. doi:10.2307/3152199

Park, C. W. B., Jaworski, J., & MacInnis, D. J. (1986). Strategic Brand Concept-Image Management. *Journal of Marketing*, *50*(4), 135–145. doi:10.2307/1251291

Park, C. W., Eisingerich, A. B., & Park, J. W. (2013). Attachment– Aversion (AA) Model of Customer–Brand Relationships. *Journal of Consumer Psychology*, *23*(2), 229–248. doi:10.1016/j.jcps.2013.01.002

Park, C. W., MacInnis, D. J., & Priester, J. R. (2009). Research Directions on Strong Brand Relationships. In D. J. MacInnis, C. W. Park, & J. R. Priester (Eds.), *Handbook of Brand Relationships*. Armonk, NY: M.E. Sharpe.

Park, C., & Lee, T. M. (2009). ParkInformation direction, website reputation and eWOM effect: A moderating role of product type. *Journal of Business Research*, *62*(1), 61–67. doi:10.1016/j.jbusres.2007.11.017

Park, J. K., & Yang, S. (2006). The Moderating Role of Consumer Trust and Experiences: Value Driven Usage of Mobile Technology. *International Journal of Mobile Marketing*, *1*(2), 24–32.

Paulhus, D. L. (1984a). *Balanced Inventory of Social Desirable Responding. PsycTESTS Dataset.* APA. doi:10.1037/t58985-000

Paulhus, D. L. (1984b). Two-component models of socially desirable responding. *Journal of Personality and Social Psychology*, *46*(3), 598–609. doi:10.1037/0022-3514.46.3.598

Payne, A. F., Storbacka, K., & Frow, P. (2008). Managing the co-creation of value. *Journal of the Academy of Marketing*, *36*(1), 83–96. doi:10.100711747-007-0070-0

Pelsmacker, P. (2010). *Marketing Communications: A European Perspective* (4th ed.). Pearson Education.

Peter, J., Paul, J., Olson, C., & Grunert, K. G. (1999). *Consumer Behaviour and Marketing Strategy* (European Edition). London: McGraw Hill.

Phau, I., & Kong, C. L. (2001). Brand Personality and Consumer Self Expression: Single or Dual Carriageway? *Journal of Brand Management*, 8(6), 428–444. doi:10.1057/palgrave.bm.2540042

Pietkiewicz, I., & Smith, J. A. (2014). A practical guide to using interpretative phenomenological analysis in qualitative research psychology. *Psychological Journal*, 20(1), 7–14.

Piller, F. T., & Walcher, D. (2006). Toolkits for idea competitions: A novel method to integrate users in new product development. *R & D Management*, 36(3), 307–318. doi:10.1111/j.1467-9310.2006.00432.x

Plummer, J. T. (1984). How Personality Makes a Difference. *Journal of Advertising Research*, 24(6), 27–31.

Poetz, M. K., & Schreier, M. (2012). The value of crowdsourcing: Can users really compete with professionals in generating new product ideas? *Journal of Product Innovation Management*, 29(2), 245–256. doi:10.1111/j.1540-5885.2011.00893.x

Polonsky, M. J., & Rosenberger, P. J. III. (2001). Reevaluating green marketing: A strategic approach. *Business Horizons*, 44(5), 21–30. doi:10.1016/S0007-6813(01)80057-4

Premkumar, G., & Roberts, M. (1999). Adoption of new information technologies in rural small businesses. *Omega*, 27(4), 467–484. doi:10.1016/S0305-0483(98)00071-1

Prothero, A. (1998). *Green Marketing: The 'Fad' That Won't Slip Slide Away*. Taylor & Francis.

Queirós, A., Faria, D., & Almeida, F. (2017). Strengths and Limitation of Qualitative and Quantitative Research Methods. *European Journal of Education Studies*, 3(9), 369–387.

Quinton, S. (2013). The Community Brand Paradigm: A Response to Brand Management's Bilemma in the Digital Era. *Journal of Marketing Management*, 29(7-8), 7–8, 912–932. doi:10.1080/0267257X.2012.729072

Radice, R. (2014). *How to Use Visual Content to Improve Social Media Results.* Retrieved November 20, 2014 from http://maximizesocialbusiness.com/usevisual-content-improve-social-media-results-16250/

Rahman, I., Park, J., & Chi, C. G. (2015). Consequences of "greenwashing" Consumers' reactions to hotels' green initiatives. *International Journal of Contemporary Hospitality Management, 27*(6), 1054–1081. doi:10.1108/IJCHM-04-2014-0202

Rao, H., Davis, F. G., & Ward, A. (2000). Embeddedness, Social Identity and Mobility: Why Firms Leave the NASDAQ and Join the New York Stock Exchange. *Administrative Science Quarterly, 45*(2), 268–292. doi:10.2307/2667072

Reed, A. I. I. (2002). Social Identity as a Useful Perspective for Self-Concept Based Consumer Research. *Journal of Psychology and Marketing, 19*(3), 235–266. doi:10.1002/mar.10011

Reicheld, F. (1996). *The Loyalty Effect: The Hidden Force behind Growth, Profits, and Lasting Value.* Boston: Harvard Business School Press.

Richins, M. L. (1994). Valuing Things: The Public and Private Meanings of Possessions. *The Journal of Consumer Research, 21*(10), 504–521. doi:10.1086/209414

Roos, I. (1999). Switching processes in customer relationships. *Journal of Service Research, 2*(1), 376–393. doi:10.1177/109467059921006

Roselius, T. (1971). Consumer Rankings of Risk Reduction Method. *Journal of Marketing, 35*(1), 55–61. doi:10.2307/1250565

Roth, Y., Brabham, D.C., & Lemoine, J.F. (2015). Recruiting Individuals to a Crowdsourcing Community: Applying Motivational Categories to an Ad Copy Test. *Advances in Crowdsourcing*, 15-31.

Ruth, J. A. (2001). Promoting a Brand's Emotion Benefits: The Influence of Emotion Categorization Processes on Consumer Evaluations. *Journal of Consumer Psychology, 11*(2), 99–113. doi:10.1207/S15327663JCP1102_03

Salwa, H., & Steils, N. (2018). Crowdsourcing: A Double-Edged Sword Outsourcing Strategy. In M. Franco (Ed.), Positive and Negative Aspects of Outsourcing. InTech.

Sánchez, C. A. (2015, June 1). *ewomcharacteristics.* Retrieved Jan 10, 2018, from brandba.se: http://www.brandba.se/blog/ewomcharacteristics

Saremi, H. Q. (2014). *Effectiveness of electronic word of mouth recommendations* (PhD thesis). McMaster University.

Satell, G. (2014). Five things managers should know about the big data economy. *Forbes*.

Sathish, M., Kumar, K. S., Naveen, K. J., & Jeevanantham, V. (2011). A Study on Consumer Switching Behaviour in Cellular Service Provider: A Study with reference to Chennai. *Far East Journal of Psychology and Business*, 2(2), 72.

Schaffers, H., Komninos, N., Pallot, M., Trousse, B., Nilsson, M., & Oliveria, A. (2011). Smart Cities and the Future Internet: Towards Cooperation Frameworks for Open Innovation. In *The future Internet* (pp. 431–446). Berlin: Springer. doi:10.1007/978-3-642-20898-0_31

Schindler, R. M., Bickart, B. (2004). Published word of mouth: Referable, consumer-generated information on the Internet. *Online consumer psychology: Understanding and influencing consumer behavior in the virtual world, 2,* 35-61.

Schütze, N. (2014). Electronic Word-of-Mouth Communication for Local Service Providers. *Technology Innovation Management Review*, 4(4), 35-42. Retrieved from http://timreview.ca/article/783

Sedkaoui, S. (2017). The Internet, Data Analytics and Big Data. In Internet Economics: Models, Mechanisms and Management (pp. 144-166). Gottinger, H.W: eBook Bentham science.

Sedkaoui, S., & Monino, J. L. (2016). *Big data, Open Data and Data Development*. New York: ISTE-Wiley.

Seiders, K., & Tigert, D. J. (1997). Impact of Market Entry and Competitive Structure on Store Switching/Store Loyalty. *International Review of Retail, Distribution and Consumer Research*, 7(3), 227–247. doi:10.1080/095939697343003

Shankar, V., Smith, A. K., & Rangaswamy, A. (2003). Customer Satisfaction and Loyalty in Online and Offline Environments. *International Journal of Research in Marketing*, 20(2), 153–175. doi:10.1016/S0167-8116(03)00016-8

Shapiro, L. M. (2010). *Severe Market Dissruption on 6ᵗʰ May, 2010: Congressional Testimony*. Collingdale, PA: Diane Publishing Co.

Sharma, S., & Crossler, R. (2014). Intention to Engage in *Social commerce*: uses and gratifications approach. *Proceeding of the XX Americas Conference on Information Systems*. Retrieved December 26, 2017, from http://aisel.aisnet.org/cgi/viewcontent.cgi?article=1695&context=amcis2014

Shenglin, B. (2017). Digital infrastructure: Overcoming Digital Divide in Emerging Economies. Zhejiang University Center for Internet and Financial Innovation: G20 Insight.

Sherif, C. W., & Sherif, M. (1967). *Attitude, Ego-involvement, and Change*. Westport, CT: Green Wood Press.

Sheth, J. N., Newman, B. I., & Gross, B. L. (1991). Why We Buy What We Buy: A Theory of Consumption Values. *Journal of Business Research*, *22*(2), 159–170. doi:10.1016/0148-2963(91)90050-8

Shiels, H., McIvor, R., & O'Reilly, D. (2003). Understanding the Implications of ICT Adoption: Insights from SMEs. *Journal of Logistics Information Management*, *16*(5), 312–326. doi:10.1108/09576050310499318

Shimp, T. A., & Madden, T. J. (1988). Consumer-Object Relations: A Conceptual Framework Based Analogously on Sternberg's Triangular Theory of Love. *Advances in Consumer Research. Association for Consumer Research (U. S.)*, *15*(1), 163–168.

Shneiderman, B. (2007). Creativity support tools: Accelerating discovery and innovation. *Communications of the ACM*, *50*(12), 20–32. doi:10.1145/1323688.1323689

Shroff, G. (2013). *The Intelligent Web, Search, Smart Algorithms and Big Data*. Oxford, UK: Oxford Univ. Press.

Simmons, G., Armstrong, G., & Durkin, M. (2011). An exploration of small business website optimization: Enablers, influencers and an assessment approach. *International Small Business Journal*, *29*(5), 534–561. doi:10.1177/0266242610369945

Sirgy, J. M. (1982). Self-Concept in Consumer Behaviour: A Critical Review. *The Journal of Consumer Research*, *9*(12), 287–300. doi:10.1086/208924

Sirgy, M. J., Grewal, D., & Mangleburg, T. (2000). Retail Environment, Self-Congruity, and Retail Patronage: An Integrative Model and a Research Agenda. *Journal of Business Research*, *49*(2), 127–138. doi:10.1016/S0148-2963(99)00009-0

Slawsby, A., Leibovitch, A. M., & Giusto, R. (2003). *Worldwide Mobile Phone Forecast and Analysis, 2003-2007*. IDC Report, No. 29586.

Sloot, L. M., Verhoef, P. C., & Franses, P. H. (2005). The Impact of Brand Equity and the Hedonic Level of Products on Consumer Stock-Out Reactions. *Journal of Retailing, 81*(1), 15–34. doi:10.1016/j.jretai.2005.01.001

Smith, M., & Treadway, C. (2010). *Facebook Marketing: An hour a day*. Wiley Publishing, Inc.

Smith, N., Wollan, R., & Zhou, C. (2010). *Social Media Management Handbook: Everything You Need to Know to Get Social Media Working in Your Business*. Hoboken, NJ: John Wiley & Sons Inc.

Solomon, M. R. (2002). The Role of Products as Social Stimuli: A Symbolic Interactionism Perspective. *The Journal of Consumer Research, 10*(10), 319–329.

Sony, M., & Mekoth, N. (2014). The dimensions of frontline employee adaptability in power sector: A grounded theory approach. *International Journal of Energy Sector*. Retrieved from http://www.emeraldinsight.com/doi/abs/10.1108/IJESM-03-2013-0008

Sony, M., Mekoth, N., & Therisa, K. K. (2018). Understanding nature of empathy through the lens of service encounter: A phenomenological study on FLE's. *International Journal of Productivity and Quality Management, 23*(1), 55–73. doi:10.1504/IJPQM.2018.088608

Statista. (2017a). *Retail e-commerce sales worldwide from 2014 to 2021 (in billion U.S. dollars)*. Retrieved January 6, 2018, from https://www.statista.com/statistics/379046/worldwide-retail-e-commerce-sales/

Statista. (2017b). *Most famous social network sites worldwide as of September 2017, ranked by number of active users (in millions)*. Retrieved January 6, 2018, from https://www.statista.com/statistics/272014/global-social-networks-ranked-by-number-of-users/

Stavljanin, V., Kostic-Stankovic, M., & Cvijovic, J. (2016). Effects of indirect advertising in video games: Adverisers' and Players' perspective. *Symposium proceedings from XV International symposium Reshaping the Future Through Sustainable Business Development and Entrepreneurship*, 889-892.

Steils, N., & Hanine, S. (2016). Creative contests: Knowledge generation and underlying learning dynamics for idea generation. *Journal of Marketing Management*, *32*(17-18), 1647–1669. doi:10.1080/0267257X.2016.1251956

Stelzner, M. (2015). *Social Media Marketing Industry report: How Marketers are Using Social Media to grow their Businesses*. Social Media Examiner.

Stern, B. B., Thompson, J. C., & Arnould, E. J. (1998). Narrative Analysis of a Marketing Relationship: The Consumer's Perspective. *Journal of Psychology and Marketing*, *15*(3), 195–214. doi:10.1002/(SICI)1520-6793(199805)15:3<195::AID-MAR1>3.0.CO;2-5

Stokes, R. (2014). eMarketing: The essential guide to marketing in a digital world (5th ed.). Quirk eMarketing (Pty) Ltd.

Sung, Y., & Kim, J. (2010). Effects of Brand Personality on Brand Trust and Brand Affect. *Journal of Psychology and Marketing*, *27*(7), 639–661. doi:10.1002/mar.20349

Swait, J., & Erdem, T. (2007). Brand Effects on Choice and Choice Set Formation under Uncertainty. *Journal of Marine Science*, *26*(5), 679–697. doi:10.1287/mksc.1060.0260

Sweeney, J. C., & Soutar, G. N. (2001). Consumer Perceived Value: The Development of a Multiple Item Scale. *Journal of Retailing*, *77*(2), 203–220. doi:10.1016/S0022-4359(01)00041-0

Tajfel, H., & Turner, J. C. (1979). The Social Identity Theory of Inter-Group Behaviour. In *Psychology of Intergroup Relations*. Chicago: Nelson-Hall.

Tang, C. M. F., & Lam, D. (2017). The role of extraversion and agreeableness traits on Gen Y's attitudes and willingness to pay for green hotels. *International Journal of Contemporary Hospitality Management*, *29*(1), 607–623. doi:10.1108/IJCHM-02-2016-0048

Tan, K. S., Chong, S. C., Lin, B., & Eze, U. C. (2009). Internet-based ICT adoption: Evidence from Malaysian SMEs. *Industrial Management & Data Systems*, *109*(2), 224–244. doi:10.1108/02635570910930118

Tan, W., Hsiao, Y., Tseng, S., & Chang, C. (2017). Smartphone Application Personality and its Relationship to Personalities of Smartphone Users and Social Capital Accrued through use of Smartphone Social Applications. *Journal of Telematics and Informatics*, *35*(1), 255–26. doi:10.1016/j.tele.2017.11.007

Tellis, G. J., Prabhu, J. C., & Chandy, R. K. (2009). Radical innovation across nations: The preeminence of corporate culture. *Journal of Marketing*, *73*(1), 3–23. doi:10.1509/jmkg.73.1.3

Terwiesch, C., & Xu, Y. (2008). Innovation Contests, Open Innovation, and Multiagent Problem Solving. *Management Science*, *45*(9), 1529–1543. doi:10.1287/mnsc.1080.0884

Thakor, D. C. (2016). The Social CRM - New Age of Business Strategy for the Organization: An Explorative Study. *Indian Journal Of Applied Research*, *6*(2), 195–197.

Thomke, S., & von Hippel, E. (2002). Customers as innovators: A new way to create value. *Harvard Business Review*, *80*(4), 74–81. PMID:12024760

Thompson, D. V., Hamilton, R. W., & Rust, R. T. (2005). Feature Fatigue: When Product Capabilities become too much of a Good Thing. *JMR, Journal of Marketing Research*, *42*(4), 431–442. doi:10.1509/jmkr.2005.42.4.431

Thrift, N. (2006). Re-inventing invention: New tendencies in capitalist commodification. *Economy and Society*, *35*(2), 279–306. doi:10.1080/03085140600635755

Tiago, O., & Maria, F. M. (2010). Understanding e-business adoption across industries in European countries. *Industrial Management & Data Systems*, *110*(9), 1337–1354. doi:10.1108/02635571011087428

Tripeadvisor. (2012). *TripAdvisor Survey Reveals Travelers Growing Greener*. Author.

Trusov, M., Bucklin, R., & Pauwels, K. (2009). Effects of Word-of-Mouth Versus Traditional Marketing: Findings from an Internet Social Networking Site. *Journal of Marketing*, *73*(5), 1–24. doi:10.1509/jmkg.73.5.90

Turban, E., Bolloju, N., & Liang, T. (2010). Social commerce: An e-commerce perspective. *Proceedings of the International Conference on Electronic Commerce: Roadmap for the Future of Electronic Business*, 33-42.

Turban, E., Strauss, J., & Lai, L. (2016). *Social Commerce: marketing, technology and management*. Springer. doi:10.1007/978-3-319-17028-2

Turban, E., Whiteside, J., King, D., & Outland, J. (2017). *Introduction to Electronic Commerce and Social Commerce*. Springer. doi:10.1007/978-3-319-50091-1

Tussyadiah, I. P. (2015). The Influence of Innovativeness on On-Site Smartphone Use among American. *Journal of Travel & Tourism Marketing*. doi:10.1080/1054 8408.2015.1068263

Uncles, M., & Laurent, G. (1997). Travelers: Implications for Context-based Push Marketing Editorial. *International Journal of Research in Marketing, 14*, 399-404.

Underwood, R. L., Klein, N. M., & Burke, R. R. (2001). Packaging Communication: Attentional Effects of Product Imagery. *Journal of Product and Brand Management, 10*(7), 403–422. doi:10.1108/10610420110410531

Van Nguyen, T. T., & Nguyen, T. D. (2016). Green Marketing Strategy-A New Trend for Businesses in Vietnam. In *Green Technology and Sustainable Development (GTSD), International Conference on* (pp. 116–119). IEEE. 10.1109/GTSD.2016.36

Van Trijp, H. C. M., Hoyer, W. D., & Inman, J. J. (1996). Why Switch? Product Category-Level Explanations for True Variety-Seeking Behaviour. *JMR, Journal of Marketing Research, 33*(3), 281–292. doi:10.2307/3152125

Vandermerwe, S., & Oliff, M. D. (1990). Customers drive corporations. *Long Range Planning, 23*(6), 10–16. doi:10.1016/0024-6301(90)90096-M

Viaene, S. (2013). Data scientists aren't domain experts. *IT Professional, 15*(6), 12–17. doi:10.1109/MITP.2013.93

Von Hippel, E. (2001). User toolkits for innovation. *Journal of Product Innovation, 18*(4), 247–257. doi:10.1016/S0737-6782(01)00090-X

Von Hippel, E., & Katz, R. (2002). Shifting innovation to users via toolkits. *Management Science, 48*(7), 821–833. doi:10.1287/mnsc.48.7.821.2817

Wang, C. (2009). Linking shopping and social networking: Approaches to social shopping. *Proceedings of the 15th Americas Conference on Information Systems (AMCIS)*.

Wang, C., & Zhang, P. (2012). The Evolution of Social Commerce: An Examination from the People, Business, Technology, and Information Perspective. *Communications of the AIS, 31*(5), 105–127.

Wang, D., Park, S., & Fesenmaier, D. R. (2012). The Role of Smartphones in Mediating the Touristic Experience. *Journal of Travel Research, 51*(4), 371–387. doi:10.1177/0047287511426341

Wang, D., Xiang, Z., & Fesenmaier, D. R. (2014). Adapting to the Mobile World: A Model of Smartphone Use. *Journal of Tourism Research, 48*, 11–26.

Wang, X. (2011). The Effect of Inconsistent Word-of-Mouth During the Service Encounter. *Journal of Services Marketing, 25*(4), 252–259. doi:10.1108/08876041111143087

Wanke, M., Bohner, G., & Jurkowitsch, A. (1997). There Are Many Reasons to Drive a BMW: Does Imagined Ease of Argument Generation Influence Attitudes? *The Journal of Consumer Research, 24*(9), 170–177. doi:10.1086/209502

Warf, B., & Vincent, P. (2007). Multiple Geographies of the Arab Internet. *Royal Geographical Society, 39*(1), 83–96.

Wasp Barcode Technologies. (2015). *State of Small Business Report.* Author.

Wathieu, L., Brenner, L., Carmon, Z., Chattopadhyay, A., Drolet, A., Gourville, J., ... Wu, G. (2002). Consumer Control and Empowerment: A Primer. *Marketing Letters, 13*(3), 295–303. doi:10.1023/A:1020311914022

Weber, L., & Henderson, L. L. (2014). *The digital marketer: Ten new skills you must learn to stay relevant and customer-centric.* Hoboken, NJ: John Wiley & Sons.

Wee, T. T. T. (2004). Extending Human Personality to Brands: The Stability Factor. *Journal of Brand Management, 11*(4), 317–330. doi:10.1057/palgrave.bm.2540176

Wei, L. Q., & Lau, C. M. (2010). High performance work systems and performance: The role of adaptive capability. *Human Relations, 63*(10), 1487–1511. doi:10.1177/0018726709359720

Westbrook, R. A. (1987). Product/Consumption Based Affective Responses and Post Purchase Processes. *JMR, Journal of Marketing Research, 24*(3), 258–270. doi:10.2307/3151636

Wigand, R. T., Benjamin, R. I., & Birkland, J. L. (2008, August). Web 2.0 and beyond: implications for electronic commerce. In *Proceedings of the 10th International Conference on Electronic Commerce* (p. 7). ACM. 10.1145/1409540.1409550

Wu, P. C., & Wang, Y.-C. (2011). The influences of electronic word-of-mouth message appeal and message source credibility on brand attitude. *Asia Pacific Journal of Marketing and Logistics, 23*(4), 448–472. doi:10.1108/13555851111165020

Yadav, M., Valck, K., Henning-Thurau, T., Hoffman, D., & Spann, M. (2013). Social Commerce: A Contingency Framework for Assessing Marketing Potential. *Journal of Interactive Marketing*, *27*(4), 311–323. doi:10.1016/j.intmar.2013.09.001

Yayli, A., & Bayram. (2012). eWOM: The effects of online consumer reviews on purchasing decisions of electronic goods. *International Journal of Internet Marketing and Advertising*, 52-61.

Yeh, C. H., Wang, Y. S., & Yieh, K. (2016). Predicting smartphone brand loyalty: Consumer value and consumer-brand identification perspectives. *International Journal of Information Management*, *36*(3), 245–257. doi:10.1016/j.ijinfomgt.2015.11.013

Yi, Y. (1990). A Critical Review of Consumer Satisfaction. In V. Zeithaml (Ed.), American Marketing Association (pp. 68–123). Chicago: Academic Press.

Yin, D., Bond, S., & Zhang, H. (2014). Anxious or Angry? Effects of discrete emotions on the Perceived Helpfulness of Online Reviews. *Management Information Systems Quarterly*, *38*(2), 539–560. doi:10.25300/MISQ/2014/38.2.10

Yoo, B., Donthu, N., & Lee, S. (2000). An Examination of Selected Marketing Mix Elements and Brand Equity. *Journal of the Academy of Marketing Science*, *28*(2), 195–211. doi:10.1177/0092070300282002

Zhang, J., & Bloemer, J. M. M. (2008). The Impact of Value Congruence on Consumer-Service Brand Relationships. *Journal of Service Research*, *11*(8), 161–178. doi:10.1177/1094670508322561

Zhang, T., Behzad, A. O., & Cihan, C. (2017). Generation Y's positive and negative eWOM: Use of social media and mobile technology. *International Journal of Contemporary Hospitality Management*, *29*(2), 732–761. doi:10.1108/IJCHM-10-2015-0611

Zhang, Y., Trusvov, M., Stephen, A., & Jamal, Z. (2017). Online Shopping and Social Media: Friends or Foes? *Journal of Marketing*, *81*(6), 24–41.

Zhihong, L., Duffield, C., & Wilson, D. (2015). Research on the Driving Factors of Customer Participation in Service Innovation in a Virtual Brand Community. *International Journal of Innovation Science*, *7*(4), 299–309. doi:10.1108/IJIS-07-04-2015-B006

Zhou, L., Zhang, P., & Zimmermann, H.-D. (2013). Social commerce research: An integrated view. *Electronic Commerce Research and Applications*, *12*, 61–68.

Zhu, K., & Kraemer, K. L. (2005). Post-adoption variations in usage and value of e-business by organizations: Cross-country evidence from the retail industry. *Information Systems Research*, *16*(1), 61–84. doi:10.1287/isre.1050.0045

# Related References

To continue our tradition of advancing information science and technology research, we have compiled a list of recommended IGI Global readings. These references will provide additional information and guidance to further enrich your knowledge and assist you with your own research and future publications.

Abtahi, M. S., Behboudi, L., & Hasanabad, H. M. (2017). Factors Affecting Internet Advertising Adoption in Ad Agencies. *International Journal of Innovation in the Digital Economy*, 8(4), 18–29. doi:10.4018/IJIDE.2017100102

Agrawal, S. (2017). The Impact of Emerging Technologies and Social Media on Different Business(es): Marketing and Management. In O. Rishi & A. Sharma (Eds.), *Maximizing Business Performance and Efficiency Through Intelligent Systems* (pp. 37–49). Hershey, PA: IGI Global. doi:10.4018/978-1-5225-2234-8.ch002

Alnoukari, M., Razouk, R., & Hanano, A. (2016). BSC-SI: A Framework for Integrating Strategic Intelligence in Corporate Strategic Management. *International Journal of Social and Organizational Dynamics in IT*, 5(2), 1–14. doi:10.4018/IJSODIT.2016070101

Alnoukari, M., Razouk, R., & Hanano, A. (2016). BSC-SI, A Framework for Integrating Strategic Intelligence in Corporate Strategic Management. *International Journal of Strategic Information Technology and Applications*, 7(1), 32–44. doi:10.4018/IJSITA.2016010103

Altındağ, E. (2016). Current Approaches in Change Management. In A. Goksoy (Ed.), *Organizational Change Management Strategies in Modern Business* (pp. 24–51). Hershey, PA: IGI Global. doi:10.4018/978-1-4666-9533-7.ch002

Alvarez-Dionisi, L. E., Turner, R., & Mittra, M. (2016). Global Project Management Trends. *International Journal of Information Technology Project Management, 7*(3), 54–73. doi:10.4018/IJITPM.2016070104

Anantharaman, R. N., Rajeswari, K. S., Angusamy, A., & Kuppusamy, J. (2017). Role of Self-Efficacy and Collective Efficacy as Moderators of Occupational Stress Among Software Development Professionals. *International Journal of Human Capital and Information Technology Professionals, 8*(2), 45–58. doi:10.4018/IJHCITP.2017040103

Aninze, F., El-Gohary, H., & Hussain, J. (2018). The Role of Microfinance to Empower Women: The Case of Developing Countries. *International Journal of Customer Relationship Marketing and Management, 9*(1), 54–78. doi:10.4018/IJCRMM.2018010104

Arsenijević, O. M., Orčić, D., & Kastratović, E. (2017). Development of an Optimization Tool for Intangibles in SMEs: A Case Study from Serbia with a Pilot Research in the Prestige by Milka Company. In M. Vemić (Ed.), *Optimal Management Strategies in Small and Medium Enterprises* (pp. 320–347). Hershey, PA: IGI Global. doi:10.4018/978-1-5225-1949-2.ch015

Aryanto, V. D., Wismantoro, Y., & Widyatmoko, K. (2018). Implementing Eco-Innovation by Utilizing the Internet to Enhance Firm's Marketing Performance: Study of Green Batik Small and Medium Enterprises in Indonesia. *International Journal of E-Business Research, 14*(1), 21–36. doi:10.4018/IJEBR.2018010102

Atiku, S. O., & Fields, Z. (2017). Multicultural Orientations for 21st Century Global Leadership. In N. Baporikar (Ed.), *Management Education for Global Leadership* (pp. 28–51). Hershey, PA: IGI Global. doi:10.4018/978-1-5225-1013-0.ch002

Atiku, S. O., & Fields, Z. (2018). Organisational Learning Dimensions and Talent Retention Strategies for the Service Industries. In N. Baporikar (Ed.), *Global Practices in Knowledge Management for Societal and Organizational Development* (pp. 358–381). Hershey, PA: IGI Global. doi:10.4018/978-1-5225-3009-1.ch017

Ávila, L., & Teixeira, L. (2018). The Main Concepts Behind the Dematerialization of Business Processes. In M. Khosrow-Pour, D.B.A. (Ed.), Encyclopedia of Information Science and Technology, Fourth Edition (pp. 888-898). Hershey, PA: IGI Global. doi:10.4018/978-1-5225-2255-3.ch076

Bartens, Y., Chunpir, H. I., Schulte, F., & Voß, S. (2017). Business/IT Alignment in Two-Sided Markets: A COBIT 5 Analysis for Media Streaming Business Models. In S. De Haes & W. Van Grembergen (Eds.), *Strategic IT Governance and Alignment in Business Settings* (pp. 82–111). Hershey, PA: IGI Global. doi:10.4018/978-1-5225-0861-8.ch004

Bashayreh, A. M. (2018). Organizational Culture and Organizational Performance. In W. Lee & F. Sabetzadeh (Eds.), *Contemporary Knowledge and Systems Science* (pp. 50–69). Hershey, PA: IGI Global. doi:10.4018/978-1-5225-5655-8.ch003

Bedford, D. A. (2018). Sustainable Knowledge Management Strategies: Aligning Business Capabilities and Knowledge Management Goals. In N. Baporikar (Ed.), *Global Practices in Knowledge Management for Societal and Organizational Development* (pp. 46–73). Hershey, PA: IGI Global. doi:10.4018/978-1-5225-3009-1.ch003

Benmoussa, F., Nakara, W. A., & Jaouen, A. (2016). The Use of Social Media by SMEs in the Tourism Industry. In I. Lee (Ed.), *Encyclopedia of E-Commerce Development, Implementation, and Management* (pp. 2159–2170). Hershey, PA: IGI Global. doi:10.4018/978-1-4666-9787-4.ch155

Berger, R. (2016). Indigenous Management and Bottom of Pyramid Countries: The Role of National Institutions. In U. Aung & P. Ordoñez de Pablos (Eds.), *Managerial Strategies and Practice in the Asian Business Sector* (pp. 107–123). Hershey, PA: IGI Global. doi:10.4018/978-1-4666-9758-4.ch007

Bharwani, S., & Musunuri, D. (2018). Reflection as a Process From Theory to Practice. In M. Khosrow-Pour, D.B.A. (Ed.), Encyclopedia of Information Science and Technology, Fourth Edition (pp. 1529-1539). Hershey, PA: IGI Global. doi:10.4018/978-1-5225-2255-3.ch132

Bhatt, G. D., Wang, Z., & Rodger, J. A. (2017). Information Systems Capabilities and Their Effects on Competitive Advantages: A Study of Chinese Companies. *Information Resources Management Journal*, *30*(3), 41–57. doi:10.4018/IRMJ.2017070103

Bhushan, M., & Yadav, A. (2017). Concept of Cloud Computing in ESB. In R. Bhadoria, N. Chaudhari, G. Tomar, & S. Singh (Eds.), *Exploring Enterprise Service Bus in the Service-Oriented Architecture Paradigm* (pp. 116–127). Hershey, PA: IGI Global. doi:10.4018/978-1-5225-2157-0.ch008

Bhushan, S. (2017). System Dynamics Base-Model of Humanitarian Supply Chain (HSCM) in Disaster Prone Eco-Communities of India: A Discussion on Simulation and Scenario Results. *International Journal of System Dynamics Applications*, *6*(3), 20–37. doi:10.4018/IJSDA.2017070102

Biswas, A., & De, A. K. (2017). On Development of a Fuzzy Stochastic Programming Model with Its Application to Business Management. In S. Trivedi, S. Dey, A. Kumar, & T. Panda (Eds.), *Handbook of Research on Advanced Data Mining Techniques and Applications for Business Intelligence* (pp. 353–378). Hershey, PA: IGI Global. doi:10.4018/978-1-5225-2031-3.ch021

Bücker, J., & Ernste, K. (2018). Use of Brand Heroes in Strategic Reputation Management: The Case of Bacardi, Adidas, and Daimler. In A. Erdemir (Ed.), *Reputation Management Techniques in Public Relations* (pp. 126–150). Hershey, PA: IGI Global. doi:10.4018/978-1-5225-3619-2.ch007

Bureš, V. (2018). Industry 4.0 From the Systems Engineering Perspective: Alternative Holistic Framework Development. In R. Brunet-Thornton & F. Martinez (Eds.), *Analyzing the Impacts of Industry 4.0 in Modern Business Environments* (pp. 199–223). Hershey, PA: IGI Global. doi:10.4018/978-1-5225-3468-6.ch011

Buzady, Z. (2017). Resolving the Magic Cube of Effective Case Teaching: Benchmarking Case Teaching Practices in Emerging Markets – Insights from the Central European University Business School, Hungary. In D. Latusek (Ed.), *Case Studies as a Teaching Tool in Management Education* (pp. 79–103). Hershey, PA: IGI Global. doi:10.4018/978-1-5225-0770-3.ch005

Campatelli, G., Richter, A., & Stocker, A. (2016). Participative Knowledge Management to Empower Manufacturing Workers. *International Journal of Knowledge Management*, *12*(4), 37–50. doi:10.4018/IJKM.2016100103

Căpusneanu, S., & Topor, D. I. (2018). Business Ethics and Cost Management in SMEs: Theories of Business Ethics and Cost Management Ethos. In I. Oncioiu (Ed.), *Ethics and Decision-Making for Sustainable Business Practices* (pp. 109–127). Hershey, PA: IGI Global. doi:10.4018/978-1-5225-3773-1.ch007

Carneiro, A. (2016). Maturity in Health Organization Information Systems: Metrics and Privacy Perspectives. *International Journal of Privacy and Health Information Management*, *4*(2), 1–18. doi:10.4018/IJPHIM.2016070101

Chan, R. L., Mo, P. L., & Moon, K. K. (2018). Strategic and Tactical Measures in Managing Enterprise Risks: A Study of the Textile and Apparel Industry. In K. Strang, M. Korstanje, & N. Vajjhala (Eds.), *Research, Practices, and Innovations in Global Risk and Contingency Management* (pp. 1–19). Hershey, PA: IGI Global. doi:10.4018/978-1-5225-4754-9.ch001

Chandan, H. C. (2016). Motivations and Challenges of Female Entrepreneurship in Developed and Developing Economies. In N. Baporikar (Ed.), *Handbook of Research on Entrepreneurship in the Contemporary Knowledge-Based Global Economy* (pp. 260–286). Hershey, PA: IGI Global. doi:10.4018/978-1-4666-8798-1.ch012

Charlier, S. D., Burke-Smalley, L. A., & Fisher, S. L. (2018). Undergraduate Programs in the U.S: A Contextual and Content-Based Analysis. In J. Mendy (Ed.), *Teaching Human Resources and Organizational Behavior at the College Level* (pp. 26–57). Hershey, PA: IGI Global. doi:10.4018/978-1-5225-2820-3.ch002

Chaudhuri, S. (2016). Application of Web-Based Geographical Information System (GIS) in E-Business. In U. Panwar, R. Kumar, & N. Ray (Eds.), *Handbook of Research on Promotional Strategies and Consumer Influence in the Service Sector* (pp. 389–405). Hershey, PA: IGI Global. doi:10.4018/978-1-5225-0143-5.ch023

Choudhuri, P. S. (2016). An Empirical Study on the Quality of Services Offered by the Private Life Insurers in Burdwan. In U. Panwar, R. Kumar, & N. Ray (Eds.), *Handbook of Research on Promotional Strategies and Consumer Influence in the Service Sector* (pp. 31–55). Hershey, PA: IGI Global. doi:10.4018/978-1-5225-0143-5.ch002

Dahlberg, T., Kivijärvi, H., & Saarinen, T. (2017). IT Investment Consistency and Other Factors Influencing the Success of IT Performance. In S. De Haes & W. Van Grembergen (Eds.), *Strategic IT Governance and Alignment in Business Settings* (pp. 176–208). Hershey, PA: IGI Global. doi:10.4018/978-1-5225-0861-8.ch007

Damnjanović, A. M. (2017). Knowledge Management Optimization through IT and E-Business Utilization: A Qualitative Study on Serbian SMEs. In M. Vemić (Ed.), *Optimal Management Strategies in Small and Medium Enterprises* (pp. 249–267). Hershey, PA: IGI Global. doi:10.4018/978-1-5225-1949-2.ch012

Daneshpour, H. (2017). Integrating Sustainable Development into Project Portfolio Management through Application of Open Innovation. In M. Vemić (Ed.), *Optimal Management Strategies in Small and Medium Enterprises* (pp. 370–387). Hershey, PA: IGI Global. doi:10.4018/978-1-5225-1949-2.ch017

Daniel, A. D., & Reis de Castro, V. (2018). Entrepreneurship Education: How to Measure the Impact on Nascent Entrepreneurs. In A. Carrizo Moreira, J. Guilherme Leitão Dantas, & F. Manuel Valente (Eds.), *Nascent Entrepreneurship and Successful New Venture Creation* (pp. 85–110). Hershey, PA: IGI Global. doi:10.4018/978-1-5225-2936-1.ch004

David, F., van der Sijde, P., & van den Besselaar, P. (2016). Enterpreneurial Incentives, Obstacles, and Management in University-Business Co-Operation: The Case of Indonesia. In J. Saiz-Álvarez (Ed.), *Handbook of Research on Social Entrepreneurship and Solidarity Economics* (pp. 499–518). Hershey, PA: IGI Global. doi:10.4018/978-1-5225-0097-1.ch024

David, R., Swami, B. N., & Tangirala, S. (2018). Ethics Impact on Knowledge Management in Organizational Development: A Case Study. In N. Baporikar (Ed.), *Global Practices in Knowledge Management for Societal and Organizational Development* (pp. 19–45). Hershey, PA: IGI Global. doi:10.4018/978-1-5225-3009-1.ch002

Delias, P., & Lakiotaki, K. (2018). Discovering Process Horizontal Boundaries to Facilitate Process Comprehension. *International Journal of Operations Research and Information Systems*, *9*(2), 1–31. doi:10.4018/IJORIS.2018040101

Denholm, J., & Lee-Davies, L. (2018). Success Factors for Games in Business and Project Management. In *Enhancing Education and Training Initiatives Through Serious Games* (pp. 34–68). Hershey, PA: IGI Global. doi:10.4018/978-1-5225-3689-5.ch002

Deshpande, M. (2017). Best Practices in Management Institutions for Global Leadership: Policy Aspects. In N. Baporikar (Ed.), *Management Education for Global Leadership* (pp. 1–27). Hershey, PA: IGI Global. doi:10.4018/978-1-5225-1013-0.ch001

Deshpande, M. (2018). Policy Perspectives for SMEs Knowledge Management. In N. Baporikar (Ed.), *Knowledge Integration Strategies for Entrepreneurship and Sustainability* (pp. 23–46). Hershey, PA: IGI Global. doi:10.4018/978-1-5225-5115-7.ch002

Dezdar, S. (2017). ERP Implementation Projects in Asian Countries: A Comparative Study on Iran and China. *International Journal of Information Technology Project Management*, *8*(3), 52–68. doi:10.4018/IJITPM.2017070104

Domingos, D., Martinho, R., & Varajão, J. (2016). Controlled Flexibility in Healthcare Processes: A BPMN-Extension Approach. In M. Cruz-Cunha, I. Miranda, R. Martinho, & R. Rijo (Eds.), *Encyclopedia of E-Health and Telemedicine* (pp. 521–535). Hershey, PA: IGI Global. doi:10.4018/978-1-4666-9978-6.ch040

Domingos, D., Respício, A., & Martinho, R. (2017). Reliability of IoT-Aware BPMN Healthcare Processes. In C. Reis & M. Maximiano (Eds.), *Internet of Things and Advanced Application in Healthcare* (pp. 214–248). Hershey, PA: IGI Global. doi:10.4018/978-1-5225-1820-4.ch008

Dosumu, O., Hussain, J., & El-Gohary, H. (2017). An Exploratory Study of the Impact of Government Policies on the Development of Small and Medium Enterprises in Developing Countries: The Case of Nigeria. *International Journal of Customer Relationship Marketing and Management*, 8(4), 51–62. doi:10.4018/IJCRMM.2017100104

Durst, S., Bruns, G., & Edvardsson, I. R. (2017). Retaining Knowledge in Smaller Building and Construction Firms. *International Journal of Knowledge and Systems Science*, 8(3), 1–12. doi:10.4018/IJKSS.2017070101

Edvardsson, I. R., & Durst, S. (2017). Outsourcing, Knowledge, and Learning: A Critical Review. *International Journal of Knowledge-Based Organizations*, 7(2), 13–26. doi:10.4018/IJKBO.2017040102

Edwards, J. S. (2018). Integrating Knowledge Management and Business Processes. In M. Khosrow-Pour, D.B.A. (Ed.), Encyclopedia of Information Science and Technology, Fourth Edition (pp. 5046-5055). Hershey, PA: IGI Global. doi:10.4018/978-1-5225-2255-3.ch437

Ejiogu, A. O. (2018). Economics of Farm Management. In *Agricultural Finance and Opportunities for Investment and Expansion* (pp. 56–72). Hershey, PA: IGI Global. doi:10.4018/978-1-5225-3059-6.ch003

Ekanem, I., & Abiade, G. E. (2018). Factors Influencing the Use of E-Commerce by Small Enterprises in Nigeria. *International Journal of ICT Research in Africa and the Middle East*, 7(1), 37–53. doi:10.4018/IJICTRAME.2018010103

Ekanem, I., & Alrossais, L. A. (2017). Succession Challenges Facing Family Businesses in Saudi Arabia. In P. Zgheib (Ed.), *Entrepreneurship and Business Innovation in the Middle East* (pp. 122–146). Hershey, PA: IGI Global. doi:10.4018/978-1-5225-2066-5.ch007

El Faquih, L., & Fredj, M. (2017). Ontology-Based Framework for Quality in Configurable Process Models. *Journal of Electronic Commerce in Organizations*, 15(2), 48–60. doi:10.4018/JECO.2017040104

El-Gohary, H., & El-Gohary, Z. (2016). An Attempt to Explore Electronic Marketing Adoption and Implementation Aspects in Developing Countries: The Case of Egypt. *International Journal of Customer Relationship Marketing and Management*, 7(4), 1–26. doi:10.4018/IJCRMM.2016100101

Entico, G. J. (2016). Knowledge Management and the Medical Health Librarians: A Perception Study. In J. Yap, M. Perez, M. Ayson, & G. Entico (Eds.), *Special Library Administration, Standardization and Technological Integration* (pp. 52–77). Hershey, PA: IGI Global. doi:10.4018/978-1-4666-9542-9.ch003

Faisal, M. N., & Talib, F. (2017). Building Ambidextrous Supply Chains in SMEs: How to Tackle the Barriers? *International Journal of Information Systems and Supply Chain Management, 10*(4), 80–100. doi:10.4018/IJISSCM.2017100105

Fernandes, T. M., Gomes, J., & Romão, M. (2017). Investments in E-Government: A Benefit Management Case Study. *International Journal of Electronic Government Research, 13*(3), 1–17. doi:10.4018/IJEGR.2017070101

Fouda, F. A. (2016). A Suggested Curriculum in Career Education to Develop Business Secondary Schools Students' Career Knowledge Management Domains and Professional Thinking. *International Journal of Technology Diffusion, 7*(2), 42–62. doi:10.4018/IJTD.2016040103

Gallardo-Vázquez, D., & Pajuelo-Moreno, M. L. (2016). How Spanish Universities are Promoting Entrepreneurship through Your Own Lines of Teaching and Research? In L. Carvalho (Ed.), *Handbook of Research on Entrepreneurial Success and its Impact on Regional Development* (pp. 431–454). Hershey, PA: IGI Global. doi:10.4018/978-1-4666-9567-2.ch019

Gao, S. S., Oreal, S., & Zhang, J. (2018). Contemporary Financial Risk Management Perceptions and Practices of Small-Sized Chinese Businesses. In I. Management Association (Ed.), Global Business Expansion: Concepts, Methodologies, Tools, and Applications (pp. 917-931). Hershey, PA: IGI Global. doi:10.4018/978-1-5225-5481-3.ch041

Garg, R., & Berning, S. C. (2017). Indigenous Chinese Management Philosophies: Key Concepts and Relevance for Modern Chinese Firms. In B. Christiansen & G. Koc (Eds.), *Transcontinental Strategies for Industrial Development and Economic Growth* (pp. 43–57). Hershey, PA: IGI Global. doi:10.4018/978-1-5225-2160-0.ch003

Gencer, Y. G. (2017). Supply Chain Management in Retailing Business. In U. Akkucuk (Ed.), *Ethics and Sustainability in Global Supply Chain Management* (pp. 197–210). Hershey, PA: IGI Global. doi:10.4018/978-1-5225-2036-8.ch011

Giacosa, E. (2016). Innovation in Luxury Fashion Businesses as a Means for the Regional Development. In L. Carvalho (Ed.), *Handbook of Research on Entrepreneurial Success and its Impact on Regional Development* (pp. 206–222). Hershey, PA: IGI Global. doi:10.4018/978-1-4666-9567-2.ch010

Giacosa, E. (2018). The Increasing of the Regional Development Thanks to the Luxury Business Innovation. In L. Carvalho (Ed.), *Handbook of Research on Entrepreneurial Ecosystems and Social Dynamics in a Globalized World* (pp. 260–273). Hershey, PA: IGI Global. doi:10.4018/978-1-5225-3525-6.ch011

Gianni, M., & Gotzamani, K. (2016). Integrated Management Systems and Information Management Systems: Common Threads. In P. Papajorgji, F. Pinet, A. Guimarães, & J. Papathanasiou (Eds.), *Automated Enterprise Systems for Maximizing Business Performance* (pp. 195–214). Hershey, PA: IGI Global. doi:10.4018/978-1-4666-8841-4.ch011

Gianni, M., Gotzamani, K., & Linden, I. (2016). How a BI-wise Responsible Integrated Management System May Support Food Traceability. *International Journal of Decision Support System Technology*, 8(2), 1–17. doi:10.4018/IJDSST.2016040101

Glykas, M., & George, J. (2017). Quality and Process Management Systems in the UAE Maritime Industry. *International Journal of Productivity Management and Assessment Technologies*, 5(1), 20–39. doi:10.4018/IJPMAT.2017010102

Glykas, M., Valiris, G., Kokkinaki, A., & Koutsoukou, Z. (2018). Banking Business Process Management Implementation. *International Journal of Productivity Management and Assessment Technologies*, 6(1), 50–69. doi:10.4018/IJPMAT.2018010104

Gomes, J., & Romão, M. (2017). The Balanced Scorecard: Keeping Updated and Aligned with Today's Business Trends. *International Journal of Productivity Management and Assessment Technologies*, 5(2), 1–15. doi:10.4018/IJPMAT.2017070101

Gomes, J., & Romão, M. (2017). Aligning Information Systems and Technology with Benefit Management and Balanced Scorecard. In S. De Haes & W. Van Grembergen (Eds.), *Strategic IT Governance and Alignment in Business Settings* (pp. 112–131). Hershey, PA: IGI Global. doi:10.4018/978-1-5225-0861-8.ch005

Grefen, P., & Turetken, O. (2017). Advanced Business Process Management in Networked E-Business Scenarios. *International Journal of E-Business Research*, 13(4), 70–104. doi:10.4018/IJEBR.2017100105

Haider, A., & Saetang, S. (2017). Strategic IT Alignment in Service Sector. In S. Rozenes & Y. Cohen (Eds.), *Handbook of Research on Strategic Alliances and Value Co-Creation in the Service Industry* (pp. 231–258). Hershey, PA: IGI Global. doi:10.4018/978-1-5225-2084-9.ch012

Haider, A., & Tang, S. S. (2016). Maximising Value Through IT and Business Alignment: A Case of IT Governance Institutionalisation at a Thai Bank. *International Journal of Technology Diffusion*, 7(3), 33–58. doi:10.4018/IJTD.2016070104

Hajilari, A. B., Ghadaksaz, M., & Fasghandis, G. S. (2017). Assessing Organizational Readiness for Implementing ERP System Using Fuzzy Expert System Approach. *International Journal of Enterprise Information Systems*, 13(1), 67–85. doi:10.4018/IJEIS.2017010105

Haldorai, A., Ramu, A., & Murugan, S. (2018). Social Aware Cognitive Radio Networks: Effectiveness of Social Networks as a Strategic Tool for Organizational Business Management. In H. Bansal, G. Shrivastava, G. Nguyen, & L. Stanciu (Eds.), *Social Network Analytics for Contemporary Business Organizations* (pp. 188–202). Hershey, PA: IGI Global. doi:10.4018/978-1-5225-5097-6.ch010

Hall, O. P. Jr. (2017). Social Media Driven Management Education. *International Journal of Knowledge-Based Organizations*, 7(2), 43–59. doi:10.4018/IJKBO.2017040104

Hanifah, H., Halim, H. A., Ahmad, N. H., & Vafaei-Zadeh, A. (2017). Innovation Culture as a Mediator Between Specific Human Capital and Innovation Performance Among Bumiputera SMEs in Malaysia. In N. Ahmad, T. Ramayah, H. Halim, & S. Rahman (Eds.), *Handbook of Research on Small and Medium Enterprises in Developing Countries* (pp. 261–279). Hershey, PA: IGI Global. doi:10.4018/978-1-5225-2165-5.ch012

Hartlieb, S., & Silvius, G. (2017). Handling Uncertainty in Project Management and Business Development: Similarities and Differences. In Y. Raydugin (Ed.), *Handbook of Research on Leveraging Risk and Uncertainties for Effective Project Management* (pp. 337–362). Hershey, PA: IGI Global. doi:10.4018/978-1-5225-1790-0.ch016

Hass, K. B. (2017). Living on the Edge: Managing Project Complexity. In Y. Raydugin (Ed.), *Handbook of Research on Leveraging Risk and Uncertainties for Effective Project Management* (pp. 177–201). Hershey, PA: IGI Global. doi:10.4018/978-1-5225-1790-0.ch009

Hassan, A., & Privitera, D. S. (2016). Google AdSense as a Mobile Technology in Education. In J. Holland (Ed.), *Wearable Technology and Mobile Innovations for Next-Generation Education* (pp. 200–223). Hershey, PA: IGI Global. doi:10.4018/978-1-5225-0069-8.ch011

Hassan, A., & Rahimi, R. (2016). Consuming "Innovation" in Tourism: Augmented Reality as an Innovation Tool in Digital Tourism Marketing. In N. Pappas & I. Bregoli (Eds.), *Global Dynamics in Travel, Tourism, and Hospitality* (pp. 130–147). Hershey, PA: IGI Global. doi:10.4018/978-1-5225-0201-2.ch008

Hawking, P., & Carmine Sellitto, C. (2017). Developing an Effective Strategy for Organizational Business Intelligence. In M. Tavana (Ed.), *Enterprise Information Systems and the Digitalization of Business Functions* (pp. 222–237). Hershey, PA: IGI Global. doi:10.4018/978-1-5225-2382-6.ch010

Hawking, P., & Sellitto, C. (2017). A Fast-Moving Consumer Goods Company and Business Intelligence Strategy Development. *International Journal of Enterprise Information Systems*, *13*(2), 22–33. doi:10.4018/IJEIS.2017040102

Hawking, P., & Sellitto, C. (2017). Business Intelligence Strategy: Two Case Studies. *International Journal of Business Intelligence Research*, *8*(2), 17–30. doi:10.4018/IJBIR.2017070102

Haynes, J. D., Arockiasamy, S., Al Rashdi, M., & Al Rashdi, S. (2016). Business and E Business Strategies for Coopetition and Thematic Management as a Sustained Basis for Ethics and Social Responsibility in Emerging Markets. In M. Al-Shammari & H. Masri (Eds.), *Ethical and Social Perspectives on Global Business Interaction in Emerging Markets* (pp. 25–39). Hershey, PA: IGI Global. doi:10.4018/978-1-4666-9864-2.ch002

Hee, W. J., Jalleh, G., Lai, H., & Lin, C. (2017). E-Commerce and IT Projects: Evaluation and Management Issues in Australian and Taiwanese Hospitals. *International Journal of Public Health Management and Ethics*, *2*(1), 69–90. doi:10.4018/IJPHME.2017010104

Hernandez, A. A. (2018). Exploring the Factors to Green IT Adoption of SMEs in the Philippines. *Journal of Cases on Information Technology*, *20*(2), 49–66. doi:10.4018/JCIT.2018040104

Hernandez, A. A., & Ona, S. E. (2016). Green IT Adoption: Lessons from the Philippines Business Process Outsourcing Industry. *International Journal of Social Ecology and Sustainable Development*, *7*(1), 1–34. doi:10.4018/IJSESD.2016010101

Hollman, A., Bickford, S., & Hollman, T. (2017). Cyber InSecurity: A Post-Mortem Attempt to Assess Cyber Problems from IT and Business Management Perspectives. *Journal of Cases on Information Technology*, *19*(3), 42–70. doi:10.4018/JCIT.2017070104

Igbinakhase, I. (2017). Responsible and Sustainable Management Practices in Developing and Developed Business Environments. In Z. Fields (Ed.), *Collective Creativity for Responsible and Sustainable Business Practice* (pp. 180–207). Hershey, PA: IGI Global. doi:10.4018/978-1-5225-1823-5.ch010

Ilahi, L., Ghannouchi, S. A., & Martinho, R. (2016). A Business Process Management Approach to Home Healthcare Processes: On the Gap between Intention and Reality. In M. Cruz-Cunha, I. Miranda, R. Martinho, & R. Rijo (Eds.), *Encyclopedia of E-Health and Telemedicine* (pp. 439–457). Hershey, PA: IGI Global. doi:10.4018/978-1-4666-9978-6.ch035

Iwata, J. J., & Hoskins, R. G. (2017). Managing Indigenous Knowledge in Tanzania: A Business Perspective. In P. Jain & N. Mnjama (Eds.), *Managing Knowledge Resources and Records in Modern Organizations* (pp. 198–214). Hershey, PA: IGI Global. doi:10.4018/978-1-5225-1965-2.ch012

Jabeen, F., Ahmad, S. Z., & Alkaabi, S. (2016). The Internationalization Decision-Making of United Arab Emirates Family Businesses. In N. Zakaria, A. Abdul-Talib, & N. Osman (Eds.), *Handbook of Research on Impacts of International Business and Political Affairs on the Global Economy* (pp. 1–22). Hershey, PA: IGI Global. doi:10.4018/978-1-4666-9806-2.ch001

Jain, P. (2017). Ethical and Legal Issues in Knowledge Management Life-Cycle in Business. In P. Jain & N. Mnjama (Eds.), *Managing Knowledge Resources and Records in Modern Organizations* (pp. 82–101). Hershey, PA: IGI Global. doi:10.4018/978-1-5225-1965-2.ch006

Jamali, D., Abdallah, H., & Matar, F. (2016). Opportunities and Challenges for CSR Mainstreaming in Business Schools. *International Journal of Technology and Educational Marketing*, 6(2), 1–29. doi:10.4018/IJTEM.2016070101

James, S., & Hauli, E. (2017). Holistic Management Education at Tanzanian Rural Development Planning Institute. In N. Baporikar (Ed.), *Management Education for Global Leadership* (pp. 112–136). Hershey, PA: IGI Global. doi:10.4018/978-1-5225-1013-0.ch006

Janošková, M., Csikósová, A., & Čulková, K. (2018). Measurement of Company Performance as Part of Its Strategic Management. In R. Leon (Ed.), *Managerial Strategies for Business Sustainability During Turbulent Times* (pp. 309–335). Hershey, PA: IGI Global. doi:10.4018/978-1-5225-2716-9.ch017

Jean-Vasile, A., & Alecu, A. (2017). Theoretical and Practical Approaches in Understanding the Influences of Cost-Productivity-Profit Trinomial in Contemporary Enterprises. In A. Jean Vasile & D. Nicolò (Eds.), *Sustainable Entrepreneurship and Investments in the Green Economy* (pp. 28–62). Hershey, PA: IGI Global. doi:10.4018/978-1-5225-2075-7.ch002

Jha, D. G. (2016). Preparing for Information Technology Driven Changes. In S. Tiwari & L. Nafees (Eds.), *Innovative Management Education Pedagogies for Preparing Next-Generation Leaders* (pp. 258–274). Hershey, PA: IGI Global. doi:10.4018/978-1-4666-9691-4.ch015

Joia, L. A., & Correia, J. C. (2018). CIO Competencies From the IT Professional Perspective: Insights From Brazil. *Journal of Global Information Management*, 26(2), 74–103. doi:10.4018/JGIM.2018040104

Juma, A., & Mzera, N. (2017). Knowledge Management and Records Management and Competitive Advantage in Business. In P. Jain & N. Mnjama (Eds.), *Managing Knowledge Resources and Records in Modern Organizations* (pp. 15–28). Hershey, PA: IGI Global. doi:10.4018/978-1-5225-1965-2.ch002

K., I., & A, V. (2018). Monitoring and Auditing in the Cloud. In K. Munir (Ed.), *Cloud Computing Technologies for Green Enterprises* (pp. 318-350). Hershey, PA: IGI Global. doi:10.4018/978-1-5225-3038-1.ch013

Kabra, G., Ghosh, V., & Ramesh, A. (2018). Enterprise Integrated Business Process Management and Business Intelligence Framework for Business Process Sustainability. In A. Paul, D. Bhattacharyya, & S. Anand (Eds.), *Green Initiatives for Business Sustainability and Value Creation* (pp. 228–238). Hershey, PA: IGI Global. doi:10.4018/978-1-5225-2662-9.ch010

Kaoud, M. (2017). Investigation of Customer Knowledge Management: A Case Study Research. *International Journal of Service Science, Management, Engineering, and Technology*, 8(2), 12–22. doi:10.4018/IJSSMET.2017040102

Kara, M. E., & Fırat, S. Ü. (2016). Sustainability, Risk, and Business Intelligence in Supply Chains. In M. Erdoğdu, T. Arun, & I. Ahmad (Eds.), *Handbook of Research on Green Economic Development Initiatives and Strategies* (pp. 501–538). Hershey, PA: IGI Global. doi:10.4018/978-1-5225-0440-5.ch022

Katuu, S. (2018). A Comparative Assessment of Enterprise Content Management Maturity Models. In N. Gwangwava & M. Mutingi (Eds.), *E-Manufacturing and E-Service Strategies in Contemporary Organizations* (pp. 93–118). Hershey, PA: IGI Global. doi:10.4018/978-1-5225-3628-4.ch005

Khan, M. A. (2016). MNEs Management Strategies in Developing Countries: Establishing the Context. In M. Khan (Ed.), *Multinational Enterprise Management Strategies in Developing Countries* (pp. 1–33). Hershey, PA: IGI Global. doi:10.4018/978-1-5225-0276-0.ch001

Khan, M. A. (2016). Operational Approaches in Organizational Structure: A Case for MNEs in Developing Countries. In M. Khan (Ed.), *Multinational Enterprise Management Strategies in Developing Countries* (pp. 129–151). Hershey, PA: IGI Global. doi:10.4018/978-1-5225-0276-0.ch007

Kinnunen, S., Ylä-Kujala, A., Marttonen-Arola, S., Kärri, T., & Baglee, D. (2018). Internet of Things in Asset Management: Insights from Industrial Professionals and Academia. *International Journal of Service Science, Management, Engineering, and Technology*, 9(2), 104–119. doi:10.4018/IJSSMET.2018040105

Klein, A. Z., Sabino de Freitas, A., Machado, L., Freitas, J. C. Jr, Graziola, P. G. Jr, & Schlemmer, E. (2017). Virtual Worlds Applications for Management Education. In L. Tomei (Ed.), *Exploring the New Era of Technology-Infused Education* (pp. 279–299). Hershey, PA: IGI Global. doi:10.4018/978-1-5225-1709-2.ch017

Kożuch, B., & Jabłoński, A. (2017). Adopting the Concept of Business Models in Public Management. In M. Lewandowski & B. Kożuch (Eds.), *Public Sector Entrepreneurship and the Integration of Innovative Business Models* (pp. 10–46). Hershey, PA: IGI Global. doi:10.4018/978-1-5225-2215-7.ch002

Kumar, J., Adhikary, A., & Jha, A. (2017). Small Active Investors' Perceptions and Preferences Towards Tax Saving Mutual Fund Schemes in Eastern India: An Empirical Note. *International Journal of Asian Business and Information Management*, 8(2), 35–45. doi:10.4018/IJABIM.2017040103

Lassoued, Y., Bouzguenda, L., & Mahmoud, T. (2016). Context-Aware Business Process Versions Management. *International Journal of e-Collaboration*, 12(3), 7–33. doi:10.4018/IJeC.2016070102

Lavassani, K. M., & Movahedi, B. (2017). Applications Driven Information Systems: Beyond Networks toward Business Ecosystems. *International Journal of Innovation in the Digital Economy*, 8(1), 61–75. doi:10.4018/IJIDE.2017010104

Lazzareschi, V. H., & Brito, M. S. (2017). Strategic Information Management: Proposal of Business Project Model. In G. Jamil, A. Soares, & C. Pessoa (Eds.), *Handbook of Research on Information Management for Effective Logistics and Supply Chains* (pp. 59–88). Hershey, PA: IGI Global. doi:10.4018/978-1-5225-0973-8.ch004

Lederer, M., Kurz, M., & Lazarov, P. (2017). Usage and Suitability of Methods for Strategic Business Process Initiatives: A Multi Case Study Research. *International Journal of Productivity Management and Assessment Technologies*, *5*(1), 40–51. doi:10.4018/IJPMAT.2017010103

Lee, I. (2017). A Social Enterprise Business Model and a Case Study of Pacific Community Ventures (PCV). In V. Potocan, M. Üngan, & Z. Nedelko (Eds.), *Handbook of Research on Managerial Solutions in Non-Profit Organizations* (pp. 182–204). Hershey, PA: IGI Global. doi:10.4018/978-1-5225-0731-4.ch009

Lee, L. J., & Leu, J. (2016). Exploring the Effectiveness of IT Application and Value Method in the Innovation Performance of Enterprise. *International Journal of Enterprise Information Systems*, *12*(2), 47–65. doi:10.4018/IJEIS.2016040104

Lee, Y. (2016). Alignment Effect of Entrepreneurial Orientation and Marketing Orientation on Firm Performance. *International Journal of Customer Relationship Marketing and Management*, *7*(4), 58–69. doi:10.4018/IJCRMM.2016100104

Leon, L. A., Seal, K. C., Przasnyski, Z. H., & Wiedenman, I. (2017). Skills and Competencies Required for Jobs in Business Analytics: A Content Analysis of Job Advertisements Using Text Mining. *International Journal of Business Intelligence Research*, *8*(1), 1–25. doi:10.4018/IJBIR.2017010101

Leu, J., Lee, L. J., & Krischke, A. (2016). Value Engineering-Based Method for Implementing the ISO14001 System in the Green Supply Chains. *International Journal of Strategic Decision Sciences*, *7*(4), 1–20. doi:10.4018/IJSDS.2016100101

Levy, C. L., & Elias, N. I. (2017). SOHO Users' Perceptions of Reliability and Continuity of Cloud-Based Services. In M. Moore (Ed.), *Cybersecurity Breaches and Issues Surrounding Online Threat Protection* (pp. 248–287). Hershey, PA: IGI Global. doi:10.4018/978-1-5225-1941-6.ch011

Levy, M. (2018). Change Management Serving Knowledge Management and Organizational Development: Reflections and Review. In N. Baporikar (Ed.), *Global Practices in Knowledge Management for Societal and Organizational Development* (pp. 256–270). Hershey, PA: IGI Global. doi:10.4018/978-1-5225-3009-1.ch012

Lewandowski, M. (2017). Public Organizations and Business Model Innovation: The Role of Public Service Design. In M. Lewandowski & B. Kożuch (Eds.), *Public Sector Entrepreneurship and the Integration of Innovative Business Models* (pp. 47–72). Hershey, PA: IGI Global. doi:10.4018/978-1-5225-2215-7.ch003

Lhannaoui, H., Kabbaj, M. I., & Bakkoury, Z. (2017). A Survey of Risk-Aware Business Process Modelling. *International Journal of Risk and Contingency Management, 6*(3), 14–26. doi:10.4018/IJRCM.2017070102

Li, J., Sun, W., Jiang, W., Yang, H., & Zhang, L. (2017). How the Nature of Exogenous Shocks and Crises Impact Company Performance?: The Effects of Industry Characteristics. *International Journal of Risk and Contingency Management, 6*(4), 40–55. doi:10.4018/IJRCM.2017100103

Lu, C., & Liu, S. (2016). Cultural Tourism O2O Business Model Innovation-A Case Study of CTrip. *Journal of Electronic Commerce in Organizations, 14*(2), 16–31. doi:10.4018/JECO.2016040102

Machen, B., Hosseini, M. R., Wood, A., & Bakhshi, J. (2016). An Investigation into using SAP-PS as a Multidimensional Project Control System (MPCS). *International Journal of Enterprise Information Systems, 12*(2), 66–81. doi:10.4018/IJEIS.2016040105

Malega, P. (2017). Small and Medium Enterprises in the Slovak Republic: Status and Competitiveness of SMEs in the Global Markets and Possibilities of Optimization. In M. Vemić (Ed.), *Optimal Management Strategies in Small and Medium Enterprises* (pp. 102–124). Hershey, PA: IGI Global. doi:10.4018/978-1-5225-1949-2.ch006

Malewska, K. M. (2017). Intuition in Decision-Making on the Example of a Non-Profit Organization. In V. Potocan, M. Üngan, & Z. Nedelko (Eds.), *Handbook of Research on Managerial Solutions in Non-Profit Organizations* (pp. 378–399). Hershey, PA: IGI Global. doi:10.4018/978-1-5225-0731-4.ch018

Maroofi, F. (2017). Entrepreneurial Orientation and Organizational Learning Ability Analysis for Innovation and Firm Performance. In N. Baporikar (Ed.), *Innovation and Shifting Perspectives in Management Education* (pp. 144–165). Hershey, PA: IGI Global. doi:10.4018/978-1-5225-1019-2.ch007

Martins, P. V., & Zacarias, M. (2017). A Web-based Tool for Business Process Improvement. *International Journal of Web Portals, 9*(2), 68–84. doi:10.4018/IJWP.2017070104

Matthies, B., & Coners, A. (2017). Exploring the Conceptual Nature of e-Business Projects. *Journal of Electronic Commerce in Organizations, 15*(3), 33–63. doi:10.4018/JECO.2017070103

McKee, J. (2018). Architecture as a Tool to Solve Business Planning Problems. In M. Khosrow-Pour, D.B.A. (Ed.), Encyclopedia of Information Science and Technology, Fourth Edition (pp. 573-586). Hershey, PA: IGI Global. doi:10.4018/978-1-5225-2255-3.ch050

McMurray, A. J., Cross, J., & Caponecchia, C. (2018). The Risk Management Profession in Australia: Business Continuity Plan Practices. In N. Bajgoric (Ed.), *Always-On Enterprise Information Systems for Modern Organizations* (pp. 112–129). Hershey, PA: IGI Global. doi:10.4018/978-1-5225-3704-5.ch006

Meddah, I. H., & Belkadi, K. (2018). Mining Patterns Using Business Process Management. In R. Hamou (Ed.), *Handbook of Research on Biomimicry in Information Retrieval and Knowledge Management* (pp. 78–89). Hershey, PA: IGI Global. doi:10.4018/978-1-5225-3004-6.ch005

Mendes, L. (2017). TQM and Knowledge Management: An Integrated Approach Towards Tacit Knowledge Management. In D. Jaziri-Bouagina & G. Jamil (Eds.), *Handbook of Research on Tacit Knowledge Management for Organizational Success* (pp. 236–263). Hershey, PA: IGI Global. doi:10.4018/978-1-5225-2394-9.ch009

Mnjama, N. M. (2017). Preservation of Recorded Information in Public and Private Sector Organizations. In P. Jain & N. Mnjama (Eds.), *Managing Knowledge Resources and Records in Modern Organizations* (pp. 149–167). Hershey, PA: IGI Global. doi:10.4018/978-1-5225-1965-2.ch009

Mokoqama, M., & Fields, Z. (2017). Principles of Responsible Management Education (PRME): Call for Responsible Management Education. In Z. Fields (Ed.), *Collective Creativity for Responsible and Sustainable Business Practice* (pp. 229–241). Hershey, PA: IGI Global. doi:10.4018/978-1-5225-1823-5.ch012

Muniapan, B. (2017). Philosophy and Management: The Relevance of Vedanta in Management. In P. Ordóñez de Pablos (Ed.), *Managerial Strategies and Solutions for Business Success in Asia* (pp. 124–139). Hershey, PA: IGI Global. doi:10.4018/978-1-5225-1886-0.ch007

Muniapan, B., Gregory, M. L., & Ling, L. A. (2016). Marketing Education in Sarawak: Looking at It from the Employers' Viewpoint. In B. Smith & A. Porath (Eds.), *Global Perspectives on Contemporary Marketing Education* (pp. 112–130). Hershey, PA: IGI Global. doi:10.4018/978-1-4666-9784-3.ch008

Murad, S. E., & Dowaji, S. (2017). Using Value-Based Approach for Managing Cloud-Based Services. In A. Turuk, B. Sahoo, & S. Addya (Eds.), *Resource Management and Efficiency in Cloud Computing Environments* (pp. 33–60). Hershey, PA: IGI Global. doi:10.4018/978-1-5225-1721-4.ch002

Mutahar, A. M., Daud, N. M., Thurasamy, R., Isaac, O., & Abdulsalam, R. (2018). The Mediating of Perceived Usefulness and Perceived Ease of Use: The Case of Mobile Banking in Yemen. *International Journal of Technology Diffusion*, 9(2), 21–40. doi:10.4018/IJTD.2018040102

Naidoo, V. (2017). E-Learning and Management Education at African Universities. In N. Baporikar (Ed.), *Management Education for Global Leadership* (pp. 181–201). Hershey, PA: IGI Global. doi:10.4018/978-1-5225-1013-0.ch009

Naidoo, V., & Igbinakhase, I. (2018). Opportunities and Challenges of Knowledge Retention in SMEs. In N. Baporikar (Ed.), *Knowledge Integration Strategies for Entrepreneurship and Sustainability* (pp. 70–94). Hershey, PA: IGI Global. doi:10.4018/978-1-5225-5115-7.ch004

Nayak, S., & Prabhu, N. (2017). Paradigm Shift in Management Education: Need for a Cross Functional Perspective. In N. Baporikar (Ed.), *Management Education for Global Leadership* (pp. 241–255). Hershey, PA: IGI Global. doi:10.4018/978-1-5225-1013-0.ch012

Ndede-Amadi, A. A. (2016). Student Interest in the IS Specialization as Predictor of the Success Potential of New Information Systems Programmes within the Schools of Business in Kenyan Public Universities. *International Journal of Information Systems and Social Change*, 7(2), 63–79. doi:10.4018/IJISSC.2016040104

Nedelko, Z., & Potocan, V. (2016). Management Practices for Processes Optimization: Case of Slovenia. In G. Alor-Hernández, C. Sánchez-Ramírez, & J. García-Alcaraz (Eds.), *Handbook of Research on Managerial Strategies for Achieving Optimal Performance in Industrial Processes* (pp. 545–561). Hershey, PA: IGI Global. doi:10.4018/978-1-5225-0130-5.ch025

Nedelko, Z., & Potocan, V. (2017). Management Solutions in Non-Profit Organizations: Case of Slovenia. In V. Potocan, M. Üngan, & Z. Nedelko (Eds.), *Handbook of Research on Managerial Solutions in Non-Profit Organizations* (pp. 1–22). Hershey, PA: IGI Global. doi:10.4018/978-1-5225-0731-4.ch001

Nedelko, Z., & Potocan, V. (2017). Priority of Management Tools Utilization among Managers: International Comparison. In V. Wang (Ed.), *Encyclopedia of Strategic Leadership and Management* (pp. 1083–1094). Hershey, PA: IGI Global. doi:10.4018/978-1-5225-1049-9.ch075

Nedelko, Z., Raudeliūnienė, J., & Črešnar, R. (2018). Knowledge Dynamics in Supply Chain Management. In N. Baporikar (Ed.), *Knowledge Integration Strategies for Entrepreneurship and Sustainability* (pp. 150–166). Hershey, PA: IGI Global. doi:10.4018/978-1-5225-5115-7.ch008

Nguyen, H. T., & Hipsher, S. A. (2018). Innovation and Creativity Used by Private Sector Firms in a Resources-Constrained Environment. In S. Hipsher (Ed.), *Examining the Private Sector's Role in Wealth Creation and Poverty Reduction* (pp. 219–238). Hershey, PA: IGI Global. doi:10.4018/978-1-5225-3117-3.ch010

Nycz, M., & Pólkowski, Z. (2016). Business Intelligence as a Modern IT Supporting Management of Local Government Units in Poland. *International Journal of Knowledge and Systems Science*, 7(4), 1–18. doi:10.4018/IJKSS.2016100101

Obaji, N. O., Senin, A. A., & Olugu, M. U. (2016). Supportive Government Policy as a Mechanism for Business Incubation Performance in Nigeria. *International Journal of Information Systems and Social Change*, 7(4), 52–66. doi:10.4018/IJISSC.2016100103

Obicci, P. A. (2017). Risk Sharing in a Partnership. In *Risk Management Strategies in Public-Private Partnerships* (pp. 115–152). Hershey, PA: IGI Global. doi:10.4018/978-1-5225-2503-5.ch004

Obidallah, W. J., & Raahemi, B. (2017). Managing Changes in Service Oriented Virtual Organizations: A Structural and Procedural Framework to Facilitate the Process of Change. *Journal of Electronic Commerce in Organizations*, 15(1), 59–83. doi:10.4018/JECO.2017010104

Ojasalo, J., & Ojasalo, K. (2016). Service Logic Business Model Canvas for Lean Development of SMEs and Start-Ups. In N. Baporikar (Ed.), *Handbook of Research on Entrepreneurship in the Contemporary Knowledge-Based Global Economy* (pp. 217–243). Hershey, PA: IGI Global. doi:10.4018/978-1-4666-8798-1.ch010

Ojo, O. (2017). Impact of Innovation on the Entrepreneurial Success in Selected Business Enterprises in South-West Nigeria. *International Journal of Innovation in the Digital Economy*, 8(2), 29–38. doi:10.4018/IJIDE.2017040103

Okdinawati, L., Simatupang, T. M., & Sunitiyoso, Y. (2017). Multi-Agent Reinforcement Learning for Value Co-Creation of Collaborative Transportation Management (CTM). *International Journal of Information Systems and Supply Chain Management*, 10(3), 84–95. doi:10.4018/IJISSCM.2017070105

Ortner, E., Mevius, M., Wiedmann, P., & Kurz, F. (2016). Design of Interactional Decision Support Applications for E-Participation in Smart Cities. *International Journal of Electronic Government Research*, 12(2), 18–38. doi:10.4018/IJEGR.2016040102

Pal, K. (2018). Building High Quality Big Data-Based Applications in Supply Chains. In A. Kumar & S. Saurav (Eds.), *Supply Chain Management Strategies and Risk Assessment in Retail Environments* (pp. 1–24). Hershey, PA: IGI Global. doi:10.4018/978-1-5225-3056-5.ch001

Palos-Sanchez, P. R., & Correia, M. B. (2018). Perspectives of the Adoption of Cloud Computing in the Tourism Sector. In J. Rodrigues, C. Ramos, P. Cardoso, & C. Henriques (Eds.), *Handbook of Research on Technological Developments for Cultural Heritage and eTourism Applications* (pp. 377–400). Hershey, PA: IGI Global. doi:10.4018/978-1-5225-2927-9.ch018

Parry, V. K., & Lind, M. L. (2016). Alignment of Business Strategy and Information Technology Considering Information Technology Governance, Project Portfolio Control, and Risk Management. *International Journal of Information Technology Project Management*, 7(4), 21–37. doi:10.4018/IJITPM.2016100102

Pashkova, N., Trujillo-Barrera, A., Apostolakis, G., Van Dijk, G., Drakos, P. D., & Baourakis, G. (2016). Business Management Models of Microfinance Institutions (MFIs) in Africa: A Study into Their Enabling Environments. *International Journal of Food and Beverage Manufacturing and Business Models*, 1(2), 63–82. doi:10.4018/IJFBMBM.2016070105

Patiño, B. E. (2017). New Generation Management by Convergence and Individual Identity: A Systemic and Human-Oriented Approach. In N. Baporikar (Ed.), *Innovation and Shifting Perspectives in Management Education* (pp. 119–143). Hershey, PA: IGI Global. doi:10.4018/978-1-5225-1019-2.ch006

Pawliczek, A., & Rössler, M. (2017). Knowledge of Management Tools and Systems in SMEs: Knowledge Transfer in Management. In A. Bencsik (Ed.), *Knowledge Management Initiatives and Strategies in Small and Medium Enterprises* (pp. 180–203). Hershey, PA: IGI Global. doi:10.4018/978-1-5225-1642-2.ch009

Pejic-Bach, M., Omazic, M. A., Aleksic, A., & Zoroja, J. (2018). Knowledge-Based Decision Making: A Multi-Case Analysis. In R. Leon (Ed.), *Managerial Strategies for Business Sustainability During Turbulent Times* (pp. 160–184). Hershey, PA: IGI Global. doi:10.4018/978-1-5225-2716-9.ch009

Perano, M., Hysa, X., & Calabrese, M. (2018). Strategic Planning, Cultural Context, and Business Continuity Management: Business Cases in the City of Shkoder. In A. Presenza & L. Sheehan (Eds.), *Geopolitics and Strategic Management in the Global Economy* (pp. 57–77). Hershey, PA: IGI Global. doi:10.4018/978-1-5225-2673-5.ch004

Pereira, R., Mira da Silva, M., & Lapão, L. V. (2017). IT Governance Maturity Patterns in Portuguese Healthcare. In S. De Haes & W. Van Grembergen (Eds.), *Strategic IT Governance and Alignment in Business Settings* (pp. 24–52). Hershey, PA: IGI Global. doi:10.4018/978-1-5225-0861-8.ch002

Perez-Uribe, R., & Ocampo-Guzman, D. (2016). Conflict within Colombian Family Owned SMEs: An Explosive Blend between Feelings and Business. In J. Saiz-Álvarez (Ed.), *Handbook of Research on Social Entrepreneurship and Solidarity Economics* (pp. 329–354). Hershey, PA: IGI Global. doi:10.4018/978-1-5225-0097-1.ch017

Pérez-Uribe, R. I., Torres, D. A., Jurado, S. P., & Prada, D. M. (2018). Cloud Tools for the Development of Project Management in SMEs. In R. Perez-Uribe, C. Salcedo-Perez, & D. Ocampo-Guzman (Eds.), *Handbook of Research on Intrapreneurship and Organizational Sustainability in SMEs* (pp. 95–120). Hershey, PA: IGI Global. doi:10.4018/978-1-5225-3543-0.ch005

Petrisor, I., & Cozmiuc, D. (2017). Global Supply Chain Management Organization at Siemens in the Advent of Industry 4.0. In L. Saglietto & C. Cezanne (Eds.), *Global Intermediation and Logistics Service Providers* (pp. 123–142). Hershey, PA: IGI Global. doi:10.4018/978-1-5225-2133-4.ch007

Pierce, J. M., Velliaris, D. M., & Edwards, J. (2017). A Living Case Study: A Journey Not a Destination. In N. Silton (Ed.), *Exploring the Benefits of Creativity in Education, Media, and the Arts* (pp. 158–178). Hershey, PA: IGI Global. doi:10.4018/978-1-5225-0504-4.ch008

Radosavljevic, M., & Andjelkovic, A. (2017). Multi-Criteria Decision Making Approach for Choosing Business Process for the Improvement: Upgrading of the Six Sigma Methodology. In J. Stanković, P. Delias, S. Marinković, & S. Rochhia (Eds.), *Tools and Techniques for Economic Decision Analysis* (pp. 225–247). Hershey, PA: IGI Global. doi:10.4018/978-1-5225-0959-2.ch011

Radovic, V. M. (2017). Corporate Sustainability and Responsibility and Disaster Risk Reduction: A Serbian Overview. In M. Camilleri (Ed.), *CSR 2.0 and the New Era of Corporate Citizenship* (pp. 147–164). Hershey, PA: IGI Global. doi:10.4018/978-1-5225-1842-6.ch008

Raghunath, K. M., Devi, S. L., & Patro, C. S. (2018). Impact of Risk Assessment Models on Risk Factors: A Holistic Outlook. In K. Strang, M. Korstanje, & N. Vajjhala (Eds.), *Research, Practices, and Innovations in Global Risk and Contingency Management* (pp. 134–153). Hershey, PA: IGI Global. doi:10.4018/978-1-5225-4754-9.ch008

Raman, A., & Goyal, D. P. (2017). Extending IMPLEMENT Framework for Enterprise Information Systems Implementation to Information System Innovation. In M. Tavana (Ed.), *Enterprise Information Systems and the Digitalization of Business Functions* (pp. 137–177). Hershey, PA: IGI Global. doi:10.4018/978-1-5225-2382-6.ch007

Rao, Y., & Zhang, Y. (2017). The Construction and Development of Academic Library Digital Special Subject Databases. In L. Ruan, Q. Zhu, & Y. Ye (Eds.), *Academic Library Development and Administration in China* (pp. 163–183). Hershey, PA: IGI Global. doi:10.4018/978-1-5225-0550-1.ch010

Ravasan, A. Z., Mohammadi, M. M., & Hamidi, H. (2018). An Investigation Into the Critical Success Factors of Implementing Information Technology Service Management Frameworks. In K. Jakobs (Ed.), *Corporate and Global Standardization Initiatives in Contemporary Society* (pp. 200–218). Hershey, PA: IGI Global. doi:10.4018/978-1-5225-5320-5.ch009

Renna, P., Izzo, C., & Romaniello, T. (2016). The Business Process Management Systems to Support Continuous Improvements. In W. Nuninger & J. Châtelet (Eds.), *Handbook of Research on Quality Assurance and Value Management in Higher Education* (pp. 237–256). Hershey, PA: IGI Global. doi:10.4018/978-1-5225-0024-7.ch009

Rezaie, S., Mirabedini, S. J., & Abtahi, A. (2018). Designing a Model for Implementation of Business Intelligence in the Banking Industry. *International Journal of Enterprise Information Systems*, *14*(1), 77–103. doi:10.4018/IJEIS.2018010105

Riccò, R. (2016). Diversity Management: Bringing Equality, Equity, and Inclusion in the Workplace. In J. Prescott (Ed.), *Handbook of Research on Race, Gender, and the Fight for Equality* (pp. 335–359). Hershey, PA: IGI Global. doi:10.4018/978-1-5225-0047-6.ch015

Romano, L., Grimaldi, R., & Colasuonno, F. S. (2017). Demand Management as a Success Factor in Project Portfolio Management. In L. Romano (Ed.), *Project Portfolio Management Strategies for Effective Organizational Operations* (pp. 202–219). Hershey, PA: IGI Global. doi:10.4018/978-1-5225-2151-8.ch008

Rostek, K. B. (2016). Risk Management: Role and Importance in Business Organization. In D. Jakóbczak (Ed.), *Analyzing Risk through Probabilistic Modeling in Operations Research* (pp. 149–178). Hershey, PA: IGI Global. doi:10.4018/978-1-4666-9458-3.ch007

Rouhani, S., & Savoji, S. R. (2016). A Success Assessment Model for BI Tools Implementation: An Empirical Study of Banking Industry. *International Journal of Business Intelligence Research*, *7*(1), 25–44. doi:10.4018/IJBIR.2016010103

Ruan, Z. (2016). A Corpus-Based Functional Analysis of Complex Nominal Groups in Written Business Discourse: The Case of "Business". *International Journal of Computer-Assisted Language Learning and Teaching*, *6*(2), 74–90. doi:10.4018/IJCALLT.2016040105

Ruhi, U. (2018). Towards an Interdisciplinary Socio-Technical Definition of Virtual Communities. In M. Khosrow-Pour, D.B.A. (Ed.), Encyclopedia of Information Science and Technology, Fourth Edition (pp. 4278-4295). Hershey, PA: IGI Global. doi:10.4018/978-1-5225-2255-3.ch371

Ryan, J., Doster, B., Daily, S., & Lewis, C. (2016). A Case Study Perspective for Balanced Perioperative Workflow Achievement through Data-Driven Process Improvement. *International Journal of Healthcare Information Systems and Informatics*, *11*(3), 19–41. doi:10.4018/IJHISI.2016070102

Safari, M. R., & Jiang, Q. (2018). The Theory and Practice of IT Governance Maturity and Strategies Alignment: Evidence From Banking Industry. *Journal of Global Information Management*, *26*(2), 127–146. doi:10.4018/JGIM.2018040106

Sahoo, J., Pati, B., & Mohanty, B. (2017). Knowledge Management as an Academic Discipline: An Assessment. In B. Gunjal (Ed.), *Managing Knowledge and Scholarly Assets in Academic Libraries* (pp. 99–126). Hershey, PA: IGI Global. doi:10.4018/978-1-5225-1741-2.ch005

Saini, D. (2017). Relevance of Teaching Values and Ethics in Management Education. In N. Baporikar (Ed.), *Management Education for Global Leadership* (pp. 90–111). Hershey, PA: IGI Global. doi:10.4018/978-1-5225-1013-0.ch005

Sambhanthan, A. (2017). Assessing and Benchmarking Sustainability in Organisations: An Integrated Conceptual Model. *International Journal of Systems and Service-Oriented Engineering*, *7*(4), 22–43. doi:10.4018/IJSSOE.2017100102

Sambhanthan, A., & Potdar, V. (2017). A Study of the Parameters Impacting Sustainability in Information Technology Organizations. *International Journal of Knowledge-Based Organizations*, *7*(3), 27–39. doi:10.4018/IJKBO.2017070103

Sánchez-Fernández, M. D., & Manríquez, M. R. (2018). The Entrepreneurial Spirit Based on Social Values: The Digital Generation. In P. Isaias & L. Carvalho (Eds.), *User Innovation and the Entrepreneurship Phenomenon in the Digital Economy* (pp. 173–193). Hershey, PA: IGI Global. doi:10.4018/978-1-5225-2826-5.ch009

*Related References*

Sanchez-Ruiz, L., & Blanco, B. (2017). Process Management for SMEs: Barriers, Enablers, and Benefits. In M. Vemić (Ed.), *Optimal Management Strategies in Small and Medium Enterprises* (pp. 293–319). Hershey, PA: IGI Global. doi:10.4018/978-1-5225-1949-2.ch014

Sanz, L. F., Gómez-Pérez, J., & Castillo-Martinez, A. (2018). Analysis of the European ICT Competence Frameworks. In V. Ahuja & S. Rathore (Eds.), *Multidisciplinary Perspectives on Human Capital and Information Technology Professionals* (pp. 225–245). Hershey, PA: IGI Global. doi:10.4018/978-1-5225-5297-0.ch012

Sarvepalli, A., & Godin, J. (2017). Business Process Management in the Classroom. *Journal of Cases on Information Technology*, *19*(2), 17–28. doi:10.4018/JCIT.2017040102

Satpathy, B., & Muniapan, B. (2016). Ancient Wisdom for Transformational Leadership and Its Insights from the Bhagavad-Gita. In U. Aung & P. Ordoñez de Pablos (Eds.), *Managerial Strategies and Practice in the Asian Business Sector* (pp. 1–10). Hershey, PA: IGI Global. doi:10.4018/978-1-4666-9758-4.ch001

Saygili, E. E., Ozturkoglu, Y., & Kocakulah, M. C. (2017). End Users' Perceptions of Critical Success Factors in ERP Applications. *International Journal of Enterprise Information Systems*, *13*(4), 58–75. doi:10.4018/IJEIS.2017100104

Saygili, E. E., & Saygili, A. T. (2017). Contemporary Issues in Enterprise Information Systems: A Critical Review of CSFs in ERP Implementations. In M. Tavana (Ed.), *Enterprise Information Systems and the Digitalization of Business Functions* (pp. 120–136). Hershey, PA: IGI Global. doi:10.4018/978-1-5225-2382-6.ch006

Seidenstricker, S., & Antonino, A. (2018). Business Model Innovation-Oriented Technology Management for Emergent Technologies. In M. Khosrow-Pour, D.B.A. (Ed.), Encyclopedia of Information Science and Technology, Fourth Edition (pp. 4560-4569). Hershey, PA: IGI Global. doi:10.4018/978-1-5225-2255-3.ch396

Senaratne, S., & Gunarathne, A. D. (2017). Excellence Perspective for Management Education from a Global Accountants' Hub in Asia. In N. Baporikar (Ed.), *Management Education for Global Leadership* (pp. 158–180). Hershey, PA: IGI Global. doi:10.4018/978-1-5225-1013-0.ch008

Sensuse, D. I., & Cahyaningsih, E. (2018). Knowledge Management Models: A Summative Review. *International Journal of Information Systems in the Service Sector*, *10*(1), 71–100. doi:10.4018/IJISSS.2018010105

Sensuse, D. I., Wibowo, W. C., & Cahyaningsih, E. (2016). Indonesian Government Knowledge Management Model: A Theoretical Model. *Information Resources Management Journal*, 29(1), 91–108. doi:10.4018/irmj.2016010106

Seth, M., Goyal, D., & Kiran, R. (2017). Diminution of Impediments in Implementation of Supply Chain Management Information System for Enhancing its Effectiveness in Indian Automobile Industry. *Journal of Global Information Management*, 25(3), 1–20. doi:10.4018/JGIM.2017070101

Seyal, A. H., & Rahman, M. N. (2017). Investigating Impact of Inter-Organizational Factors in Measuring ERP Systems Success: Bruneian Perspectives. In M. Tavana (Ed.), *Enterprise Information Systems and the Digitalization of Business Functions* (pp. 178–204). Hershey, PA: IGI Global. doi:10.4018/978-1-5225-2382-6.ch008

Shaikh, A. A., & Karjaluoto, H. (2016). On Some Misconceptions Concerning Digital Banking and Alternative Delivery Channels. *International Journal of E-Business Research*, 12(3), 1–16. doi:10.4018/IJEBR.2016070101

Shams, S. M. (2016). Stakeholder Relationship Management in Online Business and Competitive Value Propositions: Evidence from the Sports Industry. *International Journal of Online Marketing*, 6(2), 1–17. doi:10.4018/IJOM.2016040101

Shamsuzzoha, A. (2016). Management of Risk and Resilience within Collaborative Business Network. In R. Addo-Tenkorang, J. Kantola, P. Helo, & A. Shamsuzzoha (Eds.), *Supply Chain Strategies and the Engineer-to-Order Approach* (pp. 143–159). Hershey, PA: IGI Global. doi:10.4018/978-1-5225-0021-6.ch008

Shaqrah, A. A. (2018). Analyzing Business Intelligence Systems Based on 7s Model of McKinsey. *International Journal of Business Intelligence Research*, 9(1), 53–63. doi:10.4018/IJBIR.2018010104

Sharma, A. J. (2017). Enhancing Sustainability through Experiential Learning in Management Education. In N. Baporikar (Ed.), *Management Education for Global Leadership* (pp. 256–274). Hershey, PA: IGI Global. doi:10.4018/978-1-5225-1013-0.ch013

Shetty, K. P. (2017). Responsible Global Leadership: Ethical Challenges in Management Education. In N. Baporikar (Ed.), *Innovation and Shifting Perspectives in Management Education* (pp. 194–223). Hershey, PA: IGI Global. doi:10.4018/978-1-5225-1019-2.ch009

Sinthupundaja, J., & Kohda, Y. (2017). Effects of Corporate Social Responsibility and Creating Shared Value on Sustainability. *International Journal of Sustainable Entrepreneurship and Corporate Social Responsibility*, 2(1), 27–38. doi:10.4018/IJSECSR.2017010103

Škarica, I., & Hrgović, A. V. (2018). Implementation of Total Quality Management Principles in Public Health Institutes in the Republic of Croatia. *International Journal of Productivity Management and Assessment Technologies*, 6(1), 1–16. doi:10.4018/IJPMAT.2018010101

Smuts, H., Kotzé, P., Van der Merwe, A., & Loock, M. (2017). Framework for Managing Shared Knowledge in an Information Systems Outsourcing Context. *International Journal of Knowledge Management*, 13(4), 1–30. doi:10.4018/IJKM.2017100101

Soares, E. R., & Zaidan, F. H. (2016). Information Architecture and Business Modeling in Modern Organizations of Information Technology: Professional Career Plan in Organizations IT. In G. Jamil, J. Poças Rascão, F. Ribeiro, & A. Malheiro da Silva (Eds.), *Handbook of Research on Information Architecture and Management in Modern Organizations* (pp. 439–457). Hershey, PA: IGI Global. doi:10.4018/978-1-4666-8637-3.ch020

Sousa, M. J., Cruz, R., Dias, I., & Caracol, C. (2017). Information Management Systems in the Supply Chain. In G. Jamil, A. Soares, & C. Pessoa (Eds.), *Handbook of Research on Information Management for Effective Logistics and Supply Chains* (pp. 469–485). Hershey, PA: IGI Global. doi:10.4018/978-1-5225-0973-8.ch025

Spremic, M., Turulja, L., & Bajgoric, N. (2018). Two Approaches in Assessing Business Continuity Management Attitudes in the Organizational Context. In N. Bajgoric (Ed.), *Always-On Enterprise Information Systems for Modern Organizations* (pp. 159–183). Hershey, PA: IGI Global. doi:10.4018/978-1-5225-3704-5.ch008

Steenkamp, A. L. (2018). Some Insights in Computer Science and Information Technology. In *Examining the Changing Role of Supervision in Doctoral Research Projects: Emerging Research and Opportunities* (pp. 113–133). Hershey, PA: IGI Global. doi:10.4018/978-1-5225-2610-0.ch005

Studdard, N., Dawson, M., Burton, S. L., Jackson, N., Leonard, B., Quisenberry, W., & Rahim, E. (2016). Nurturing Social Entrepreneurship and Building Social Entrepreneurial Self-Efficacy: Focusing on Primary and Secondary Schooling to Develop Future Social Entrepreneurs. In Z. Fields (Ed.), *Incorporating Business Models and Strategies into Social Entrepreneurship* (pp. 154–175). Hershey, PA: IGI Global. doi:10.4018/978-1-4666-8748-6.ch010

Sun, Z. (2016). A Framework for Developing Management Intelligent Systems. *International Journal of Systems and Service-Oriented Engineering*, 6(1), 37–53. doi:10.4018/IJSSOE.2016010103

Swami, B., & Mphele, G. T. (2016). Problems Preventing Growth of Small Entrepreneurs: A Case Study of a Few Small Entrepreneurs in Botswana Sub-Urban Areas. In N. Baporikar (Ed.), *Handbook of Research on Entrepreneurship in the Contemporary Knowledge-Based Global Economy* (pp. 479–508). Hershey, PA: IGI Global. doi:10.4018/978-1-4666-8798-1.ch020

Tabach, A., & Croteau, A. (2017). Configurations of Information Technology Governance Practices and Business Unit Performance. *International Journal of IT/ Business Alignment and Governance*, 8(2), 1–27. doi:10.4018/IJITBAG.2017070101

Talaue, G. M., & Iqbal, T. (2017). Assessment of e-Business Mode of Selected Private Universities in the Philippines and Pakistan. *International Journal of Online Marketing*, 7(4), 63–77. doi:10.4018/IJOM.2017100105

Tam, G. C. (2017). Project Manager Sustainability Competence. In *Managerial Strategies and Green Solutions for Project Sustainability* (pp. 178–207). Hershey, PA: IGI Global. doi:10.4018/978-1-5225-2371-0.ch008

Tambo, T. (2018). Fashion Retail Innovation: About Context, Antecedents, and Outcome in Technological Change Projects. In I. Management Association (Ed.), Fashion and Textiles: Breakthroughs in Research and Practice (pp. 233-260). Hershey, PA: IGI Global. doi:10.4018/978-1-5225-3432-7.ch010

Tambo, T., & Mikkelsen, O. E. (2016). Fashion Supply Chain Optimization: Linking Make-to-Order Purchasing and B2B E-Commerce. In S. Joshi & R. Joshi (Eds.), *Designing and Implementing Global Supply Chain Management* (pp. 1–21). Hershey, PA: IGI Global. doi:10.4018/978-1-4666-9720-1.ch001

Tandon, K. (2016). Innovative Andragogy: The Paradigm Shift to Heutagogy. In S. Tiwari & L. Nafees (Eds.), *Innovative Management Education Pedagogies for Preparing Next-Generation Leaders* (pp. 238–257). Hershey, PA: IGI Global. doi:10.4018/978-1-4666-9691-4.ch014

Tantau, A. D., & Frățilă, L. C. (2018). Information and Management System for Renewable Energy Business. In *Entrepreneurship and Business Development in the Renewable Energy Sector* (pp. 200–244). Hershey, PA: IGI Global. doi:10.4018/978-1-5225-3625-3.ch006

*Related References*

Teixeira, N., Pardal, P. N., & Rafael, B. G. (2018). Internationalization, Financial Performance, and Organizational Challenges: A Success Case in Portugal. In L. Carvalho (Ed.), *Handbook of Research on Entrepreneurial Ecosystems and Social Dynamics in a Globalized World* (pp. 379–423). Hershey, PA: IGI Global. doi:10.4018/978-1-5225-3525-6.ch017

Trad, A., & Kalpić, D. (2016). The E-Business Transformation Framework for E-Commerce Architecture-Modeling Projects. In I. Lee (Ed.), *Encyclopedia of E-Commerce Development, Implementation, and Management* (pp. 733–753). Hershey, PA: IGI Global. doi:10.4018/978-1-4666-9787-4.ch052

Trad, A., & Kalpić, D. (2016). The E-Business Transformation Framework for E-Commerce Control and Monitoring Pattern. In I. Lee (Ed.), *Encyclopedia of E-Commerce Development, Implementation, and Management* (pp. 754–777). Hershey, PA: IGI Global. doi:10.4018/978-1-4666-9787-4.ch053

Trad, A., & Kalpić, D. (2018). The Business Transformation Framework, Agile Project and Change Management. In M. Khosrow-Pour, D.B.A. (Ed.), Encyclopedia of Information Science and Technology, Fourth Edition (pp. 620-635). Hershey, PA: IGI Global. doi:10.4018/978-1-5225-2255-3.ch054

Trad, A., & Kalpić, D. (2018). The Business Transformation and Enterprise Architecture Framework: The Financial Engineering E-Risk Management and E-Law Integration. In B. Sergi, F. Fidanoski, M. Ziolo, & V. Naumovski (Eds.), *Regaining Global Stability After the Financial Crisis* (pp. 46–65). Hershey, PA: IGI Global. doi:10.4018/978-1-5225-4026-7.ch003

Turulja, L., & Bajgoric, N. (2018). Business Continuity and Information Systems: A Systematic Literature Review. In N. Bajgoric (Ed.), *Always-On Enterprise Information Systems for Modern Organizations* (pp. 60–87). Hershey, PA: IGI Global. doi:10.4018/978-1-5225-3704-5.ch004

van Wessel, R. M., de Vries, H. J., & Ribbers, P. M. (2016). Business Benefits through Company IT Standardization. In K. Jakobs (Ed.), *Effective Standardization Management in Corporate Settings* (pp. 34–53). Hershey, PA: IGI Global. doi:10.4018/978-1-4666-9737-9.ch003

Vargas-Hernández, J. G. (2017). Professional Integrity in Business Management Education. In N. Baporikar (Ed.), *Management Education for Global Leadership* (pp. 70–89). Hershey, PA: IGI Global. doi:10.4018/978-1-5225-1013-0.ch004

Vasista, T. G., & AlAbdullatif, A. M. (2017). Role of Electronic Customer Relationship Management in Demand Chain Management: A Predictive Analytic Approach. *International Journal of Information Systems and Supply Chain Management, 10*(1), 53–67. doi:10.4018/IJISSCM.2017010104

Vergidis, K. (2016). Rediscovering Business Processes: Definitions, Patterns, and Modelling Approaches. In P. Papajorgji, F. Pinet, A. Guimarães, & J. Papathanasiou (Eds.), *Automated Enterprise Systems for Maximizing Business Performance* (pp. 97–122). Hershey, PA: IGI Global. doi:10.4018/978-1-4666-8841-4.ch007

Vieru, D., & Bourdeau, S. (2017). Survival in the Digital Era: A Digital Competence-Based Multi-Case Study in the Canadian SME Clothing Industry. *International Journal of Social and Organizational Dynamics in IT, 6*(1), 17–34. doi:10.4018/IJSODIT.2017010102

Vijayan, G., & Kamarulzaman, N. H. (2017). An Introduction to Sustainable Supply Chain Management and Business Implications. In M. Khan, M. Hussain, & M. Ajmal (Eds.), *Green Supply Chain Management for Sustainable Business Practice* (pp. 27–50). Hershey, PA: IGI Global. doi:10.4018/978-1-5225-0635-5.ch002

Vlachvei, A., & Notta, O. (2017). Firm Competitiveness: Theories, Evidence, and Measurement. In A. Vlachvei, O. Notta, K. Karantininis, & N. Tsounis (Eds.), *Factors Affecting Firm Competitiveness and Performance in the Modern Business World* (pp. 1–42). Hershey, PA: IGI Global. doi:10.4018/978-1-5225-0843-4.ch001

von Rosing, M., Fullington, N., & Walker, J. (2016). Using the Business Ontology and Enterprise Standards to Transform Three Leading Organizations. *International Journal of Conceptual Structures and Smart Applications, 4*(1), 71–99. doi:10.4018/IJCSSA.2016010104

von Rosing, M., & von Scheel, H. (2016). Using the Business Ontology to Develop Enterprise Standards. *International Journal of Conceptual Structures and Smart Applications, 4*(1), 48–70. doi:10.4018/IJCSSA.2016010103

Walczak, S. (2016). Artificial Neural Networks and other AI Applications for Business Management Decision Support. *International Journal of Sociotechnology and Knowledge Development, 8*(4), 1–20. doi:10.4018/IJSKD.2016100101

Wamba, S. F., Akter, S., Kang, H., Bhattacharya, M., & Upal, M. (2016). The Primer of Social Media Analytics. *Journal of Organizational and End User Computing, 28*(2), 1–12. doi:10.4018/JOEUC.2016040101

Wang, C., Schofield, M., Li, X., & Ou, X. (2017). Do Chinese Students in Public and Private Higher Education Institutes Perform at Different Level in One of the Leadership Skills: Critical Thinking?: An Exploratory Comparison. In V. Wang (Ed.), *Encyclopedia of Strategic Leadership and Management* (pp. 160–181). Hershey, PA: IGI Global. doi:10.4018/978-1-5225-1049-9.ch013

Wang, F., Raisinghani, M. S., Mora, M., & Wang, X. (2016). Strategic E-Business Management through a Balanced Scored Card Approach. In I. Lee (Ed.), *Encyclopedia of E-Commerce Development, Implementation, and Management* (pp. 361–386). Hershey, PA: IGI Global. doi:10.4018/978-1-4666-9787-4.ch027

Wang, J. (2017). Multi-Agent based Production Management Decision System Modelling for the Textile Enterprise. *Journal of Global Information Management*, *25*(4), 1–15. doi:10.4018/JGIM.2017100101

Wiedemann, A., & Gewald, H. (2017). Examining Cross-Domain Alignment: The Correlation of Business Strategy, IT Management, and IT Business Value. *International Journal of IT/Business Alignment and Governance*, *8*(1), 17–31. doi:10.4018/IJITBAG.2017010102

Wolf, R., & Thiel, M. (2018). Advancing Global Business Ethics in China: Reducing Poverty Through Human and Social Welfare. In S. Hipsher (Ed.), *Examining the Private Sector's Role in Wealth Creation and Poverty Reduction* (pp. 67–84). Hershey, PA: IGI Global. doi:10.4018/978-1-5225-3117-3.ch004

Wu, J., Ding, F., Xu, M., Mo, Z., & Jin, A. (2016). Investigating the Determinants of Decision-Making on Adoption of Public Cloud Computing in E-government. *Journal of Global Information Management*, *24*(3), 71–89. doi:10.4018/JGIM.2016070104

Xu, L., & de Vrieze, P. (2016). Building Situational Applications for Virtual Enterprises. In I. Lee (Ed.), *Encyclopedia of E-Commerce Development, Implementation, and Management* (pp. 715–724). Hershey, PA: IGI Global. doi:10.4018/978-1-4666-9787-4.ch050

Yablonsky, S. (2018). Innovation Platforms: Data and Analytics Platforms. In *Multi-Sided Platforms (MSPs) and Sharing Strategies in the Digital Economy: Emerging Research and Opportunities* (pp. 72–95). Hershey, PA: IGI Global. doi:10.4018/978-1-5225-5457-8.ch003

Yusoff, A., Ahmad, N. H., & Halim, H. A. (2017). Agropreneurship among Gen Y in Malaysia: The Role of Academic Institutions. In N. Ahmad, T. Ramayah, H. Halim, & S. Rahman (Eds.), *Handbook of Research on Small and Medium Enterprises in Developing Countries* (pp. 23–47). Hershey, PA: IGI Global. doi:10.4018/978-1-5225-2165-5.ch002

Zanin, F., Comuzzi, E., & Costantini, A. (2018). The Effect of Business Strategy and Stock Market Listing on the Use of Risk Assessment Tools. In *Management Control Systems in Complex Settings: Emerging Research and Opportunities* (pp. 145–168). Hershey, PA: IGI Global. doi:10.4018/978-1-5225-3987-2.ch007

Zgheib, P. W. (2017). Corporate Innovation and Intrapreneurship in the Middle East. In P. Zgheib (Ed.), *Entrepreneurship and Business Innovation in the Middle East* (pp. 37–56). Hershey, PA: IGI Global. doi:10.4018/978-1-5225-2066-5.ch003

# Index

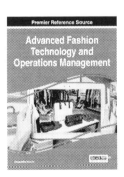

Ensure Quality Research is Introduced to the Academic Community

# Become an IGI Global Reviewer for Authored Book Projects

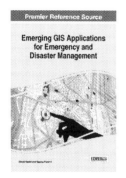
Premier Reference Source

Emerging GIS Applications for Emergency and Disaster Management

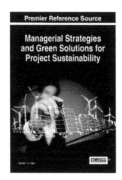
Premier Reference Source

Managerial Strategies and Green Solutions for Project Sustainability

Premier Reference Source

Comparative Approaches to Using R and Python for Statistical Data Analysis

Premier Reference Source

Solutions for High-Touch Communications in a High-Tech World

## The overall success of an authored book project is dependent on quality and timely reviews.

In this competitive age of scholarly publishing, constructive and timely feedback significantly expedites the turnaround time of manuscripts from submission to acceptance, allowing the publication and discovery of forward-thinking research at a much more expeditious rate. Several IGI Global authored book projects are currently seeking highly qualified experts in the field to fill vacancies on their respective editorial review boards:

## Applications may be sent to:
development@igi-global.com

Applicants must have a doctorate (or an equivalent degree) as well as publishing and reviewing experience. Reviewers are asked to write reviews in a timely, collegial, and constructive manner. All reviewers will begin their role on an ad-hoc basis for a period of one year, and upon successful completion of this term can be considered for full editorial review board status, with the potential for a subsequent promotion to Associate Editor.

If you have a colleague that may be interested in this opportunity, we encourage you to share this information with them.

Printed in the United States
By Bookmasters